"If ever a theologian should provide a memoir of his journey, Tom Oden is the one. *A Change of Heart* is the record of that phenomenal sojourn intersecting the lives of countless theologians and religious leaders. And as readers of the relentless Oden would expect, the pages of this book fly by on the winds of Oden the wordsmith. This is the montage of a master artist."

Paige Patterson, president, Southwestern Baptist Theological Seminary

"Tom Oden is one of the most remarkable Christians of our time. This is the story of how he has lived through, contributed to and helped to overthrow several revolutions during his long and fruitful life. Deeply rooted in Wesleyan spiritual traditions, Oden shows us the meaning of grace in a human life—grace that shatters in order to restore and bring joy. Those of us who know and love this great theologian will be delighted to read the story of his pilgrimage thus far. The whole church will be blessed by it."

Timothy George, founding dean of Beeson Divinity School of Samford University and general editor of the Reformation Commentary on Scripture

"In a century when intellectuals abandoned the Christian faith in droves, one intellectual had the courage to embrace it. A movement liberal at forty, at eighty Tom Oden had become the champion of the classic Christian consensus. *A Change of Heart* tells the story of one of the twentieth century's most courageous intellectual and spiritual journeys."

Roberta Green Ahmanson

"Tom Oden's *A Change of Heart* chronicles his own odyssey through modernity back home to the fathers he never knew—until he read them, prayed with them and learned the riches of the timeless faith at their feet. This book invites readers to join him in this odyssey. As one who has been privileged to travel the last part with him, I can truly say they will not be disappointed in the journey Tom Oden is inviting them to undertake with him."

Joel C. Elowsky, associate professor of historical theology, Concordia Seminary St. Louis; research director, Center for Early African Christianity

"In this memoir Tom Oden explores his theological career with specific reference to his transition from Christian liberalism to evangelical Christianity. In the process he describes the many theological issues that dominated his era, focusing on the World Council of Churches as a lightning rod. Oden's view that theology should not be at the whim of every passing fashion, or that current affairs should not be the litmus test, deserves careful consideration even by those who disagree with him. Oden offers a touching description of the passing of his wife after a bout with cancer. The book is a record of an important theological voice of his generation, one that brings to focus the wide-ranging religious influences of the day."

Lamin Sanneh, D. Willis James Professor of Missions and World Christianity, Yale Divinity School

A Change of Heart

A PERSONAL AND
THEOLOGICAL MEMOIR

◈

Thomas C. Oden

IVP Academic

An imprint of InterVarsity Press
Downers Grove, Illinois

InterVarsity Press
P.O. Box 1400, Downers Grove, IL 60515-1426
World Wide Web: www.ivpress.com
Email: email@ivpress.com

*InterVarsity Press® is the book-publishing division of InterVarsity Christian Fellowship/USA®, a movement of
students and faculty active on campus at hundreds of universities, colleges and schools of nursing in the United States
of America, and a member movement of the International Fellowship of Evangelical Students. For information about
local and regional activities, write Public Relations Dept., InterVarsity Christian Fellowship/USA, 6400 Schroeder
Rd., P.O. Box 7895, Madison, WI 53707-7895, or visit the IVCF website at www.intervarsity.org.*

Cover design: Cindy Kiple
Interior design: Beth McGill
Images: Photo of Thomas Oden: InterVarsity Press

ISBN 978-0-8308-4035-9 (print)
ISBN 978-0-8308-8019-5 (digital)

Printed in the United States of America ♾

Library of Congress Cataloging-in-Publication Data

Oden, Thomas C.
 A change of heart : a personal and theological memoir / Thomas C.
Oden.
   pages cm
 Includes bibliographical references and index.
 ISBN 978-0-8308-4035-9 (pbk. : alk. paper)
 1. Oden, Thomas C. 2. United Methodist Church (U.S.)—Biography.
I. Title.
 BX8495.O34A3 2014
 230'.76092--dc23
 [B]

                                                                    2014033341

P 23 22 21 20 19 18 17 16 15 14 13 12 11 10 9 8 7 6 5 4 3 2 1

Y 34 33 32 31 30 29 28 27 26 25 24 23 22 21 20 19 18 17 16 15 14

To Edrita

The love of my life
who helped me hear God's footsteps

Contents

Preface

All school work came to a halt when every kid in my third grade class went out to the cotton fields during harvest time. A faded yellow school bus took us a few miles out of town to "pull bolls." We sang and laughed at the thought of briefly escaping from the classroom.

I dragged a long white denim sack my grandmother had made for me. It had a harness to loop over my shoulder which allowed me to pull it through the long rows of cotton as I stripped the cotton fibers from their shell. The barbed husk of the boll was there to protect the soft cotton fibers I was pulling out. The trick was to get the cotton out without getting our hands bloody from the sharp edges of the cotton husks.

A single row of cotton was a quarter mile long and took a long time to work, but row after row we worked as fast as we could. We competed to see how many pounds of cotton we could pull in a single day. Then we dragged those long, heavy sacks full of cotton to one of the Ford Model T trucks, where it was weighed and soon taken to the cotton gin. An overseer supervised the weighing, and we were paid cash immediately. For a third grader it was the most money I had ever had in my pocket. Though exhausted, I also felt like I had accomplished something big.[1]

Then there was baseball. It was the sweet spot of my life. Maybe it was because Mickey Mantle and I were born on the same day and year in Oklahoma, but I have always been captivated by the game of baseball. Whenever Mantle and Joe DiMaggio were on the same field, my ear was glued to the radio.

I kept up with the St. Louis Cardinals when Dizzy Dean was pitching, Enos Slaughter was hitting over .300, and Johnny Mize was breaking records for home runs. I always thought of baseball as the perfect game. It contains the exact combination of distances and speeds to make a competition both fair and unpredictable. Even today I still love watching the story of a game unfold with all of its maneuvering and strategizing.

I was blessed by baseball, but more so blessed by a grandmother who prayed for me every day, even though I did not pay much attention to all of her prayers. I always knew that she and God would be there for me. In her own way she led me to believe that sooner or later I would get some hint from God about doing something I could do that really needed to be done. She planted seeds of belief in me which let me trust that providence was at work in my life, and that our free choices are being encouraged by God's grace.

part one

Early Years

The 1930s

Prairie Dawn

DUST BOWL BEGINNINGS

Jackson County. The flat land made me aware of the big sky. From the top of the water tower you can see for miles. My childhood was spent in a small town in the short grass country of Oklahoma. The town of Altus sits in the middle of windy wheat fields and silently grazing cattle.

Nearby are ancient granite mountains in the distance that turn purple in the late evening sun. The Navajo Mountains are about six miles away to the east and the Quartz Mountains fifteen miles to the north. The Oklahoma red granite mined there is the oldest and finest anywhere.

Before statehood this was fertile grazing land for nomadic Native American tribes like the Comanche and Wichita, who once roamed these plains looking for buffalo. Finding and collecting arrowheads was my first venture into the world of discovering that ancient hidden world. I felt the privilege of holding a bit of history in my hand.

During the frontier years from 1866 until statehood in 1907, six million Longhorn cattle rambled through our county grazing on prairie grasses all the way from Abilene, Texas, to Abilene, Kansas, on the Old Western Trail. Our family acquired the deed to some property that touches the slopes of one of the Navajo Mountains where the North Fork of the Red River meanders south as if it were looking for Texas. It became a place for family retreat, natural wonder, conservation and exploration for turtles, wildflowers, and an occasional porcupine.

Altus was as far from the centers of power as you could get in Oklahoma, hidden away in the extreme southwestern corner of the state. The dirt roads in the county were often impassable after the prairie thunderstorms. After World War II a few were asphalted. Many nearby towns that were once thriving have virtually disappeared. Only a few lonely remains of farmhouses still stand. Many rural churches and schools have almost vanished as well, and some are used for barns or storage.

Everything in Altus was within walking distance. It was an eight-block walk to get a haircut downtown and a three-block walk to the park, tennis courts and high school. Beyond that was a sea of wheat fields and cattle ranches.

No one famous or wealthy lived in my hometown. They were farmers, laborers and small-town folk. Life was not easy, but the love we had in our family felt like all we needed. We did not think of ourselves as restricted or left behind. This was the center of the world so far as I was concerned. We lacked nothing essential.

Everyone knew that if they were going to make something of their lives, they would have to do it for themselves. No one attributed success or failure to a person's environment or external causes. They assumed that most outcomes were due to the effort of the person or lack of it. If someone messed up, we would more likely ponder how a hurtful habit might be a lesson for us to avoid.

A "can do" spirit was what most clearly characterized that independent and confident small town. But the lack of rain and an abundance of dust depleted farm incomes. That led to many homeless men on the move looking for odd jobs. Strong and good men on the road to somewhere would knock on our door needing food, but they were always willing to work for it. Even though they were on the move, all we needed to know was that they were persons who had fallen on hard times and were hungry. We never turned any of them away. My mother would always find something to feed them, usually what we would be eating that day.

They were not asking for anything more than leftovers or a cup of coffee or a few crackers or bread. I never remember them asking for money, probably because there was almost no money circulating. Often business exchanges occurred by bartering goods or services. Mom often reminded me that each one of those people in need was made in God's image. They were people portrayed in the movies as hobos, but we never used that word. I knew they were hardworking people who couldn't pay their mortgages and had to leave good farms as the banks were foreclosing on them and disrupting long-laid plans.

Dust storms were a regular part of my childhood. I can still smell and feel the looming approach of a thousand foot high wall of heavy gray dust rolling in unexpectedly. We would all run inside to try to seal the windows with newspapers we attached by pins and masking tape to keep as much dust as possible out of the house.

We conserved and reused everything. In that sense most everyone in our town would have been considered ecologically minded by necessity, but without any fancy words. We carved many of our own toys. When the rubber on the slingshot broke, I would look for an old inner tube and a tree branch to start over and make a new one.

Dad purchased a set of small leather-bound books containing the shortened versions of classics such as Hamlet, Rousseau and the ballads of Robert Burns. One of them was Emerson's *Self-Reliance*. I read it at an early age, maybe ten. Because of Emerson's book, self-reliance became a key aspiration in my search for character.

Despite everything, I considered Cypress Street the world's best place to be. Still do. We were on no main route and seldom locked our doors. I saw pictures in the newspapers of soup lines in the cities. We much preferred to be in dust-coated Oklahoma than in a Chicago food relief line or a crowded Hooverville camp in California.

The gentle warmth of family. Almost every kid on my street came from a close-knit family at a time when family meant everything. My family's small red brick, steep-roofed English cottage had two bedrooms, but to us it always seemed to have plenty of space for everyone. We had hideaway folding beds for visitors and family. On holidays the house could sleep as many as seventeen. That was good because we had an extended family that stretched from Tippecanoe County, Indiana, to Las

Cruces, New Mexico. I was among the youngest, near the bottom of the pecking order, so I was often consigned to "sleeping at the foot of the bed." I was always happy to be a small kid in a large family.

My small world was my big family. My identity stemmed out of theirs and I wouldn't have been me without them. I remember my childhood much like William Butler Yeats described himself in his early days in Sligo as "a boy with never a crack in my heart." I felt complete as a child, lacking nothing important. And I learned that delayed gratification was part of every worthy endeavor.

Growing up, I was intrigued by the stories told around our fireplace about my grandmother's grandfather, Elijah Walker, who was the first merchant to set up a small trading post in Northern Alabama to buy and sell foods, tools and goods among the Creek Indians. Even more exciting were Civil War stories about my great-grandfather John C. Oden, whose military record shows he was captured four times in battles that ranged all the way from Richmond to Natchez. Each time—either by release or escape—he returned to his own unit, led by Colonel Thomas Bluett, after whom my grandfather was named and later I was named.

My grandmother Sallie Elisa Walker rode into Arkansas on a Conestoga wagon. Just after the Civil War, while she was still a young girl, her pioneer father, Andrew Jackson Walker, gathered up his growing family from around Talladega, Alabama, and set out for the West, where they hoped to mine for gold or find tillable land.

After several days on the road, as the wagon pulled up to the ferry on the Tombigbee River, there was a horrible accident. When the wagon tipped, Sallie's brother Thad fell off and was crushed by the wagon wheel. Grieving, the family stopped to mourn and bury their little boy. Sallie did the only thing she could do; she climbed back in the wagon and with her heartbroken family headed due west on the rough roads toward Little Rock.

From there they headed south to Clark County, where some of their Alabama friends and family had settled. In November of 1876 they arrived at the village of Amity for what they thought would be a short stop. Heavy snows began to fall and they could not continue. They stayed in

Amity, which became the ancestral home of the Oden family. Sallie grew up and fell in love with my grandfather Thomas Oden, the son of a Presbyterian minister. Their marriage united two evangelical Christian traditions which would influence their family from then on: Cumberland Presbyterian and Wesleyan Methodist.

My grandfather Clark, my mother's father, was a railway man all his life. About the same time the telegraph was invented by Edison, my grandfather landed a job delivering newspapers on board the Indianapolis and Bellefontaine Railroad, which led to his learning telegraphy and eventually to his life as a railway agent. He moved his family from Pendleton, Indiana, gradually west to assignments in the Texas Panhandle, then to Nevada and finally back to Oklahoma.

Grandfather Clark was a loyal union man with lengthy seniority in the Brotherhood of Railway Workers, which at that time was among the nation's strongest labor unions. Granddad's most prized possession was his official railroad time piece, his round Hamilton watch, which he kept in his vest pocket on a gold chain. Since human lives as well as reliable arrival schedules were at stake in the railroad business, he lived by the clock. His passion for railroading was passed on to all his family, especially to his two sons, both of whom became university teachers in fields related to the technology and history of railroads.[1]

I inherited this same love of the railroad. I often would go down to the Katy station in Hollister to visit with my grandfather at his busy railway office. I remember the special sound of an almost nonstop telegraph tapping out Morse code. Through the incessant hum of dots and dashes, Granddad was the first in town to learn of wars, elections, tornadoes or the St. Louis Cardinals' scores.

My father was born in 1895 on an eighty-acre farm near the Caddo River in Arkansas. When I visited that old family farm as a kid I came away with touching memories of how my dad had grown up on the frontier. There was a small frame house which had at its center a red brick fireplace with crackling cedar firewood I can still smell burning. My grandfather built that house with his own hands.

In his smokehouse I got a sense of how the pioneer family had lived, by preserving with salt brine the pork or beef they had raised or the fish or fowl they had hunted. I watched my tall, lanky grandfather Oden feed the stock with alfalfa feed he himself had grown, and draw fresh, cold water with a rope and bucket out of a well he had dug and an improvised pump he had installed on his own back porch. My grandfather was a hard scrabble farmer who played the fiddle and talked politics with a quiet, wry wit. My dad and his brothers and sisters along with their parents worked this farm, repairing their own tools, planting and mowing, and living largely within a bartering economy.

I have wondered what might have prompted a Presbyterian farmer and his Methodist wife to name my father Waldo Talmage Oden. They used to read by candles they themselves had made from beeswax or animal-fat tallow. Possibly they read somewhere about Peter Waldo, who was the medieval preacher who founded the Waldensians, or Reverend T. DeWitt Talmage of the Brooklyn Tabernacle, who was the leading Presbyterian holiness preacher of his day.

Dad was the first one in his family who managed to get a higher education. His Latin teacher in his Arkansas one-room school thought he did well enough to encourage him to become a lawyer, which he did by pressing further westward into Oklahoma. He attended the University of Oklahoma Law School in its earliest years, graduated in 1920, and then went on to the University of Chicago Law School. After passing the bar, he settled into his law practice back in Oklahoma. He in turn assisted all of his brothers with their education.

For ninety years there has been an Oden Law Firm in Jackson County led by my father and brother Tal, continuing a firm that had been founded before statehood. When asked what he did, my dad would answer drolly, "Just a country lawyer." But I found out he was one of the best when I saw his trial record. He went to the courthouse almost every day and litigated cases for clients in trouble, many from small farms.

As a boy I spent many hours around my dad's office watching him do his legal work and seeing him help people from all sections of our community. Dad's county seat law firm served all layers of society and every aspect of the human condition. Lacking cash, clients would often barter for legal services with chickens, cattle, mineral rights and garden products. From the back seat of a courthouse bench I watched my father reason with judges and juries, settle disputes, defend mostly under-privileged clients and embody the rule of law. I also relish the memory of my father checking the conditions of seeds or roots of his maize crop, singing tenor in church or reading into the late evening a thick maroon-covered mortgage history of a client's property.

I treasured my time at Dad's office. I liked the smell of the leather of the books, the quietness and the invitation to learn. Thick books were on every wall, floor to ceiling, protected by glass enclosed bookcases. His most valuable possessions were his books. I loved to tiptoe into his hushed library and spontaneously read on any random page of any of his weighty volumes of the *Corpus Juris*.

Mom completed Dad in so many ways, bringing joy and confidence into our home life. Throughout my life I saw my mother face economic hardship, wartime conditions and tests of character that always seemed to make her stronger. She could be tough, but in a most gentle way. Her childhood was spent in Amarillo, Texas, during its boisterous cowhand days. She told us that some of the ranch hands would ride into town on Saturdays shouting and shooting their guns into the air, but her parents always kept her safe in the house until they had gone.

Everyone who heard my mother's voice felt her warmth. She took quiet pleasure in performing unnoticed random acts of anonymous kindness. To her final days she was forever hosting, caring, listening and serving. Still she beams her lightness into my dusky evenings, showering her special form of glory on me. I don't ever recall a speck of guile or despair in her character.

I was born in the fall of 1931, when the Dust Bowl was just beginning and Hoover was president. Those were the difficult days between the Crash of 1929 and the election of Franklin Roosevelt. Since there was no hospital in Jackson County except for a small clinic in Dr. Allgood's house a block away, I was born in the smaller of the two bedrooms of our house.

I showed up as little brother to a very bright big brother (Tal) with round glasses who would become a lawyer like our father. Later a little sister (Sarah) would appear who would have to be strong enough to contend with two big brothers. Happily the three of us have stayed very close over the years.

At five I was finally old enough to become a Cub Scout. Tal had already earned his First Class Badge and had his eye on getting a whole sleeve of merit badges. Each step required a difficult task and an examination providing proof of having learned something useful. I followed the Cub Scout Motto, "Do your best." We learned to tie knots, camp out, cooperate and tough things out. I memorized the Scout law, which says "A Scout is trustworthy, loyal, helpful, friendly, courteous, kind, obedient, cheerful, thrifty, brave, clean, and reverent." These ideals have never been erased from my consciousness.[2]

I entered Mrs. Highsmith's kindergarten the same year I became a Cub Scout. Mrs. Highsmith had converted a double garage at the back of her property into a place for preschool education. We learned about getting along together, singing, nature, numbers, game playing and truth telling. In the rhythm band I got to play the sticks. Others more fortunate got to play the tin whistle, drums or ocarina.

My next school, the Old Washington School, was a far cry from Mrs. Highsmith's garage. Built at the time of statehood, its creaking stairs symbolized the passing generation of original Jackson County pioneer settlers. A four block walk from my house, the school was to me an awesome building of bright red brick looming high above me, with its soaring Victorian ceilings and heroic pictures of Washington and Lincoln. Its most conspicuous feature was an out-of-the-window second floor fire escape—a long tube-like slide plunging down to the dirt playground at a 45-degree angle. In my classroom on the first floor, we envied the luckier older kids upstairs who got to go down the slide during fire drills.

My teacher, Miss Peetry, was young, warm, considerate and, yes, beautiful. She made everything at school interesting. I fell in love not only with learning but, in a six-year-old's way, with Miss Peetry. My world there was fun, safe, wholesome and nourishing. My best friend was a reserved kid in overalls named Ralph Blaine, whose shyness matched my own. It was good to have a friend who could understand my quiet ways.

A house full of music. As the son of an Arkansas country fiddler, Dad always desired a house full of music. This is what he discovered in Mom, a woman with a heart full of music. Throughout my youth the house was always pulsating with music of all kinds—classic, country, hymns and popular songs. We had music students in our living room almost every day with Mom guiding countless five-year-old fingers through the first steps of Haydn and Mozart. My mom especially reached out to talented young African American students, some of whom went on to college music degrees and became professional musicians. I enjoyed seeing the proud faces of parents who came into our living room to hear their children's recitals.

Everybody in my family frequently played instruments, sang harmony and put together skits. We all learned early to read music, understand rhythm and improvise chords. All three of Mom's sisters were musicians, and every summer they made a train trip to Chicago for music lessons. My grandfather provided harp instruction for Louise; violin for Mary and Catherine, piano for my mother, Lily, and flute lessons for Dave and Ira. Grandfather Clark owned the first movie theater in the village of Duke when the earliest silent movies were being shown. Duke Theater combined live music with those films. It was a stage for amateur performances and homemade vaudeville entertainment. His daughters performed as "The Clark Sisters," with my mother at the keyboard.

Growing up in my family meant small fireside performances on many nights. While none of us in the immediate family chose music as a profession, all of us have been lifelong musical enthusiasts. Tal was good enough at bassoon while in high school to get an invitation to serve as bassoonist in the Oklahoma City Symphony Philharmonic Orchestra under the direction of Maestro Victor Alessandro. Now in his eighties, Tal still has a huge repertoire of sing-along songs, musical comedy, country and folk songs, and entertainment gigs for Valentine's Day dinners, family reunions, Rotary Clubs, and church meetings, available anytime for any occasion, always funny and ready at the drop of a hat.

It was through music that I first learned to reason. The reasoning process in music occurs through rhythm, melody, chords, progressions, transitions and grace notes. From a young age I grasped intuitively that I could apply musical modes of mental organization to anything else I studied. When I tried to explain this to others, I found them mystified, but to me its reasonableness was self-evident. Thanks to my mother I was playing a simplified form of Beethoven's "Für Elise" at five. As I grew I found every kind of music appealing, from Leadbelly to Shostakovich.

GROWING UP

Finding purpose. At ten an epiphany happened to me on a summer night when my cousins and I were sleeping outdoors on blankets. As I lay on the grass looking toward the sky for comets and constellations, I found myself involved in a deep and puzzling thought process about *space*. I wondered what was beyond the edge of the universe. Really beyond. If the world was measurable, and we could imagine an edge to the universe, what could be "beyond"?

Then I wondered what might have happened before the earliest point in *time*. I wondered what "before time" could ever possibly mean, and puzzled about what might exist after the last moment of time. I realized much later that Augustine had already pondered this. Though I did not know that I was raising the question of the mysterious relationship between finitude and infinity, I recall how deeply affected I was by the twin mysteries of space and time.

In our family the day began with "Upper Room" devotional readings with our parents before breakfast. We always said grace before each meal. Scripture, prayer and thoughtful conversation were woven into the daily fabric of our family life. I memorized passages of Scripture like Psalm 1 and 1 Corinthians 13. These gems still return to my memory at unexpected times. We also gathered with Grandmother Oden in the living room just before bedtime to hear a passage of Scripture read, usually a chapter. Then we would get on our knees and pray. Grandmother began with fervent petitions for the family, the lost, the poor and the spiritual health of the nation.

Dad taught the men's class at church during most of his adult life. I remember him on Saturday evenings pouring over *Peloubet's Select Notes*, a commentary for teachers. I still treasure thumbing through his leather Bible, tattered and underlined over many years of teaching, with some of his marginal notes still intact.[3]

All Methodists back then knew that everyone had a calling that would give purpose and meaning to their lives, but I wasn't sure what mine might be. With two musical grandfathers, a piano teaching mother, a barbershop quartet singing father and a big brother who was a musical whiz, it seemed to me at first that music might be my calling. At thirteen I set a goal of learning how to play every instrument in the orchestra (I did it—except for the strings). I began arranging quartet and orchestra scores on a small scale at age thirteen. As an aspiring composer I got a lot of practice at writing and arranging musical scores for quartets and singing performances, and by fifteen I thought that composing might be my calling. The idea of a vocation in ministry was first planted in my mind at about age ten by Brother Hiram Brogan, a retired minister in our church. Every Sunday he wore the formal dress of black tie and tails in the tradition of Southern Methodist ministers at that time. He always held before me the thought that I might grow up to be a minister. His school teacher daughter Bessie thought so too, but I assumed they were just being nice.

For a long time I was unclear about what ministers did on days other than Sunday. Then came the summer when I was invited to drive around the tobacco farms of rural Tennessee all day with my Uncle Thurston, who was making annual visits to his congregations as their Methodist district superintendent. That trip provided an exciting glimpse of parish ministry I had not seen before. Affable, jolly and generous, Thurston smoked good cigars despite Methodist rules. The day I was with him, he was traveling around his district to encourage those congregations to meet their projected goals, take care of each other and have some fun doing it. As I was warmly welcomed everywhere, I began to wonder about being something like him. Other times I vaguely imagined that I wanted to be a lawyer. Either way, all I ever really wanted was to end up with a house full of books.

The 1940s

A World at War

AFTER PEARL HARBOR

My small and sheltered world changed abruptly on Sunday, December 7, 1941, the day Pearl Harbor was attacked.

How our country changed drastically. In an instant our nation was at war. Even though I was only ten, my childhood was over. The peaceful skies had been swept away.

From then on my growing-up years would be spent in the state's largest city during the bloodiest international war in history.[1] Four million American troops were sent out to fight for us. They were heroes to us, and we loved and honored them wholeheartedly. Thousands died and many more were wounded. I did know they were dying for us. So, back home in safety, total effort was required of each one of us. I understood this, as did all of the kids I knew. Everyone had to stop everything they had been doing for an all-out defense of our country.

I remember exactly where I was when I first learned of Pearl Harbor. On that wintry day we were driving home from church. From the weighty conversation in the front seat, we learned that something was happening in Hawaii. In particular, the Battleship USS Oklahoma was ablaze. I did not know anything about Hawaii, but I did know that our sailors on the Oklahoma were jumping from flames into the water.

We drove to grandmother's house in Hollister later that afternoon, with all of the conversation in low tones. As I listened to every word, I knew my life would never be the same. Our family often sang while we were traveling in the car. Someone broke out with

> O Columbia! the gem of the ocean
> The home of the brave and the free. . . .
> Thy mandates make heroes assemble.
> When Liberty's form stands in view.

Since first grade I had known every word of it. Now I was singing it with all my heart.

As we returned home, we huddled in the back seat of the car watching the wheat fields go by. I now knew that Dad would try to reenlist in the Army he had served in World War I. I wondered how we would live. We were still reeling from the Great Depression.

Dad immediately volunteered for military service but was turned down for age and health reasons. He was forty-six years old in December 1941. Everybody who was unable to serve in the regular army was eager to find some way to help out in the war effort. Dad was asked to chair the local draft board, a hard assignment because he had to decide about farm boys going off to war. Although my dad had strong leanings against international entanglements, often referring to the Monroe Doctrine, he answered the call however he could. We remained in Altus until December 1942, when Dad was called by the federal Office of Price Administration (OPA) to Oklahoma City as a prosecutor against black market offenders, to search out and stop law breakers. The laws broken had to do with regulating urgently needed war materials such as rubber, oil, metals, food and resources for the fighting servicemen.

No one in our family wanted to move from Jackson County, leaving behind our friends, but we all wanted to do our part. So in mid-winter our family bundled up and headed for Oklahoma's capital city. My world shifted quickly from rural to urban, peace to war, childhood to adolescence. No longer was my frame of reference quiet Jackson County with its cotton fields and courthouse. Now I lived in a bustling capital city in a perilous world. Radio became my link to the events, and I learned geography by following battle sites. I kept up with the course of the war like I had always kept up with baseball.

My family, like everyone else, got ration stamps for gasoline, sugar, butter, meat and many other food products, and spent them cautiously. Except for a few violators, almost everyone respected those temporary but necessary rules in order to speed needed goods to the battlefront.

On each car a ration sticker showed what level of priority you had in the war effort. Farmers who produced food were in a higher priority than merchants. In the Christmas season of 1943, we drove to New Orleans to spend the season with Aunt Louise's family. We ran short of gas stamps and, while counting our ration stamps, had to coast down hills to conserve gasoline on the way back from New Orleans.

The housing shortage was tight. We were fortunate enough to be able to squeeze our family of five into a two-bedroom bungalow in the outskirts of far northwest Oklahoma City. We had our piano in the living room. There were two moveable folding beds for guests. Some stayed for a long time. Cousin Dorothy Dean Baker stayed as a guest for about a year during the war while she served as a secretary at Tinker Air Force Base, where bombers headed for war and where Douglas made C-47s. Typically our family invited at least one soldier to our family table every Sunday after church.

We had a victory garden in the back yard and a chicken coop behind the garage. The posters reminded us "Our food is fighting." We raised our own vegetables and planted fruit trees. Unfortunately deer and rabbits found our garden to be very tasty.

Our house was only steps away from a clay creek bed that fed into Will Rogers Park, which became my playground, my world to possess and my place to dream. My next door Native American friend Larry Wolfkill joined me in exploring the bluffs and hills. It was the perfect place for adventurous boys, like an enormous back yard. The park offered great stretches of grassy running space, picnic tables, huge oaks and a swimming pool. In the late evening we found crayfish by turning over rocks in the stream, watching them scurry away as they propelled themselves backward.

During the next years I walked over a mile to Taft Junior High School

every day, rain or shine. Taft offered a highly rated curriculum of three
years of preparation for Classen High School, one of the most rigorous
high schools in the state.

I was fortunate to begin learning Latin at thirteen years old. Few
schools in Oklahoma offered it, but fortunately mine did. The grounding
gained by Latin helped me later in historical studies, theological study,
the study of ancient writers and later with my hobby of collecting rare
books. The curriculum prepared me for later university studies in philosophy, literature and history.

Always making do. We easily found ways to entertain ourselves. The
strict limitations we learned from the Depression years were carried over
into the war years. We continued to spend little, save as much as we could
and give a fair share to whoever was in need, including Uncle Sam.

It was not unusual for kids to walk long distances to school during
the war because there was no gasoline. The snarled public bus routes
did not make it much easier. Walking was just the way you got from
one place to another. You did not expect to be picked up or delivered.
On Saturdays we went to downtown movies whenever we had ten cents
and bus fare.

As air conditioning did not yet exist, we engineered our own device
for cooling the house in the summer. The best we could do was to pipe
a spray of fan-cooled water dripped on straw that had been packed between chicken wires. I can still remember the refreshing fragrance of the
wet straw on a scorching day of dry heat. Those makeshift air coolers are
not to be confused with the refrigerated air conditioners that would
come some years after the war. Oklahoma heat was ordinarily so dry that
this worked well enough even on 100 degree days, which were frequent
in August. We drank lemonade sitting directly in the airflow, breathing
the cool breeze. When refrigerated air conditioning finally arrived, few
could afford it. Our family did not get a refrigerated air conditioner until
1950 or a television set until 1956.

After folding newspapers at five in the morning, I zipped around the
neighborhood on my bike trying to land the folded paper within reach
of the customer's front door. The paper boy was paid by the number of

weekly collections made. The most dreaded part for me was collecting the money. I had to screw up my courage to knock on the door. Later I would graduate to mowing lawns with a push lawnmower.

My brother was fortunate to land an exciting job downtown with Captain Ribble of Ribble Boat Works. He learned the skills of boat making at a very early age. Later he and I built our own boat in our garage. It was a small dory for fishing. When it leaked, we caulked. As time went on we caulked it again. It was always an adventure to take it out. But it was ours, and we made it, leaks and all.

In those days agile boys were hired to set up the pins at the bowling alley and then perch above them. Just after a bowling ball would hit the pins and send them flying, we would immediately jump in the perilous pit where the balls fell, reload them, and then jump out of the way before the next ball came smashing through. It was exhilarating each time the ball came roaring down the alley. When Dad found out what I was doing for forty cents an hour, he insisted that I look for a safer job.

I found ways to help out the troops: collecting glass bottles, gathering metals for military use, and putting out circulars on cars and doors for wartime causes. I saved tinfoil from gum wrappers, which were turned into reflective materials released from bombers to jam enemy radar. During air raid drills at school we sang songs like "Coming in On a Wing and a Prayer" and "Praise the Lord and Pass the Ammunition." I relished playing John Philip Souza marches in the school band, stepping along to such rousing marches as "Stars and Stripes Forever," "El Capitan," and "Semper Fidelis."

Tal worked on warplane production at Tinker Air Force. I made model airplanes that mimicked the P-51 Mustangs I so admired. I was enthralled with the sleek shape of the fighting planes. New designs of fighters, tankers and bombers were coming out month after month. With light balsa wood and thin paper I built model airplane replicas of P-48s and B-24s. From soft wood I carved out the likenesses of fast-flying P-38s and lethal B-25 Mitchell bombers. I could identify almost every profile of an airplane or ship that was out there fighting for us.

At school we bought war stamps that we pasted in books that eventually were intended to lead to the purchase of a war bond. At a quarter a stamp, we glued them into our war bond stamp book until we had enough to purchase an $18 bond, which eventually matured for $25. It took forever to make a full stamp book. The bonds yielded 2.9 percent interest, cashable after ten years. Dad put my war bond books in a safety deposit box. By 1949 I had almost forgotten about them. When I was getting ready to go to college I cashed them all out for $125.

We kept in touch with all our scattered family by what we called round-robin letters. Mom would set up the old upright Royal typewriter on the dining table, stuff into it about four carbon copies in a tight sheaf, and type away about all the family news. The recipients would forward these treasured carbon copy letters to others in the extended family. They often went through a half dozen hands.

In 1944 Dad had a heart attack. At age forty-nine he was put on a regimen of total rest. Grandmother Clark stayed with us for weeks during his recovery. For a while my two grandmothers rotated for periods of time in our house in order to help Mom care for Dad. After three months of absolute bed rest, Dad returned to his task of law enforcement.

Chopin and political imagination. Then came Chopin. He had a deep effect on my political imagination. In 1945 I saw the movie on the life of Frédéric Chopin—*A Song to Remember*. I had already been playing Chopin on the piano, but the epic film made me want to learn much more. I resolved to learn to play every piece of Chopin that I was capable of learning, although many were far beyond my competence.

The film was the story of a romantic idealist musician and virtuoso composer with a social conscience. I related to this idealism strongly. We were living in wartime, as was Chopin. While the film was being produced, Poland was in fact under the heel of SS troops and Nazi tanks. I was enthralled by the ordered freedom of Chopin's creations. I loved everything Chopin wrote, from preludes to nocturnes, mazurkas to waltzes, and etudes to concertos. His inventiveness penetrated to my core in a way no other composer had ever done.

But Chopin had another quality that also captured my imagination. His music had an underlying political inspiration. It reflected the heroic political idealism to which I was beginning to aspire. His music was my first intellectual passion. It fired my buoyant imagination and elevated my view of what music could do to the soul. As a boy who already had a large dose of romanticism I began to read poetry in the tradition of Wordsworth, Shelley, Keats and Kipling. Reading and memorizing poetry was far more important in my school years than any time since, but I was more than ready to absorb it then. Chopin gave musical voice my idealism. It was soaring, inventive and passionate. Chopin thought he was writing music for Poland. I thought he was writing for me.

To further this idealism I became interested in public speaking. On the shy side, I needed to push myself toward more winsome public communication skills. I read books on making speeches, the great orations, and on winning friends and influencing people. They did not make me a better person, but they made me a more confident communicator. I learned that I was able to draw people together and challenge them to do more than they had imagined. I became maximally involved in the youth activities of the Epworth League for Methodist young people, where I received ever-expanding doses of social justice aspirations.

Leroy dies in the battle for the Saar River. I followed the frightful stages of the war avidly, both on the radio and by reading the papers. We prayed for the troops through battle after battle, from Tunis to Normandy to Berlin. We followed the Pacific War intensely from the Solomon Islands to the Coral Sea to Bataan to Guadalcanal to Saipan.

My much-admired cousin Leroy was a hulking football tackle at Mountain View High School on the slopes of the Wichita range. He was amiable, funny and strong. On Thanksgiving Day in 1944 we had our last touch football game with all the cousins in front of the parsonage where Leroy's father, my Uncle Walker, was pastor. Leroy motivated me to play tough and smart. I still remember the long pass I caught from him and his whoop of approval. That was the last time I saw Leroy. He shipped off with the 45th Thunderbird Division when it was called into active combat. By that Christmas he was in France headed to the Saar River area. Within sight of the end of the war he was killed in heavy combat near Saarbrücken in January 1945. This was during the hard winter of the Battle of the Bulge, only four months before the war in Germany was over.

Personally I was hit harder by Leroy's death than by anything else in the war. I could not believe we had lost him. He had seemed indestructible. After Leroy's death, the 45th Infantry Division moved through the Saar Valley and smashed through the Siegfried Line.

Soon after the Allied Forces liberated the Nazi concentration camp at Buchenwald, Franklin D. Roosevelt died suddenly at Warm Springs, Georgia. I was walking home from school on April 12 when I stopped off as usual for ice cream at the little drug store half way home. There I heard of FDR's death. I arrived at home in tears feeling like a member of my family had died.

THE RETURN HOME

War's end and the taste of peace. Germany surrendered unconditionally on May 7, 1945. The neighborhood went wild with joy. We joined in street celebrations, fireworks, singing and nonstop exultation. There were many tears. We went to church that evening to pray for our soldiers' safe return.

I continued to watch the battles as the war persisted in the Pacific until the Battles of Okinawa and Wake Island. Although I did not know it, the first atomic bomb was being tested not far away in the New Mexico desert at the Trinity site.

We were stunned when on August 7 we heard about the bewildering Hiroshima atomic bomb, and then the one at Nagasaki two days later. On August 15 Emperor Hirohito announced Japan's unconditional surrender. On VJ Day, the whole nation once again danced, celebrated, and wept for joy.

The war had been a time of maximum effort, ending in euphoric relief. When the United Nations Charter was signed, I felt like I was living in a safer and saner world.

Mom's cousin George Seeger was released from a German POW Stalag. As an artist, while imprisoned in the Stalag, he used his own hair for a brush and found a way to make paintings in the prison camp using whatever materials were available. He sent one of those wonderful paintings to Mom. She hung it in our living room near the front door, reminding us of the sacrifice cousin George had made for our freedom. That dark painting was very small, but I felt awe each time I passed by.

For me it was time to reinvent my future. In the summer of 1946 our family moved back to our hometown of Altus, which had been only slightly changed by the war. The air base was much larger, now with huge hangers for transport aircraft. I rejoined my friends in my sophomore year. I was back in my element, quickly connecting with my old pals. Dad resumed his law practice, and Mom had her piano classes once again in our living room.

My return to Altus was all the more touching to me when I saw the open cemetery for the castaway airplanes from the war. They were being brought to Altus Air Force Base to be torn apart and melted down for scrap. Salvage crews also ripped out the usable electronic equipment for meltdown. Tal was on one of those wrecking crews.

I treasured the site of those broken planes. I knew that the guys in those planes had fought for me and my freedom, and that many had died. Colorful graffiti revealed the spirit, humor and hopes of the flight crews. Heavy flack damage from enemy anti-aircraft barrages showed the desperate battles they had fought. These were the real remnants of planes I had been previously venerating by fashioning their shapes into model airplanes out of balsa wood and paper. Now their last resting place was minutes from my house. With each round of the tractor on the far side of the airport, where I was planting wheat and cultivating fields that abutted the graveyard, I pondered their sacrifice.

The most famous B-17 bomber of the war, the "Memphis Belle," came to rest there. Two movies were made of its exploits. It had completed twenty-five combat missions intact.

I played a decent game of tennis, but it brought me no sense of triumph. I was at the age when I was feeling the need for a little glory. In the summer before my junior year I was determined to go out for football. I spent a hot summer working out, pushing weights and running long distances on the irrigation ditches with my tennis partner Billy Kirk Reid.

I did all the football coach asked, pushing weighted sleds, running laps, stepping through tires and doing jumping jacks and pushups. Coach was trying to get all of us toughened up. One day in practice I didn't hit hard enough and didn't run fast enough. Coach Broiles mimicked my lackluster way of doing pushups. He was right. At 126 pounds max, no matter how hard I tried, I was just too skinny to ever be a good football player. Most of the guys were in the 140-200 pound range. I left football and went back to music where I excelled.

The next season I rejoined the football team as its manager, which meant that I basically got to be the water boy, but I took the job seriously. I got to be close to glory, travel with the guys and stand in their shadows so close I could feel the glow. I was an efficient team manager, accepted and enthusiastic.

The most prized symbol in the school was an athletic letter jacket. Anyone with a jacket was in. I didn't think that it was possible for a manager to get a letter jacket, but I was wrong. When we celebrated a winning season banquet in a hotel ballroom filled with boosters, I was in for a surprise.

After all the jackets had been distributed, I heard my name called. To my complete shock I was called up to the podium to be presented with a prestigious football letter jacket. I received it and wore it with pleasure, however ambiguously I had earned it.

But that was not the end of the story. After rejoining the band, I became its president. I received a band jacket with a musical symbol on it at the senior banquet. Now I was the only student in Altus High who had two jackets. My tender soul could hardly handle that much glory. I took turns wearing them, but was always aware I had not really earned them in the normal way.

Driving stakes on a road crew. The only summer job I could find back in Altus after the war was with the Dunlop tire store, where trucks would pull up to the back to get tires changed. Mr. Duncan thought I could handle tire repairs. Truck tires were a hassle. I learned to use the hydraulic jack to lift the vehicle up, and then I wrestled tires off the rim with a heavy iron rim separator. I pried them loose from the frame with brute strength, disconnecting the inner tube from the outer tire, and then found out what was wrong, and repaired it with pressed hot glue.

Some tires weighed more than I did, which made my job difficult. They sometimes stuck to the rims like cement. I did acceptable work, but decided this was not the job for me.

For a while I was on a crew applying hot tar to flat-roofed buildings. We went up on tall ladders, pulled heavy materials up by a pulley, heated foul-smelling tar and spread it on evenly with push brooms. I did not last long at the tar business. The best thing I gained from the experience was that my respect deepened for tough, resilient, working people.

The hardest physical work I ever did, apart from farming, was driving stakes on a highway road crew. I was assigned to swing a twelve-pound ballpein sledgehammer on stakes for a state highway survey crew charged with bridge construction and maintenance. It was an Oklahoma summer of record heat, with many days over 100 degrees. The survey crew was staking out boundaries for waterways and roadways. This paid better than other jobs and increased my upper-body strength, so I was an eager employee. Each day the crew truck would pick me up at 6 a.m., take my crew out to its distant location, drop us off in the heat, and then we would work hard until 11:30 a.m.. After a merciful lunch break in a rural restaurant, we would work three or four more hours in the blistering afternoon sun. The senior crew of surveyors carefully marked where my stake belonged. All I had to do was take my sledge hammer and pound it down into the ground. It sounded easy, but what I didn't figure on was that the clay soil in the summer was so baked it seemed like rock.

Our crew was working a few miles out near the one-street farm town of Gotebo, where everyone toiled mightily just to survive. The town had only one mom-and-pop café with a large airplane propeller-size fan for cooling. They knew what their thirsty customers wanted. Their super-large 16 ounce tin cans of sweetened ice tea served with a handle soldered on the can were to us like a godsend. The road crew gave me the opportunity to get to know tough workers who did not ever complain. I enjoyed being with all of them, the crew and the people.

What I learned from hardscrabble dirt farming. In my high school years and early college years (1947–1951), Tal and I raised five seasons of wheat crops, four seasons of maize, four of cotton and two of alfalfa. We were learning all the time, working long hours without any guarantee that we would be successful in raising those crops.

Dad needed an experienced farming partner to work the land he had been acquiring over the years. He never believed in paper or stock investments, and thought the only thing worth owning was land. Dad found an experienced sharecropper named Clarence Bowman. Mr. Bowman was a steady, modest, resilient farmer who always wore a crumpled straw hat and faded blue overalls. He and his wife raised a houseful of children in the small farmhouse on our irrigated farm, which featured dairy cows, jackrabbits, chickens and lots of sweat. The Bowmans lived rent free in the house, splitting profits with Dad by agreed-upon shares.[2]

Tal and I assisted Mr. Bowman doing whatever he thought we needed to do. We spent long days plowing, planting, cultivating, irrigating and finally harvesting. We had to learn how to set a straight furrow, monitor what was happening in the plant root systems under the topsoil, check for insects and diseases, and apply manure to stimulate growth. Mr. Bowman used few words. He was unhappy when we did not catch on quickly as he expected us to do exactly what he said and figure things out for ourselves. We also got a basic introduction to farm equipment maintenance with our International Harvester Farmall tractor.

Farmers in Jackson County were vulnerable to crop failures and bank failures. Any who went bust began again from scratch with whatever they had.

Dad was attorney for the legal and legislative needs of the Jackson County Irrigation Authority. It was among the first in the state to develop a large gravity flow irrigation project where water flowed downstream from the distant reservoir in the Quartz Mountains through ditches with controllable dams to be released gradually into the rows of our fields. We learned how to start the flow of water by suction tubes from the irrigation ditches. Tal and I were responsible for 160 acres of land under irrigation, plus several other unirrigated plots of land outside the Irrigation District.

I loved working with farm people. They were unpretentious, straightforward and guileless. For several growing seasons their world was my world. Tal and I had an arrangement with Dad that if we could make crops grow, he would help provide us with a path to college, which I knew was a good deal. We were also expected to help support ourselves in college by whatever jobs we could find.

The day came when my task was to clear out wide swaths of robust Johnson grass whose roots went deep around the tender cotton roots to choke the life out of them. I was sixteen, armed only with a hoe. Johnson grass is the most insidious weed on the prairie. I could hoe it to ground level, but that did little good if the roots remained intact.

Through this ordeal I learned something about myself. I decided I did not want to work that hard for a living. I liked a lot about farming, but it was in the Johnson grass patches that I decided my future had to be with books and ideas, not muscle and sweat.

It was on a 99 degree day with a hoe in calloused hands, with sweat obscuring my vision, with my face caked with dirt, that I quietly promised myself to become a more attentive and deliberate student. It was a cotton field epiphany. God was hedging my way with a wall of Johnson grass. Happily, I had already acquired a taste for reading.

From Handel to Hank Williams. My vocation of writing began when I created a comic column in the school newsletter spoofing all things related to the high school. My pen name was "Flash." I enjoyed writing in a way that sparked laughter.

My most rigorous class in high school turned out to be the most beneficial for me. It was Mrs. Peterson's demanding course on public speaking. I gained confidence to speak in public under her no-nonsense mentoring. This also gave me an opportunity to hone my research skills and make public presentations confidently.

At fifteen I organized a German polka band called "The Hungry Five," which featured comic skits. We played for family, neighborhood and church, and later created our own impromptu Spike Jones impressions, playing gigs wherever we could find an audience. We got some laughs and made some amusing and unconventional noises. Soon we formed a barbershop quartet, who provided entertainment at service clubs, school assemblies and church basements. We found venues for singing everything from Gospel to Handel. Our repertoire of comedy numbers was in a kitschy lampoon style.

With my guitar I sang virtually every song Hank Williams ever wrote, twanging and yodeling as much like Hank as I could, singing with a cracked voice "Lonesome Blues," "I'm So Lonesome I Could Cry" and "I Can't Help It." The same with Roy Acuff and Patsy Cline. I did all this without missing a beat on Haydn, Schumann and Stravinsky. My favorite songs were those of Rogers and Hammerstein, from *South Pacific*, *Oklahoma!* and *Carousel*. I found it easy to learn to play a bit of ukulele, harmonica and ocarina (sweet potato). We also had a full-size harp in our living room, which Mom taught to special students, and which I did my best to learn.

During my high school senior year, my hometown of Altus was chosen by *Look* magazine as "The All-American City," and I felt it was, with a population of little more than five thousand, which was the optimal size, according to Plato's *Republic*, of the ideal *polis*.

The 1950s

Love and Learning

◈

COLLEGIATE YEARS

Hurdling left. I packed off to the University of Oklahoma in late August 1949. My brother, Tal, was far more than a typical roommate. He was a reliable guide to the challenging new world of the university. I decided not to follow him in joining a college fraternity because I wanted to be able to claim my own time and not get trapped in the party subculture. Having plowed cotton, I now had to learn how to plow through books, cultivate consistent ideas, and bring them all into positive outcomes.

From my first memories Tal had always led the way and I had followed. At the university he was my role model for scholarship, performance, music and politics. He was always tirelessly ready to give his time to help and advise me. Along with my dad, he gave me a role model for becoming a man.

Tal and I roomed together the first year in a place we jokingly called "the White House," a clapboard garage that had been turned into a boarding room in Mrs. Packard's backyard. It was large enough only for our bunk beds plus a place to hang Tal's twenty-two caliber rifle and my guitar. We saw it as barely more than a "room and a path," but favorably situated near our classes. Mrs. Packard presided over a hungry dining table of students of many languages and cultural settings. They ranged from freshmen like me to graduate students from places like Iran and Venezuela.

The White House was a block from the campus to the west and a block to the Santa Fe Railroad to the east. Four times a day the quiet campus was filled with the abrupt whistles, clanging and clattering of trains thundering by. Since I had grown up loving the rumblings and echoes of trains, I felt very much at home.

This tiny living space became the war room for the great proletarian uprising we not only expected, but in some vague way sought, even if only in our fantasies. I lit my pipe with aromatic tobacco, strummed my guitar while singing labor protest songs, and talked endlessly with well-bred co-conspirators of an imagined revolution.

Tal and I stayed at the White House until the spring of 1950, when we began working as dishwashers for Mrs. Slade's boarding house. During Easter of 1951 Tal married a terrific woman who was to become one of the dearest friends in my life, Jane Hazlett. While Tal was busy establishing a life with Jane, I was plunging more deeply into ideas than relationships.

I lived at Mrs. Mary James' house the next year, which was close to University Theatre and three blocks from the tennis courts. Mrs. James's nephew, Charley Mahone, had invited me to room and board there. Charley was a top student headed for a PhD in clinical psychology and eventually for postgraduate study with Anna Freud at the Tavistock Clinic in London. From Charley I got my first glimpse into the theories and ideas of psychoanalysis.

My first meeting with a university official was with Dean Glenn Couch. He had a practice of choosing several first-year students to guide personally, and he chose me. Three years earlier he had selected Tal out of the freshmen students as a bright advisee working toward an accelerated pre-law program.

When the dean asked me what I wanted to study in college, I said probably law or preparation for graduate school. That was all he needed to hear. The dean told me that they had just the program for me, which was called Letters. This was a new liberal arts program initiated that fall in which you were allowed to read, with the adviser's guidance, whatever you wanted to read in literature, history and philosophy. At that moment

I knew I was in the right place. From then on I never had any regrets and never went through any struggle in choosing a major.

Letters was an honors program for those who would be likely candidates for graduate studies in the humanities. It encouraged students to develop a self-designed curriculum in independent interdisciplinary study.

This program allowed me to choose the best professors in almost any sequence. It was not until overall academic standings were calculated at the end of my first year that I got word that I had unexpectedly been elected to the freshman honor society, Phi Eta Sigma. That group immediately sent me off to Houston to represent the University of Oklahoma as a delegate to their 1950 National Convention. It was for this reason that I had my first airline flight.

The youthful Dr. Clayton Feaver, who had received his PhD at Yale under the great Professor H. Richard Niebuhr, was hired to teach religion and ethics at OU just as I got there. He became the first of a long string of early mentors for me who studied or taught with Richard Niebuhr at Yale (among others were Albert C. Outler, Paul Ramsey and James Gustafson). Being Feaver's first Letters student was an honor. He introduced me to Augustine, Aquinas and Calvin. I am happy to report that in the next half century my niece Amy Oden and her niece Sarah Taylor Oden would also graduate from the OU Letters program.

Books and ideas were intriguing not only for me but for many in my family, which had more than its share of professors, lawyers and clergy. While I was at OU, my Uncle Dave was teaching at Purdue, my Uncle Ira was in a PhD program at Berkeley and my Uncle Hen was teaching at Southern Methodist University's School of Law. My cousin William E. Oden was getting his PhD in history at the University of Wisconsin, on his way toward becoming president of one of the branch campuses of the University of Texas. And my cousin (later Bishop) William B. Oden would soon be headed for Harvard and a PhD at Boston University. Many more family PhDs would follow in the next generation.

With my special opportunity in Letters at OU, I could now read to my heart's content in poetry, the novel, the events of human history and the many ideas to be examined. I read E. E. Cummings, Shakespeare, Plato and tried to read Spinoza. I spent hours at Rickner's Book Store, looking for whatever new or used books I could afford. I devoted endless hours to wandering freely around the open stacks of the great Bizzell Library, the largest research library in the state. The library was magical, built in a red-and-white turreted style similar to Windsor Castle, with spacious, walnut-paneled reading rooms and a half million books. I was a happy bookworm feasting through long rows of shelves. I was especially drawn to library sections that dealt with the meaning of history.

In those early, delicious days of free-spirited reading, I was peculiarly drawn to the agnostics and atheists, partly to let them test my belief system, which they did. There I met Friedrich Nietzsche and found him to be the most poetic and rhetorically powerful of all the philosophers (until I later read Søren Kierkegaard). In the psychology section I read Sigmund Freud, who forced me to question everything I had learned beforehand about psychological dynamics, abnormality, dreams and sexuality.

But it was Marx who stormed into my imagination, especially on the labor theory of value, the class struggle and economic determinism in history. First I read early Marx material: his theory of alienation and critique of private property in his 1844 papers, his vision of proletarian revolution, and his *Theses on Feuerbach*, where he argued that the task is not to interpret the world but to change it.

This prompted me to search into the antecedents of Marxist socialism (Saint-Simon, Robert Owen and Proudhon) and its later interpreters in Lenin, Trotsky and Norman Thomas. I studied Marx's influence on sociology (Émile Durkheim and Max Weber), philosophy (Herbert Marcuse), psychology (Wilhelm Reich), and political theory (Harold Laski). Their weaknesses would gradually become evident in the sad histories of their disastrous consequences, as in Ukraine, the Gulags and Cambodia. I was a Marxist utopian dreamer for a decade before I learned the vulnerabilities of Marxist theories. As I looked back, it was full of deeply flawed arguments, but they were central to my thoughts in the fifties. I let their words saturate my mind before I went to seminary, and they remained in my mind like a ghost well beyond my years at Yale.

The ideas I most loved were expressed by three in particular: the will to power (Nietzsche), the desire to understand the sexual roots of all behavior (Freud), and the search for radical social change (Marx). Even today when I speak of modernity, I am pointing especially to those three prototypes of modern consciousness.

The love of my life. The fifties began for me at the Acacia Christmas Dance in 1949. Until then I had only seen Edrita Pokorny from a distance as a star of the OU School of Drama on the grand proscenium of University Theatre. The Acacia Dance was one of the major social events of the season, but not something I normally would have attended. Pastor Ray Anderson linked me up with Nina May Allen, who was visiting Edrita in Norman. Edrita wanted someone to escort her childhood friend to the big dance. Since I had met Nina May the previous summer at Turner Falls Camp, I happily agreed. As it turned out, I got to dance a few times with Edrita and found myself amiably drawn to her.

At the next Sunday night gathering of the Wesley Foundation, about thirty students gathered for a simple dinner, some square dancing and singing. Edrita, already recognizable as the ascending star of theater studies, had come to escape from a very busy schedule of rehearsals. I had seen her perform in *The Women* by Claire Booth Luce in the fall of 1949 to a full house at the huge Holmberg Hall at OU, and knew she received rave reviews for her performance. I had also seen her in several other major fall productions. Now, wonderfully, here she was, showing up at this Methodist student center informal get-together.

After the square dancing ended, mild-mannered Pastor Ray signaled it was time to offer thanks and eat. Being a slow mover, I gradually made my way to sit down on a folding chair, but Edrita pulled the chair away from me. Her timing was exquisite, and I found myself sitting on the floor looking up at her laughing gleefully with everyone else. To me, she was the most gorgeous girl in the room, a beautiful natural blond who was elegant in every way, but also playful, affable, gracious and almost totally unaware of her striking beauty.

We hit it off from the beginning, and I was smitten. She was quick-witted, while I was drolly amusing. She could tell stories that made people collapse with laughter, often long stories with many twists and turns, and with an unerring sense of timing.

It seemed as if we were seldom apart after that evening at the Wesley Foundation gathering. I thought of myself as an avant garde social radical, while she was totally dedicated to her craft as an artist, both in acting and directing. We were so different. She probed every inward feeling or motivational approach to deepen her capacity to portray a character. This made for absorbing conversations between the two of us.

As an artist she deepened my aesthetic sensibilities. She was also a gentle and effective critic. I quickly found that she was becoming everything to me. She provided practical ballast to my volatile idealism, and my life was brightened by her presence, brilliance and love.

My story cannot be told without her as she was a crucial part of my intellectual and spiritual formation. We were only nineteen when we met, but our story together would last for the next forty-six years.

I quietly became drawn toward the idyllic picture of marrying her and becoming a bookish country parson with her by my side. We dated as often as possible between January and July 1950 when she went abroad with a traveling theater troupe to Europe. She had been invited to join an ensemble for a traveling summer of performance and study in Europe called the Greasepaint Caravan for Peace, run by the National Methodist Student Movement. This troupe was directed by Joe Love and Ruth Love, who virtually invented theatrical experimentation in Methodist worship, with special interests in how the dramatic arts might be utilized for social change. This was an early form of the "community theater movement."

I found that my sense of self-worth soared with Edrita by my side. She walked every step with me in my interior debate about whether or not I would go into the ministry, law or writing, and we corresponded heavily throughout her time in Europe. I spent that summer at Perkins School of Theology in Dallas getting credentialed for a pre-ordination trial preaching appointment. I was so relieved when she returned. At some point I came to realize that she had kept all of my letters neatly wrapped in a pink ribbon, which pleased me so much. I was just nuts about her.

When I was offered the opportunity to serve a rural church as student pastor, Edrita and I talked it over and decided it could be a trial run into parish ministry. I was so grateful that she took to parish life so winsomely and endearingly. When she could break loose from her heavy practice and performance schedule, she would join in that tiny parish. She often accompanied me in the 1946 Dodge I bought in order to travel twenty-six miles between my first church at Ninnekah and the university.

By early 1951 I needed some time to push through my ambivalences regarding both marriage and vocation. I had a decisive conversation with my dad, who had fortunately come up to Oklahoma City on legal matters just at the right time to talk this through with me. I got from him all I needed for my breakthrough decision.

Edrita's best friend in Ada was Phyllis Evans. During our courtship Phyllis married a Methodist minister in a rural parish. That was a happy serendipity for us because Phyllis gave Edrita a glimpse of what marriage to a minister might mean. Fortunately for me, Edrita could see herself very happy in that picture.

In April when the white dogwoods were blooming all over Norman, we went together to a crowded Resurrection Day service. After the service and finally alone in the foyer of the church, we found ourselves talking in a room filled with flowers. In a rare moment of impulsive clarity, I reached for one of those plain wooden usher's chairs and asked her to sit down. I got down on my knees and asked her to marry me. Both life vocation and life companionship were settled on that Easter day. We set our wedding date for August 10. Living alone like a church mouse in a spare attic room in McFarlin Church with only the bare necessities—a toaster and peanut butter—I counted the days until Edrita would become my wife.

Edrita had the exceptional opportunity of starring opposite David Niven in New York in a Sunday night radio presentation of the Philip Morris Playhouse on Broadway in May before our August wedding. She had won a competition to represent the University of Oklahoma in the dramatic story of *The Seventh Veil* at the central studios of CBS Radio in Manhattan. This was her first major theatrical performance beyond the university. It was an honor for the university and a great pleasure for me to hear her play a costarring role opposite a great British and Hollywood film actor before a nationwide audience. It was a demanding role, and she played it superbly.

In our parish that Sunday evening the congregation gathered with me for a special evening service after which we all huddled around a radio and listened to Edrita perform. When she was back on campus, she received the coveted Buffalo Mask Award for being the outstanding student in theater arts. She continued to be frequently cast in university productions and was easily recognized for her accomplishments on the campus.

After a honeymoon in the Ouachita Mountains, we settled snugly into a small upstairs garage apartment tucked in behind the large brick mansion of Law School Dean Judge John G. Hervey. It was an idyllic honeymoon hideaway for the two of us.

We loved our parish ministry at Ninnekah. I was picking up the knack of what it meant to preach. I read books on homiletics and studied the sermons of others. I quickly learned that I had to tone down my social radicalism at the pulpit if I was to be an effective minister in a rural setting. The farmers in Ninnekah were diligent, independent, loyal and resourceful. Since I had raised several crops in Jackson County, I had no difficulty identifying with them, calling on them at their homes, visiting and counseling them in my simple way.

People expected home pastoral visits and missed them if I did not show up now and then. As the pastor I was treated like a member of the family. I went out on lengthy rounds of visitation and would find them in their ordinary living situation doing whatever they were doing. I found rural ministry very compatible with my temperament. Edrita cheerfully adapted to her new role as a pastor's wife.

The choices Edrita and I made the first two years of college made an impact on the rest of our lives. All the challenges I took, she took with me, and we grew closer together at every turn. We decided to undergo a rigorous graduate education that would prepare us mutually for a life of making a family together and being able to engage in the work of ministry and in the life of learning.

Every turn a left turn. Even though I had been totally committed to the war effort during the war, I quickly became a pacifist after the first atomic bomb blast. Once I connected with my church's national youth movement, I began to see the vision of a world where all weapons would be banned, opening the way for a world government that would seek social justice and where peace and sanity would prevail. In that teenage dream of mine, the world court in The Hague would make just decisions on international conflicts, and the newly born United Nations would bring the entire world together into one peaceful planet. Without a second thought, I began to march lockstep with antiwar and pacifist sentiments and social revolutionary ideas.

Within one month after Hiroshima, I was pledged to the principles of far-left pacifism. Most of the arguments turned out to be oversimplified, as I later learned, but as a youth they appealed to my romanticist idealism. It seemed simple: totally disarm now, pursue peace, seek justice, trust the power of reason to overcome conflicts between nations, refuse to cooperate with the military-industrial complex, and expose the money trail to learn who had been benefiting from war economically.

As it turned out, my church sent their youth to summer camps more to gain a vision of social justice than of personal religious experience. I was elected to represent Oklahoma at a regional church youth camp in Fayetteville, Arkansas. There the national youth leadership outlined their plan for the future and taught us about the labor movement, grasping capitalists and the need for total disarmament.

From then on my intellectual trajectory was poised for leaping much further to the political left. That meant Henry Wallace and the Farmer-Labor wing of the Democratic Party. Those hurdles happened abruptly, and my course was set early. The national Methodist youth movement was a world of its own, with extensive organization and strong political convictions. It was designed for propaganda that promoted social change according to the Social Gospel vision pouring out of the theological schools. My distant ideological mentors for that dream were socialist candidate Norman Thomas, pacifist pioneer A. J. Muste and British Hyde Park preacher Donald Soper. I got this indoctrination second- and thirdhand from reading and from going to youth conferences on all levels—local, district, conference, jurisdictional and national levels. As a teenager I was not sufficiently self-critical to see any unintended consequences, and such talk was not encouraged.

Between 1946 and 1956, every turn was a left turn. I had to fend off temptations toward anarchism. I was more deeply drawn into the vision of an egalitarian society shaped by radical social engineering, Marxist historical and sociological interpretation, and resource redistribution.

Everything imaginable seemed possible for my young mind, and I was well rewarded for my utopian thoughts by those older leaders of my church. Resistance to all of those ideas simply didn't occur either on my part or on the part of people I knew, including family and friends. I was on a mission to make the world a much better place and felt empowered to actually transform our society.

My job as regional youth leader was to take the Social Gospel message to the other district and state camps and gatherings. At the Turner Falls youth camp in Oklahoma in the summers of 1948 and 1949 I was already beginning to be an activist leader within the conference system. This took on special significance when I was elected to go to the national conference of nine thousand Methodist youth in Cleveland in January 1949, when I was seventeen years old. There I was introduced to a left-leaning political agenda blessed by the church youth leaders I trusted. I was challenged to enter the ministry, but not to a ministry of Word and Sacrament or of evangelization or soul care. The national Methodist Youth Movement was enthralled with the imagination of a revolution that we thought would essentially replace the traditional gospel. I was so excited to help lead the way as I wanted to plan others' lives for them and thought I could do that for them better than they could for themselves. Looking back now, I see the ego and self-serving agenda into which I was caught up, but I didn't see any of that back then.

My first practical adventure into radical politics was to become an activist in the World Federalist Movement also at age seventeen. I organized an oratorical contest for my church as a senior in high school. I hired the largest hall in town for the meeting and invited all the youth leaders in the district, but almost no one showed up. Undaunted, I pressed on.

I do not remember ever hearing a pacifist or politically leftist sermon in my home church. But it did not take me long to begin to pick up more clearly the pacifist idealism from the national leaders of the International Fellowship of Reconciliation, the World Federalist Movement and the Methodist Federation for Social Action. I would later come to understand that Boston University School of Theology had produced the most articulate Methodist pacifists which had been led by their pacific bishops. Among Presbyterians and Congregationalists most came from Union Seminary in New York or Chicago Divinity School. They were active in the late forties and went viral in the fifties.

I consistently found the pacifist dream intimately connected with the dream of wealth redistribution. My fellow dreamers and I thought we had better ideas than did the masses we imagined we were protecting. In our hubris we thought we were embodying great intelligence and common sense that surpassed all traditional ideas.

During the war I knew only a few who had serious moral reservations about the war, but Hiroshima ended that. The pacifists appeared like mushrooms out of the dust and smoke of Nagasaki. The physicists who had built the bomb were having second thoughts and the intelligentsia was troubled. If the pacifist spirit was slumbering during the war, it was wide awake in postwar America, even in remote and culturally conservative Oklahoma.

A few of us like-minded students found each other my first year at The University of Oklahoma. We started singing the songs of labor and socialism in a conspicuous place on the campus, but mostly we just loved to sing. Yet some of us loved even more the ideas about which we sang: world revolution against profit motive, private property and the economics of war. We unthinkingly assumed it would be a revolution without firing a shot, based purely on rational ideas. We truly believed that we would do this on moral persuasion alone of the sort we saw modeled in Gandhi.

With my five-string banjo, I blithely sang the new hymnody that came straight out of the labor left. The revolutionary songs in 1950 replaced the hymns I had sung in the 1940s, and I was very comfortable with that.

All the leftist students at the university suffered through the bitter climate of accusations that characterized the McCarthy period. Many Methodists were accused of procommunist sympathies. I assumed and feared that the FBI might have a file on me as a student activist.[1]

Participation in the Army Reserve Officers' Training Corp was mandatory, so I bit my tongue and spent hours marching with a wooden rifle. I did not score well in mechanical rifle assembly, hence my worst grade in college turned out to be in military science. My friend Charley and I discovered that we could get exemptions from marching if we registered to be on a university sports team, so we both signed up for the tennis team. Charley climbed up the tennis team ladder as quickly as I descended it, but we managed to escape the fate of marching with an imitation weapon.

Because of the Korean War, men between eighteen and thirty-five were required to be in a lottery draft for two years. I registered for the draft but was never called. My friend Pete Hitt was killed during that terrible winter in Korea in 1950. This left me to wonder if his death might be redeemed or made right by my pacifist life. I thought maybe I should have been there with him, much like I had felt about my cousin Leroy buried near the Siegfried Line. My guilt at not doing enough for my country fueled the flames of my revolutionary heart.

The church as an instrument for political change. I went into the ministry to use the church to elicit political change according to a soft Marxist vision of wealth distribution and proletarian empowerment. Edrita could sense that I was on a long and uncertain path. She was always more conservative than I, but she did share my basic social values and was willing at least to let me test my political follies.

I was enamored with every aspect of the 1950s' ecumenical Student Christian Movement. My dad had participated in it in his early twenties when it was oriented to world mission. He had raised money for the very campus church building that introduced me to political radicalism: McFarlin Church in Norman.

Whenever I read the New Testament after 1950, I was trying to read it entirely without its crucial premises of incarnation and resurrection. That required a lot of circular reasoning for me to establish what the text said. I habitually assumed that truth in religion was finally reducible to economics (with Marx) or psychosexual motives (with Freud) or self-assertive power (with Nietzsche). It was truly a self-deceptive time for me, but I had no inkling of its insidious dangers.

My views on wealth redistribution were shaped largely by knowledge elites who earned their living by words and ideas—professors, writers and movement leaders. Like most of the broadminded clergy I knew, I reasoned out of modern naturalistic premises, employing biblical narratives narrowly and selectively as I found them useful politically. The saving grace of God on the cross was not in my mix of life-changing ideas.

My university was probably less liberal than most other universities. My best political mentors, like John Paul Duncan, were less volatile, less drawn toward radical possibilities, less ideological than I. I can now sadly say that I enjoyed my radical idealism to the fullest extent possible and actually rejoiced in being more extreme in my thinking than almost anyone I knew.

Like Tal I was reasonably skilled in networking and political strategizing, but he was never as far left as I was seeking to be. He studied political science and history in preparation for a life in the law profession. I gravitated toward his best teachers, especially those leaning farthest to the left.

When E. Stanley Jones, Methodism's most conspicuous author, visited Norman in 1952, I sought an individual conversation with him. We talked about vocations, both his and mine, as I was struggling to decide between pastoral ministry and teaching. He encouraged me to keep studying and praying until I got resolution. I thought I might undertake a ministry similar to his involving evangelical missions in India coupled with active social service.

Shortly after that I had the opportunity to meet Martin Niemöller, one of the founders of the Confessing Church movement, who opposed the Nazification of the German Protestant churches. I probed his mind as I chauffeured him from Norman to Tulsa for a public lecture. He was an international leader of the pacifist movement and a brave opponent of

Hitler. Pastor Niemöller had been willing to suffer imprisonment rather than abandon his commitment to the freedom of the pulpit to preach the gospel, and had been imprisoned at Dachau until the allied troops arrived in 1945. His antiwar activism and his resistance to anti-Semitism were for me a model of the kind of ministry to which I aspired.

Songs of an imagined revolution. My Jewish friend Bob Simha, from New York City, was the only person I knew who could really play the five-string banjo. Bob had traveled on the Hudson River Sloop with Pete Seeger, the folk song master himself. Bob taught me how to pick and improvise on the instrument so as to get the optimal combination of percussion, rhythm and ingenuity from every stroke. Having played guitar, I adapted to the five-string banjo whose fifth string gave me the opportunity for many more rhythmic variations than I would have had with strumming instruments.

Every Sunday midday our group of would-be revolutionaries gathered to sing labor protest songs at the South Oval at OU, across from the Bizzell Library entrance. We sang labor movement songs, solidarity songs and songs that spoofed the political right. We sang the songs of Leadbelly, the Weavers, Josh White and Odetta. Those are names hardly recognizable today, but in my youth they were the pioneers of the American folk music tradition upon which Joan Baez, Bob Dylan, and Peter, Paul and Mary would later build their recording careers.

Our largest storehouse for songs was the far left *Students for Democratic Action Songbook.* I still cherish that little weather-beaten mimeographed book. It contains a treasured depository of folk, labor and socialist songs, including protest songs, African American spirituals and Appalachian poverty songs. We sang about the penniless, the struggling masses, the oppressed and the labor organizers, all of whom were being tormented by corrupt capitalists.

The confluence of music and literature with socialist and labor history were all woven into the same fabric of social advocacy. All my close friends were left-wing Democrats involved in liberal church social action efforts, mostly Presbyterians, Methodists or Disciples of Christ. Some of us organized the first meeting of the noncommunist SDA (Students for

Democratic Action), a student branch of the Americans for Democratic Action. Luminaries such as Eleanor Roosevelt, Arthur Schlesinger and John Kenneth Galbraith led the SDA nationally.

The core of our folk singing group met at least twice weekly, often at Bob and Nancy Smith's house, to sing and fantasize about how we were going to remake the world. We talked of revolution, but always with the premise that we would be the clean hands and blue sky idea elites rather than combatants in the trenches.

All of us were youth from churches of mainline Protestantism, joined under the umbrella of the National Council of Churches. We believed we were "on the side of history."

We were the core of those activist students who were intensely involved in the largely innocuous actions of the student senate, of which I was vice president. We were the ones that ran for offices, schmoozed with political bigwigs, asked tough questions to visiting speakers and performed our protest songs on any occasion.

I was especially moved by the music and temperament of fellow Oklahoman Woody Guthrie because he articulated in music what I felt in my heart. I liked his plain singing, easygoing spirit and the down-to-earth pathos of his songs. Woody grew up in Okemah, Oklahoma, and Pampa, Texas, near my hometown of Altus. While he was "on the road," I was singing his kind of songs in his style, with my five-string banjo. While he was unwittingly co-opted by the Communist Party, I was more than willing to be co-opted by the SDA socialists.

I found Saul Alinsky's teaching of socialist pragmatism and political opportunism extremely useful as I made plans to co-opt religious structures as instruments for the fundamental transformation of society. I was slow to grasp the crass moral callousness of Alinsky's methods. Alinsky, a Chicago poverty community organizer, became a model of tough-minded, no-nonsense social transformation. His *Reveille for Radicals* had great appeal for a pastoral idealist like me and would also have a decisive effect on Hillary Clinton and Barack Obama in the years that followed. Both of them came from the Alinsky-led Chicago school of push-and-shove politics.

I learned from Alinsky to think of everything in terms of class conflict. Alinsky's project to build grassroots peoples' organizations was based on polarized thinking between the oppressed and the oppressors. Today it is referred to as "class warfare," a metaphor that comes right out of the core of the Marxist historical vision of the victory of the proletariat against the bourgeoisie. Alinsky's goal was the redistribution of power with himself as the chief distributer. He taught me that radicals precipitate the social crises by strategic deception, surprise attacks on vulnerabilities, direct action and rhetorical cover-up. He taught me how to distinguish liberals from radicals. I preferred the radicals. Liberals talk. Radicals organize.

I read Rousseau's *Social Contract*, the Marx-Engels *Correspondence* and Thomas Jefferson on the *Necessity of Taking up Arms* and his deistic New Testament (*The Life and Morals of Jesus of Nazareth*). My head spun with visionary ideas, but it was not until I read Howard Fast's novel *Citizen Tom Paine* that I became inwardly identified with the revolutionary struggle. While writing that book, Howard Fast joined the Communist Party.

In college I lost the capacity for heartfelt, extemporized prayer. I would have considered it gauche to pray spontaneously aloud with other college sophomores. I had also left behind my love of the church's Scriptures, prayers and especially its hymns, but I always knew they would be there if I went back to find them.

I first read William Butler Yeats with Dr. Stanley Kaufman in the fall of 1952. Edrita and I took that course together. Yeats became a lifelong literary companion for me both in the poetic arts and in political imagination. It was Yeats who lifted my imagination to quiet recognition of the power of the word, as did Shakespeare.

I wanted to learn better how to write, so I took several courses at the Creative Writing Laboratory led by William Foster Harris. He stimulated within me a passionate interest in writing novels and stories, as well as a desire to write more simply, winsomely and truthfully. An experienced teacher of fiction writing, Harris was a timely guide for ushering me confidently into the world of writing. He went over with me every line I wrote, critiquing, encouraging and cajoling.

After writing many short stories, I was allowed by Harris to write my first novel in my junior year on the biblical figure Amos the prophet, entitled *Let Justice Roll.* It was a fictional version of my political ideas. My second novel was written in my senior year on the story of John the Baptist, titled *Dayspring.* Both had strong social justice motifs. Mercifully they have remained unpublished manuscripts and the readers have been spared. I owe a great debt to Harris. I learned the habits of the writer: merciless editing for economy, redrafting, lively imagination and especially rising early for lucid thought. My model as a writer was Thomas Wolfe's passionate, self-disclosing, moving prose.

My early mentors in reading the Christian classics in primary sources were Cortez A. M. Ewing in the history of political theory. and Clayton Feaver in Western philosophy and religion. They provided my first glimpses into Augustine, Theodore of Mopsuestia and Abelard. These would prepare me for studies with Outler at Perkins and Niebuhr at Yale.[2]

The theologian who guided me toward a dialogue with culture was Paul Tillich, especially in *Theology of Culture.* It provided the theological rationale for the years I spent in the psychology-and-religion dialogue.

I had great admiration for Ho Chi Minh as an agrarian patriot ten years before America's entry into the Vietnam war. Like many Social Gospel Methodists in the fifties, I identified strongly with the Vietnamese national independence movement against the French colonialists, which our government supported. By the time the anti-Vietnam War protest movement heated up in the 1960s I had already been a sympathizer favoring Ho for years. In the early 1950s Ho appeared to be a gentle, benign anticolonialist.

Many of the social theorists I was avidly tracking in the 1950s were from the Marxist-oriented Frankfurt School: Georg Lukács, Theodor W. Adorno, Herbert Marcuse and Ernst Bloch. Among those were also psychoanalysts trying to blend Marx and Freud, such as Wilhelm Reich, Helene Deutsch and Karen Horney. I especially had great admiration for four leading religious leaders—all Protestant pastors: Harry Ward,[3] A. J. Muste, Norman Thomas[4] and John Swomley.[5] All were socialists and pacifists.[6]

I cared deeply, as did many pastors and bishops, about those pacifist collectivists who never won an election or even wide acceptance in the local churches, but who held sway in the growing church bureaucracies. When in 1950 the *Reader's Digest* attacked "Methodism's Pink Fringe," they were targeting the very leaders with whom I most identified.

Those who encouraged my social illusions seemed to me to be the very best representatives of the church and the university. I had little resistance to going astray from those I trusted most.

Abandoning the patrimony. I have been asked why I abandoned my patrimony and why I sublimated so quickly all that I had earlier learned about classic Christianity. It was because I loved the illusions and blithely ignored their consequences. As a result I caused unintended harm, but I was less sensitized to the harm I was doing to others than the harm I thought others were doing to the voiceless poor. While I imagined I was being critical and rational, I was actually ignoring my best critical abilities.

I imagined I had a share in transforming human history. While examining the motives of capitalists and warlords, I did not examine my own motives. The biblical words for this are egocentricity, arrogance and moral blindness. I confess now that I became entrapped with the desire for upward mobility in an academic environment that would generate ideas for a regulatory society.

One reason for writing *A Change of Heart* is in part to alert people to question the realism of those collectivist and unexamined illusions. Those who test them critically will be less likely to be hurt by them or to hurt others. The wrongs I failed to recognize in my youth have had ripple effects that I will never completely know, but on the last day I will be accountable for them.

Looking back, I now know God has accompanied me on a long, circuitous path in order to help me arrive finally on the narrow road to experience the reliability of classic Christianity. My major learning has been the rediscovery of Christmas (incarnation) and Easter (resurrection).

I now understand that I would never have been able to become a plausible critic of the absurdities of modern consciousness until I myself had experienced them. I did not become an orthodox believer or theologian until after I tried out most of the errors long rejected by Christianity. If my first forty years were spent hungering for meaning in life, the last forty have been spent in being fed. If the first forty were prodigal, the last forty have been a homecoming.

Until the end of the 1960s I do not recall ever seriously exchanging ideas with an articulate conservative. They were there, but not on my scope. I systematically avoided any contact with those who would have challenged my ideology.

Civil rights activism before the Birmingham jail. My engagement with the pursuit of racial justice stems back to the struggles within the racially divided Methodist church in 1949–1952 during my high school and college years before the Rosa Parks bus-ride arrest of December 1, 1955. Martin Luther King Jr. was still in school during those years and had not begun his activist Birmingham period.

The Central Jurisdiction of the Methodist Church was the only racially separated jurisdiction, composed of all-black annual conferences which existed within the Methodist family. I was a teenager when I became conscience-stricken that we had two Methodist Churches in Altus, one white and the other black. Dad had for years been a pro bono defender of the black church regarding any questions of property rights, financial difficulties or construction codes. Alma and Dan Thomas were members of that church, whom we had come to love during the many times they were in our house. Their church was right on the railroad tracks while ours was downtown. I felt it was unreasonable and unconscionable to have the one body of Christ split into two races.

That sense of outrage came to a head when in 1949 Tal and I were both involved in a controversy with conference leadership over whether the youth camp owned by the Oklahoma Methodist Conference at Turner Falls would permit Central Conference access to camp facilities. We both sought to organize resistance to those elders who considered this issue too controversial to introduce into conference legislation. We were ultimately successful, but not quickly and not without repercussions. That struggle was being played out before and after I became a postulant for ordination in the West Oklahoma Conference, and through it I learned how to stand up at the right time for simple justice.

The National Association for the Advancement of Colored People (NAACP) had annual national conventions for legislative purposes. In 1952 the 43rd NAACP National Convention was held in Oklahoma City, and I felt privileged to attend it. All the luminaries of the civil rights movement gathered there for national decision making: Thurgood Marshall, Bayard Rustin, Roy Wilkins and Oklahoma's own civil rights stalwarts Clara Luper, James Stewart and the great Roscoe Dunjee of the *Black Dispatch*. I witnessed the debate in which the pivotal resolution was passed stating unalterable opposition to "the expenditure of federal or local funds for health activities, hospitals, playgrounds, or any other agency or institutions without definite safeguards against discrimination because of race, creed, color, or national origin." That resolution became a pattern for later decisive legal changes in the 1960s.

THE SEMINARY EXPERIENCE

From college to seminary. Edrita and I enjoyed a very fulfilling senior year at OU. Edrita had been selected to the Mortar Board National College Senior Honor Society. I had a strong intellectual partner for the challenges ahead. Honors came unexpectedly to me as well when I was elected to OU's PE-ET, an academic circle of the top ten senior men in the university. All of that was topped by the unexpected news that I had been elected to Phi Beta Kappa. I went to the Methodist Annual Conference in Tulsa and learned that we had been appointed to the tiny parish of Whitebead, Oklahoma, a seventy-five-year-old parish founded when Oklahoma itself was only four years old.

My mother had studied piano in the 1920s at Canyon College in Texas. After three years of study, nearing her degree, her family moved to Oklahoma, where she taught music in a small high school near Altus. After years of child raising, my determined mother went back to complete her last year in college. Ironically she and I completed our college degrees on the same day.

In considering a seminary, my choice came down to the University of Chicago Divinity School or Southern Methodist University's Perkins School of Theology. In the winter of 1953 I went to Chicago to see what it had to offer. It felt to me to be more pretentious and elitist than I preferred. Lodged in Frank Lloyd Wright's celebrated Robie House on the University of Chicago campus, I tried to give the University of Chicago a fair hearing, but found it was not for me.

I had already spent one summer on the Perkins campus and knew some of its faculty. The atmosphere on the campus was electric with the works of Kierkegaard, Bultmann and Hartshorne being energetically deliberated. Ultimately I chose Perkins because it had a brilliant young faculty that featured Albert Outler, who had been teaching at Duke and Yale. In addition I was drawn to the brilliance of existentialist Joe Mathews and Bultmannian Edward Hobbs.

At Perkins Edrita and I lived only one block from the home of my much-loved Aunt Catherine Akin in the neighborhood where I had spent so many pleasant days visiting as a boy. There was a creek bed a block from her house where my cousin Jodie and I used to look for minnows and worms for fishing. That creek bed became the site for the new Martin Hall for married couples, where Edrita and I as newlyweds came to live for three very happy years.

Perkins was a young seminary aspiring to the level of academic reputation held by Duke and Yale. The faculty was very young, dazzling and challenging. The faculty was largely from Yale, Union, Duke and Chicago.

Edrita was soon snapped up as a model for the John Robert Powers Modeling School, where she also taught modeling, voice and diction, acting, fashion, poise, and the social graces. She also took on ingénue roles as an actress in community theater productions.

I became youth minister for the Central Congregational Church in downtown Dallas. The Congregationalists and Evangelical Reformed denominations were in the process of uniting to become the United Church of Christ. That gave me my first ecumenical exposure to another church slightly more liberal than the United Methodists.

In the summer of 1954 Edrita and I flew to Chicago to attend the Second Assembly of the World Council of Churches, the Evanston Conference, only six years after the WCC was born in 1948 at Amsterdam. I had been selected as a delegate of the InterSeminary Movement to serve as a youth observer. I watched with awe as the procession of distinguished delegates marched into the opening service. At age twenty-two we were meeting leading world ecumenical luminaries: W. A. Visser 't Hooft, Eugene Carson Blake, Edmund Schlink and Paul Minear. Even President Eisenhower made an appearance in Evanston while we were there.

I wanted to be a part of those who were bringing separate church bodies into cooperation, mediating conflicts and leading in social justice matters. I wanted to be in the company of people who wanted to "speak truth to power." I wanted to learn from them, network and strategize.

Having learned in college that I could compete in advanced studies, I now wondered if I wanted to be a parish pastor or a theological scholar. I aspired to write, so I sought to become an ordained minister who would also be a writing theologian.

I yearned for the whole vision of truth in history, but in fact limited myself by reading only that which involved the radical edge of modern experimentalism. My earliest research and writing focused on "the now," on experienced meaning in the present. I was drawn to the study of psychotherapies because I thought that they might illuminate for me some of my own inner incongruities and prepare me for ministry. They did bring me closer to an understanding of inward experience and feeling, but no closer to tested human wisdom. I continued to rely upon the frame of the Marxist vision of the whole human scene, especially as it had been mediated to me through the Student Christian Movement. For me they offered a plausible view of the dynamics of history, but largely as it was viewed as an economic conflict between the haves and have-nots.

Soon I was reading voraciously, especially on the meaning of universal history. That meant not just history up to now but also according to apocalyptic writers, which included the future of history—not merely the future so far as we could see but so far as God sees, beginning to end. I had this love for integration of the truth into a single world-historical perspective. My chief personal mentor was Albert Outler. Like him, I loved the life of the mind, of study, of writing and interpreting all that I could come to understand in its interconnected wholeness.

My most transformative learnings in seminary were under the

guidance of existentialist Joseph W. Mathews, especially in seminars on Luther and Kierkegaard. I learned how to read a theological work with utter inward seriousness about myself, as if it were directed toward me. I had never really met the mind and heart of Luther except through sketchy secondary sources. With Mathews I struggled with every sentence of Luther's most important essays—"The Ninety-Five Theses," "The Freedom of a Christian," "To the Christian Nobility of the German Nation," "The Babylonian Captivity of the Church" and "The Bondage of the Will." I took Luther's teaching deep into my soul, but filtered it through a secularized frame of reference. It had a profound effect upon me.

The deep plunge into Kierkegaard. What followed was a deep plunge into Søren Kierkegaard. Once I got inside Kierkegaard's moving narrative of Abraham in *Fear and Trembling*, lived with it and breathed its spirit, I was forever formed by it. I must have read *Sickness Unto Death* a half dozen times before I really grasped the stages on the road from despair to freedom. The journey of the soul became more fully defined for me in *Stages Along Life's Way*.

From that time onward I had an exceptional literary companion for my lifelong journey ahead. Kierkegaard's existential analysis of soul and body in spiritual tension, his brilliant writing and his passionate view of the Christian life pursued me and overtook me. I learned how to teach seminars by following Mathews's stormy and confrontational pedagogy, and this prepared me to teach Kierkegaard seminars for the next fifty years.

During those intellectual endeavors I was also learning to be a pastor. Edrita and I were serving small rural churches, enjoying the down-to-earth people with whom we felt so much at home. When I preached my last sermon at Whitebead, Oklahoma, in May 1954, I had carefully prepared a sermon on Paul's farewell to the Ephesian elders (Acts 20:13-38). My plan was to begin by reading the whole chapter ending with "What grieved them most was his statement that they would never see his face again. Then they accompanied him to the ship" (v. 38). I had grown so close to this congregation that when I got to that last sentence, I could not finish it. I choked and then tried again, but I couldn't do it. My tears were flowing as I was overcome with grief at losing my relationship with those wonderful people. Edrita intervened with some fitting remarks about how much they had meant to us.

In my last year of seminary Edrita accepted the position of director of the Dallas Little Theatre. When she needed a janitor, I volunteered. That was spring of 1956 after I had completed all of my class work. I found that pushing a broom was what I needed to get grounded once again. I enjoyed the entertaining arts community and being close to Edrita, who was always a matchless professional.

As time passed I realized that Richard Niebuhr best exemplified the love of comprehensiveness and wholeness that I was seeking. I dreamed of attending Yale in order to study under him. In his writings he proved himself an interdisciplinary thinker of the widest range and highest integrity.

While still in seminary, I had my first opportunity personally to meet him, the eminent teacher of my teachers, Albert Outler and Joe Mathews, and it was memorable.[7] Perkins had developed the reputation of a place where exciting theological education was happening. When Richard Niebuhr visited Perkins in my middle year of theological education, I was chosen as one of three students to meet and talk with him about how we were experiencing our theological studies and what we were missing. That encounter with him was a gift of special providence which drew me closer to Yale. I remember the interview with Niebuhr as if yesterday. He was a very gentle man. His distinguishing facial feature was a highly wrinkled forehead, which gave the visual first impression of enormous wisdom packed into that head with his deeply furrowed brow. He asked quiet and penetrating questions and I was instantly impressed by his range of ideas presented in ordinary language.

I finished my seminary courses a semester early, leaving me with seven undisturbed months to prepare for Yale. I asked Outler what I should do to prepare for my PhD studies. His answer was to read, read and read, and that, of course, was much to my liking. He helped me build a reading list that included Plato, Aristotle, Augustine, Thomas Aquinas and Calvin. He insisted that I not rely on secondary sources. I was to let the texts speak to me in their own voice, person to person, as if the author was living under my roof.

I filled my days gladly with reading, marking and learning at my own pace the *Timaeus, Phaedrus, Theaetetus* and *The Republic* of Plato. Then I dug into Aristotle's *Nicomachean Ethics* on the nature of the good, on intellectual and moral virtue, on the golden mean, on pleasure and pain, on friendship, and into his *Politics* on the good community. I carefully read Outler's magisterial translation of Augustine's *Confessions*, and his *Enchiridion on Faith, Hope, and Love*, which was one of the best reads of my life. Those months proved to be my most valuable stretch of sustained learning. However, I was still regrettably reading those classics through modern existentialist and psychoanalytic eyes.

In the summer of 1956 I served two small churches in Jackson County, Oklahoma. Edrita and I were living with my parents and traveling out to the Methodist circuit at Prairie Hill and High Point. I found that they were ministering to my soul more than I was to them. I learned so much about the reality of Christian community by being in their midst. They were unassuming, humble, meek and capable of quiet wisdom. Prairie Hill was too small to have even a store or gas station. It was a warm, lovely church on the open prairie surrounded by wheat and alfalfa farms. There were only about a dozen families total. But it was there that I learned how much love the people had for their pastor and their church, how much they longed to be taught and led in righteousness, and how they sang and prayed from the heart.

On weekdays I put in long hours with concentrated work in close quarters. My home church in Altus had generously given me a space in which to study quietly in a small, isolated room on the second floor, where I worked with my pipe in my teeth. One day I became extremely nauseated with tobacco toxicity. That revulsion caused me to instantly quit smoking and never smoke again. That sudden renunciation taught me that long-reinforced habituation could change in a moment.

YALE

I was accepted for PhD studies at both Yale University and Columbia University/Union Seminary in New York. Competition was fierce in both cases. I chose to do my doctoral study at Yale chiefly because of

H. Richard Niebuhr. I had already learned a lot of Yale theology from
Clayton Feaver, Albert Outler and Joe Mathews. I was honored to receive
the Moore Fellowship from the Perkins faculty, which provided resources for graduate studies for one year.

Edrita and I were expecting our first child. We arrived in New Haven
in August 1956 and began the search for housing, which was hard to find
near the university at reasonable cost. Willing to put sweat equity into
the rent, I decided to work as janitor of the Unitarian Universalist Church
only two blocks from Divinity Quadrangle and the library. We were provided one large room on the second floor, with a kitchen downstairs that
had pots and pans large enough to cook for an army. In that setting we
took great joy in caring for our first child, Clark, who was born December 21, 1956, at Yale New Haven Hospital. Edrita's mother, Arita Pokorny, came from Oklahoma to help with the new baby. Clark was an
unusually contented and cheerful baby, and was adored by the Unitarian
Universalist parishioners. A year later we moved into Yale's splendid new
housing for married students.

Only four students were admitted to the PhD program in theology
and ethics in 1956. When we had our first meeting with our chief advisers, H. Richard Niebuhr and his young associate James Gustafson, we
were all apprehensive, but our heightened anxieties were quickly reduced
when Niebuhr remarked that we had been carefully selected, and he
expected none of us to fall short.

Hans Frei, George Lindbeck and James Gustafson were all young
faculty members at Yale. All three became incredibly valuable advisers
for me during my years in the Yale Graduate School. I was especially
fortunate to have Hans Frei as an inimitable mentor in Barth studies.
Born in Breslau, Germany, to Jewish parents, Hans was baptized Lutheran and upon the arrival of the Nazi regime in Germany was sent to
a Quaker school in England. He completed his dissertation at Yale just
as I arrived. George Lindbeck became my guide in the study of Thomas
Aquinas and medieval theology. He was born in China of Lutheran missionary parents, studied at Yale and Paris, and completed his dissertation the year before I started at Yale. James Gustafson was six years

my elder and the one with whom I most fully identified. Those three young teachers (along with David Kelsey, who ran the divinity school bookstore at the time) would form the core of the movement later called the "Yale School," focusing on how the biblical narrative impinges on communities of believers.

In my first year I worked closely with the Yale Divinity dean Liston Pope. In his social ethics seminar I had the privilege of studying the conservative Austrian thinker Frederick Hayek's *The Road to Serfdom* and compare his thoughts with the early essays of Karl Marx. He was the first teacher to introduce me to the awesome works of Nicolai Hartmann, teacher of Martin Heidegger and Hans-Georg Gadamer. I reveled in Hartmann's brilliance in my early months at Yale.[8] Hans Frei at first seemed formidable until I learned he had a gentle spirit and possessed an enormous breadth of learning. Since I was captivated by Bultmann, I hesitantly entered Frei's Barth seminar, where my eyes were opened to an alternative to Bultmann and existentialism.

Yale at first felt tedious and a little boring when I compared it with the exciting dialogue in which I had been immersed in Perkins Seminary. Passionate, probing interpersonal engagement with others seemed to be missing in my graduate studies, and this led to a period of doubt and grief for me.

Teaching at Yale College. By November of my first semester, I wondered if I had made a mistake by coming to Yale. I heard about the famous international colloquies taking place at Drew University featuring Hans Jonas, Rudolf Bultmann, Heinrich Ott and other luminaries, mostly focused on existential theology. One of my closest classmates at Yale was Jeff Hopper, son of the dean of the Drew Graduate School, Stanley Hopper. Jeff kept me up to date on those exhilarating events at Drew. The more I learned, the more I wanted to visit with some of the remarkable faculty there. I especially wanted to meet Bernhard Anderson, Carl Michaelson and Will Herberg.

So on a rainy Friday in December 1966, I took off for a whole day to visit Drew. This prompted me seriously to consider shifting into the PhD program there. Unable to see Herberg, I had two appointments scheduled:

one with Dean Stanley Hopper and one with theologian Carl Michaelson. I was amused in my appointment with Hopper that he wanted to talk more about Carl Jung and literary criticism than about curriculum. He invited and encouraged me to apply to Drew.

Then I visited Carl Michaelson for an astonishing conversation. His basement office was crammed with stacks of books in every cranny. Finding him winsome and empathic, I explained my experience of isolation and ennui at Yale. He wanted to know if I had done much with Richard Niebuhr, and I had to admit that I had not done much as yet. When I told Michaelson I was seriously considering a move to Drew, he looked at me sternly and said, "Go back to Yale. Work with Niebuhr. You won't regret it."

I left Michaelson with a feeling of bewilderment. As I drove back to New Haven, his advice began to soak in. He was right that I had given neither Niebuhr nor Yale a fair chance. I remembered Michaelson's parting words: "Do not throw away the opportunity to work with America's greatest living theologian."

Arriving back at Yale, I asked for an appointment with Niebuhr. After I described to him my trip to Drew and the reasons for it, he wanted me to stay at Yale. He told me he had hoped that I would be his assistant in instruction for the coming semester, and I quickly told him I would be honored to do this. I asked him if he would consider guiding me in an individual tutorial, a reading course in theological ethics, and he suggested a tutorial on Augustine and Calvin. That made up my mind instantly and I gladly remained at Yale. It was a pivotal moment for me.

A few days later I got word that Niebuhr had nominated me not only to be his teaching assistant in the divinity school but also for a graduate teaching assistantship in the Yale Undergraduate College. I became an assistant in instruction to Professor William Christian in the department of religious studies, where I got a much deeper exposure to process philosophy than I had gotten with Schubert Ogden at Perkins. I plunged into the works of Alfred North Whitehead.

William Christian was Yale's expert in process philosophy, especially Whitehead. He was a quiet, considerate, brainy, tweedy fellow. Working with him prepared me to deal with the many talented process theologians with whom I would soon spar more seriously, including John Cobb, Pieter de Jong, the brilliant Catherine Keller and Schubert Ogden.

The break with pacifism. The pacifist spell was broken by three events in fall 1956: the Hungarian Uprising, Reinhold Niebuhr's critique of pacifism, and Robert Batchelder's dissertation on Hiroshima. In late October 1956, brave students in Hungary were standing up against Soviet tanks. Worker's councils demanded withdrawal from the Warsaw Pact, but the tanks were swift and devastating. Hungary was the first crack in the repression that had silenced freedom in Eastern Europe. As I watched students resisting tanks, I realized that unjust power had to be met with justified resistance. Those intrepid students on the streets of Budapest offered me a model of courage completely different from my earlier pacifism. I realized that moral decisions required something more than theories and ideas.

Reinhold Niebuhr, Richard's brother, had rejected pacifism in 1939, but I did not find his arguments persuasive until the Hungarian Uprising. Niebuhr argued that the trouble with pacifism was that it tried to live in history as if it were without sin. In his stunning essay "Why Is Communism So Evil?" Reinhold Niebuhr argued that its utopian illusions provide it with a moral façade for its most unscrupulous political policies. That hit me hard. That was the second major jolt to my own pacifist fantasies.

My personal break with pacifism also occurred in extended conversations with my close friend Robert Batchelder, also in the PhD program at Yale. I had been in daily dialogue with him as we both wrote our dissertations in theological ethics under Richard Niebuhr's direction. He had taken on the assignment of assessing every angle of the events and moral judgments made in Truman's decision to employ the atomic bomb to end the war. He made a thorough fact-based study of the number of lives saved and the risks that would have been present if Truman had not given approval for the dropping of the bomb. These facts convinced him and me that the alternative would have been a prolonged ground war that would have cost many more Japanese and American lives. I was convinced that it was a proper and prudent decision. The alternative would have been even more disastrous. His argument appeared later in his book *The Irreversible Decision*.

The individual tutorial with Niebuhr on Augustine and Calvin was timely for me, ending all doubts about my purpose at Yale. Niebuhr proved to be a searching mind, probing Socratic questions on issue after issue. I discovered more clearly the profundity and range of Niebuhr's intellect. He was a rigorous editor, attentive to every flaw in my thinking and writing. His careful critique of the papers I submitted helped me correct many shortcomings. He coached me in the accurate presentation of evidence, dispassionate objective reasoning and clear argument.

My first teaching assignment at Yale was much more demanding than I had anticipated. Yale College was at that time all male, exclusive and boisterous. These were the "little lambs who had gone astray," but somehow I learned to deal with the temper of the talented students at Yale, which was often smart, funny and sometimes narrowly disdainful. I was twenty-five, and they were only a few years younger. When I spoke I sounded like a rustic Oklahoman, while they were from wealthy families of the East Coast. It would take me some time to get a little polish.

By the middle of the spring term of 1957 I more clearly defined my trajectory and moved toward a selection of topics for the daunting comprehensive examinations. They focused on the literature of the Reformation, Søren Kierkegaard and a general field examination in theology and ethics. I took those exams in May 1957. When Niebuhr read them, he thought I needed "a little more mellowing," and, of course, he was right. I was not ready to write a dissertation. I received my MA that year and immediately dug in again for comprehensive examinations in 1958 and happily passed them all.

I had an appetite for wholeness within the complexities of data. Niebuhr embodied that temperament and took me step by step into the vast world of interdisciplinary reflection, always allowing the sociological imagination, psychological insight and historical perspectives to work together to penetrate a proximate vision of the whole.

Niebuhr wanted all of his graduate students to have some serious interdisciplinary competence beyond theology, so I chose to be responsible for the arena of psychology of religion. I hoped to correlate aspects of contemporary psychotherapies with a philosophy of universal history. The psychology that prevailed in my college years was predominantly Freudian psychoanalysis, but my clinical beginning point in the late 1950s had turned to Rogerian client-centered therapy. The psychology that prevailed in my Yale years was predominantly the empirical social psychologists like Kurt Lewin and Musafer Sherif. I gradually assimilated those views in order to work on a critique of therapies and assess them all in relation to my major interest in the meaning of history.

In the late 1950s I sought to develop a workable integration of a therapy of personal self-disclosure with a theology of divine self-disclosure, with special reference to the polarities I had found in the wide space between Carl Rogers and Karl Barth. From early days of college reading in humanities, I was always more interested in interdisciplinary questions than in any narrow field specialization.

I was surprised that I was chosen as a Kent Fellow in 1957, among a remarkable class that included Michael Novak, Jacob Neusner, Ian Barbour, John Maguire and Vince Harding, each of whom were destined to have conspicuous effects upon their fields of study. The Kent Fellows would become recognized as unexcelled leaders among university professors with interests interfacing the study of religion. This community of discourse became crucial in my intellectual formation. The circle of Kent colleagues drew me into ever widening spheres of interdisciplinary inquiry.[9]

My fascination with Rudolf Bultmann's demythology project was very evident in the mid-1950s and continued throughout my Yale years. The works of Kierkegaard, Heidegger and Bultmann became the prevailing sources for all I sought to do. The Hebrew and Christian sacred texts came alive through existential interpretation of the faith that formed among Jesus' followers—reported first in oral tradition from which the written tradition was derived. But I started to wonder if it was the biblical writers I was absorbing or was it Bultmann.

I was writing and speaking in defense of what I thought was a moderate Bultmannian position in theology. Bultmann had rightly resisted the German liberalism of Adolf Harnack, who sought to base Christian teaching on the moral imitation of the historical Jesus. The Jesus of history was constantly being contrasted with classic Christian dogmas about the incarnate and risen Christ, Lord of glory. Bultmann's answer to Harnack was to translate every Gospel passage into what he regarded as its demythologized existential meaning.

Through this unusual route, I learned to take the New Testament texts very seriously, but still only within the presumed framework of modern naturalist ideologies. Regrettably, the Scripture texts I had loved as a child had become buried in my secularizing consciousness, but now they found a new life with me. Bultmann showed me the way back into an intense engagement with the sacred texts, but not fully into its own premises of revelation. He was investigating historically the memory of the community remembering Jesus, not the Jesus of the text, who was understood by classic Christianity as truly God, truly human. I carelessly assumed Bultmann's method would remain decisive for every serious interpreter of Scripture.

In the summer of 1957 I proposed a dissertation topic: a comparative study of theological ethics in Rudolf Bultmann and Emil Brunner. When I brought this to Niebuhr, he wisely amended it to *The Concept of Obedience in Bultmann and Barth*. This led to my spending a major amount of my time in my second year reading through Barth's *Dogmatik* with special reference to his ethics, and working closely with Hans Frei in his Barth seminar. Both Barth and Frei came to exercise enduring influence on my educational formation. On my dissertation committee happily were three inestimable mentors: Niebuhr, Frei and Gustafson.

In the Christmas season of 1957 I returned to Oklahoma for the wedding of my sister, Sarah, to a young Episcopal priest, James Hampson. They were headed for seminary in the Episcopal Theological School adjacent to Harvard, where Sarah would work as an assistant to the distinguished sociologist Talcott Parsons. Jim, a Southerner from Shreveport, would be initiated into New England Episcopal parish life. They spent many years of ministry in Providence and the Boston area. His appointment to the Episcopal parish in Wenham, near Gordon College, brought them in close touch with leading evangelical faculty members in their pews and church leadership, including Elisabeth Elliot and Addison Leitch. They were instrumental in drawing Jim and Sarah into the cutting edge of evangelical intellectual leadership, with friendships with Tom Howard and J. I. Packer.

My ongoing relationship with Jim Packer, FitzSimons Allison and many other brilliant Anglican evangelicals would not have happened without Jim Hampson. His early influence on me in my transition from modern to classic Christian teaching was immense. While I was trying to demythologize Scripture, he was taking its plain meaning seriously. His strong evangelical preaching led him to become one of the founding sponsors and supporters of Trinity School of Ministry in Ambridge, Pennsylvania, along with Peter Moore, Bishops Alfred Stanway and John Rodgers, and later its board chairman for many years.

Teaching at Southern Methodist University 1958–1960. In January 1958 Joseph Quillian, the dean of Perkins School of Theology, made a trip to New Haven to talk with me about my future plans in teaching. His purpose was to see if I had any interest in coming back to my alma mater, Southern Methodist University, as an assistant in instruction during the time I would be completing my dissertation in absentia. Perkins needed someone to teach a basic course in philosophy and logic for seminary students who had no college philosophy, and to serve as preceptor in the core course on theology and ethics team taught by four impressive colleagues—Albert Outler, Schubert Ogden, John Deschner and Van Harvey.

At that point I had received only one request for a job interview, which had come from Smith College in Northampton, Massachusetts, one of the "Seven Sisters" of the Ivy League. After some pondering, I made a decision that would affect all of my future work and writing in more ways than I could ever have anticipated. It was a decision between seminary and college teaching. More so it was a decision between the two very different cultures of New England and the Southwest. I chose seminary teaching in Texas, which was a decision some of my colleagues on the East Coast thought was foolish. From then on, as long as I was in the Southwest, I would feel the sting of the silent condescension and stereotyping by Eastern elites who disdained southwestern American culture. Many viewed as inconsequential everything that happened west of the Hudson River. What they disparaged was exactly what I loved, the easy-going, unpretentious, common culture of my native landscape in Oklahoma and Texas.

In June 1958, Edrita, Clark and I moved back to Oklahoma for the summer to take a three-month appointment in a Methodist parish in Lexington, near Norman. By late August we were on our way to Dallas to begin two very agreeable years of seminary teaching, dissertation writing and enjoying our new baby in an apartment only two blocks from my office.

I had two very productive and delightful years of teaching at SMU's Perkins School of Theology while completing my dissertation in absentia. I was humbled to be assigned to a teaching team composed of inter-nationally recognized scholars, each one very different—a classic historical theologian (Outler), a process theologian (Ogden), a Barthian ecumenist (Deschner), and a skeptical, positivist, almost believing philosophical theologian (Harvey). The encounter between four great minds offered me an inspirational learning environment in the practice of teaching theology. I accepted the rhythm of team teaching and took it with me to future teaching assignments.

Unexpectedly, I was asked to serve as assistant to Robert Elliott in his core course in pastoral care. Under Elliott I deepened my reading range in Freud, Jung and especially Carl Rogers. Elliott was a splendid mentor for me in grasping the spirit and dynamics of client-centered therapy. Under his guidance I found experiential validation for the wisdom of Rogers' three conditions for constructive personality change: internal congruence, empathy and unconditional positive regard. I found that where those conditions were met, positive constructive psychological changes were likely.

Richard Niebuhr appointed soft-spoken Professor David Shipley as my residential mentor for the completion of my Yale dissertation on Barth and Bultmann. The demanding labor I did in writing my disser-tation on the two leading German theologians of the day would in time bear fruit in two major writing projects of the sixties: *Radical Obedience: The Ethics of Bultmann* and *The Promise of Barth: The Ethics of Freedom.*

I finished the dissertation draft in January 1960, submitted it confidently and within three weeks received a searching nine-page letter from Richard Niebuhr. Though he affirmed my basic argument, he insisted on major stylistic revisions. I had picked up many deadly writing habits common to graduate students—long sentences, technical terms and affected phrases. Decherd Turner, founding director of Bridwell Library, graciously agreed to go over the wordy dissertation manuscript sentence by sentence to correct those errors and reduce repetition. His friendship gave me the great and unmerited gift of a conscientious librarian ready to serve selflessly, a treasure I will never forget. With this literary cleansing, my dissertation was approved in time for spring semester graduation in May 1960.

Once accepted, I sent the first half of the dissertation to Rudolf Bultmann as a courtesy with an invitation to respond to any points in my analysis and critique if he wished. I was speechless when I received a long letter from Bultmann, who had diligently examined the details of my arguments. His letter became a featured part of the publication in 1964 by Westminster Press of *Radical Obedience: The Ethics of Rudolf Bultmann: With a Response by Rudolf Bultmann.*

That book, more than any other, launched my career as a serious theologian. But it also led to my reputation as a situation ethicist, ironically just about the time I was beginning to disavow situation ethics. It took a long time for me to convince others that the trendy *Situation Ethics* of Joseph Fletcher in 1966 was quite different from the far more profound radical obedience of Rudolf Bultmann. Fletcher's was a popularized moral relativism while Bultmann's focused on a laborious historical critical picture of the ethic of Jesus.

I left Perkins for a new appointment in August 1960. I said goodbye to old friends, valued mentors and to an intense decade of learning and personal growth.

The 1960s

The Church of What's Happening Now

How different I now was from the uncertain boy who entered The University of Oklahoma University in 1949. Edrita and I were both twenty-eight years old when we were at last ready to settle in to my first full-time teaching position. I was confident and poised for a career of teaching and writing.

TEN YEARS AS A MOVEMENT THEOLOGIAN

Choosing the quiet life. The first location we considered was the off-campus Faith and Life Community at the University of Texas at Austin, where they wanted me to join their faculty in 1960. It was an academic version of the renowned Iona community in Scotland, where there once stood a great medieval monastery whose monks lived according to a daily order of worship, work and hospitality.[1] But this community was charged with existential intensity.

We first visited the community in Austin on the invitation of my former ethics professor Joseph Wesley Mathews. Under his leadership the Ecumenical Institute at the University of Texas was one of the boldest experiments in lay theological education.[2] It provided the pattern for the Ecumenical Institute of Chicago. The core theological curriculum was shaped by Kierkegaard, Bultmann, Camus, Sartre and Tillich. Joe's confrontational teaching style made sparks fly everywhere he went. I was awed by his energy, candor and courage.

Edrita and I were both deeply impressed by what Joe and Lyn were doing in Austin, but upon reflection we reluctantly decided that the match wasn't quite right. The feverish pace of the Faith and Life Community did not provide the space and time I needed to become a writing scholar.

Instead, we chose a remote place where I could begin my teaching journey: Phillips Graduate Seminary in Enid, Oklahoma.[3] Seminary teaching came closer to offering the life of the mind that I was seeking. In that tranquil environment we would nurture our family life and raise our children in a small, low-profile town with an ecumenical seminary that was drawing students from all over the continent. Most of them came out of the Alexander Campbell and Barton Stone tradition of the lay led congregations that formed the Christian Church (Disciples of Christ).

For the next decade in Enid we savored our quiet life, our friends and especially our little ones. Clark was three, Edward came in 1961, and Laura in 1963. When Laura came, she changed the whole dynamic of the family. She was a small girl in a neighborhood of larger boys, and out of necessity learned basic skills of diplomacy by the time she was three. While juggling parenting tasks Edrita found time to teach theater at Phillips University, directing productions for the college associated with the seminary.

In Enid my teaching colleagues were graduates of excellent PhD programs (Chicago, Yale and Vanderbilt) and presided over by Stephen J. England, a splendid Yale PhD dean, who expected a high level of performance and enabled it with strong and thoughtful direction. The faculty was like an extended family. Scholars, wives and children all met regularly for backyard barbeques. We had a high sense of shared mission and a desire to talk through burning issues with varied viewpoints respected.[4]

I benefited immensely from ongoing conversations with Don Browning, author of *Atonement and Psychotherapy*, who came from the University of Chicago shortly after I arrived at Phillips. My closest colleagues there were less far left politically than I, and I learned from all of them. I covered core courses in historical theology, ethics, and pastoral care. I offered annual seminars on John Wesley for the numerous Methodist, Wesleyan and Holiness tradition students, and contemporary

Protestant ethics featuring Kierkegaard, the Niebuhrs, Bultmann, Barth and Tillich. In my course "The Social Implications of Christian Ethics" students engaged in local hands-on case studies on poverty conditions, housing, hunger, racial discrimination and the sociology of power grids in the city. I constantly experimented with teaching methods, team teaching and using Human Relations Training Laboratory methods to stimulate self-disclosure.

Questions about God's existence, self-disclosure, saving action and almighty power reminded me of my inadequacies. For me, the *theo* in theology had become little more than a question mark. I could confidently discuss philosophy, psychology and social change, but God made me uneasy.

I was asked in 1961 to edit a short work by the German theologian Eberhard Müller, *The German Evangelical Academies and Church Renewal.* This became the first of six studies on church renewal published by the Student Christian Movement.[5] The North American forms of that movement were innovative, dedicated and led by young theologians eager to transform the troubled urban world they inherited. It fell to me to describe and explain the varieties of experimental theological academies emerging up in many universities and urban locations.

Soon I felt like a traffic officer on a busy city cross street where traffic was coming in from all sides. That was the heyday of the lay theological renewal in Europe and of urban ministries to the poor in North America. From then on my responsibilities as an editor continued to multiply. Those of us in that movement were convinced that we were providing models for the church of the future.

In addition to my teaching, writing and editing, I was asked to shepherd a growing number of students at Phillips who needed a mentor on their path to Methodist ordination. I was completely at home in the Methodist tradition, particularly in Oklahoma, where I had grown up as a Methodist. My family had been deeply involved in Methodist leadership, with my uncle serving as a district superintendent in Tennessee and my dad as a district lay leader in Oklahoma. My brother Tal continued the tradition and was elected at a very early age to important

legislative roles in the General Conference, which determined the rules
for the huge Methodist bureaucracy. He was elected again and again.
From 1962 to 2008, Tal became a trusted parliamentarian in the general
legislative sessions of the United Methodist Church. He was elected
more times than any other person in the church's history. As an attorney
he served long terms on the General Boards of Education and Ministry,
responsible for policy in the seminaries, and in the General Board of
Global Ministry, which oversaw world missionary policies and practices.[6] My connections to the Oklahoma Methodist organization helped
me guide others toward ordination and readiness for ministry.

Back on the farm. Edrita was frugal and patient, but she needed appli-
ances we couldn't afford. We were living prudently, and I did not like to be
in debt. By late April 1961 I decided that I needed to make some additional
income during my summer vacation. I began to imagine how I might use
my previous work experience in farming to make Edrita's life easier.

We were in the heart of wheat country and a bumper crop was expected that spring. Having raised several crops of wheat, I got the bright
idea that I could purchase a wheat harvesting combine and offer harvesting services to local wheat farmers. I watched the crews of harvesters
streaming north from Texas, harvesting all the way to Canada on
Highway 81, and I knew there were needs for more harvesters. That
meant I would have to make a risky investment in heavy machinery with
the hope of a reasonable reward. A combine (mower and harvester of
grains) was an extremely complicated and temperamental machine
having hundreds of moving parts with dozens of scissor blades, but I felt
confident in my ability to handle one. My goal was to buy Edrita a dishwasher with the profits I would realize from harvesting wheat.

As I shopped for a combine I found only one in my price range. The
new combines crowding the highways were shiny, comfortable, air con-
ditioned and plush. Mine ended up being a ten-year-old, self-propelled
Massey-Ferguson that could do the job if I could keep it running. I ad-
vertised in the newspaper: "Local combine available for harvest."

My colleague, Professor Loren Fisher, was an expert in ancient Near
Eastern languages who could read Ugaritic, Hebrew, Greek, Egyptian

hieroglyphs and more. He had been on several archaeological expeditions to Ras Shamra in coastal Syria in search of evidences of the earliest alphabets. He also happened to have grown up on a farm in Northern California. We both knew our PhDs would not help us get the crop in, but fortunately for me he was as eager to get back into the fields as I was and agreed to be my truck driver.

Wheat farmers get especially nervous at harvest time. You have to wait for the wheat to ripen; then when it ripens you have to go into the fields at the precise time of full maturity for the grain. If it rains you cannot go in because 3,000 pounds of combine would get stuck in the mud.

In addition, I needed a place to park the thirteen-foot combine I had bought. A farmer a mile away from the seminary let us use some of his field for parking. Then we waited for someone, anyone, to call. Finally just at the time when the wheat was ready for harvest, we got a few calls. The first came from that farmer who had given us a place to park our combine. He had a twenty-acre plot of land within sight of the tower of Seminary Hall. Unruffled, I fired up the big red combine and began cutting in wide swaths. With only a few minor breakdowns, it all worked. After dark on that first day I came home with my face blackened with so much dust and sweat that Edrita and Clark at first did not even recognize me at the door.

Unfortunately, a few days later we tore up the shaft of the cutting blades on the combine. In the shop we found that repairing it would cost the same as the down payment but with rain threatening, we had no choice but to persevere.

We finished the second job and went to a third, a bigger field of high, ripe, golden wheat. We worked incredibly hard for two and a half weeks. When the last round of wheat was augered into the truck, I gave the signal for Loren to head off for the grain elevator. As he pulled away, I noticed that he was dribbling a small, steady flow of precious grain from the back corner of the truck. I shouted for him to stop. I ran to catch up, but he didn't hear me. Later when we went to settle with the farmer, we found out that he was so pleased he had harvested a larger yield than he had expected that he was not upset about the lost grain.

Fortunately I was able to sell the combine back to the dealer from whom I had purchased it. I worked harder that June than I had worked since my days of fighting Johnson grass. I was relieved after final calculations when I learned that I had almost exactly broken even. Edrita was grateful that we had not gone further in debt and that Loren and I had come out of the experience still alive. She did not get her dishwasher that year, and I never again went back to farming.

Theology in search of legitimation. Back at my teaching and editing jobs I imagined the new world we were trying to create would be enduring and absolutely better than any world we had inherited. For me, if an idea was purported to be new, it looked a lot better than any idea that seemed to be old. Most theologians I knew were trying to discover some new way of looking at the old ideas of God, humanity, sin and salvation. I was there to teach theology, but theology itself was in search of legitimation. What I was really doing might more accurately be described as promoting Rogerian psychology, wealth-distribution, demythology and existentialist ethics than studying God. Theology was desperately in search of a method, whether it was borrowed from cutting-edge philosophy, social theory or political life, as long as it didn't begin with revelation.

Those were the years of my maximum participation in the international ecumenical student movement, the World Council of Churches and the National Council of Churches. For years I had a pricey biweekly "overall subscription" to all of the World Council literature from Geneva. I regularly read almost every journal and document published by the Council. I was only interested in that form of ecumenism that had some social value. My major aim was to track social change advocacy and lay movements of church renewal. I was floating on the wave of secularization. Theologians were undertaking the ironic task of deconstructing the old religion in order to create a new religion.

I functioned as a movement theologian, continuously shifting from movement to movement toward whatever new idea I thought might seem to be an acceptable modernization of Christianity. This required me to be constantly on the move, networking, editing, writing, strategizing and serving as an information adviser for student movement leaders. This was admittedly a massive departure from classic Christianity, which I recognized but ignored. If theology required reasoning out of God's self-disclosure, I was certainly not doing that—rather the opposite.

In my seminary teaching I appeared to be relatively orthodox, if by that one means using an orthodox vocabulary. I could still speak of God, sin and salvation, but always only in demythologized, secularized and worldly wise terms. God became the Liberator, sin became oppression and salvation became human effort. The trick was to learn to sound Christian while undermining traditional Christianity.

In my writing and editing I was busy informing and alerting covert community organizers to new trends, ideas and strategies that might be useful to their engagement in social change. Unfortunately, I had no interest in critiquing the outcomes or assessing the social consequences of the ideologies that substituted for theology, since I was completely convinced that they were self-evidently true and self-justifying.

My first real encounter with conservative evangelicals did not go well for them or for me. Serving as my seminary's faculty adviser to the Inter-Seminary Movement (ISM), I led a small delegation to a large regional meeting of ISM students at the Southwestern Baptist Theological Seminary (SWBTS) in Ft. Worth. SWBTS was and is the largest seminary in the nation. They were Baptist conservatives, and our delegates were ecumenical liberals. Asked to deliver a plenary address during their chapel hour before a vast audience of about a thousand students, I prepared an avant garde speech more suited for a rally than a worship service.

When I entered that huge space, I faced the largest crowd I had ever addressed and felt like a goldfish in a swarm of piranhas. The president, Dr. Robert Naylor, who was a man with a gentle spirit and fixed convictions, introduced me. My prepared remarks were focused on the work of Dietrich Bonhoeffer, whose prison letters were being widely read by theological students at the time. I explained and defended Bonhoeffer's concept of "religionless Christianity." Deep into a romanticized view of secularization under the tutelage of the Dutch theologian Gerardus van der Leeuw, the prevailing slogan was "Let the world set the agenda." In the austere atmosphere of that most conservative Baptist seminary, I proceeded to set forth an appeal to "worldly theology" as a new and promising basis for seminarians of different viewpoints to come together. My stated purpose was to advance Christian unity, but that's not what happened.

As I finished my presentation, President Naylor rose, quieted the restless audience and expressed polite appreciation for the intent of my address. He then began extemporaneously and with genuine rhetorical elegance to take on point by point the substance of my speech. In his warm, congenial and pastoral way, he deftly refuted practically every argument I had made. After the service, with great charm President Naylor again grasped my hand warmly and expressed his gratitude for my presence on Seminary Hill. I went away feeling trounced by an aging wise man of gracious and articulate Southern culture. That encounter helped me realize that conservative evangelical thinking was capable of real intellectual force, contrary to all of my previously fixed stereotypes of it.

Situation ethics. Situation ethics was entering its heyday. Its core conviction was that the command of God is revealed in the now, and only in the now, and hence not disclosed in any durable rule ethic. Established rules and long-standing precedents were widely considered irrelevant, and what was relevant was making Christianity acceptable to modern assumptions about the truth. The history of moral wisdom was being junked, and I was functioning as a junk dealer.

In an attempt to contribute seriously to the theological underpinnings of existential ethics, I wrote my first essay for the *Ecumenical Review* in 1961. The question was, "Is the Demand of God Ambiguous?" I argued no, it is not ambiguous, because it is unambiguously being made known in the moment. Only then were the conditions for obedience understandable and knowable. I was convinced that leading theologians Barth and Bultmann were similarly focused single-mindedly on "what's happening now."

When that essay was translated into German and appeared in the leading German journal in theological ethics, *Zeitschrift für Evangelische Ethik*, I got calls from the media looking for a potential story. That media flurry occurred before Joseph Fletcher published his popular book *Situation Ethics*, which featured shallow, sentimentalist assumptions entirely different from those of Bultmann or Barth. The media loved situation ethics because it was a chic popularization of an ethic without rules and fit perfectly into a permissive society. I was labeled an advocate of situation ethics, and the label stuck.

In 1963 I got a letter from Roland Tapp, acquisitions editor of the Westminster Press, who wanted to come to Oklahoma to visit with me. Westminster had an avid interest in books on the new morality. I had submitted a sample of the Bultmann section of my dissertation to the publisher, Paul Meacham, with the thought that they might wish to publish it in some revised form. Tapp visited our home in Oklahoma eager to publish it with minimal change. That was the beginning of a long relationship with Westminster, and even more the beginning of a lasting friendship with an excellent editor.

As I continued to be asked by the ecumenical Student Christian Movement of the early 1960s to be a motivator for theological innovation, I found ways of spinning that task toward a theology grounded in existential thought and only thinly veiled Marxist analysis.

God and the gods. Many protoconservative views were already embedded in my mind. For example, in the early 1960s I had developed an analogy between the Christian year and salvation history. That was a liturgical analogy that I had never seen anyone thoroughly explore.[7] It became a staple feature of many of my lectures and writings of the early 1960s. The core of that correlation was simple: Advent, Christmas and Epiphany are analogous to humanity's waywardness, God's action, and the response of the good community. Lent, Easter and Pentecost/Trinity are analogous to the same sequence of human fallenness, God's grace and human accountability. In that way the six seasons of the Christian year summarized the key theological motifs of Christian teaching.

Another example of hidden orthodox memory was found in Richard Niebuhr's powerful essay on "God and the gods." When Edrita and I first read this together, we realized that we could not live without some object of devotion which would render our life meaningful and make life worth living. Further, we came to understand that when a creaturely value becomes perceived as absolutely necessary for our existence, we have a god in our life. This distinction between God and the gods was operative in all that I was doing in the 1960s.

With this premise I was able to develop an interpretation of the human condition experienced in time as anxiety, guilt and boredom. That logic appeared in published form first in my 1962 short book called *The Crisis of the World and the Word of God*.[8] The human predicament in time was viewed as anxiety for the future, guilt over the past and boredom in the present. That threefold relationship to time solved hundreds of problems for me. That implicit construct then received much fuller refinement in *The Structure of Awareness*. It reappeared in almost everything I subsequently wrote.

Accordingly, Christian freedom centers on being freed from anxiety about the future through the act of trusting in God who transcends our gods.

Christian freedom in relationship to the past is centered on being freed from guilt over past acts through the forgiveness of God.

Christian freedom in relationship to the present consists of being freed from boredom which despairs over anything meaningful happening now, and is cured by hearing and obeying the command of God in the moment.

The benefit of these three freedoms—from anxiety, guilt and boredom—is that we are permitted to live freely to love in the now, since we have been made free through the gift of a new future and a new past and a new perception of our present. Since we are no longer preoccupied with the anxious future and the guilty past, the momentous call of The Now can be heard and answered responsively. That was such a simple correlation that I wondered why I had not already heard anyone discuss it. Even when I looked for some hint of its simple clarity, I could not find it in the literature either of psychology or religion, so I pursued it doggedly.

To explain further, time makes relative all of our presumed absolutes. There must be a reality in relation to which all of those gods are relative. It matters less what that reality is called than that it be recognized as enduring beyond all of our idolatries. Call it "the way things are" or "the

Final Reality with which each of us must deal." By whatever name, that One is the Destroyer of all those gods which appear to make our lives worth living but don't. Even when I tried to give this reality no name, I found that it reappeared as the Nothing out of which all things come, and the Future into which all things return. I was meeting the Source and End of all things. I experienced this One as the original and final word about life. In the Bible I was learning that that One had broken through our idolatries by the power of his love, so that I might learn to say with Job 13:15, "Though he slay me, yet will I trust him." Throughout all my secularized wandering, I knew I had met and trusted that One.

A community of persons in history had come to understand this Slayer of our idolatrous values as friend. I could see hazily that the faith of that Jewish-Christian community had come to cling not to creaturely goods and finite causes but to that final reality. I knew, even in my way-wardness, that I belonged to that community who confessed that that One can be trusted because he has made himself known as Father. When I compared that One to anything else I could conceive, I found with Anselm that nothing greater can be conceived.[9]

I was able to confess the Apostles' Creed, but only with deep ambiguity. But I stumbled over "he arose from the dead." I had to demythologize it and could say it only symbolically. I could not inwardly confess the resurrection as a factual historical event. I was assigned the task of teaching theology, but when I came to the resurrection, I honestly had to say at that stage that it was not about an actual event of a bodily resurrection but a community's memory of an unexplained event. I could talk about the writings of the people who were remembering and proclaiming it as the saving event, but I could not explain to myself or others how Christianity could be built on an event that never happened.

That turned the New Testament into a puzzle of historical investigation about an event that never occurred. I doggedly continued to teach that the disciples' memory of Jesus' resurrection enabled us to understand ourselves anew as the recipients of a new present.

This unrisen Christ was coupled with an ethic that held that the demand of God appears only in the present. It was uniquely given anew each moment. To listen to the need of the neighbor who meets me concretely is to listen for the call of God. That was the basis for a situational view of ethics. The requirement of God was discernible in the present since the neighbor always meets us with genuine needs.

That was my credo in my early thirties. It was new birth without bodily resurrections and forgiveness without atonement. *Resurrection* and *atonement* were words I choked on. That meant that the gospel was not about an event of divine salvation but about a human psychological experience of trust and freedom from anxiety, guilt and boredom. For me that passed for theology, but I remained uneasy about its insufficiencies.

Shared trajectories: Alinsky and Hillary. When I later tried to explain my early views to students in their twenties, I found that the easiest way to connect was to show how closely my ideological history paralleled Hillary Rodham Clinton's in her Smith College days. That context helped those students grasp immediately where I was coming from. Although I never met Hillary Rodham, and though she was younger than I, she was reading my essays and working out of the same sources and moving in the same circles as I had been.

Hillary and I had the same sociopolitical mentors: Saul Alinsky and Joe Mathews. My former Drew colleague, ethicist Donald G. Jones, had been her high school pastor who had drawn her into the circle of activist Methodists. The core curriculum of Mathews's Chicago Ecumenical Institute (whose antecedent was the Austin Faith and Life Community discussed earlier) was where she learned to combine existential theology with political activism. I was a writer for her core curriculum. Our trajectories mirror the same story of many Methodist social activists. We shared the same working sources, which were Tillich's cultural analysis, Bultmann's demythology, early feminism and especially Saul Alinsky. Her educational trajectory was remarkably parallel to mine with Yale, Methodist Student Movement activism, experimental ecumenism and Chicago-style politics as prevailing features, which were always moving leftward politically. Although we traveled along the same path, we never once connected personally, but I provided some theological rationalizations for her and others for this brand of situational ethic.

We were both eager to learn from Saul Alinsky, the pragmatic Marxist urban Chicago community organizer. Her Wellesley thesis was "There Is Only the Fight: An Analysis of the Alinsky Model." It was so favorably received by Alinsky that she was offered a job at his foundation. I have thoroughly examined her thesis, which was kept under lock and key for years. I see in it a parallel of my own responses during that era. I admired Alinsky enough to covertly try to make his unprincipled amoralism work in the church. His strategies were cynical power manipulations in the tradition of Lenin.

Alinsky took great joy in thumbing his nose at classic moral teaching. Clinton's view of historical determinism came from the same utopians I had idolized. She saved, as did I, all the old copies of every issue of *Motive* magazine, the Methodist student movement predecessor of much of her religious and political radicalism. *Motive*'s editors, Roger Ortmayer and B. J. Stiles, were old friends of mine and valued colleagues. I trusted that magazine because I thought it was the voice of the "prophetic church." I became an avid supporter of feminism under the powerful advocacy of this magazine, which was the first religious journal to set forth the analogy between the oppression of blacks and the oppression of women.

During this transitional period I began to recognize that I was not the rootless radical I had imagined myself to be. That surfaced when I appeared on television with my old friend Charles Curran, who was a theological expert at the Second Vatican Council at the time when I was an informal Protestant Vatican II observer. The producers expected the distinguished Catholic theologian to take the viewpoint of classic Catholic teaching and I, as the liberal Protestant, was supposed to argue for situation ethics.

As it turned out we found ourselves debating as if I was the Catholic and he was the liberal Protestant. They had not counted on Curran moving left while I was moving right. I had been typecast as an apologist for situation ethics, and Curran was regarded as an expert on Catholic rule ethics. I could see an ironic reversal unfolding as I argued for natural law ethics and he argued for a highly contextual ethic. Charley was eventually removed from the faculty of Catholic University of America in

1986 as a dissident against the church's moral teaching. I began to question my role as an activist reformer and was inwardly moving toward classic Christian teaching on natural law and public order involving such issues as abortion, parental responsibility, divinely created gender differences and sexual accountability to God's way of ordering creation as male and female.

Empathy and incarnation. By the time I had my last seminar at Yale with Hans Frei, I had grasped the significance of Barth's principle of the analogy of faith, which said that humanity is fully understood only in relation to the Word revealed in the incarnation. Even though I did not see the incarnation as a historical event, I understood that way of reasoning by analogy.

The analogy that wouldn't go away was: as God enters into our human history as incarnate flesh, so we enter into the experienced world of others. The question I asked myself was whether psychotherapy, which depended on empathy, could learn from the good news of God's entering into the human sphere as a human being. Even though I had searched the literature and found nothing, I had a hard time believing that such a simple analogy as that between incarnation and empathy could have been so long overlooked. All during the early 1960s I was teaching classes in both pastoral theology and systematic theology, so I was preoccupied with exploring the deep and hidden correlations between two presumably separate worlds: theology and psychotherapy. It took me several years to pull my thoughts together in *Kerygma and Counseling*, which was written in 1964 and published two years later. It explained the most significant and vivid correlation I had identified in my earliest years of teaching. It was the hidden kinship between Karl Barth and Carl Rogers. They seemed to live on two different planets, but for me they had a deep kinship. My first step into the international discourse was a symposium which featured that finding. It came about through deliberation with Professor Andre Godin, who had taught psychology of religion at the Gregorian in Rome and later at the Lumen Vitae Institute of the University of Louvain in Belgium.

He put together a team of French psychologists and theologians to critically review my study called "Insight and Revelation." This symposium was published as a booklet in 1965 in *Nouvelle Revue Theologique* under the title "Experience Therapeutique et revelation: un Symposium." Those French scholars were the first in Europe to consider carefully the heart of my proposal for the unrecognized kinship between Barthian revealed theology and Rogerian humanistic therapy. The French properly understood the proposed analogy between human empathy and God's incarnation before any in North America.[10] This proposal elicited scholarly deliberation in Europe among both Catholics and Protestants.

At the same time I was writing on the uncharted theme of unconditional acceptance, a theme I found in Carl Rogers. I argued that it was a fitting description of the forgiving God, and that unconditional love corresponded directly with commonly acknowledged assumptions in effective psychotherapy.

Soon I began to hear the phrase *unconditional love* on the lips of homilists and priests as applied to God, first in Europe and then in America. The Rogerian idea of unconditional acceptance was being viewed as unconditional love of not only persons but more so God. This phrase quickly entered into the common vocabulary of psychological literature, sermons and books, especially for pastoral writers struggling to find ways of making God's forgiveness plausible.

Before Rogers I could find no books or articles that had been written on "unconditional positive regard" or "unconditional love." It is a phrase that apparently had emerged popularly in the early 1960s. Even Pope John Paul II would soon be preaching that God "loves us all with an unconditional, everlasting love." Carelessly, I had invited pastors and theologians to equate the unconditional positive regard that had proven to be a reliable condition of effective psychotherapy with God's unconditional forgiving love for humanity.

In doing so, I had absentmindedly and unfortunately disregarded all those powerful biblical admonitions on divine judgment and the need for admonition in pastoral care. Few of these homilists mentioned the wrath of God against sin as Jesus did.

I had drifted toward a Christ without a cross and a conversion without repentance. It still makes me wince to hear sermons today about God's unconditional love that are not qualified by any admonition concerning the temptation to permissiveness. I had absorbed Tillich's powerful sermon from *The New Being* on "You Are Accepted," where Christian faith hinged primarily on our willingness to "accept our acceptance." But acceptance by whom? Tillich believed we were accepted by the "Ground of being." This was an idea, not an event in history. In Tillich's "acceptance" there was no actual cross or resurrection, but only the idea or concept of acceptance. This resulted in a permissive John the Baptist and a dehistorized Christ, who was a useful moral example of absolute acceptance. That is not what the New Testament had in mind.

The favorable reception of these essays prompted me to develop my thesis more fully in *Kerygma and Counseling*. During the early 1960s I read everything I could get my hands on regarding viable links between psychological and theological wisdom.

I was relying largely on Carl Rogers's approach to client-centered therapy, which hinged on three key conditions of constructive psychological growth: empathy, internal congruence and unconditional positive regard. Within these premises I began to probe the early signs of existential psychology then arising in Germany.

My deeper desire was to see how these three conditions related to the heart of Christian teaching on the incarnation.[11] It was easier for a secular audience to understand unconditional acceptance than incarnation. Barth's doctrine of analogy opened the door to develop the connection: God the Father's incarnate coming in Jesus was for believers analogous to the empathy required in constructive psychological growth.

Before I left for my sabbatical year in Heidelberg, I was working intensely on finishing *Kerygma and Counseling*. Though not published until 1966, it was entirely complete and submitted before I left for Germany. Joachim Scharfenberg was the leading German psychoanalyst who was writing on the interface between theology and therapy. He had previously operated largely out of a Freudian set of premises, but increasingly he and Hans-Joerg Koeppen were intrigued by my correlation between incarnation and empathy.

After *Nouvelle Revue Theologique* in French and *Psychotherapie und Seelsorge* in German, and following the ensuing discussion of *Kerygma and Counseling*, I was often asked to explain the analogy to pastors and counselors.[12] These challenges prompted me to define my research in Germany for my first sabbatical leave in 1965–1966: to study firsthand the emerging movement of existential philosophy and psychology as seen in Ludwig Binswanger, Victor Frankl and the later writings of Martin Heidegger.

THE HEIDELBERG YEAR: 1965–1966

Our family of five packed up for a year in Heidelberg. Laura was two, Edward was four, and Clark was eight. I had received a grant as a Danforth Cross-Disciplinary Fellow for that academic year. I had arranged to meet Pastor Adrian Geense at the Student Christian Movement Center of the University of Heidelberg on Ziegelhausen Strasse overlooking the River Neckar.[13]

A week later we settled comfortably into our little apartment at the foot of the path leading up to the Heidelberg Castle in the neighborhood of the Kornmarkt, the oldest part of the medieval city, which had been officially founded in 1386. Our next door neighbor, the gentle and amiable Frau Heilman, faithfully took care of the rose garden that we all enjoyed so much in our patio entrance.

Günther Bornkamm, the famous New Testament scholar and dean of the Heidelberg University graduate studies in theology, welcomed us warmly to the university. A visit to Bornkamm's residence was a pleasant way to begin my work at Ruprecht-Karls Universität in Heidelberg. We reminisced about our mutual friends in Texas, whose food relief work after the war was well-remembered.

We loved living near the Neckar River at the base of the steep hill under the castle which stood high above Heidelberg. Our children played with the neighborhood children. Our boys would push their scooters all the way to the top of the winding walkway and coast triumphantly down to the Altstadt. We bought bread, cheese and tea in the Kornmarkt, where grains had been traded since the eighth century. We attended church at the fifteenth century neo-Gothic Peterskirche, the oldest church in Heidelberg. I was able to walk to lectures and seminars in the narrow streets which were laid out centuries before Hegel was born.

We ordered in advance a new Volkswagen Kombi Microbus right out of the Wolfsburg factory. We were thrilled with our boxy all-purpose green bus with thirteen windows. While we were in Germany we were able to tour all the way from Sweden to Scotland to Italy, as well as make a major expedition from Heidelberg to Vienna to Istanbul to Damascus to Jerusalem to Marseille and back to Heidelberg, roughing it all the way. To sleep our family of five in the Microbus, Clark perched on a VW hammock above the front seats and the two smaller children took floor shelf space at the head and foot of the improvised bed where Edrita and I slept. This was the happy design of the Microbus that became the familiar symbol for the hippie generation.

Conversations with Bultmann, Barth and Pannenberg. My first theological excursion out of Heidelberg was to the home of Professor and Frau Dr. Bultmann in Marburg in a visit prearranged before my coming to Germany. Frau Bultmann welcomed me into their warm, book-filled living room. She made delicious chocolate Mozartkugeln cookies, which we had with mint tea. Professor Bultmann was eighty-one, in good health and ready for a conversation on our mutual interests. I found it easy to talk with this unpretentious and notable scholar.

I thanked him for so carefully responding to my study of his ethics in the book *Radical Obedience: The Ethics of Rudolf Bultmann.* He confirmed that it was the first substantial treatment of his views on ethics. I talked with him about German theology, the future of theology and invited his assessment of my sabbatical research.

With Frau Bultmann present during all of our conversation, Professor Bultmann wanted to hear news about our mutual friends, John Cobb and Schubert Ogden. We discussed unresolved issues of my book, especially about Bultmann's roots in Kant and Kierkegaard regarding the concepts of moral discernment, hearing, obeying and responding. I attempted to raise the troubling question of the Christian doctrine of the resurrection, but Bultmann parried it by focusing on the tradition of the resurrection memory rather than its fact. I was surprised that Professor Bultmann was as aware as he was of current developments in theology in North America. However, he did not seem to have as much interest in existential psychology and theology as I thought he might.

In the years before coming to Heidelberg I had been intrigued by the work of the great existential psychologists of Europe: Ludwig Binswanger, Karl Jaspers, Victor Frankl and J. H. van den Berg. All were in their later years when I was in Heidelberg. My main research goal was to meet as many of them as possible and read them thoroughly. I also wanted to meet participants in the Kreise der jungen Bultmanntheologen, the circle of Bultmann scholars, with whom I expected to find much in common.

Existential psychology was an emerging school in Germany before it much later became a recognized approach in England with R. D. Laing. There were no significant American contributors, and in 1965 there was as yet no American literature on existential psychology at all. The subject would become active about ten years later in America.[14] This research was for me a continuation of my previous inquiries into Kierkegaard, Nietzsche and Heidegger, who were among the major antecedents of existential psychology.

My central location for researching all aspects of the theory and practice of existential psychotherapy was the Psychiatrisch und Psychologisch Institute at the School of Medicine at Heidelberg, with additional interactions with Frankl in Vienna and J. H. van den Berg in Leiden.

I received a friendly handwritten note from Martin Heidegger, the central underlying figure in German existential philosophy and psychology, indicating his regret that he would not be in Freiburg at the time I was passing through on my way to Rome.[15] I had poured over his work and the results of my study of Husserl and Heidegger would find detailed expression in my book *The Structure of Awareness* three years later.

I drove to Leiden for an illuminating and detailed conversation with J. H. van den Berg, whose earlier works on social psychology and *A Phenomenological Approach to Psychiatry* played a key role in the development of existential psychological practice. One of his major contributions was his theory of social neurosis.[16]

Shortly after our arrival in Europe, Westminster editor Roland Tapp again visited our family in Heidelberg on his way to the Frankfurt Book Fair. Our encouraging conversations led to a plan for a basic outline of my next Westminster book project, *Contemporary Theology and Psychotherapy*, which developed the themes I was actively working on in Heidelberg.

I had written Karl Barth indicating that I would call when I came through Basel on my way to the Second Vatican Council in Rome, and he had encouraged me to stop by, knowing that I was preparing a full-length book on his ethics. I called at his home in the morning, only to learn from his son Markus that he was in the hospital and would not be home for another week. I had met Markus Barth at Pittsburgh Theological Seminary a year earlier, so when I called, he suggested that I go ahead and visit his father at the hospital. I was grateful for the opportunity to talk with this great man, the leading Protestant theologian of the twentieth century.

I found Barth sitting in bed clothes and bathrobe in a chair beside his bed in the hospital with a makeshift desk made out of two hospital tables end on end. On another smaller table was a small shelf of books. The only titles I recognized were Catton's *History of the Civil War* and an issue of *Zeitschrift für Evangelische Ethik*.

My most distinct first impression was of his wry smile, his ever-present pipe and his bright twinkling eyes. At eighty he radiated friendliness, quiet wisdom and a warm personal interest in me.

I wrote three questions on a card that I gave to him. The first was on the possible influence of his *Kirchliche Dogmatik* volume II/2 on the development of Bonhoeffer's *Ethics*. He answered firmly that he did not think the two works could be easily compared, since Bonhoeffer's work was published posthumously in an unfinished form, and his was a deliberate part of a larger systematic work. But he seemed confident that Bonhoeffer had known nothing of volume II/2 before 1942. I was surprised and still remained a little unconvinced. I pointed out their almost identical views on the concepts of command and obedience. I suspected that Bonhoeffer had obtained the manuscript of II/2 prior to writing his essays. Barth admitted the similarity but did not think

Bonhoeffer had followed his argument in any significant way.

My second query was about his view of the analogy of faith (the process of reasoning analogously from God's self-disclosure to human knowledge) in contrast to the traditional analogy of being (which reasons from the general concept of being to the being of God). I asked how far it could be applied to ethical reflection and especially to issues regarding the interface of theology with the social sciences, specifically psychology and the practice of psychotherapy. I proposed that his view of reasoning analogically from revelation to creation was relevant not just to a general theory of knowledge but also to moral and psychological reflection. He agreed, citing his teaching on marriage, asking if I thought its analogical reasoning was clear. In answering yes I explained that my primary interest was in the method of the analogy of faith. I thought it was a potentially powerful means of dealing with questions of culture, including personal transformation and psychological health.

When I asked if it could be applied to psychotherapy, he listened and nodded his head frequently but with a perplexed facial expression. Then he said he had never seen this attempted. I had brought along a copy of my essay "Experience Therapeutique et revelation: un Symposium." It spelled out my understanding of how his teaching on the incarnation, without his knowing it, has illuminated the concept of empathy as taught by Carl Rogers. He had barely heard of Rogers but immediately grasped the analogy. I felt that he was blessing the effort to employ the analogia fidei to therapeutic growth and that he was intrigued with the analogy between empathy and incarnation. I told him I would send him the fuller version of that thesis in *Kerygma and Counseling* as soon as it was published. He gently warned me against veering too far from the central task of theology as the study of the Word of God revealed.

That led to my third question on the role of self-affirmation in Christian teaching. When he asked for clarification, I explained my conviction that love of the neighbor is rooted in an appropriate form of self-affirmation that was only possible in the light of grace, and that God's affirmation of fallen humanity calls for a fitting response of self-affirmation. His face turned very serious for the first time, and he somberly remarked: "The self must give itself to the neighbor. You must not base Christian ethics upon the self-absorbing idea of self-affirmation." With forefinger high he said, "Proceed cautiously. The only source of love of the neighbor is the Word which God speaks affirming both you and the neighbor, not any self-affirmation one gives to oneself. The wellspring of love is God's sheer gift, never a possession by virtue of one's own self-relation. The love of the neighbor overcomes all self-love." That was said passionately. I countered that Scripture as well as most psychotherapists held that there was no firm basis for self-giving if you have nothing to give, as we see in Jesus' dictum to "love thy neighbor as thyself," but I agreed to take to heart his admonitions. When I noted I had taken enough of his time, being keenly aware of his physical limitations, he continued to probe for details of my work in the psychiatric department of Heidelberg, and wondered about my concerns and intentions in my trip to Rome.

Two of his statements imprinted on my memory. On the use of the analogy of faith he said intently, "Probier! Probier! Probier!" (Try! Try! Try!). Second, he wanted to underscore that the church must "live by the Holy Spirit," not the spirit of the times.

As I prepared to leave the hospital, I wished him good health from all his American friends and followers, and reminded him of the remarkable contributions he had made to us all. He then said he was aware of age, but, in heartfelt words, he said he was pleased to have lived a full life and was not complaining about his limitations. His temperament throughout my visit was deeply joyous, alive, full of grace, generosity and delight.

He grasped my hand as I was parting and said drolly, "Say hello to the pope." I laughed and replied that I would greet our friends in Rome on his behalf. With a little hand wave and a smile, I left him and closed the door.

Upon returning to Heidelberg, I was pondering the two encounters I had just had with the two greatest Protestant theologians of the twentieth century. Shortly thereafter I got word from J. W. Lippincott Publishers of Philadelphia that they would like for me to write a book on a major contemporary theologian. I turned immediately to Karl Barth's ethics as my subject. It was in a series edited by Martin Marty on the promise of major theologians for the future of Christianity. I decided to revise substantially the Barth section of my dissertation as a basis for development of a full-length treatment of Barth's ethics under the title *The Promise of Barth: The Ethics of Freedom*.

Not long after my book on Bultmann was published, I began to have increasing reservations about what had been given up in order to find a demythologized Jesus. As the controversy over situation ethics intensified in North America, I was growing more cautious about Bultmann's single-minded stress on the "moment"—the situation at hand, which was the key feature of his Christian ethic. That had been the central thesis of my dissertation on Bultmann and Barth: God's command is revealed unambiguously in the now.

Prompted by Carl Braaten, I began reading Wolfhart Pannenberg's work on *Offenbarung als Geschichte* before it was translated into English as *Revelation as History*. It reset the terms of discussion for many of the best young theological students in Germany. I read it in amazement as he presented a much more powerful critique of both Barth and Bultmann than I had conceived in my dissertation.

Pannenberg offered brilliantly crafted historical arguments that allowed me to get beyond the situation "ethic of the moment" in which I was tangled. Bultmann had narrowed history to the moment of existential encounter in the now. Oppositely, Pannenberg extended the focus of history to its broadest frame: creation to consummation. That forever redefined my trajectory.

The premise from then on was that universal history is revelation. That meant the study of the whole of history in what the Bible calls revelation. The crucial point is that the "whole" includes the end. Only through grasping the end of human history was its beginning understandable. For me that was a stunning idea: the meaning of history was known through the end of history. For Christians the meaning of the end of history was anticipatively revealed in the history of Jesus. Here was what I had been looking for. The New Testament taught the meaning of universal history, seen in the light of the events of the life, death and resurrection of Jesus, and promised final judgment. To my amazement Pannenberg presented evidence-based arguments that the resurrection of Jesus was the decisive event in history pointing to the end of history. Nobody before Pannenberg had made that connection as clearly as he did.

During my year in Heidelberg, John Cobb of Claremont was in Mainz. He took the train down to Heidelberg to discuss with me the implications of Pannenberg's work for the future of theology. What a wonderful man was John Cobb. He was brilliant, principled and caring. He and I read the Pannenberg initiative in very different ways. He saw in Pannenberg an integral theological mind rooted in the Hegelian desire to interpret the wholeness of history. I agreed but saw Pannenberg rather as a challenge to both Bultmannians and Barthians who had neglected universal history viewed as revelation. Cobb was editing a new book for Harper on Pannenberg's remarkable ideas and wanted me to translate the essay by Pannenberg which constituted his response to all the other essays of that book.

After I made my translation, I sent it to Pannenberg and he invited me to come to Mainz to discuss my work and his future projects. I had recently read *The Feminine Mystique* by Betty Friedan, the first of an outpouring of feminist books. Much impressed by this new movement, I tried to explain feminism to Pannenberg. I joined with Friedan in consciousness raising for the women's movement, especially for fair treatment in the workplace. I urged Wolfhart and Hilke to learn more about American feminism since it seemed to me that it was destined to influence Western culture powerfully. Without having heard any of the feminist arguments or passions, they were wary of that entire development. I now find it ironic that I was the first person to attempt to persuade Pannenberg to take nascent feminism seriously. Looking back, this could be a scene for a situation comedy. The feistiness of that conversation would only become apparent ten years later when I could more clearly see the moral hazards of some types of feminism.

Hilke was the one most skeptical of where feminism might take us. As she graciously took time to guide me through the Romanesque Mainz Cathedral built in A.D. 975, my advocacy of feminism was never mentioned. She was more interested in hearing about my family heritage in the Odenwald.

Observer at the Second Vatican Council. In Rome in the autumn of 1965, key documents of Vatican II were under intense debate. It was the season for perfecting many documents that had been approved in principle, but awaited further refinement in translations. This was the last session of the Vatican Council.

My chief seminary mentor Albert Outler was there officially as an designated Protestant Observer. Albert put me directly in touch with the Ecumenical Secretariat, led by Cardinal Bea, and there I met the Paulist Father Tom Stransky, who became a good friend and an ongoing Catholic partner in dialogue. He arranged for me to be admitted to the session of Vatican II as a friendly unofficial observer at the time the Latin draft for the *Dogmatic Constitution on Divine Revelation* was being debated. It was being amended looking toward final voting and approval in November. *Lumen Gentium* (Light of the Nations) was also being finalized for publication at that time.

As I entered the nave of St. Peter's Basilica, I was ushered through a sea of bishops and cardinals to a seat very near Pope Paul VI. I sat almost directly under the celebrated canopy soaring above the altar, the famous Bernini *Baldacchino*, the largest piece of bronze art in the world, a vast free-standing colossus of four columns with spiral fluting adorned with olives, bay and acanthus leaves looming high above the altar. It marked the location of the ciborium honoring St. Peter's martyrdom on that very spot in the largest space within the world's largest church. The enormous dome of the basilica was directly above us. The grave of St. Peter was directly below us deep underneath the cathedral in archaeological remains dated to the first century.

I got the Latin text draft of the document on revelation in advance, along with the Latin drafts of *Lumen Gentium* and other Vatican documents either in preparation or under debate. I relied on Ed Gagney, a young Paulist priest sitting beside me, to whisper-translate the proceedings, which were largely in Latin. The debate that autumn while I was there centered on crucial Vatican documents on the apostolate of the laity and the relationship with the Jews. It was 1965, the year of the council when so many of those history-making documents were being completed. I was privileged to be present when many of those documents were just beginning to be made available in French and English.[17]

I came away from Vatican II profoundly challenged, newly respectful of the conciliar process. From that point on, classic conciliar consensus became an impassioned issue for me.

At Vatican II my mind was growing through the embryonic beginnings of a reversal of moral conscience unlike any I had known. I found myself increasingly critical of the Freudian psychoanalysis that had long shaped my interest in personal behavior change. I better recognized the long captivity of Protestant pastoral care to contemporary psychology and became a critic of the very accommodation to modern consciousness that I myself had advocated throughout the preceding decade.

Back in Heidelberg, a brilliant circle of American theological colleagues had found each other that year, including Egil Grislis of Duke and Karl Donfried of Smith College. They provided me with an ongoing conversation on theology that kept me informed about many research efforts going on in Germany. Among the youngest on the Heidelberg New Testament faculty was Dieter Georgi, who generously welcomed our family to his home. We were introduced to German Christmas customs and foods at their house. Dieter became for me a model of independent text-based research focused on primary sources. That method would prove important for my later textual work in patristic exegesis (interpretation of Scripture). He was the kind of New Testament theologian who attended carefully to the text of Scripture, aware of all its historic and cultural determinants, but focused strictly on what the Greek texts said and meant.

Dieter invited me to attend the annual meeting of the Bultmann-Kreise, the circle of Bultmannian scholars who met annually. In January of 1966 we drove to a small village guesthouse to meet the inner circle of the second generation of Bultmann scholars. Among them were some who would come to dominate the departments of New Testament studies in European and American universities in the ensuing decades. The group was dedicated to advancing and critiquing the influential initiatives Bultmann had taken toward the demythology of the New Testament. The more I heard, the more my interest in Bultmann ebbed since it appeared to me that the inner circle was more intent upon acceptance within the historical guild than in listening to the wisdom of the text.

I was invited to a seminar on theology and psychology at the Ecumenical Institute in Bossey, Switzerland. I reported to them the research I was doing at the Heidelberg Institute. One of the leaders was Russian Orthodox Metropolitan Anthony Bloom with a full white beard, who my two-year-old daughter, Laura, mistook for Santa Claus. Dear Bishop Anthony played the role of Santa Claus each time he saw her.

After one of the late afternoon sessions I walked down the winding hill to the village pub with David L. Edwards of Oxford, who at that time was the editor of SCM Press. After working so long with SCM leadership in North America, I found him a trove of information on the strengths and weaknesses of the ecumenical Student Christian Movement, which he had served as general secretary. At that time we both were still drawn to the prosecularization model of Christian theology and found it better actualized in the ecumenical SCM than anywhere else. When I sketched out the core categories for the structure of awareness in time, he encouraged me to develop it into a book, which I did during the next three years.

TRAVELS TO ODENWALD AND JERUSALEM

Connecting with my family in the Odenwald Forest. The only thing I knew about my family in Germany was my recollection of Grandmother Clark talking about her distant German relatives who lived in the area of Reichenbach, Hesse Darmstadt, Germany. It was one of the tiniest spots on a very large-scale map. When I got to Heidelberg I started planning a visit with them.

My great-grandfather, George Seeger, came from the tiny village of Reichenbach in the Oden Forest just before the Franco-Prussian War of 1870. With spare resources he had bid goodbye to his family of stonecutters in the mountains of the Oden Forest, where the family had lived for untold generations. Determined to make it on his own to America, he arrived in Baltimore with 25 cents.

Our family set out to connect with the Seeger family in Reichenbach. We were encouraged when we walked around the cemetery and found numerous gravestones marked with the family name, Seeger. After inquiries we found that some of my relatives still lived in an apartment over the General Store, which had once been a blacksmith and stonecutter's shop for who knows how long.

The blacksmith shop was on Nibelungenstrasse, the street of the ancient Teutonic myth of Siegfried and Brunhilde. We were warmly greeted, wined and dined. Relatives came from out of the hills to see us. We met the eldest member of the family, Jacob Seeger, who turned out to be a cousin of my great-grandfather. That was the first reunion of the American and German Seegers in a hundred years. I had with me a genealogical tree of my family, and they had a detailed "Stammbaum" of their family. Then came the moment of recognition when we laid out those two trees together. It was easy to make the connections. At last it dawned on me that my great-grandfather Seeger's blacksmith shop in Lafayette, Indiana, was a continuation of the blacksmith shop in Reichenbach. Both sides had been unaware of the connection until that day.

When my mother and I years later visited Reichenbach, we were entertained by a folk-singing musical group led by some of the family. We saw the village Lutheran Church where my great grandfather had been baptized, and the cemetery where the family was buried. We also went to the ancient Ratskeller for *Gemütlichkeit* in a large gathering of the extended family.

Throughout the sabbatical year we as a family of five traveled all over Europe, packed snugly in our VW Microbus. The close quarters were challenging, but it provided a unique opportunity for our children to see many sites from the Tivoli to the Cologne Cathedral, from the Swiss Alps to the Low Countries, from the Regensburg to Stonehenge. They learned a lot of history that year. The children sang their way through the Brenner Pass and we camped out on top of one of the Seven Hills of Rome.

The expedition from Heidelberg to Jerusalem. In early spring we packed up our family for a long expedition. Our objectives were Vienna, Yugoslavia, Greece, Turkey, Lebanon and Syria. Our final destination was Jerusalem.

Packed high on our VW roof rack was an abundant supply of necessities for two months or more: milk that would not spoil, clothes for all climates, tenting and camping gear of all sorts, and toys and books for the children. We were accompanied by another family all the way to Istanbul—Dr. Charles Baughman and his family from St. Paul Seminary in Kansas City. He was also on sabbatical in Heidelberg. Together we roughed it all the way from Germany to Turkey with no hotels, few showers and lots of memorable encounters.

Our first stop was Vienna, where I had scheduled a visit with the great Austrian psychiatrist and Holocaust survivor Viktor Frankl. He was crucial to my study year since he was the best known existential analyst. Eight years older than I and already world famous, he warmly welcomed me and inquired about my research. We talked freely about his groundbreaking insights that came directly out of his death camp experience in which he had found meaning in even the most demoralizing, death-laden circumstances. It was in prison that he learned that no one could take away his inner freedom, even under the worst conditions of slave labor. His attitude toward his environment had been in his own hands. No matter how confined externally in body, he had remained free to take his own voluntary attitude toward all that happened.

His work would later spawn the humanistic psychology movement in North America in which I participated both through writing for its journal and testing its therapeutic approaches in small group processes. Dr. Frankl escorted me into his library, where he had gathered all his extant articles, most in German, and graciously offered that I take any that might fit into my research interests.

From Vienna we turned south to travel through the entire length of Yugoslavia from Zagreb through Belgrade to Skopje. At that time Yugoslavia was a sternly ruled communist country under Marshal Tito. We were wary as we passed by guarded street corners with Kalashnikov AK-47 assault rifles in evidence. We traveled through a whole gamut of ethnic communities, from Slovak and Croat to Serbian and Macedonian. In Greece we sought out the Byzantine churches in Thessaloniki. While driving through Thrace we heard news that Syria was in a state of revolution.

We arrived exhausted in Istanbul and needed some recovery time. For several days we explored the ramparts, sites and souks of Istanbul. We marveled at the magnificence of Hagia Sophia and Justinian's architectural achievements. In Istanbul I made a visit to the American Embassy for their advice on the Syrian crisis and the news was disheartening. Despite State Department counsel, we decided nonetheless to proceed on the course we had previously set. We had come too far to be turned back by the Ba'ath Revolution. There on the Bosphorus Strait, European Turkey ends and Asian Turkey begins, separating the two subcontinents. We sadly parted with the Baughman family, who had decided to go west to Ephesus and stay out of Syria. My family headed across the vast plains of Anatolia. We proceeded south toward the southern Turkish coast and hoped we could get through the Syrian border guards.

Our first stop after Istanbul was Izmit, ancient Nicomedia, with its Hellenistic ruins and Palace of Diocletian. We drove through many cities whose names appear in the New Testament in the regions of Bithynia, Galatia and the Anatolian plains, on the way to Cilicia and Tarsus. The overnight facilities were far apart. We made our way to the Taurus Mountains and found them to be vast, steep and beautiful. The snow and ice, however, were dangerous, and I could hardly see anything as I drove. I continued to drive into the darkness until at last I was passed by a large BP oil truck with bright backlights. I followed those lights through the hazardous winding mountain passes of the Cilician Gates for many kilometers until we finally arrived at the city of Tarsus as there had been no place to stop on the road. In Tarsus we saw the ruins of the port city where Paul was born.

Our main stop in the south of Turkey was the early Christian sites of Antioch, where Ignatius had been bishop and where John Chrysostom had preached in the Great Cathedral. South of Antioch we visited the garden of Daphne with its waterfalls and forested valley, once inhabited by sumptuous Roman villas. We proceeded south toward the hazardous Syrian border, where we heard that the Ba'ath Revolution was just beginning.

The day was waning and our gas tank was almost empty as we neared the border. There were no nearby cities and no petrol stations as we were in a remote mountainous region. Syrians refugees were fleeing north into Turkey back then just as they are today.

It was unnerving not to be able to find fuel. Finally we had no option but to pull off the main road where the tiny village of Kulac was nestled about six miles from the highway. Unfortunately it was so small that there was no filling station there. As we pulled into the settlement, excited children ran up to us shouting and chasing us. I said, "petrol?" They shook their heads no.

Fortunately an elderly man with a white beard approached the bus and took me into a drab one-room general store which had almost nothing for sale. He took out a ten gallon vessel of gasoline. With a pair of iron scales, like the old scales of justice that had measured weight against weight in ancient times, he added lead weights on one side and poured out two gallons of petrol on the other side. Gratefully I gave him Turkish currency. He grinned widely through his broken teeth as he happily pocketed much-needed cash. Then he gestured that we were welcome to stay, but the late afternoon light was declining and we needed to reach the Syrian border. By that time the whole village of children and adults had turned out for what seemed to be a major event and watched us head back on the rocky road to the highway that would take us to the Kasab boundary crossing.

Entering Syria during the Ba'athist coup d'état of 1966. We arrived at the Syrian frontier customs office only days after the beginning of the revolution. It was the bloodiest coup Syria had experienced since 1949, and the unrest was still simmering. The army units under Hafez al-Assad had abruptly seized power, declaring a form of Ba'athism which promoted the vision of a pan-Arab Greater Syria.

At the Syrian border crossing we were met by two guards armed with heavy automatic weapons and they asked us for passports. The guard took my passport, handed it to another guard and came back to inspect. As he peered into the bus he saw our two-year-old blond Laura sitting between Edrita and me. His eyes lit up as he motioned to me that he wanted me to pass her through the window to him. I glanced at Edrita who seemed to sense the inevitableness of the situation. I felt I had no choice. Laura was her charming self and was completely unafraid. I let her climb over the steering wheel, and as I handed her over to the armed guard, he immediately left with her, disappearing into the border control shack. We waited in horror.

All he wanted to do was show her off to his fellow soldiers and then he brought her back out smiling. He handed her back to me and I passed her to Edrita. I looked through my back mirror as we pulled out, very grateful we had survived that experience and had made it into Syria.

Driving south along coastal Syria, we arrived at the port city of Latakia as night was falling. We located a grocery store to replenish our dwindling supply of bread and fruit.

Our appearance in Latakia was widely noted, but there was no sign of hostility. We stayed overnight there near the Mediterranean shore. Latakia had enjoyed several centuries of Christian presence before the Arab conquest in 638. We were able to see the chief architectural landmark of Byzantine Christianity in the city, the basilica built by Justinian after devastating earthquakes had destroyed the earlier church.

Our main site in North Syria was the ancient city of Ras Shamra, ancient Ugarit, once a Neolithic village which had urban occupation from the late Bronze Age to the Iron Age. I had heard for years about Ugarit from my close colleague Loren R. Fisher at Phillips Seminary. He could read ten languages and had been on archaeological digs at Ugarit, after which he had written about the Ras Shamra cuneiform tablets and artifacts unearthed from its extensive library.

The Ras Shamra site was off the coastal road a few kilometers. Right away we could tell that the excavation site at Tell Shamra was huge. Loren had been digging there in 1958 with Cyrus Gordon when he shared in the discovery of the Claremont Ras Shamra Tablets. As my family and I pulled into the site early that morning, no one was there. All the informational signs were in Arabic. We saw a limping man approaching us after we had been wandering around the site for a while. He could speak only a little English but volunteered to be our guide and pointed out ruins of the ancient city.

We walked over the vast ruins of the former ninety-room royal palace. The libraries of Ugarit contained clay tablets written in Sumerian,

Hurrian, Akkadian and finally Ugaritic—a previously unknown language before recent digs. The cuneiform tablets using the ancient Ugaritic language were from the period of 1450–1200 B.C. Ugaritic, Mycenaean and Cypriot pottery shards were strewn all about. I realized I was stepping over ruins of the auspicious place where the first written language was likely invented and archived, and where one of antiquity's earliest libraries had been unearthed.

When we finally got to Lebanon, we found it to be even more dangerous than Syria. We had planned to stay at American University in Beirut but found that it was closed as there had been conflicts and threats around its perimeter the previous day.

The university security guards were polite but could not offer us safety. They took us to a relatively secured area near the university complex and allowed us to camp there. We learned that there had been fighting in that area the night before. That night in Beirut was the most fearful of our entire expedition as we could hear armored vehicles and shouts nearby.

We were on our own in our Microbus and could expect no police assistance. Our only option early the next morning was to get out. We pressed west over Mount Hermon and reentered southern Syria on our way to Damascus. Again the border between Lebanon and Syria was heavily guarded on top of Mount Hermon, but we were flagged through, much to our relief. In the capital city there were few tourists due to the revolution, but there was sufficient police protection so that we were able to visit some ancient parts of the central city without alarm. We were awed by the beauty of the Ommayid Mosque, built in A.D. 634, considered the fourth holiest site in Islam. The site on which the mosque was built is linked with the earliest days of Christianity. In Byzantine times, before Islam, that central city location had been the site of the Orthodox Basilica of St. John the Baptist, first built in the times of Constantine for a Christian congregation that predated the Nicene Creed.

In New Testament times Saul of Tarsus had journeyed to Damascus to persecute and kill Christians when he had been blinded by a light from above. He was led by hand to the Street Called Straight where he met Ananias, who had been sent by the Spirit to take care of Saul and baptize him as Paul. We were able to locate the traditional site of the Street Called Straight. We found the Chapel of St. Ananias, which was thought to be on the site of the most ancient Christian church in that area. Though often rebuilt, it remains one of the earliest still-standing church locations of Christian history, with services continuing to be held there.

Damascus has many treasured locations of early Christian memory. One was the oratory of the head of John the Baptist, revered by both Christians and Muslims. Another was by the Keissan Gate that memorialized St. Paul's Window, recalling an event reported in Acts in which Paul was fleeing from soldiers seeking his life. He was let down at night in a basket by rope.

Security was far more stable in Damascus than it had been in Beirut, and safer in Jordan than it had been in Syria. We soon left Damascus driving south toward Amman, Jordan, and stopped at the magnificent Roman site of ancient Gerasa, Jerash, presently one of the cities of the Decapolis noted in the New Testament, where many columns still stand. In the winter season it was quiet with only a few visitors. We strolled along its long colonnaded central street, its forum, its ruined temples and its hippodrome, all surrounded by a largely intact city wall. In the center of Jerash were remains of an early Christian basilica dating back to the A.D. 300s. More than a dozen churches had been built in Jerash in the fifth and sixth centuries, where some of their magnificent mosaic floors have survived. From Jerash we drove on to Amman, looking eagerly toward our hoped for crossing, the River Jordan, and driving on into Jerusalem.

Jerusalem and Qumran. We had been advised that since we were Americans, we might be stopped abruptly either at the Allenby Bridge over the River Jordan or the Mandelbaum Gate. If that had happened, that might have been the end of our lengthy expedition of 1,828 miles from Heidelberg.

Our heavily loaded VW Microbus had a noticeable German tag, which we hoped would obscure our American identity as we crossed into disputed territory. Strewn along the highway were tattered evidences of the earlier Palestinian-Israeli conflicts: damaged tanks, jeeps and signs that indicated recent points of conflict.

The Mandelbaum Gate marked the division between the Israel and Palestinian armies in the war-torn city of Jerusalem. We went through its heavy security, braced for trouble at any moment. Since any traveler with an Israeli stamp on their passport would have been turned back, we carefully avoided that scenario. Fortunately we made it through with the German tag on the Volkswagen and trouble-free passports. We were relieved to set foot on Israeli soil, even though in 1966 it was still a virtual battle zone. We were in Jerusalem when much of Mount Skopus and many parts of the old city were under Palestinian control. We headed for the American School of Oriental Research (ASOR) just outside of the Damascus Gate in the Palestinian quarter of the old city.

The five of us climbed out of the cramped bus, took a deep breath and stretched our legs with relief. The long trip had been exhilarating, but we felt much more elation as we finally arrived at our destination in the Holy City. We felt victorious over circumstances and over our own anxieties.

We were welcomed into the safe walls of the ASOR in an area of Jerusalem that was heavily populated by Palestinians. Two elderly, white-bearded guards secured the property as they had been expecting us.

Two eminent American colleagues were research residents at ASOR at that time, and their families greeted us warmly. They were James and Anita Robinson of Claremont Graduate School and Paul and Nancy Lapp of ASOR. The year prior to our coming to Jerusalem, the Bab edh-Dhra site had been excavated by Paul Lapp.

The ASOR was only a three-minute walk to the Damascus Gate of the old city. When I went to the antiquities market, some of the artifacts of Bab edh-Dhra (ancient Sodom) had already found their way to one of the dealers. I asked Paul Lapp about their authenticity and legality. He confirmed their genuineness and indicated that they were legitimately available if stamped as approved for sale by the Israeli government. So I legally acquired four ceramic bowls from the Early Bronze Period (3100–2900 B.C.), unblemished in their original excavated condition. James Robinson had recently obtained access to the Nag Hammadi documents.

He was very busy working on their identification and interpretation. He was thrilled to be one of the first to gain access to them at a very early stage of their study and classification. My nine-year-old-son Clark and I joined Jim in a rigorous mountain climb to the steep rocky slopes above Qumran to see if we could reach one of the famous Qumran caves where scrolls had been found. We discovered that only some remains of a plaster floor remained in the cave. We came down from the mountain above Qumran with bleeding hands, but elated that we had reached and inspected one of the relatively unstudied Qumran caves.

We were in Jerusalem a year before the Six Day War, when Syria was pursuing a mutual defense agreement with Egypt. The Palestine Liberation Organization had stepped up its guerilla activity, and Israel was under siege. Israel's borders were suffering repeated sporadic Arab attacks. In the north they were observing heavy Syrian military activity in the Golan Heights. Many parts of the West Bank of Palestine were virtually inaccessible to travelers.

While residing in the American School, our family made daily trips out to emerging digs of biblical cities. We were carefully advised by ASOR faculty about where to go and where not to go. It was judged reasonably safe to go to Jericho, Bethlehem and Hebron, plus many sites in the western parts of Israel and the Galilee.

As a boy I had marveled at the story of David and Goliath. Now our children were picking up smooth stones at the valley of Elah, where David had killed Goliath. In Jericho we climbed around the spectacular remains of the excavations by Kathleen Kenyon into the grain silos of the seven-thousand-year-old city, one of the oldest continuous settlements in human history. The Bible I had learned as a child, distinguished from the Bible I had learned in historical-critical studies, was coming alive for me in a palpable way.

Near Bethel we happened upon a colorful West Bank Palestinian wedding. We traveled leisurely over the Galilee: Nazareth, Capernaum and Tiberius. We visited sites south of Jerusalem to Bethlehem, Tekoa, the Herodian Castle and accessible parts of the Judean Desert, where so many of the earliest Palestinian monasteries were located. Gazing down upon the Plain of Sharon from the heights of Megiddo (Armageddon), I pondered the end of history as the key to understanding the beginning, progression and prophesied ending of history,

We visited my archaeologist friend Jim Ross (formerly of Drew, then of Alexandria) while he was digging at Tel Gezer, a city far northwest of Jerusalem that had been conquered by Joshua and rebuilt by Solomon. He set me to work with a trowel and a brush, digging, scraping and cleaning artifacts from the Iron Age. It made me wish I had spent more time in archaeological digs. All of those experiences gave me a sensory feeling of contact with the history I longed to see in a larger perspective, and it deepened my awareness of historical continuity.

Bethlehem in the spring of 1966 was safe, not crowded, and had many Christian families in residence, unlike today. Our family explored the town, its people, its food and its sites freely and unhurriedly. We returned to visit the ancient Church of the Nativity and its surroundings. It was and still is one of Christianity's oldest churches, dating to Helena, the mother of Constantine. The site harks back to the earliest Christian memory of Jesus' birth, death and resurrection. Underneath the basilica we knelt in the Grotto of the Nativity, an underground cave that enshrines the traditional site of the Nativity, where Jerome is thought to have studied, lived and worked on his translation into Latin of the Hebrew Bible.

I told my children that my own personal story as a child had been shaped by the story of the calling of Samuel at the house of Eli in the temple of Shiloh. That story had prompted me as a boy to reflect upon my own vocation. Now amazingly my family was trekking on the slopes of Shiloh and Ephraim.

As a young pastor I had preached on the story of Elijah at Mount Carmel, where he had overcome the priests of Baal in a test of miraculous power. Now, my family was visiting Mount Carmel. I had preached on the biblical narratives of the raising of Lazarus in Bethany. Now we were walking leisurely through the streets of Bethany tasting the food and meeting the people. I had preached on the transfiguration on Mount Tabor and found myself climbing its slopes. I had preached on the calling of the disciples at Capernaum. Now we were on the shores near Capernaum, where we collected shells from the waters where Jesus, Peter and the disciples had sailed and fished. Our children searched for Roman coins stuck on the eroding slope of the coastal bluff adjacent to the great amphitheater of Caesarea Maritima.

By sea from Haifa to Genoa. After Caesarea we had to make our way back to Haifa, where we had an appointment to load our dusty VW bus onto a mid-sized ship of Hellenic Lines on its way to Athens and Marseille. After weeks of encrusted travel we were ready for the comforts and conveniences of a Mediterranean sea voyage. Our bus was stored in the interior of the ship.

Suddenly our living quarters changed from cramped bus travel to invigorating sea air and great Greek cuisine. We loved the transition from the Judean desert to a comfortable Greek Mediterranean sailing vessel with a small swimming pool and time to unwind and take in the brisk sea breezes. Our destination before returning to Heidelberg was Geneva, Switzerland, where I had been invited to assist the World Council of Churches staff as it was holding its World Conference on Church and Society in April 1966.

Our first Mediterranean stop was at the port of Limassol, where the ancient city of Kourion is perched high on a cliff overlooking the sea. Next was the Greek island of Rhodes off the coast of southern Turkey. In its harbor once stood one of the Seven Wonders of the World, the Statue of Colossus. At the Archaeological Museum of Rhodes we tried in vain to interest our children in the splendid sculpture from the archaic, classical, Hellenistic and Roman periods, but after weeks of travel they were more interested in running, dodging, exploring and discovering shards.

From Rhodes to Athens we went through stormy seas where the ship reeled so much that the food slid off the tables. The crew had to belt our children to dining chairs. Like riding on a roller coaster, they thought it was great fun. As the storm got worse, it called to mind the episode reported in Acts 27 when Paul, on his sea travel from Caesarea to the Aegean Sea, had faced gale force winds that almost took the whole ship and crew to the bottom of the sea.

Watching an ecumenical train wreck with Paul Ramsey. Conference

Secretary Paul Albrecht was the person who had invited me to help on the staff of the Geneva Conference. Up to that point I had been a loyal participant in WCC leadership, chiefly by writing and editing various books and tracts for the ecumenical Student Christian Movement.

Liberation movements were being actively promoted by the WCC leadership. Leftist politics of the sort I had previously supported were now presuming to lend an aura of quasi-prophetic relevance to the ecumenical movement. Bureaucrats were setting utopian, political objectives for all churches everywhere, but their ideological interest was evident from the outset. Meanwhile totalitarian collectivist regimes were being given a moral pass. Collectivist rhetoric such as that by which I had previously been enthralled was now being proposed as a norm for all Christian believers all over the world.

With the call to repentance, faith and discipleship reduced to political action, the WCC's special vocation had become to change all societies fundamentally through politics and wealth transfer. One Genevan official reported that "the churches should be more active in promoting a worldwide revolutionary opposition to the capitalist political and economic system being imposed on new nations by Western industrialized countries." From then on they vowed that "the WCC would not condemn those who in their context resorted to violence as the only possibility for realizing justice." The newfound ecumenical purpose of WCC was to engineer a "common response by churches to injustice and inequality, violence and war, and environmental destruction," but it neither sought nor found any consensus about the biblical ground of such concerns. Deputy General Secretary Konrad Raiser summarized, "As Christians we are called to act; we cannot wait until we have reached complete agreement in terms of analysis or with regard to the theological, ethical and ecclesiological implications." The most urgent question was "whether the transformation of society should be achieved through quiet efforts at social renewal or through the use of revolutionary methods, such as the violent overthrow of an existing political order."[18]

I found myself naively marching behind maverick sociologist Margaret Mead in a protest demonstration on Geneva's streets. It was a protest against capitalism and in support of a plan to redistribute world income. I was finding that the confessional glue that had held the modern ecumenical movement together was becoming leftist politics just at the time I was in the slow process of recognizing their disastrous consequences. All of this poured out of my heart in an instant during that protest march when I finally grasped that I was in the wrong place.

In Geneva I was relieved to meet my friend Paul Ramsey of Princeton, whom I still consider the greatest ethicist of the generation following Richard Niebuhr. Paul and I met at the bar of the International Hotel each evening to review the day's highlights and follies. Paul was exasperated at the moral shallowness and naiveté of the World Council. His opinions on the WCC would soon appear in print in the definitive book on the struggle for the soul of ecumenism titled *Who Speaks for the Church?* We were witnessing the crackup of modern ecumenism. At first we laughed over its absurdities, and then we grieved over what we were seeing in Geneva. No matter how excited the WCC leadership was about their boldness, they did not get it—their actions were causing everyone else to turn away.

The more I watched the spectacle, the more I knew I was coming to a fork in the road. The road was modern ecumenism, born in 1948 in Amsterdam in the time of my youth and recklessness before 1966, which virtually ended for me on those Genevan streets. I was finally coming to understand that my generation of ecumenists had deeply disrupted the fragile unity of the body of Christ in an attempt to heal it. I felt to some extent personally responsible.

I had been party to tearing down church institutions that could not easily be replaced and moral traditions that would take decades to rebuild. What was replacing the received ecumenical confession was a diffuse vision of supposed positive political change built largely on a Marxist view of inevitable historical change, proletarian revolution and crony wealth redistribution. My generation of idealists had been uncritically convinced we could build something better, more faithful, more humane than all that we had received from all of the previous generations. I could see that what was emerging was nothing like what we had anticipated.

I have never been the same after Geneva. I lost confidence in those I had trusted. I had traveled with ecumenists from the idealistic days of the college student Christian Movement to the InterSeminary Movement to the exhilaration of the second World Conference at Evanston, only to experience Geneva as a vast breakdown of classic Christian social teaching.

Later, I went to the follow-up Conference on Church and Society at Detroit in 1966. The worst features of the Geneva Conferences were multiplied in the Detroit Conference.[19] Detroit was Geneva on steroids. It shocked me into recognition that an organization I had trusted to unite believers could cause so much division.

I left Detroit with revulsion in my soul. If those idealists had grasped the necessity of bringing their ideals into useful and viable outcomes, that would have been understandable. But I knew that political manipulations and arrogance were doing irreparable harm to the very churches they sought to reform.

Back in Heidelberg in the spring of 1966, I sought an audience with the eminent philosopher Hans Georg Gadamer, who had written extensively on hermeneutics, historical method and the nature of understanding. I invited him for a personal visit at our little apartment with Edrita juggling our three children in a small space. He appeared at our doorway exactly on time. I began our conversation by noting the great affection I had for Nicholai Hartmann's work, upon which Gadamer had based his early work, and this struck a chord of nostalgia in him.

As I tried to explain to Gadamer what I was researching at Heidelberg, I began to realize that he personally knew virtually all the figures I was studying: Heidegger, Bultmann, Barth, Hannah Arendt, Carl Friedrich von Weizsäcker, Karl Jaspers, Heinrich Ott and Pannenberg. But he was mystified as to how they might relate to my theological interest in the practice of psychotherapy. As he left, I felt like a novice in the presence of a true philosophical giant, trying to explain to him the elements of something I thought he already understood.

We said goodbyes to our neighbor Frau Heilman, the Georgi family and our circle of sabbatical-year friends as we left Heidelberg. As I departed, I realized that the purpose for my coming there had changed, and that my journey had been reenergized by Barth, Vatican II, the expedition and Pannenberg, none of them on my original sabbatical agenda.

THE STRUCTURE OF AWARENESS

After Heidelberg. Before boarding the great ocean liner Queen Mary for New York, our family spent the last weeks of the sabbatical in England. Our nostalgic trajectory in the south of England included Canterbury, Stonehenge, Westminster, Bristol and Oxford. In London I attended the World Methodist Conference in historic Westminster Central Hall. There I met the core international leadership of Methodist scholars and bishops. I identified more fully with the African and East European Methodists than with the American delegates. The full-scale collapse of the World Council of Churches in Geneva in 1966 had not yet affected the Methodists, but cracks were beginning to appear.

The last stop before boarding the Queen Mary for New York was Nottingham, for an unforgettable visit with the brilliant psychiatrist Frank Lake. He was high on my list of existential psychologists relevant to my sabbatical study in Europe. Having read a draft of *Kerygma and Counseling*, he was eager to see what I had been doing in Germany. He had served in India as the director of the Christian Medical School at Madras, teaching in psychiatry before returning to England to found the Clinical Pastoral movement in 1962.

Over many years Frank Lake became a true friend. I read his magnificent book *Clinical Theology*, which provided, as the subtitle says: "A Theological and Psychiatric Basis to Clinical Pastoral Care." That conversation with Frank Lake alone would have made my summer in England worthwhile. He had brought together classic Christian biblical teaching with the profound practice of a type of psychiatry that had a warm pastoral focus. Lake was the greatest Christian analyst of anxiety, despair and anomie since Kierkegaard, all embedded intentionally in a strongly biblical frame of interpretation.

After that visit I spent months reading, pondering and lecturing on Lake's deep and moving books. He became a model for me in the search for cohesion in interdisciplinary study. He prompted me to push through to the publication of *Contemporary Theology and Psychotherapy*, and to begin a process that eventually would lead to a major book project with Harper and Row titled *Pastoral Theology: The Essentials of Ministry*.

Upon embarking from Portsmouth, my head spun with all the memories of the Heidelberg year. We docked in New York, took our Microbus to Providence, Rhode Island, where my sister and her husband were serving an Episcopal parish. There I learned more of Jim's lively associations with Anglican evangelicals Michael Green, John Stott and J. I. Packer. I could see a deep grounding in Scripture and tradition occurring in that community.

Surviving a decade of recklessness. In the three years after my year in Heidelberg, during the period from 1966 to 1969, I set my mind to completing the books I had begun in Germany: *Contemporary Theology and Psychotherapy, The Promise of Barth: The Ethics of Freedom* and *The Structure of Awareness.* Of those literary efforts, the one in which I became most invested was *The Structure of Awareness.* It gathered together the fragments of my lengthy and productive studies in existential psychology and theology.

No sooner had our family settled back into the relaxed pace and open spaces of Oklahoma life than I was faced with an unexpected vocational decision. Peter Berger of Hartford Theological Seminary wanted me to teach in his department. I was much impressed by his early book *The Rumors of Angels,* and its winsome style of writing became a model I tried to emulate. After much anguish, I reluctantly wrote Berger of my decision to stay in quiet Oklahoma and continue writing on all that was happening in the journey of my mind.

I had become aware that I was headed directly against the radical stream of the 1960s. I had enjoyed being part of its vision and had relished the feeling that I was leading others in new ways of thinking and believing, but my heart now knew that movement was not my future.

The resolve to write in my own voice. I loved the whole process of writing: research, drafting, redrafting, listening carefully to editors, benefiting from reviews and defending my ideas in the public sphere. From a small ecumenical seminary in Oklahoma, I knew I would have to stay on track deliberately to gain a hearing as a competent teacher and writing scholar. I also knew that I was missing a historical depth in pre-Reformation writings.

I loved Shakespeare's pursuit of fitting words, Luther's obedience of faith, Calvin's passion for Scripture, Kierkegaard's psychological analysis, Yeat's poetic imagination, Hartmann's phenomenology of value, Reinhold Niebuhr's political realism and Rogers's care for persons. This was the cluster of intellects of the 1950s and 1960s that most occupied my mind, that I had deeply absorbed and had fueled my determination to focus on the life of the mind rather than on becoming a lifelong captive to political activism. I wanted to write in a way that brought these together. I had not given myself an easy assignment.

My resolve to write was strong, just when my commitment to demonstration politics was weakening. George Wallace was a controversial candidate for president who held a rally in our town, Enid. I had joined a group of protesting picketers against the racist history and candidacy of Wallace. I had long hair as did others nearby. Wallace had drawn laughter when he pointed directly to us with the remark "The only four letter words hippies did not know were w-o-r-k and s-o-a-p." I was growing weary of the effectiveness of demonstration politics. The rowdiness of the summer of 1968 ended in the November election of Richard Nixon.

The pivotal event that best epitomized the deteriorating political culture of the late sixties for me was the Democratic National Convention of 1968, where the war resistors with whom I had once identified threw feces at the Chicago police.

Our culture was in the process of changing, and I was now riding on the crest of a giant wave of stirring ideas: The hermeneutic thought of Dilthey, Gadamer and the later works of Heidegger provided me with a method of describing the contours of my own consciousness. From the sociologists of knowledge, from Karl Mannheim to Peter Berger, I was learning how to think of Christianity as a community living always within a changing social world. Those mentors provided me with a method to analyze the formal structures of my own consciousness of time and relationship. After Heidelberg, I was determined to develop my own method of theological reasoning. This would require a full-length argument. It was my first attempt at systematic theology based on an examination of my own internal experience of my relationship to time.

Mapping the structure of awareness in time. Since first reading Nicholai Hartmann, I had been pondering how to accurately describe my existing relationship to my past, my present and my future. The story of my relationship to God, my false gods, my anxieties and my guilt was linked to my relationship to the inescapable flow of time.

I was searching for my relationship to the One who had given me life and who had outlived all of my creaturely values that I had in some way worshiped as gods. I wanted to understand how those idolatries had shaped my relationship with my neighbor and with the natural world. I sought an integral vision of past, present, future, God, self and the natural world. The outcome of this reflection is what I called *The Structure of Awareness*.[20]

The rudiments of that vision had already been sketched in my first published book, *The Crisis of the World and the Word of God*, in 1962. It was a short book I had written for the Methodist Student Movement for its national conference. I realized that it needed filling out, and I was now ready to pursue it to its depths.

Bear with me on a brief departure into the workings of my mind back then. I was intrigued with describing the human predicament in terms of seven basic, existential relationships. *Existential* refers to those relations in which every human unavoidably exists:

the future (not yet)
the past (having already occurred)
the present (Now!)
the Unconditioned (the One who gives us life)
one's own self (I exist in a relationship with myself)
other persons I meet (the neighbor)
the natural and historical environment (the world)

Those relationships summarized my structure of awareness. My thesis was that those seven relationships were intrinsic to human existence. Three of those were temporal relationships:

the imagined future, which led to anxiety
the remembered past, which led to guilt
the experienced Now, which led to boredom

Anxiety, guilt and boredom are all intensified by idolatry.

Those three were exhaustive of all possible relationships to time.

Then there were four more forms of personal relationship: the relation to the Giver of all things, to myself, to other human beings and to the natural world. My relationship with the inorganic world was entirely different from my relationship with persons. I believed those seven to be exhaustive of all possible personal relationships in the spatial order within time. All other ancillary relationships can fit into these simple and familiar categories.

I knew that my anxiety was a distrust of anything the future might bring that would challenge my idolatries (revolution, money, sex, power, etc.). The good function of my imagination had become twisted by my gods. In moments of maximum anxiety I was convinced that my gods could not deliver me, and I despaired over the loss of them.

The Bible spoke to me of a saving event that called me to receive the future as a gift, since the Giver of the future had become revealed as ultimately not threatening beyond the death of my finite gods.

Similarly, guilt is a relationship to my past in which I have denied values and gods considered necessary for my existence. I became free from guilt when I realized a way had been provided by God for those idolatries to be forgiven and redirected.[21]

By analogy, I related to my present with boredom when values I had idolized were inaccessible to me; but I was free from boredom when I realized a way had been provided by God to receive the present as a gift of grace.

No one to my knowledge had written on that integrated structure as a system for self-examination. That construct offered a plain explanation of my relationship to time and personhood. It illuminated many problems I myself faced. Since I had not found any philosopher, psychologist or theologian who had utilized that basic frame, I began to wonder if that conceptual structure was something I was called to clarify for myself, if not for others.[22]

The intensive group experience and the élan of the late sixties. That led me into several years of exploring the group therapy movements that focused on self-disclosure. All of those diverse movements could be seen under the category of the intensive group experience.

Psychiatrist Frank Lake invited me to give lectures at Oxford in St. Catherine College to bring those thoughts to expression for the core leadership of the Clinical Theology Association. Interacting with Lake brought me to a closer appreciation of his work as a therapist and teacher, especially of his emerging work in primal therapy and regression analysis.[23]

While in Oxford for those lectures, I found my way into the open stacks at Waterford's bookstore near the train station. I spent a whole day in the poorly lit third and fourth levels of those dusty stacks. The amazing availability in Oxford of rare books that had been published three or four centuries earlier enthralled me. I enjoyed the vellum bindings, the aesthetics of fonts, the mystery of identification and the language challenges—in short, everything having to do with early printed books. Finally I settled upon a Latin concordance printed in the seventeenth century and bound in its original vellum. Rare books have been my collecting passion ever since. They have helped me retain my linguistic skills while learning something of the history of printing, plus they have provided me with wonderful glimpses into past times.

Edrita and my son Edward accompanied me from Oxford to Edinburgh and to St. Andrews in pursuit of Ed's passion for golf. I returned with new energy and a determination to finish the manuscript of *The Structure of Awareness*, which was published in 1969.

When I was asked to serve, in addition to my teaching, as an interim minister for a small Congregational church in Carrier, Oklahoma, a rural town near the seminary, I accepted because I wanted to get back in touch with parish life, preaching and pastoral care.[24] In parish life I relearned the basic goodness of the laity, the holiness of a worshiping community and the desire to live accountably to God. Those were priceless recognitions. I learned that even with all the deteriorations in the church denominational bureaucracies, there was stability, love and generosity in the churches. They restored my love for and confidence in the local church.

As a reflection of the down-to-earth stability of the faithful laity, I wrote on *The Visibility of the Church* (1969), which developed a critique of the "underground church" and of popular expressions of the supposed invisibility of the church.

The New Age movement of the late 1960s was for me exhilarating. It came as swiftly as it disappeared. The Green Revolution and the heyday of the Human Potential movement moved at top speed. Everyone was talking about peak experiencing and self-actualization. The air was fueled by the revolutionary passions of the sixties, Vietnam, situational ethics, the new morality, sexual experimentation and anti-parent spleen.

My book *The Intensive Group Experience* came out of the fantasies and anguish of the Human Potential movement. It put the movement in historical perspective, pointing to its roots in eighteenth century Jewish Hasidism and Wesleyan small group holiness movements.

In the late 1960s I was following the writings of the most experimentally oriented psychotherapists.[25] In addition to the Bethel National Training Laboratories, the center of experimental action was Esalen near Big Sur in a spectacular site near the coast of California. I was most interested in learning more about Gestalt therapy. I plunged into this wild and unpredictable scene of the Human Potential movement as it was beginning to impact the suburban churches. My aim was to do investigative reporting on the most experimental of all of those hothouse group processes. Houston was the place in the Southwest to find those experiments in full bloom. To participate directly in them I took a six-month sabbatical. I found them on the campus of the Houston Medical Center, which included the University of Texas Medical School, M. D. Anderson Cancer Center, Texas Heart Institute and one of the largest VA Hospitals on the continent.

I was selected for a half-year grant from the Association of Theological Schools. Edrita, Ed and Laura accompanied me for my semester in Houston under a project of the American Theological Association. I focused on new research at the Veteran's Hospital and the Houston Medical Center involved in the emerging therapeutic theories of Gestalt analysis and role reversal empathy. The high point of my New Age days did not last long, but it did offer a powerful set of experiences that for a time enlivened my imagination. I signed on for supervised clinical training in the psychiatric ward of the VA Hospital. I worked both in the open ward and the closed ward. I was also serving that semester as Visiting Professor of the Institute of Religion. I learned of Rolfing massage techniques from Esalen teachers. My two closest partners in dialogue at the Institute were Dominican Friar Benedict Ashley and Kenneth Vaux. Father Benedict had gone through many experimental stages before returning to classic Christianity in the Dominican Order. Kenneth Vaux was among the nation's premier theological ethicists.

In the long halls of the VA Hospital, I learned the basics of pharmacological treatment of severely troubled patients, observing both the usefulness and abuses of those medications. In the psychiatric ward, I saw patients who were there for long-term stays. My closest mentors in the psychiatric wards were Dr. Walter E. (Buzz) O'Connell and Dr. Philip Hanson. O'Connell was working with addicted patients and those suffering from post-traumatic stress disorder. Highly eclectic, he belonged to the burgeoning school of humanistic psychology, with special interests in natural high theory and practice, and psycho-spirituality. He and Phil Hanson led intensive group interaction processes in which people were being prepared to reenter society.

I had already been introduced to primitive forms of psychodrama in the literary tradition of Sophocles's *Antigone*, Shakespeare's *King Lear*, Goethe's *Lila*, Stanislavski, Sigmund Freud's dream analysis, Jung on active imagination and Alfred Adler's will to power and inferiority complex analysis. It was not until my VA internship that I could observe the positive and negative therapeutic outcomes of J. L. Mareno, Viola Spolin, Fritz Perls and Wilhelm Reich. I was especially drawn to techniques of psychodrama: doubling, role reversals, mirroring and soliloquy. I found the most promising approaches were role reversal therapy and psychodrama in the stream of Jacob and Zerka Moreno.[26]

Working as a clinical trainee in the locked psychiatric ward of the VA hospital, I led (under Dr. Hanson's supervision) a group of individuals who voluntarily entered a process designed to help them adjust to the outside world. We sought to teach them empathy by guiding them imaginatively into attention to another's experience. That was sometimes called drama therapy, where the techniques of mirroring, storytelling, plot, voice, movement, play and imagination were central features.

Transactional Analysis was at the height of its popularity, with its simpler version of Freudian views of ego, superego and id, translated by Eric Berne into the language of adult, parent and child. After Eric Berne wrote *Games People Play* in 1964, it became a fad among suburban church pastors and laity. In Houston in 1969, I met Thomas Harris, who popularized Eric Berne's transactional analysis in his book *I'm OK— You're OK*, which was widely pushed by counseling pastors across the country. I couldn't resist writing a spoof on Transactional Analysis called "Who Says You're OK?" I parodied Transactional Analysis in an interpretation of Paul's epistle to the Romans using TA insider jargon. Those were incorporated into my Harper book called *Game Free*. My reticent connection with Transactional Analysis appeared in two books, both from Harper and Row, *Game Free: The Meaning of Intimacy*, and *TAG: The Transactional Awareness Game*, along with a series of cassette tapes on the meaning of intimacy.

Since the Human Potential movement was almost entirely devoid of historical insight, I set forth a previously unexamined thesis on the historic roots of the encounter culture. I showed evidence that they had been found in the eighteenth-century Hasidic and Wesleyan movements of experimental groups seeking to aid each other in holy and responsible living. The book was called *The Intensive Group Experience: The New Pietism*. Core parts of that thesis were offered in "How Hasidic, How Wesleyan Is Our Encounter Culture?" in the *Journal of Humanistic Psychology* and *Intellectual Digest*. I was invited to a National Council of Churches (NCC) Conference on Leadership, where the ecumenical leaders wanted to learn more about some standard techniques of the Human Potential movement: deep breathing, body relaxation and group trust exercises.

So what sort of theologian had I turned into? I was still trapped in the role of the "movement theologian" but without the narrow political focus. The extreme trajectories of Charles Davis, Matthew Fox and Jim Nelson were far to the left of my own at that time, but nevertheless I was working with their questions. They had all taken a sharp turn away from classic Christianity and toward the feverish search for something else to justify a denuded Christian faith.

Most oddly I was drawn to the early Social Interaction Analysis of the young Harvard social psychologist Timothy Leary. That was before he was distracted by LSD experimentation and psychedelic drug usage. His graphs of interaction patterns became a major source for my book *TAG: The Transactional Awareness Game*. He provided a much improved pattern for sorting out types of interpersonal transactions. Amid the widespread interest in game theory, I developed a board game called the *Collusion Spectrum*.

The board game I devised was so complicated that almost no one could play it. The publishers at Harper were interested in it, so I developed it as a short book with a board game attached. Today on eBay the game is categorized as "vintage retro."

Its goal was to provide a more accurate descriptive means of sorting out types of human interactions, relying heavily on the empirical data of major social psychologists, chief of whom was Timothy Leary. He would end up sadly and famously as an advocate for psychedelic drugs.

Earth Day '69. The zenith of these popular movements for naturalistic idealism was for me the first Earth Day in Texas, which happened in Houston one year before Earth Day went national. Hermann Park was near the Texas Medical Center, where I worked. I went to a teach-in near McGovern Lake on the first day of spring.

The protest placard summed up a decade: "Make Love Not War." Seeking to conserve the earth's natural environment, we walked among gnarly oak trees. I sat on a park bench near the outdoor amphitheater to read a handout copy of *Socialist World*—a propaganda piece of which I hadn't seen a copy in several years, but its themes were all too familiar to me. The paper was saturated with labor-left messianic rhetoric. I thought back two decades to my Norman Thomas days, when I actually was a socialist. I felt overcome with relief and embarrassment that I had come so close to being trapped in that world. As the tumultuous decade was coming to a close, life on the cutting edge was draining me. I was experiencing a revulsion against self-preoccupation, narcissism and anarchy.

For some reason I had in my pocket that day my India paper edition of the 1662 Book of Common Prayer, which I had purchased at Blackwell's bookstore in Oxford. I turned to the collect for the day. Under the shade of a majestic gnarled tree I read out loud: "Almighty Father, who has given thine only Son to die for our sins, and to rise again for our justification; Grant us so to put away the leaven of malice and wickedness, that we may always serve thee in pureness of living and truth; through the merits of the same thy Son Jesus Christ our Lord. Amen." My eyes filled with tears as I asked myself what had I been missing in all of my frenzied subculture of experimental living.

The challenge to teach graduate studies in the New York area. Amid that funk of uncertainty in Houston, I received an invitation to consider coming to join the faculty of one of America's leading graduate schools at Drew University in Madison, New Jersey, where few of them knew me apart from my writings. What they knew of me was my literary record as a centrist Bultmannian, an education experimentalist and an actively publishing scholar. They liked it that a Bultmannian had ventured into the world of experimental psychotherapies.

Drew Graduate School had a lofty reputation in the fifties because of the Drew Colloquium, which had brought world theological leaders to speak on the most hotly contested themes of that day.[27] Now in 1968 Drew had become the scene of a huge conflict between the Drew University administration, headed by President Robert Oxnam, and the theological faculty. The issue was the control and allocation of Drew endowment funds, which had earlier been accrued mostly to the seminary.

Professor James M. Ault had been brought in from Union Seminary in New York as theological dean to heal that fissure. I got a call from him asking me to help them rebuild that faculty, as many had resigned. At the time I was in my most fluid and unpredictable phase. I had recently published *The Structure of Awareness*. I was in my tenth comfortable year at Phillips and was not looking for a new challenge, because my family was so happily settled in the community and university.

But when we visited Drew, Edrita and I found the village of Madison a very livable environment with good schools and direct links with Manhattan. The university welcomed us heartily and offered me an opportunity to be a part of the total rebuilding of a once-great faculty, now somewhat dispirited. I could see that my perspective would be significantly enlarged by being in the multicultural New York atmosphere.

part two

Change of Heart

The 1970s

The U-Turn

◆

The town of Madison offered the best of both worlds: the quietest village in Morris County in the shadow of the greatest city on earth. We were in a lovely neighborhood amid huge trees and welcoming neighbors. Most of them commuted every day into Manhattan.

LIFE AT DREW

The university was set in a lush evergreen 186-acre campus in a deep oak forest that had remained virtually untouched since the Ice Age. Drew had been a theological seminary for sixty years before it became a university with graduate programs in theology, which were comparable in reputation to Princeton and Yale. The Drew campus is only a one hour ride by train, bus or Holland Tunnel into Manhattan. Madison had been steadily connected to Manhattan by rail since 1836.

New faculty appointees were expected to be publishing scholars who would contribute to the ongoing international dialogue on religion and culture—which they did, especially in the fields of archaeology, biblical studies, history and theology. The Drew faculty had been known for gathering together distinguished scholars since the days the *McClintock and Strong Cyclopedia* was begun in 1853.

With a library of more than a quarter million volumes, I was in my element. That unique library held the largest collection of Wesleyan and

Methodist archival documents in the world. I loved being within an hour of some of the greatest libraries in the world: Columbia University, NYU, Union Theological Seminary, Jewish Theological Seminary, Fordham and Princeton. The logistics of my work as an author was made much simpler by having near at hand the major publishers of North America, most with international publishing operations. The Princeton University Press, with whom I published two books, was only an hour away to the south, and Harper and Row was an hour away in mid-Manhattan.

I began my thirty-three years of service at Drew University in 1970, called as a tenured professor at age thirty-nine. I shared Dean Ault's vision of a revitalized theological faculty impacting international scholarship, but I had no premonition that Drew would change me more than I would change Drew.

On December 31, 1969, the last day of the decade of the sixties, our family arrived in a freezing rain to the home we had bought in New Jersey. With an inch of ice covering our driveway, we got a nippy introduction to New Jersey winter weather.

I regretted that moving our family put us at such a long distance from our much-loved extended family. Laura was a kindergartner, Edward was in the third grade, and Clark was just entering junior school in Madison. Our children came to love their new neighborhood, only a hundred yards from the university and within walking distance to their schools.

Edward was our athlete. Always the out-front leader, he was the pitcher in Little League baseball and quarterback in football. As a preteen he became an avid reader by reading what he was passionate about reading—as long as it was the *New York Times* sports section. Soon he would be memorizing thousands of sport statistics. I marveled at the capacity of young minds to absorb information.

Clark was fortunate that the state-of-the-art technology center of Bell Labs was nearby—the premier research institution of AT&T, whose headquarters were only a few minutes from Madison. These were the labs where the transistor was invented, the first computers assembled and wireless cell phones developed. Clark was happy to be invited to join a special Explorer Scouts advanced electronics laboratory program at AT&T in Whippany. Suddenly he found himself surrounded by cutting-edge electronic equipment in a special hands-on program. The troubled condition of public schools was a drag on Clark, so we allowed him to complete high school on his own through homeschooling and distance learning. In our basement, surrounded by electronic equipment, Clark became a genuinely self-taught individual, learning all he could learn about his passion: the dynamics of sound. Later Clark graduated with a degree in electrical engineering.

At six Laura started dance classes. Born to be a performer, she was adorable. I wished that I had danced with my daughter long before I did at her wedding. I myself have cherished a hidden desire to be a soft-shoe dancer. Picture Astaire singing, "I wanna be a dancin' man, / While I can, / Gonna leave my footsteps on the sands of time, / If I never leave a dime."[1]

Then picture Bill Robinson and Shirley Temple tap dancing on the stairs in *The Little Colonel*. I wish that could have been Laura and me.

Edrita, who had been happily teaching and directing theater at Phillips University, was delighted to be only sixty-five minutes away from Broadway. All of the family was happy about living near the incomparable cultural assets of Manhattan's sports, music, theater, visual arts and intellectual life.

A Jewish mentor for the recovery of classic Christianity. The premier teacher in the Drew Graduate School was without doubt social philosopher Will Herberg (1901–1977), the brilliant, diminutive, forceful, bearded Russian Jew who had come to teach at Drew in 1955.

I had never met a mind so brilliant, a wit so quick and an analyst more probing. When I asked him to talk about his youthful days as a communist youth organizer, he always changed the subject.[2] Just as I had been enthralled by the utopian ideals of Marxism, Will Herberg as an idealistic youth had taken it much further a generation before by actually joining the Communist Party, which was not unusual among Russian immigrant Jewish families of the 1920s.[3] After thirty years of activism in the Communist Party and the labor movement, his heart was changed into becoming a powerful anticommunist critic, writer and conservative college circuit lecturer. He had experienced American communism inside and out before rediscovering his lost Jewish roots.

His presence at Drew made all the difference for me. Thirty years my elder, he was willing to think critically and empathically with me, a much younger colleague, about my vocation. Providence surely played a role in my life when he was placed as a formidable obstacle in my path.

We both understood the difference between Jew and Christian: One was expecting the Messiah; the other had met the Messiah. Disillusionment with utopianism drew Herberg toward the classic teaching of Judaism in a way amazingly similar to how I was being gradually drawn to classic Christian teaching. I found him to be intensely loyal to his Jewish tradition while being deeply empathic with his Christian students.[4] Though Herberg was not a Christian, he made it possible for me to become one.

By reading his published works hidden away in the Drew archives, I found that before 1929 he had followed the Comintern line until the 1930s when American-oriented Communists began to have serious rifts with the rigid Soviet party leadership. His independent spirit led him to break away from the strictly Soviet-dominated center of the party. With American Jay Lovestone he had struggled as a freethinking communist against Soviet dominance of party policy. He remained a communist until August 23, 1939, when the Hitler-Stalin Pact made it morally unbearable for a Jew to remain in the party.[5]

I read his essays written during the years after 1939, when he was a leading noncommunist spokesperson and political advocate for the International Ladies' Garment Workers Union.[6] His abrupt disavowal of communism came when he was thirty-nine years old, the age I was when I first met him.

During that transition, Herberg had weighty conversations with Reinhold Niebuhr on theology and seemed on the verge of converting to Christianity. Niebuhr urged him to rediscover his Jewish roots by studying Judaica at the Jewish Theological Seminary, which was just across the street from Union Theological Seminary. An irony worth noting: Herberg became a Jew by listening to a Christian; I became a Christian by listening to a Jew.[7]

I had heard him speak at the University of Oklahoma in 1953. It was the first time I had ever heard the word *atonement* treated seriously. Herberg was constantly out there on the American university lecture trail challenging the Marxist view of history and the fantasies of utopians.[8]

After meeting Will, I began to read the passionate critics of communism. It was not until I read Arthur Koestler's *Darkness at Noon* that I got a glimpse of how insidious the promises of communism were. The circle of eminent writers who left communism included André Gide, Ignazio Silone and Stephen Spender.

Will was an astute Socratic questioner and a scrappy debater, unafraid to face tough and awkward intellectual encounters. Pushing university students to examine the unexpected consequences of their idealistic passions, he spoke out fearlessly for Hebraic biblical teachings on idolatry and salvation history. He loved the role of out-front controversialist interlocutor, and his university audiences loved to see him play it to the hilt.

Herberg was the master teacher on the university faculty, influencing generations of graduate students in interreligious dialogue, philosophy and theology. He passionately communicated the sacred tradition of Scripture that Jews and Christians share together. Both Hebrew and Christian Scriptures affirm salvation history as the basis for social criticism. As a Jewish social philosopher, he drew many Christians, including me, toward a deeper understanding of their own Christian faith.

Dean Bernhard Anderson brought Herberg into the Drew Graduate School faculty to teach Judaica and social philosophy. The fit was perfect. That feisty gadfly was every inch a teacher. No one in his seminars could get by with cheap reasoning. He did not often speak of his own personal history of activism because he considered that his time spent as a Marxist was a lost cause, but one that prepared him to expose its illusions. Despite the huge range of his writings, only a few times did he offer a glimpse of his own personal narrative.[9]

When I first set foot on the Drew campus I was eager to meet him. I first saw this sixty-nine-year-old man trudging along the sidewalks of Drew with a heavy briefcase of books on his way to teach a graduate seminar. When we met on a cold rainy day, we immediately became friends, and he invited me over to his apartment across the street for tea that very day. Every wall of his modest apartment was filled with books of every genre. Herberg's wife, Anna, had passed away some years before I met him, though she went through all of the transitions of life with him, from organizing Young Workers to returning to Judaism to teaching.[10]

The faceoff with Herberg at Convent Station: The instant of recognition. My change of heart began to happen in my first month at Drew. Will and I hit it off immediately, but it was not until he met Edrita that he was most impressed with me. She was a dazzling raconteur, quick-witted and ready for banter. The three of us set up a biweekly schedule of luncheon meetings in which Will and I went at it, with Edrita serving as an active moderator who often softened the decibels.

The decisive moment of our confrontation was inevitable. Soon after our first meeting, I had given Will a copy of my recently published book *Beyond Revolution*, and he had read, marked and intensely responded in copious marginal notes. I received his annotated copy as a gift after his death, and it has become one of my most prized possessions.[11]

Two weeks after that the three of us were having lunch in the balcony section of Rod's Restaurant in Convent Station. Will was trying to show me that the errors I was making were much deeper than I had realized. I tried to defend myself. Suddenly my irascible, endearing Jewish friend leaned into my face and told me that I was densely ignorant of Christianity, and he simply couldn't permit me to throw my life away.

Holding one finger up, looking straight at me with fury in his eyes, he said, "You will remain theologically uneducated until you study carefully Athanasius, Augustine and Aquinas." In his usual gruff voice and brusque speech, he told me I had not yet met the great minds of my own religious tradition.

He explained that he had gone through a long season of restitution after his erratic days and found it necessary to carefully read the Talmud and the Midrashim to discover who he was. Likewise he felt that I would have to go to a quiet place and sit at the feet of the great minds of ancient Christianity to discover who I was.

Herberg reminded me that I would stand under divine judgment on the last day. He said, "If you are ever going to become a credible theologian instead of a know-it-all pundit, you had best restart your life on firmer ground. You are not a theologian except in name only, even if you are paid to be one."

In an instant of recognition, I knew he was right, I knew he had said that because he cared deeply about me. His words burned into my conscience. That was the opening bell that led to a bruising personal dialogue about my self-deceptions. All of its implications were not realized instantly, but my reversal began then and there on that very day, that very moment.

I asked myself, *Could it be that I had been trampling on a vast tradition of historical wisdom in the attempt to be original?*

From her eyes I knew that Edrita understood what Will was saying. Later she coolly asked me what I was going to do about it. At the time I did not have an answer. I had read some Augustine, Aquinas and Luther, but I had never crawled through patristic texts with a listening heart. I had never truly inhabited that timeless, sacred world.

Although that recognition occurred in an instant, it took years to take root and grow. I had to assimilate it, let it stew and find my own way to recovery.

Why did it take a Jew to turn me to Christianity? I had heard many dire warnings against colluding with conservative ideas of continuity and moral accountability. How did he get through to me so instantly? Why did I get so few warning signals from Christians against the long-range consequences of pacifism, collectivism and naturalism? Why did I have to wait for a former socialist Jew who had been though those illusions himself to confront me with how futile they are? I had received little encouragement from Christians to inquire deeply into the greatest minds of the earliest Christian tradition.

How the Sacred Texts Began Interpreting Me

The 180 degree change of course. I plunged into reading the earliest Christian writers: Polycarp, Ignatius and Justin Martyr. I wanted them to feed my soul.

The maturing of my change of heart took place only gradually through quiet reading in early mornings in a library carrel, allowing myself to be met by those great minds through their own words.

While reading Augustine's *City of God* on the ironic providences of history, I finally grasped how right Solzhenitsyn was about the spiritual promise of Russia. And while reading Cyril of Jerusalem's *Catechetical Lecture* on evidences for the resurrection, I became persuaded that Pannenberg had provided a more accurate account than Bultmann of the event of resurrection.

While reading the dialogues of fourth-century Sister Macrina and the women surrounding Jerome, I now could trace the profound influences of women on the earliest and richest traditions of spiritual formation, especially in monastic and ascetic disciplines.

While reading John of Damascus on the providence of God in *The Orthodox Faith*, I realized that the reordering of theological ideas I thought I was just then discovering had been well understood as a stable and received tradition in the eighth century.

While reading John Chrysostom on voluntary poverty, I discovered that the existential freedom Viktor Frankl had experienced in the Nazi concentration camp had been anticipated by fourth-century Christian teachers, martyrs and confessors.

And so it went. All of that happened while I was reading, just reading. I was being guided by the Spirit toward an integral sense of Scripture based on the consensus of the early Christian interpreters of sacred Scripture.

Every question I previously thought of as new and unprecedented, I found had already been much investigated. That led to deeper conversations with Orthodox, Catholic and evangelical graduate students and colleagues, whose voices I had not been hearing.

Soon I reveled in the very premises I had set aside and rationalized away: the preexistent Logos, the triune mystery, the radical depth of sin passing through the generations, the risen Lord and the grace of baptism.

As I worked my way through the beautiful, long-hidden texts of classic Christianity, I reemerged out of a maze to once again delight in the holy mysteries of the faith and the perennial dilemmas of fallen human existence. It was no longer me interpreting the texts but the texts interpreting me. I was deeply moved.

The classic texts reshaped my mind. Soon I was asking how God could become truly human without ceasing to be God. I wondered how human freedom, when so distorted by the history of sin, could become radically atoned on the cross. I questioned that if God was almighty and incomparably good, how could God allow sin to have such a persistent grip on human social processes. And I wondered how the incomprehensible God could make himself sufficiently known to finite human minds. I wanted to understand how God was and is one, if God is Father, God is Son and God is Holy Spirit. I wanted to know how the faithful can mirror the holiness of God within the history of sin. Not a new question, or a dull one, in the list.

Herberg did not answer all of my questions, but he put me on to the road where the answers could be found: classic Christian teaching out of Scripture. By that simple admonition, he did more for me intellectually in the early months of our close friendship than did any other person in my lifetime, by requiring me to ground my thinking in classic wisdom. As I took a deep dive into the early church fathers, they corrected my modern prejudices.

If asked then what my future would be like, I would have guessed completely wrong. I had been unprepared to grant sacred Scripture its own premises: divine sovereignty, revelation in history, incarnation, resurrection and final judgment.

I had put too much uncritical trust in contemporary methods of historical study and behavioral engineering. Now I was seeing interpersonal transactions in relation to the creation, redemption and consummation of universal history. That change in perception was momentous for me.

I came by grace to grasp the distinctive way of consensual reasoning that had ripened within classic Christianity. I became fascinated with the social dynamics of orthodoxy, the process of transmitting apostolic tradition and coming to trust the reasoning of classic consensual teaching. Those who absolutely adored absolute toleration began to notice I was suffering fools a little less gladly.

I was elated to realize that there was nothing new in what I was learning; I was only relearning what had been relearned many times before from the apostolic witnesses. I was amazed that the intergenerational wisdom of the ancient community of faith was completely accessible within modernity. There was no need for apology to university colleagues, no need to diminish my learnings by requiring them to conform to transient modern assumptions. There it was, still pulsating as a living, caring community that had survived unnoticed underneath the illusions of modernity.

My life story has had two phases: going away from home as far as I could go, not knowing what I might find in an odyssey of preparation, and then at last inhabiting anew my own original home of classic Christian wisdom. The uniting theme of the two parts of my life can only be providence. For confessing Christians it is a familiar story of a life unexpectedly turned around by an outpouring of grace.

My life has passed through the core phases of the history of modern social change, politics, technology, philosophy and religion. Some may find that my story mirrors their own experience. Putting that mirror in another's hands is my motivation to write it accurately just as it occurred. Those societal changes have affected everyone in our times, but at the same time the perennial story of salvation awaits anyone ready to hear it.

Finding an orthodox foundation. I had been enamored with novelty. Candidly, I had been in love with heresy. Now I was waking up from this enthrallment to meet a two thousand year stable memory.

Since meeting and dwelling with the Christian exegetes through their writings in their own words, I came to trust the very orthodoxy I had once dismissed. I found myself living within a much larger community of discourse populated not just by modern companions but radiant minds of many past generations from varied cultures spanning all continents for two thousand years. Through this discipline I became even more relevant, not less relevant, to modern partners in dialogue. As I began to immerse myself in classic Christian texts, I found myself standing within the blessed presence of the communion of saints of all generations. They were the antiphonal choir with whom I was singing.

I experienced more crosscultural freedom of inquiry. Long-ignored theological ideas came alive—like divine foreknowledge, revelation in history, demonic temptation, the lives of saints and angelic succor. I felt incomparably blessed to receive that inheritance.

Today the thoughts and prayers of the great minds of the worshiping community are my daily bread. They feed my soul. The patristic writers reveal an amazing equilibrium in their cohesive grasp of the whole course of human history through the sacred texts. They give me what I had long yearned for since I was ten: an inclusive sense of the whole of human history, beginning to end. The classic Christian mind is at home in every conceivable cultural setting.

A door was opened by a Jewish friend for me to take a path into classic Christian wisdom, but I had to take it on my own. It was not an act of defiance but an act of joy when I was turned aside from the path I was on. I was ushered into a new awareness that no human wisdom is more reliable than the actual history in which God is omnipresent. All my subsequent writings flowed directly out of that wellspring.

I do not believe I would have been prepared to serve as a critic of modernity without having first entered fully and honestly into its flawed premises. The One who had been guiding my life into such a deep immersion into modernity was the same One who was now guiding my life toward giving up its illusions for classic tested truths.

All I needed to do was to listen to the texts of the story of salvation as viewed through the eyes of its most reliable consensual interpreters. The more consensual, the more trustable.

No modern ideology has such a lengthy continuity of witness. Scientific inquiry has had little more than two centuries to establish its orthodoxy. The apostolic consensus has had two millennia. My questions about decaying modern culture were being decisively shaped by the communion of saints who have lived through far deeper crises than this modernity.

My search drew me toward new friends and unexpected recognitions: Gregory of Nyssa on the body-soul interface, Vincent of Lérins's *Aids to Remembering*, the classic Christian ecumenical doctrinal definitions of the first five centuries, and the balanced pastoral counsel of Gregory the Great.

Herberg taught me to read them slowly and thoroughly in their own words, not in secondary diluted interpretations of them. He knew that I would become lost in supposed relevance without that solid textual grounding.

In the early months of my quest in 1970 I came across the late-fourth-century treatise by the Christian physician Nemesius of Emesa, *Peri Physeos Anthropon* (On the Nature of the Human). I was amazed to realize how much wisdom was thoroughly grasped by that little known Syrian physician. His teaching of the integrated human person was built upon a Christological analogy between the incarnation and the body-soul interface. He taught that the best way to understand our humanity was through the disclosure of the truly human in the incarnation. Here was a brilliant psychologist whose psychology was transformed by the body-soul relationship manifested in the life of Christ.

I brought Nemesius with me to class and read portions. Students marveled as he described the structure of the living human body, the position and function of its diverse parts, and the relationship between the body and the soul as they are engaged in complex activities such as imagination, memory, thought, desire, sense perception and the emotions. Nemesius concluded that the human body-soul composite functions best when the body serves as an instrument for the soul.

At length it dawned on me that ancient Christian psychological wisdom could be the basis for a deeper critique of modern narcissistic psychology than I had yet seen from within modernity. That recognition was the beginning of a long sequence of similar findings.

By Christmas 1970 I had found my way into the fifth-century *Aids to Remembering*, the *Commonitory* of Vincent of Lérins. It provided me with the most accurate description to date of how the faithful had arrived at consensus. Only then did I see explained for the first time in a clear and descriptive way the consensual path for receiving the truth that I had already glimpsed operating in the Great Ecumenical Councils. From Vincent I gained the essential foothold in defining ecumenical teaching as that which had been believed everywhere, always and by all.

From then on my reasoning gradually became a straightforward matter of identifying those apostolic teachings which believers from all places and times confessed and believed with one voice and for which they had been willing to die. That form of reasoning awakened in me a deeper form of critical reasoning that could penetrate and discern the deficits of modern naturalism. I became better prepared to recognize the strengths and weaknesses of modernity by viewing them in the light of consensual Christianity. At last I realized that the world was best viewed from the vantage point of the glory of God revealed in history. The seed of the Word was being planted precisely within the fertilized soil of ever waning cultures.

Everywhere there was wonder in the creation itself—in time, providence in history, the penetration of grace and freedom, sin in believers and radical judgment at the end of history. The lamp of Scripture illuminates every dark corner "making all things new."

After pondering Vincent, I was motivated to do a straight through read of the fourteenth volume of the Nicene and Post-Nicene Fathers, a report of the decisions of the Ecumenical Councils and early regional councils. I couldn't put it down, and I have never been the same since. There I first grasped the logic of orthodox theological method.

Those quiet days were among the most important of my life. That spiritual exercise of reading conciliar reasoning affected literally everything I would touch as a teacher, writer and editor from then on. That is where it first dawned on me that God the Spirit was guiding the decisions of those who were consensually remembering the testimony of his coming in the flesh. I saw how boundaries of reliable doctrine were defined by worldwide consent, and how the Spirit nurtured and enabled unity.

THE DREAM OF UNORIGINALITY

The tombstone said "He made no new contribution to theology." In the season of Epiphany 1971 I had a curious dream in which I was in the New Haven cemetery and accidentally stumbled upon my own tombstone with this puzzling epitaph: "He made no new contribution to theology." I woke up refreshed and relieved.

I was uplifted to see such an unexpected epitaph prefigured in a dream. That striking image signaled to me that I no longer had to produce something new in theology in order to find a reliable foothold in theological discourse. It took no small effort to resist the constant temptation to novelty.

Since the first time I ever thought of becoming a theologian, I was earnestly taught that my most crucial task was to "think creatively" in order to "make some new contribution to theology." Nothing at Yale was drummed into my head more steadily than the aspiration that the theology I would seek would be my own and my uniqueness would imprint it.

But this dream prompted me to begin to try to follow the strict rule of Irenaeus that Christian truth must avoid any temptation to "invent new doctrine." New doctrine meant ideas that would presume to improve on the apostolic testimony. No concept was more deplored by the early Christian writers than the notion that the task of theology is to "innovate." Innovation was for them equivalent to something "other than" (*hetero*) the received apostolic teaching.[12] What the ancient church teachers least wished for Christian teachers is that they would become focused on self-expression or become an assertion of purely private inspiration, as if those might claim to be some decisive improvement on apostolic teaching.

I set about trying scrupulously to abstain from creating any new doctrine. It was the best decision I had made as a theologian. It was hard for me, but immensely productive. I realized that I could be a theologian simply by reflecting accurately out of the great minds of Christian teaching. That was 100 percent more fruitful than the expression of my own imaginings. For once and for all, I knew my calling would be fulfilled through building bridges between the classical Christian consensus and the lost reality of the modern world. It was not me proposing the consensus but me being found by it.

The most oft-quoted interpreters of Scripture are easily recognizable from the empirical fact that they have been most consistently and widely reconfirmed. Many are orthodox, but eight have been most often designated as most universally received: the four great ecumenical

Doctors of the Church of the Eastern tradition (Athanasius, Basil, Gregory of Nazianzus and Chrysostom) and the four Doctors of the Church of the West (Ambrose, Augustine, Jerome and Gregory the Great). They were the ones most consensually remembered, who most accurately gave expression to the faith that was already well understood by the apostles and celebrated by the worshiping community under the guidance of the written Word. Their names have been commended by subsequent Ecumenical Councils as reliable interpreters of Holy Writ. All were widely respected East and West in the formation of classic Christianity.

None of them viewed themselves as creative geniuses. They knew that it was the community itself that had been made brilliant by the Spirit. The most moving of those writers, to me, were Athanasius and Augustine. Both of them were refined like gold out of the cauldron of early Christianity in Africa.

The twelve books I wrote in the 1960s were not all wrong, but flawed by the fervent desire to accommodate to modern worldviews. By 1970 I could see the tremendous harm caused by some of the follies I had promoted. I do not repudiate them overall, but now see the shortcomings of their hidden assumptions that were common to that time.

Making reparations. My past visions of vast plans for social change had irreparably harmed many innocents, especially the unborn. The sexually permissive lifestyle, which I had not joined but failed to critique, led to a generation of fatherless children. The political policies I had promoted were intended to increase justice by political means but ended in diminishing personal responsibility and freedom. Many of the seemingly humane psychological therapies I had supported may have made people more miserable, less able to choose wisely or to seek the virtues required for happiness

Since true guilt was seldom mentioned in modern secular ethics, I had to learn to repent, to see my own arrogance and to acknowledge my limitations. My education and my permissive church had not taught me repentance, but the prayers of the ancient Christian writers brought me to repent over willed sins and receive the grace of forgiveness, provided I made reparations.

In the summer of 1970 as I was dodging traffic on Manhattan streets with an old leftist friend talking about what we had done, I blurted out, "Have you thought about how reckless we were? How we tossed out institutional achievements that had been centuries in the making?" He was speechless. He had never thought about it.

Advent is a season of repentance and hope. By the middle of Advent in 1971, I was remembering many of the actions I had voluntarily taken without thinking of their consequences. By the end of Advent I was hoping for forgiveness and renewal.

By the season of Christmas of 1971, I realized that my once solitary journey was accompanied by millions of millions of ancient and modern believers who shared in the company of the prophets and apostles and believers throughout time. By the season of Epiphany of 1972, I was pledged to present nothing new or original in basic Christian teaching that would have my initials stamped on it as if it were mine. I have honored that pledge, and it has been immensely gratifying for me. Ever since then I have remained deeply committed to the surprisingly relevant idea of unoriginality.

Resetting the agenda. Good friends grew uneasy as they saw me moving in a traditional direction. Some of my dearest friends still wonder why I changed my mind. They could not see that it was my heart that was renewed, not my mind. Over time it became evident to all who knew me that I was on a path quite unlike the path that had brought me to graduate teaching.

Most colleagues viewed my reversed direction as disastrous academically, and they urged me to reconsider. They thought I was throwing away a Phi Beta Kappa key, a Yale PhD and a promising writing career in academia, and in a way I was. To become an articulate Christian believer in a modern university is to become a pariah to many. My friends were seeing this from within their social locations in the university. I was looking at the university from the vantage point of a different social location: the community of faithful consensus sustained over two millennia.

As I continued to investigate the psychological and social dynamics of modern ideas and events, I was experiencing a growing distaste for anarchy, pretensions of discontinuity, revolutionary talk and non-historical idealism. Some wondered if I was going through a midlife crisis. To me it was a midlife breakthrough. I was forty. My next forty years would be entirely different.

Theology is the study of God. The study of God is simply to be enjoyed for its own incomparable subject, the One most beautiful, most worthy to be praised. Life with God delights in its very acts of thinking, reading, praying and communing with that One most worthy to be beheld, pondered and studied, not for its written artifacts or social consequences but for joy in its object.

During those days of vocational discernment, what was changing in me was the recognition of the unchanging character of God. I was recognizing that our experiments of fallen freedom were being held together by God's constancy.[13]

God is more than a means to an end for social change, and no literature has more contemporary social significance than the earliest Christian writers who were closest in time to the incarnation. Defending the unchanging gospel, Paul warned: "Even if we or an angel from heaven should preach a gospel other than the one we preached to you, let him be anathema" (Gal 1:8).

My previous relationship to Scripture had been a filtering process which permitted those sources to speak to me only insofar as they could meet my conditions, my worldview and my assumptions as a modern person. Now I was finding that the fertile and prolific seed of orthodoxy could grow in the arid atmosphere of modern culture, even in academia. I pledged to resist the temptation to quote modern writers less schooled in the whole counsel of God than the best ancient classic exegetes. Set apart for unoriginality, I had a contrarian task in the university I loved.

I was becoming aware of the providence of God working within my former Freudian-Existentialist-Marxist past. I was celebrating that turbulent history as having been taken up into a more inclusive understanding of history.

In the study of social continuity, I was turning now to neglected modern observers such as Alexis de Tocqueville, Adam Smith and

Edmund Burke. Previously I had had no exposure whatsoever to the intellectual history of conservative thought, which I had stereotyped as backward and mean-spirited. Meanwhile I wondered why the durability of the classic Christian consensus had remained unexplained and virtually ignored in the academy.

How I overcame my education. I had worked hard to get an education, but now I had to work even harder to overcome the education I got. Once I grasped that I had to desensitize fixed habits of years of a well-meaning but contaminated education, I realized that the task ahead would be much harder. If I was going to remain an effective teacher in a university system that had many flaws, I would have to learn how to make classic rational and Christian arguments in ways plausible to my colleagues. As examples, I did this by applying the social location arguments to critics of religion unaware of their upward mobility aspirations. I applied to behaviorists the growing evidences for intelligent design. I applied to political utopians the evidences of the consequences of utopian thinking. And I had to learn to do this in a congenial way.

I especially had to rethink my own errors. When I wrote an essay on "The Priority of Pardon to Penitence" in 1969, I was following a premise of Karl Barth's theology, that God's eternal forgiveness is already a gift prior to our receiving it. Now I was realizing that this argument left an opening for an easy temptation to take God's forgiveness entirely for granted without repentance and faith. Later when I wrote *The Transforming Power of Grace*, *The Good Works Reader* and especially *Corrective Love*, I deliberately tried to correct this serious omission.

I had previously written an essay for the *Zeitschrift für Evangelische Ethik* on the question "Is the Demand of God Ambiguous?"[14] which stated that the will of God is not known in rules but only in the existing moment. I had followed a Bultmannian form of contextual ethics that had become ingrained in me in the 1960s. It focused on the moment as the only situational teacher of the will of God. This left me without an adequate grasp of the proper functions of moral constraint. If I took seriously the premise that the moment will reveal what to do, then I had left the discipline of ethics with nothing to do. I had thrown away the instruction of the law, which guides conscience and leads to repentance. That had huge consequences for sexual ethics.

In another one of my earlier books, *Kerygma and Counseling*, I had grasped the analogy that as the therapist brings human empathy to the troubled, so God brings divine empathy to the human condition of guilt, anxiety and boredom. At first I wanted to make use of the incarnation as a means of thinking about how to connect Christianity with constructive psychological change. That put God in a secondary role as an optional helper to a human process. It reduced the incarnation to a convenient analogy for therapeutic empathy, ignoring that God indeed is the incomparably empathic One who illumines human empathy.

I could teach the analogy from counseling to kerygma better than the analogy from kerygma to counseling. When the idea of incarnation was used pragmatically, the biblical analogy from God to humanity was trivialized. Only when I learned to reason analogically from the incarnation of God to human empathy did I get the full impact of biblical reasoning. If the incarnation was not an actual event in history but merely an idea in our heads, the biblical reasoning had not yet been grasped. Only by going down that pragmatic road to its dead end was I able to rediscover the simplicity of the mystery of the incarnation.

I was going through a cycle of learning, unlearning and relearning. That is best seen in my joyful reception, then in my sophisticated rejection, then later in my embracing the hymns of my childhood. When I first sang them, I knew naively that God had come in the flesh. Then I learned that God had not really come in the flesh but rather in some symbolic sense acceptable to modern assumptions. At last I learned to recover the uncomplicated truth that God precisely becomes human in the flesh, dies for me, rises again and saves me from my sins. All these are viewed by consensual Christianity as historical events.

I had joined one movement after another, whether political, therapeutic or philosophical, and found some way to present it in a diluted Christian vocabulary. Now I was observing that classic Christianity had survived the death throes of thousands of supposed modernities. That helped me to see the huge difference between modern legalistic inclusivism and the more inclusive embrace of the Creator for all creation. This was the 180 degree turn that began with the fire in Herberg's eyes.

REGROUNDING PASTORAL CARE

During the 1970s I faced the passionate defensiveness of those still devoted to accommodating pastoral practice to psychotherapeutic fads. That was the start of what would soon include many areas where wise classic perspectives clashed with the prevalent modern assumptions.

The task of the pastoral counselor was then commonly viewed as ferreting out what was currently happening or likely to happen in the sphere of emergent pop psychologies and adapting them as much as possible to the work of ministry. There were dozens of chapters of that story, most of which I had lived through.[15]

In those adaptations, classic Christian pastoral care was usually ridiculed as out of date and an obstacle to progress. Updated pastoral theology had become little more than a mimic of current psychological vogues. Often those movements were bad psychology to begin with, as psychologist Paul Vitz astutely demonstrated in his book *Psychology as Religion*. As an offender myself, I had to test out those options before recognizing their limitations.

I slowly realized that the traffic on that bridge was moving only one way: from psychological speculation to enthralled religious accommodation, as if Christianity had no psychology of its own. I remembered Nemesius. Theology's listening to psychology has been far more accurate, empathic and attentive than has psychology's listening to classic Christian teaching of soul care. The bridge would never be built by the complete acquiescence of classic Christianity to the reductionist assumptions of psychology.

Only when I learned to trust the classic Christian consensus on care of souls, as seen in Cyprian, Augustine and Gregory, did I see the way ahead. That testing was a slow process for me throughout the 1970s.

Every generation of believers has access to the vast store of practical wisdom bequeathed by Christian antiquity. Each generation is called freely to enter the vault and simply listen. Some have the duty to protect that vault and transmit its wisdom to future ages with fresh insights into its unchanging power. Many in my generation were refusing to enter the vault and some tried to burn it down, but it survived the fires of modernity as it had survived so many times before.

Outcome studies on the effectiveness of psychotherapy. The Finch Lectures at Fuller School of Psychology in January 1971 provided my first major opportunity to pursue the classic corrective to many of my earlier efforts. Since the renewal of pastoral practice was a territory I had been exploring throughout the previous decade, it was the place for me to begin to work toward an agenda for pastoral theology, which took a full decade to congeal.[16]

The outcome studies of the effectiveness of psychotherapy provided new empirical evidence for a deeper critique of popular psychology. They showed the weakness of the most typical psychotherapeutic practices. I was prompted to dive into this behaviorist literature as I was preparing this major lecture series in California.

This was my first serious exposure to dialogue with thoughtful evangelical scholars who knew the psychotherapeutic literature exceptionally well. It would lead to a chain of consultations, dialogues and decisions that brought me closer to mainstream evangelical life and thought.[17]

These lectures were published with critical respondents under the title *After Therapy What?* They anticipated many of the themes with which I would deal throughout the 1970s. But the most important event for me was examining the new behavioral studies of the effectiveness of psychotherapy. They weaned me away from many previous illusions.[18]

In preparation for those lectures I researched the large accumulation of controlled studies on therapeutic outcomes and client deterioration by the highly respected behavioral psychologists Hans Eysenck, Allen Bergin, Hans Strupp, Jerome Frank and my clinical mentor Philip Hanson.[19] The cumulative impact of over three hundred of those studies convinced me that the average psychotherapy cure rate was not better than the spontaneous remission rate.

The average outcomes of all types of therapy approaches turned out to be the same rate of recovery as that which occurred merely through the passage of time, approximately 63 percent. Indeed, those studies found that symptoms would disappear spontaneously about two thirds of the time without any therapeutic intervention.

Up to that point I had been convinced that psychotherapies on the whole were exceptionally effective. The psychologists themselves did not know that their cure rates barely matched the rate of spontaneous remission, which was the rate of recovery achieved by doing nothing. That finding was coupled with the alarming specter of "client deterioration," which showed that 10 percent of the patients found their condition worsening under the care of professional psychotherapists.

Those empirical facts took me aback. I had spent two decades trusting the assumed effectiveness of psychotherapies, but now I had actual rigorous empirical evidence of their average ineffectiveness. At Fuller I grasped the sobering implications of those behavioral studies, especially for pastoral care and theology. They elicited a substantial shift of direction for me toward a critique of many common psychotherapeutic assumptions.[20]

When I tried to introduce that evidence to key leaders of pastoral care circles, most were incredulous. Not one of the leading pastoral writers up to the time of my Fuller Lectures had even mentioned them or apparently even known of them. This had led pastors for years to be wildly optimistic about secular therapeutic outcomes.

The outcome studies were not mere opinion or theory but fact-based, empirically supported data from a large number of controlled scientific studies in numerous university psychology departments. The evidence had been accumulating for a long time but had been almost systematically ignored by pastoral counselors and fee-based therapists whose legitimacy hinged on the shaky assumption that they were usually effective. Those uncertain therapies had become virtual idols to pastoral caregivers.

The accommodation of pastoral care to psychotherapy gradually bottomed out proportionally as those studies were taken seriously. They prompted a decisive reversal in my thinking about the viability of psychotherapy itself.[21]

The Graduate School of Psychology at Fuller was building a talented young faculty, and as it turned out, they wanted me to help them build it. They had been reading *Kerygma and Counseling* and *The Structure of Awareness*. I was tempted to join that faculty, Edrita resisted, and together we made the wiser decision to stay at Drew.

My academic field location at Drew was theology and ethics, but since I had been writing throughout the 1960s on pastoral issues, I became an active participant in the revitalization of the program for graduate students in psychology and religion. That once important graduate degree at Drew had declined in the late 1960s. Since my writings prior to Drew had focused significantly on psychotherapeutic issues, I was asked to help renovate it by teaching a seminar on the history of the care of souls. This prompted me to dig much deeper than before into the early history of Christian care of souls, admonition and discipline. That research fitted precisely into what I wanted to pursue in response to Herberg's challenges. I plunged into neglected figures in the history of psychology like Nemesius and John Climacus.[22]

As I pushed deeper into that literature, I realized that the pivotal figure of the Western pastoral tradition was clearly Gregory the Great. His work *Pastoral Care*, once essential but long ignored, had served as an indispensable guide to pastors and counselors for more than a millennium. So I took Gregory the Great as the prototype figure for pastoral care and in a short book analyzed his seminal *Book of Pastoral Rule* (A.D. 590) in detail, commending it as a model for present-day pastoral counsel.[23] Spiritually and biblically grounded in the Benedictine tradition, it was full of wisdom. It provided a distinct care-giving method that remained pertinent amid all of the modern fads.[24]

THE POLITICS OF REPENTANCE

Conscience and dividends. I participated in a protest demonstration against apartheid at the South African Embassy in Washington, D.C. Our placards called for disinvestment in corporations that were shielding the apartheid government policies. That drew me further into more serious ethical inquiry on how church organizations might engage international corporations regarding their public responsibility.

The remarkable consultations held at the Institute on Religion and Public

Life in New York became my academic and spiritual home during the years when I was getting my new bearings. My intellectual habitat was becoming less the university than the circle of theologians formed principally around Lutheran Richard Neuhaus, conservative Jews Midge Dechter and David Novak, and the wise Catholic voices of Avery Dulles and Michael Novak. Other key partners in dialogue in the Washington, DC, area were Ernest Lefever and George Weigel in the Ethics and Public Policy Center. I grew especially close to the leaders of the Institute on Religion and Democracy and in time would become chairman of their board. [25]

Through those conversations I was drawn into a lifelong friendship with Richard Neuhaus. He had a great gift for bringing seminal minds together. Much of that dialogue revolved around the intellectual agility, theological depth and light-hearted hospitality of Neuhaus himself.

Among that New York circle, former socialists like Norman Podhoretz, Will Herberg and Irving Kristol were becoming leading advocates of free economies and limited government, sometimes dubbed "neocons." Along with many evangelical and Jewish partners in dialogue, I was reading widely in the history of economic freedom and conservative political theory, an arena from which I had previously been heedless.

After decades of avid absorption of ideas on controlled economies and regulatory policy, I now found myself diving into sources that my university education had not thought important enough for me to read—classic levelheaded conservative writers like Richard Hooker, Edmund Burke, James Madison, Alexis de Tocqueville and John Henry Newman. The more I read from Thomas Soule, Nathan Glazer and Russell Kirk, the more I realized how uneducated I actually was. I had not planned to write anything more on public policy until I received an unexpected invitation from Dr. Ernest Lefever of the Ethics and Public Policy Center in Washington. He wanted me to come to New York to meet a circle of New York friends of the Center. He hoped I would consider writing a book for the Center on the incessant political activism of the National Council of Churches, and challenged me to make a thorough investigation of the ideological assumptions underlying those initiatives.

Alinsky-type actions and techniques were being employed by the social action bureaucracies of Episcopalians, Presbyterians and especially Methodists. Some of my old friends in the UM General Boards of Social Concerns and Global Ministry were among the most aggressive activists. Their Marxist historical and economic assumptions intensified the radicalism that believed profits were evil and that international corporations had no legitimate function. Demonstrators and activists of all stripes were busy picketing and protesting the board meetings of Nestlé, Dole, United Fruit and military suppliers. Methodists were leading the charge in financing those NCC protests.

I had no problem with protesters exercising their free speech rights, but I had questions about the ideological undergirding of what they were saying. It ranged from soft Marxist polemics to utopian outrage. Their protests were very predictable for liberation groups of the time. I viewed the protection of property rights as an intrinsic aspect of human dignity. If there is no right to property, intrusions on human dignity will ensue. I investigated mountains of paper flowing out of church agency activism reports, strategic studies and action plans attacking concentrations of property. Ironically these protests were being paid for by the reluctant local church laity of the mainline who were growing more interested in the financial accountability of those boards.

So I, as a former scoffer of capitalism, set about writing *Conscience and Dividends*, defending economic freedom and property rights under the guidance of conscience shaped by classic Christian social teaching.[26] I thought the church activists needed to better understand Protestant pluralism, democratic values and local church membership opinion. Many church members were dismayed that their views were overlooked or distorted. Self-perpetuating social action bureaucrats in high offices were often dismissive of the views of their grassroots constituencies, whom they were called to represent. The liberal denominations have repeatedly had difficulty in constraining their boards and agencies.

Sadly, I had participated directly in the emasculating of many vitalities of the classic religious tradition I had received. In the early 1970s I became a political penitent, keenly aware of the destructiveness of my former political history.

I had spent years arguing for statist economics, convinced that it had elitist motives and potentially totalitarian consequences. I had been an admirer of Ho Chi Minh and even Mao in his early period. I had turned a blind eye to the terrible consequences of Marxist tyranny in Ukraine, the Gulags, and in China and Cambodia.

My U-turn did not require that I cease being a political being, but my excesses required a long period of silence. I knew I had to go through a season of political contrition that required some specific behavioral reparations. I knew that all penitents are invited to the Eucharist, and political passions must not stand in the way of Holy Communion.

I made efforts to restore what had been damaged. Conscience required that I do what I could to repair the systems I had harmed.

The evidence of a modern culture in precipitous decline was obvious in high youth suicide rates, violent crime, deepening sexual addictions, gangs controlling drugs and two million abortions per year. I found that some of the damage done has been irreparable. An abortion, like a murder, cannot be undone.

Edrita and I had parented our children up to this point in a way characterized by a soft ethic of support for self-actualization, pardon and freedom. Our children had been raised in a loving environment with few boundaries. Those permissive parenting values were common in that time. Looking back, it might have been better for our children to have had a tougher teaching of sincere repentance and reparation, which would have been fitting to the reality of divine pardon. Now I could see that my role as a parent had been dominated by a flawed view of situation ethics without rules. My children knew they had a loving father but I could have been a better one had I made the boundaries clearer. What was missing was classic Christian teaching of original sin and the function of the law that brings conscience to repentance.

As the excesses of ever more radical forms of feminism emerged, I grew to value the humane reasoning of classic Christian feminism. Earlier I had been an avid defender of Betty Friedan and Germain Greer, and had not even objected to Simone de Beauvoir's views of open marriage. But it was classic Christian feminism that offered the most profound corrective that could protect the interests of children. Biblical teaching called for cohesive families whose happiness was based on the bonding of one female and one male in a durable relationship of covenant fidelity in love, committed to protect the life and well-being of their offspring. Fatherless children were the strongest argument against hedonic sexual experimentation.

The culture of life. Prior to the time of my turnaround, I had been teaching social ethics to young pastors. In classes I had been providing a rationale for their blessing convenience abortions. I had not yet considered the vast implications of its consequences for women, families and society, but most of all for the lost generation of irretrievably aborted babies. When I tried to explain to God why I had ignored those consequences, the answer kept coming back to me: no excuse. I had been wrong, wrong, wrong. The situation ethics on which those abortion arguments were made were unprincipled and careless of human life.

Abortion became an unavoidable issue for me when women seminary students who were struggling to understand their own abortions came to my office for counsel. They were grieving over loss. They were among the best students I had. They had thoughtlessly become trapped in sexual activity as "flower children" committed to making love, not war. They did make love, but a subtler war ensued. It was a war against children. I belatedly recognized that millions of innocent lives were being destroyed on behalf of a narcissism that was careless of its consequences. Taking life was being argued simply on the basis of arbitrary individual choice and convenience. I experienced an overwhelming wave of moral revulsion against the very abortion-on-demand laws I had once advocated.

The protection of the prenatal child had been swallowed up in a wave of advocacy for free choice, overriding the incomparable value of life and overlooking the irreversibility of death. Deliberate killing of babies in the womb had become the new normal. That was a shock and still is. That realization produced a numbing loss of confidence in a whole series of permissive policies I had previously struggled to achieve. The abortion issue was my wake-up call.

As I awakened, I realized that some mainline Protestant theologian needed to stand up for the rights of the unborn. Not many Protestant theologians at that time were openly pro-life because that would have caused loss of face with some feminists. But there were two Methodist theologians who just happened to be my valued friends, Albert Outler and Robert Nelson, who guided me through. That was an early phase of a series of acts of political repentance for me.

Before conception we have a moral choice as to what we will do with our bodies. After conception we do not have a choice to take away the life our bodies have created. Men do not have a choice to be nonfathers and women do not have a choice to be nonmothers after conception. After conception more than two human beings are involved. After *Roe v. Wade*, my conscience would consent only to being responsibly pro-choice before conception and pro-life after conception.

In Austin, Texas, on leave in 1976, I was invited to a private luncheon to converse with Sarah Weddington, the attorney who had argued the *Roe v. Wade* decision before the Supreme Court in December 1971, which was finally decided on January 22, 1973. She was a smart, youthful, feminist attorney. Her client, Norma L. McCorvey, the "Jane Roe" in *Roe v. Wade*, was at that time a leader in the fight for convenience abortions. (Fast forward: Years later in 1995 she revealed she had falsely testified that she had been raped and turned against the very court that had made a judicial precedent for abortion on the basis of her plea. In 1995 McCorvey was baptized and became actively pro-life in a life-affirming ministry to women who have had abortions but have suffered with unresolved grief and depression. Notably she taught forgiveness in a unique way by helping those women understand that their children are waiting in eternity to welcome them with open arms.) I tilted inconclusively with Sarah Weddington.

In April 1975 I was on the busy set of the NBC News production studio in New York face to face with Barbara Walters to discuss the ethics of treatment termination. Karen Ann Quinlan, a twenty-two-year-old who became unconscious one night after arriving home from a party, had collapsed into a persistent vegetative state in Morristown in my New

Jersey county of Morris. That brought end-of-life decisions to the forefront of national attention. Miss Walters was only two years older than I but already a highly experienced national broadcaster. She was expecting a theologian like me, with a reputation for being a situation ethicist, to support pulling the plug on Karen Ann Quinlan.

Miss Walters did not get the story she wanted from me. I set forth classic arguments on the duty to protect life consistent with the time-honored Hippocratic Oath to do no harm. In the following months the media was obsessed with talk of the right to end life deliberately by withholding the means of life to patients in a coma. For months the news was focused on living wills, miracles, the physician's duty to preserve life, the court's intrusion into medical decisions, and who speaks for a coma patient. I was forced to decide whether to follow the almost unanimous popular opinion or give serious reasons why life itself was a unique form of value not comparable to any temporal value. I aligned with the traditional magisterial Vatican against a host of liberal North American Catholic voices.[27]

April 18, 1975, was the day of the first broadcast of the *Robert MacNeil Report*. I was his first guest. I remember climbing up the unsightly stairs of the cramped 42nd Street quarters of the Public Broadcasting Station. That was before he partnered with Jim Lehrer in the *MacNeil-Lehrer Report*. In that interview I was the only Protestant theologian I knew to publicly raise serious objections to liberal treatment termination of those who were not brain dead according to the Harvard Criteria.

I called together a group of practicing physicians and ethicists, and we set to work on formulating the Drew Criteria for Treatment Termination, which was designed to complement the Harvard Criteria on Brain Death. The Drew University Interdisciplinary Study of Treatment Termination generated scientific and statistical evidence that sought to help families make moral judgments regarding end-care treatment.[28]

In an interview with Chris Wallace in July 1975, I argued that the most popular conceptions of a legal living will attempt in vain to anticipate extraordinarily complex unknowable future contingencies. I explained that due to so many variables in any given future situation, it is virtually impossible to anticipate and qualify them as a general rule applicable to all future circumstances.

The National Right to Life movement wanted to hear more of my view on this subject. They invited me to their national convention in Boston in 1977 to discuss how end-of-life issues correlate with beginning-of-life issues. I wrote "Beyond an Ethic of Immediate Sympathy" for the *Hastings Center Report*.[29] On the ten-year anniversary of the papal encyclical *Humanae Vita* in 1978, I attended a conference at Princeton on abortion and euthanasia. There I met many of the Ratzinger Circle of younger American theologians. An amazing number of them would become leading theologians, bishops, archbishops and cardinals in the next three decades, and several became friends of mine.[30] In regular luncheons with my dear friend Father C. John McCloskey and my closest colleague James O'Kane, as well as with the Neuhaus Circle, I entered more deeply into camaraderie with articulate, young, traditional Catholics.

Through those debates on abortion and treatment termination I came to the resolute conviction that life is of incomparable value since it is the precondition of all other human values. It is on a wholly different plane morally than the relief of suffering, which itself is in the service of life. The faithful are given a specific promise that God "will not let you be tested beyond your strength" (1 Cor 10:13).

Classic Christianity After the Collapse of Modern Ideologies

Classic teaching in modern times. Modernity refers to a posttraditional, postmedieval, postfeudal historical worldview marked by industrialization, secularization, naturalistic reasoning and expanding technology. The term *modernity* (*modernité*) was coined by Baudelaire to point to the ephemeral experience of life in an urban metropolis.

When my graduate students had trouble identifying which school of modern theology I was defined by, I playfully began using the term *paleo-orthodox*. At first it seemed like a quip, but like the term *young fogeys* it stuck. In a world in which theology had become a frenetic search for the newest of the new, the emerging young fogeys remembered that what had been forgotten was the oldest of the old. They were perceived to be like fogeys except they were not old. Most were under thirty. Paleo-orthodoxy in my view simply means classical consensual Christianity.

The almost comic term *paleo-orthodoxy* was an act of contrarian defiance to distinguish classic Christianity from neo-orthodoxy, a dominant theological movement of the 1950s–1960s that had virtually forgotten the patristic writers. Neo-orthodoxy was a set of theological attempts to remain modern while rescuing selected ideas of classic Christianity acceptable to modernity.[31]

It is a matter of historical fact that orthodoxy emerged out of consensual reflection on Jewish and Christian Scripture in the first four centuries and has remained substantially in place ever since. It was received by believers around the world and sustained largely unchanged for the past twenty centuries. To be orthodox is to be grounded in the earliest consensual classic Christian teaching.

The most concise way to explain my *Agenda for Theology* (1979) was by defining three common prefixes: *paleo, neo* and *post*. To be *paleo* it must be unapologetically focused on ancient wisdom and unafraid to say why. It is paleo in defiance of everything that is compulsively neo.

Something is *neo* or modern if it is current, up-to-date, contemporary and new. An obsession with the modern turns into a constant flight to stay ahead of the next thing.

Modern refers to a time, a mentality and a malaise. Think of a target of three concentric circles: the *outer* circle was the overarching intellectual ideology of the waning historical period that has lasted from the French Revolution to the Vietnam War—or more precisely from 1789 to 1968.

The *middle* circle was a mentality found especially among the intelligentsia and knowledge elites which assumed that recent ways of knowing are self-evidently superior to all premodern alternatives. If you do not recognize that mentality, you can easily find it in *The New Republic, Atlantic* and more popularly in magazines like *Self, Vanity Fair, Rolling Stone* and *Motor Trend*.

But what was the central *target* of the term *modernity*? The *inner* circle of the target of modernity is the time after 1968, revealing the last-stages deterioration of the ideologies underlying modernity. If you compare those modern journals before 1968 and after 1968, you will find a tone of increased desperation, despair and frenzy. Why 1968? It was, in my view, the peak year of cultural reversal. After that, the new normal was the rapid deterioration of the leading ideologies that had prevailed before 1968.

But what does *post* refer to? Postmodern refers to the period *after* the dominance of Darwinian, Freudian, Nietzschean and Marxist ideologies and all their children. The premodern world prevailed before the French Revolution. The postmodern world has been prevailing since the late 1960s. No worldview lasts indefinitely. What we call modernity will not last.

Four typically modern figures that identify the four movements going downhill since 1968 are naturalistic reductionism (Darwin), narcissistic hedonism (Freud), autonomous individualism (Nietzsche) and property redistribution by elites who factor their own interests first (Marx).

Future historians will look back on the 1960s and recognize more clearly that all of those ideologies were by then in a state of steep decline. Their appearance of vitality had hidden their deeper despair.

Today the intellectual descendants of those figures are all on the defensive in the culture despite reports to the contrary. Meanwhile they desperately maintain the denial fantasy that they are still, despite evidences, on the leading edge of history. Modernity in this third sense is a false optimism about the future of modern ideologies.

It is hard for those trapped in the modern spirit even to imagine the ancient, since the defining expectation is that the moral foundations of the modern period will live into the deep future and maybe endlessly.

The hypothesis that I sought to defend in *Agenda for Theology* is: these times we live in are the last days of the controlling ideologies of the modern period.

After architecture had shed the term *postmodern*, philosophy sought to catch up with it. The secular idea of postmodern that appeared a decade after I was writing is entirely hypermodern. When *postmodern* became corrupted into a popular philosophical fad, it entirely missed the vulnerabilities of the underlying cultural idols which I was resisting. Lyotard's *postmodern* has proven to be an ephemeral phase that has already largely disappeared. It never took the death of modern ideologies seriously enough. The fact that consensual Christianity will outlive Lyotard, Foucault and Fukayama will soon be easily recognizable. I regard virtually all of these so-called postmodern writers as desperately ultramodern.[32] If they tell you they are post, they are usually ultra.

When I say post I really mean post, that is, the period after the collapse of the leading modern worldviews.

The collapse of the underpinnings of modern life. Although other dates may be pinpointed, there are plausible evidences that the death of modernity occurred in 1968. That was the year of the Tet Offensive, the assassinations of Martin Luther King Jr. and Robert F. Kennedy, the My Lai Massacre, and the riots at the Democratic Convention in Chicago.

By the time I met Herberg in 1970 the wheel of history had already turned toward postmodernity. He knew it. I knew it. The evidence:

- Freud's psychoanalysis was less effective than the spontaneous re-mission rate.

- The societies that most closely followed Marx became the poorest.

- The biogenetic evidences of intelligent design were mounting.

- Nietzsche's assertions had totalitarian consequences.

The tipping point was reached in 1968, but it only became more recognizable in the ensuing years. I found myself living in an era that was beginning to be postmodern in the sense that the four leading modern ideologies had turned out to be losers, but the media elites could not see their deterioration. The renewal of the classic Christian consensus within modernity (or more precisely postmodern paleo-orthodoxy) is more than a private or personal perception. It was a historical event of growing consciousness. The faithful were neonates in a world in which modern ideologies were dying.

Those who persist in thinking that these ideologies are infinitely promising are by definition modern. If you think these ideologies are dead or irreversibly dying, you are postmodern. I struggled with the university when it became hopelessly defensive about all the underpinnings of modern consciousness.

I myself grieve over many aspects of the waning of the modern period, which has created a more dangerous world than modernity itself. The good news is that the seeds of God's good news are planted already in every dying culture. What is ahead of postmodernity? No one knows, but whatever it is, it will not succeed in destroying the deep roots of Christian memory.

The gift of classic Christianity will only be received when people are ready to receive it, understand it and be comforted by it. In order for that to happen, they must be willing to let modern consciousness collapse of its own weight. This recognition is happening on a person-by-person basis.

It is in the real world that the Christian story of salvation is unfolding. That story is best told in the Bible. The redeeming Word is always at work in the world. A deceased modernity is not an ultimate threat from within the long view of history. The gist of my turnaround is a celebration of this actual history.

Modernity has only lasted less than a dozen generations, while orthodox Christianity has already flourished for more than four hundred generations and shows no sign of fatigue. Yet orthodoxy seems like a newcomer in the university and to the cultural elites, since that is where it has been most forgotten.

The list of modernities since the patristic period that have been transcended by orthodoxy is too long to describe here. Tribalism, feudalism, nominalism and social utopianism provide examples.

I was focused on measuring the durability of worldviews. I was finding the modern ideologies to be dead except for their aftereffects. Outside the university the culture already knows the failures of modernity in broken families, malfunctioning government policy and defective education. Inside the university there are few signs of recognition. Those signs are easily recognized, however, by single mothers desperately seeking placement for their children in long lines of lotteries for urban educational alternatives and charter schools.

Repentance is one of the least favored words in the modern vocabulary, especially in the university. I have loved spending my life in the university, but I know it well enough to see its vulnerabilities. The academy is already struggling to survive the breakdown of modern ideologies to which it has become so indebted. It will survive, but it will be one of the last institutions to give up its illusions.[33]

The concept of heresy does not exist because it might offend someone. The only actual heresy that might cause someone to gasp would be to mention the word *heresy*. The providential reason God allows heresy among the faithful, according to the ancient Christian writers, is to challenge the worshiping community to correct its exaggerations so as to bring it back into the balanced consensus.

After modernity what? Genuinely postmodern Christian theology had not yet reached its defining moments of maturity until George Lindbeck's work *The Nature of Doctrine: Religion and Theology in a Postliberal Age* in 1984, and Richard Neuhaus's *The Catholic Moment: The Paradox of the Church in the Postmodern World* in 1987, and in the works of Carl Braaten and Robert Jenson. All of them had been thoroughly immersed in modern consciousness before they found in classic Christianity the deepest critique of modernity's illusions.

I began searching for a more reliable grounding for the study of sacred texts. That grounding came only when I recognized the reasonableness of the ancient consensual Christian tradition. It had a more reliable critical method based on historic consensus, which implies centuries of human experience. It had remained surprisingly stable while passing through innumerable cultures for two millennia. The orthodox critique of modernity occurred by asking persistent Socratic questions to the guild of biblical scholars who had previously controlled the gateways to the sacred texts.

I had devoted years to reading in the Dibelius and Bultmann critical literature (form criticism, existential analysis, redaction criticism), only to realize belatedly that it was distracting me from my central pursuit. It finally dawned on me that these accommodations lacked depth in historical understanding. My own critical capacity had been dulled by the very modern assumptions I had considered to be state of the art "critical."

Social location analysis helped me understand what was driving historical and literary criticism. It was the despairing need to seek upward social mobility in the secularizing university.

Historical-critical methods in the university today have in fact often emerged out of a history of biblical criticism. Some of the most influential early critics were biblical critics, followed by secular modes of examining texts.[34] The intent of the early phases of historical criticism was to ask legitimate questions like when and where a particular text originated, how, why, by whom, for whom it was written, what sources were used in its composition, how the text was preserved and transmitted.

The point at which modern criticism became ideological advocacy was when it did not allow the ancient writer his own worldview but rather judged that worldview from the viewpoint of an assumed absolutely reliable worldview of scientific forms of knowing spiritual realities. To view biblical texts as having purely human rather than supernatural origins is not to grant the ancient writer his voice. Modern critical methods based on flawed ideologies now rule inquiries into literature, philosophy and history. They have produced an era of flawed attempts that often stood in the way of grasping the meaning of history viewed as a whole. Their form of criticism is easily spotted as they began by ruling out the key premises of historical revelation, apostolicity, catholicity, holiness and grace, which are all necessary to understand the sacred texts that best convey the meaning of universal history.

Well-meaning modern biblical critics warned me that patristic criticism was precritical. That opened a door for me to enter into a more decisive discussion regarding the critique of criticism. The issue was whether *critical* is defined narrowly in the terms of the modern experience alone or more inclusively in terms of the whole range of human historical experience. The latter was my task. If the term *critical* is limited only to that which modern consciousness says is critical, that is precisely the self-deception that required correction.

Paul Ricoeur provided a model for this in describing a "second naiveté" that examined modern critical arguments but saw that these led to an unexpected openness to God's work in history. This critical agenda assumes a much longer time frame than a decade or a century. It looks toward universal history. Articulating that agenda set the course for all of my subsequent inquiries.[35]

Losing Will. Will Herberg's active intellectual life continued until his final illness beginning in 1976. He heroically continued to teach his seminars as he became very ill. Suspecting some neurological illness, my colleague Don Jones and I took our neurosurgeon friend Henry Liss over to Herberg's apartment to provide a preliminary assessment. We knocked repeatedly on Will's door. We waited a long time to allow him to shuffle down his stairs to the doorway. When he finally arrived, he was withdrawn and defensive. He seemed to sense something ominous unfolding, so he locked the screen door. We tried to persuade him to let us come in and talk about his condition, his absence from class, missing appointments, occasional lack of coherence and loss of memory, but he closed his door. Whatever Will was facing, it was clear that he wanted to face it alone. A few days later Don found a way of getting him to the emergency room, even though he resisted. Edrita and I visited him that afternoon in the hospital. Diagnosed with a late-stage brain tumor, he was bewildered and alarmed. We were devastated.

How could it be? That magnificent brain! Gone. I visited him repeatedly in the nearby nursing center. Soon he was totally unresponsive. When he died of brain cancer on March 27, 1977, Protestants, Catholics and Jews mourned. With Will gone, I wondered how I could move ahead without him.

Soon after Will's passing, our own family was distraught by a series of medical crises. Edrita was diagnosed with life-threatening breast cancer in 1978. I was stunned. She was the one who held our family together. She had three surgeries to try to arrest it. As a sturdy survivor, she remained upbeat, noncomplaining and very active. She fought a twenty-year battle with this insidious disease.

Laura was a cheerleader in her junior year of high school. At the height of her young life in February 1979, she was faced with a very serious melanoma diagnosis. She then required two surgeries in 1979 to prevent further spread of the cancer to her lymph nodes. That left her with a serious and long-term case of lymphedema, which required wrapping her leg in cloth bands every night, which she patiently did for many years.

Finally, our most athletic son, Edward, had a serious golf accident in the summer of 1980, which caused total loss of vision in his right eye. This was days before his leaving for college. He was swinging a two iron off the first tee when his golf ball hit a hidden concrete marker and bounced right back to his eye. He was in the hospital in the days just before he left for his first year at Southern Methodist University. Undaunted, he studied history at SMU and decided in his senior year to enter law school at Washington and Lee University.

The pace of life was interrupted, but did not stop during these health impediments.[36] Also new challenges that I had to address were brewing in the seminary.

The Struggle for the Soul of Theological Education

The declining future of liberal theological education. The highly respected dean who had brought me to Drew, James Ault, was elected to the episcopacy sixteen months after I arrived.[37] After that, I enjoyed working with a series of able graduate school and seminary deans. I had a very good personal relationship with the presidents and general university administers during the majority of my thirty-three years at Drew. I was an active participant in many decision-making processes. Whenever possible I asked to be relieved of administrative roles since I viewed my vocation as teaching and writing. However, when asked, I served in the trenches of university committees facing major decisions, such as search committees for deans and presidents, long-range planning, budgeting, admissions, departmental committees and the faculty senate.[38]

I was honored to be a part of Drew Seminary, which was one of the two oldest theological schools serving the United Methodist Church. The growth years of seminary education were the 1950s. As my years of teaching ended, the denomination's membership was in the process of declining rapidly from 9 million to 7.7 million, with the largest loss of members in urban areas and especially in two regions: the Northeast and the Pacific West.[39]

I viewed myself as a loyal theologian seeking to be faithful to my ordination. The venues where I kept in touch with current issues in Wesley studies were the Wesleyan Theological Society and the Church Holiness Society. In Cambridge I had a period of residence in the Methodist theological college, Wesley House. I also participated in the formation of the Wesley Studies section of the American Academy of Religion. I helped form the Charles Wesley Society for the purposes of study, preservation, interpretation and dissemination of Charles Wesley's poetry and prose.

Conflicts grew throughout the late 1970s when the Methodist General Conference ordered a study showing which theological institutions would be least likely to survive the chronic decline in numbers and the ensuing shortage of funds. Soon a subtle competition for survival emerged between the thirteen Methodist seminaries. Some of the self-standing seminaries in Denver, Ohio, Kansas City and Washington, DC, were included on the list of potential casualties. The real shock, however, was that two of the most prestigious and best endowed UM seminaries appeared on the list as well—the seminaries of Boston University and Drew University.

I was expected to help bolster Drew's case with the national United Methodist leadership and with the Council of Bishops. I accepted the duty of attending General Conferences and trying to secure the seminary's future, but I soon found myself weary of the distracting work of political fence-mending. All thirteen seminaries survived, but some barely. The prevailing emphasis remained on social activism and obsessive political correctness. No Methodist seminary was reaching out for evangelicals. Not one. I actively argued that if the General Conference would allow at least one of the thirteen seminaries to reach out intentionally and actively for evangelicals and conservatives, it would grow exponentially. No seminary was ready to take that obvious step. The numbers of students at Asbury Theological Seminary continued to grow from 700 to 1,400 even while the average graduating class of the UM Seminaries was around 90. Asbury did not get any funding from the UM General Conference because it was regarded by the educational bureaucracy as too conservative, too Wesleyan. Yet it was producing more pastors for local Methodist ministries than any other Methodist-related seminary.

The conflict was essentially between a growing conservative laity and a declining liberal clergy, led by politically correct majorities in the theological schools and bureaucracy. My warnings fell on deaf ears. The faculties had little interest in listening to the troubled laity.

Empirical studies gave proof that the denomination's seminaries were failing. A shocking Longitudinal Clergy Study on continuance of theological graduates in pastoral work after their graduation brought the bad news. It was directed by Rolf Memming, who had a PhD in empirical sociological studies before coming to seminary. For the first time we had solid evidence of a very high dropout rate among young clergy, men and women, but especially women.[40] The dropout rates among probationary clergy in some conferences ranged as high as 40 percent. I argued without avail that if the seminary appointed only a few new faculty who could connect with evangelical students, that would solve our struggle for registrations and tuition. Meanwhile the new faculty appointments were all in the opposite direction. Most new appointments were made to left-leaning scholars who were dedicated to their ideologies and who either ignored, loathed or demeaned evangelicals.

The stalemate was perceived by laity as the arrogance of seminaries unwilling to listen to many if not most of the laity, who were unconvinced of the wisdom and prudence of the activists' stands on egalitarian language restrictions, abortion, sexual ethics and lack of financial accountability. But the conflict was oppositely perceived by liberal seminary faculties as the ignorance and backwardness of the churches they were called to serve. If a business enterprise had such a failure rate, the administrators would have been promptly fired by the board. But the bishops applauded the liberalization, seminary trustees didn't want to rock the boat, and pastors who had been ordained were virtually ensured a stipend for life. The system was unsustainable.[41]

Caught in the squeeze of the call to eliminate the weakest seminaries, my seminary administrators thought I might be able to influence policies favorable to the seminary. I was one of the few Methodists on the faculty, so it fell to me to meliorate the problem. The problem was funding, registrations and dropouts. I had a growing conscience about the effectiveness of American theological education in mainline Protestantism generally, not just in my seminary alone.[42] I tried to be loyal to my seminary, but found it difficult to get a hearing with the trustees, who were the only ones that could make a difference.

The election of my cousin, William B. Oden, as bishop of the United Methodist Church and later as president of the Council of Bishops, brought me an unexpected sense of relief. After that I enjoyed an undeserved measure of respectability with the Methodist bishops that I would not have had otherwise. My loyalty to my church tradition never wavered, but I wondered if that loyalty might at some point require more explicit resistance. This part of the story requires a flashback.

Engaging process theology and evangelical theology. My on-and-off encounter with process theology began in my Perkins days in 1955 when I had a seminar with Herndon Wagers on Whitehead. I was left mystified by his view that all matter has some level of consciousness, and by his view of a growing and changing God with good intentions but limited power. When I served as teaching assistant at Yale College under Professor William Christian, a leading expert on Whitehead, I once again tried to engage in dialogue with this perspective.[43]

My unavoidable clash with process thought intensified when I team taught in a course with my brilliant colleague Schubert Ogden at SMU. We were both Bultmannians at that time, but I was never a convinced process theology advocate. Ogden and I had exchanged our sharply different views on some of his opinions in *Christ Without Myth* and on Bultmann's *Essays*.[44]

While on leave at the University of Texas in 1976, I had an opportunity to converse informally with the gentle and wise Charles Hartshorne, whose students in process philosophy had become my colleagues over many years. I experienced in Hartshorne a caring and thoughtful mind, well prepared to deal with the issues with which he was thoroughly familiar. But I did not experience in him a desire to enter into the forbidding arena of classic doctrinal inquiry, especially when it involved the

language of revelation, sin and salvation. When I told him I was preparing a volume for Princeton University Press on the parables of Kierkegaard, we spent some enjoyable time recollecting stories from the
Kierkegaard corpus. My serious purpose with Hartshorne was to explore
whatever he might be thinking about the project of Wolfhart Pannenberg
on history as revelation and how it might relate to process theology at
that time, as it was being developed by John Cobb. His response was
guarded, admitting he knew little about Pannenberg but had high trust
in John Cobb.

My closest theological teaching partner at Drew was Pieter de Jong,
my dean and convenor of the Graduate Department of Theology. Pieter
taught the process theology seminar at Drew with a special interest in
relating process thought to the cosmic evolutionary ontology of Teilhard
de Chardin.

After Pieter's passing, the brilliant young Catherine Keller replaced
him. As one of John Cobb's most talented PhD students, she was thoroughly committed to the assumptions and arguments of process thought,
with special interests in its relevance for feminist thought and a theology
of liberation. She won many adherents to imaginative process reasoning.
I found her always to be generous and an empathic partner in dialogue,
even though our assumptions were quite different.

On a different path, in 1976 A Fund for Theological Education (AFTE)
was founded by Albert Outler and Ed Robb for the specific purpose of
assisting young classical Christian scholars to study at the finest universities in Germany, Scotland, England and North America. I was involved
from the beginning. Aware that many graduate programs in North
America had drifted into ideological advocacy, the Fund committed its
energies to assist evangelical doctoral candidates to study in preferred
study locations with classically grounded and highly competitive PhD
programs such as Oxford, Cambridge, Notre Dame and Duke. Serving
on the selection committee with Ted Campbell of Duke, we hoped to
bring into the faculties of American educational institutions some new
voices with unexcelled credentials in biblical and historical studies to
teach classic Christianity while also showing evidences that they had

fully grasped current knowledge in their own field. Very quickly this effort had an extraordinary record of achievement against great odds. It supported many brilliant, classically oriented students. In time they were accepted to serve on the leading faculties of universities and seminaries.

The first public event that featured AFTE's basic concerns was held at Notre Dame in 1979, a week-long "Colloquy on the Loss and Recovery of the Sacred." Keynoted by Albert Outler, it brought together leading Catholic voices such as Leo Jozef Cardinal Suenens and Father George Tavard with outstanding Protestant theologians like Lutheran Martin E. Marty, Orthodox Alexander Schmemann and Leonid Kishkovsky, as well as evangelical theologians like Carl Henry and Richard Lovelace. Notre Dame's president, Theodore M. Hesburgh, moderated this remarkable ecumenical gathering, out of which came many lasting friendships for me.

My first contact with Carl Henry, founding editor of *Christianity Today*, happened at this Notre Dame Colloquy. He was widely acknowledged as the preeminent evangelical theologian of his time. He told me that he had read *Agenda for Theology* with keen interest. He became my mentor in evangelical theology along with J. I. Packer and Timothy Smith. Dr. Henry was a member of the American Theological Society (ATS), the most distinguished group of Catholic, Protestant, Orthodox and Jewish theologians in America.[45] To my knowledge Carl Henry was at that time the only conservative evangelical in that illustrious company, and it was he who generously sponsored my entry into that society. I gladly accepted and entered into conversation with many brilliant theologians who became lifelong friends. There I formed enduring friendships with Paul Ramsey, Avery Dulles, Geoffrey Wainwright, Charles West and Karlfried Froelich.

In the late 1970s, my friend Stan Gundry of Zondervan Publishing House met regularly with me every year for an extended conversation at the American Academy of Religion. One year when we met in New Orleans for AAR, we talked about my possible participation in the Evangelical Theological Society (ETS), and he as a board member urged me to join. I had already been pondering the need to bridge the chasm between conservative evangelicals and mainline moderates. It seemed to me to be an ecumenical mission that I could handle, but I realized I would take flak for it. When I consulted with the noted historian Timothy Smith of Johns Hopkins about how he handled criticisms of his participation in ETS, he told me simply to stay attentive to Wesley himself as the model evangelical, which is what I did. Without his encouragement I would never have considered joining an organization that was stereotyped negatively in both Wesleyan and liberal circles.[46]

At that time I could hardly find anyone in ETS who was from a mainline liberal school like Drew. Most in the ETS leadership were conservative Reformed or Baptist, and a few were generic fundamentalists.[47] Many were distrustful of any form of ecumenism, but in the next twenty years that would change.

At that time no evangelical seminary to my knowledge featured a specified chair in patristic studies. Years later when I went to my last ETS meeting, the best evangelical seminaries in North America had qualified offerings in patristic studies, with Wheaton, Asbury, Dallas, Baylor, Gordon-Conwell and Fuller among them. I watched and shared in that amazing transformation of the evangelical theological curriculum. Soon highly qualified evangelical patristic scholars were taking leading roles in the Oxford Patristic Conference and the North American Patristic Society. I was glad to have been an early proponent of that reversal.

As an evangelical-catholic voice in a mainline liberal seminary, I increasingly became involved in church renewal within the mainline Protestant denominations. This put me in touch with the Methodist renewal efforts like Good News, the Association for Church Renewal and later with multidenominational evangelical, Catholic and Jewish research and publishing groups like the Ethics and Public Policy Center, the Institute on Religion and Democracy in Washington and the Institute on Religion and Public Policy in New York.

I was invited by Stan Gundry to be a part of the editorial board of the Zondervan imprint called the Francis Asbury Press. Wesleyan and Arminian scholars at that time had few opportunities for scholarly publications apart from their denominational presses. Through many editorial meetings at Zondervan in Grand Rapids, I connected with many leading Wesleyan and Reformed scholars. My publishers at that time (Harper, Abingdon and Westminster) had little interaction with either traditional Catholics or conservative evangelicals. I was witnessing a breakthrough in publishing for mainline evangelicals.

I was beginning to realize that I had two quite different reading audiences: the Harper centrist liberals and the Zondervan centrist evangelicals. Ironically those two great publishing houses would later merge under the larger international group called HarperCollins.

My faculty colleagues were embarrassed that I was even talking with conservative evangelicals, much less working with them on writing projects. I found the evangelicals to be more welcoming and inclusive than the liberals, who were so frequently speaking about inclusion but with a narrower view of inclusiveness largely defined by gender and ethnicity. Evangelical and Catholic inclusiveness transcended those divisions and went deeper into transcultural classic Christianity.

CELEBRATING THE UNBROKEN ECUMENICAL CONSENSUS

Discerning the history of consent. Even though I could find no one in the academy who was interested in deliberate unoriginality, I was able on my own to move forward with that as my central purpose. As I developed what became by far the most productive period of my life, I was welcomed into a community of recollection of the oldest history of consent in Western culture. What at first seemed to be something I had "discovered" turned out to be the opposite of discovery but rather the recognition of what had already been discovered again and again. It was humbling to recognize a tenet so contrary to everything I had been taught about the importance of individual creativity.

In an era focused on change, the value of historic continuity had been left largely unstudied. I read sociological analyses on what holds communities together over time—over long periods of time, over centuries, over millennia. I searched the literature on stability, permanence, constancy, reliability and steadiness. I looked in vain in the literature of modernity for an answer. Instead I found dozens of shelves of books on social change, but almost none on social durability. Some philosophers of universal history like Hegel and Toynbee grasped the reality of social continuity but they were dealing with cultural and national patterns of continuity, not three millennia of continuity in a scriptural canon and liturgy held intact through innumerable different cultures and times. Hegel imposed upon history a pattern of dialectical reasoning that finally proved unconvincing. Toynbee flooded my mind with the varieties of human cultures but not what had held them together over centuries. He was more astute in grasping what made them decay than in what made them cohere.

Consent was not ecumenical if it was not found worldwide in all twenty centuries. The clergy did not create this consent; it was achieved by an act of the worshiping community confirmed by the laity in song, prayer and Scripture. If all of the clergy in Christian history had agreed on a point of Christian doctrine that had received no universal consent by the worshiping community, it would not be ecumenical consent.

Whenever I came upon those points where it seemed that the apostolic consensus had lost its way or broken up irretrievably, I discovered that by looking more deeply into the most consensual interpreters of the sacred text, the truth proved itself to be self-correcting under the guidance of the Spirit. That premise, that the Holy Spirit sustained the right memory of the truth revealed in history, was to me counterintuitive at every step. Yet the constant course correction of the community was the most remarkable aspect of the history of ecumenical consent.

That consensus was expressed in the first generation of apostles at Jerusalem in A.D. 49 and then tested and confirmed in their writings and in the great ecumenical councils. From the outset, triune teaching has stood at the core of Christian faith, since the texts demanded it. The decisive assumption is that the Spirit is guiding the faithful. No one described that better than Vincent of Lérins, who showed that the method of consensus had been in effect before he described it. He had listened to the phenomena of consent in order to describe it. He had listened first to the unified consent of the apostles and only then to the wisest interpreters of the apostles who had gained the widest consent from the worldwide people of faith.

The laity discerned all along that what they had heard in the apostolic testimony was true. The foremost minds of Christian consensual teaching made clear what the worshiping community already knew. Through culture after culture this close unity was sustained.

Those who walk steadily within the apostolic consensus look to dwell intellectually and morally inside its premises without wavering. They find themselves blessed by a deep grasp of truth based on those who worship the unchanging God revealed in Jesus by the power of the Spirit. That is a special form of empirical inquiry called intergenerational evidence.

The spiritual and intellectual trajectory of the 1970s. The capacity of classic Christianity to utterly change a life is confirmed by the many lives it has changed. There are millions of those narratives, with my story being only one. Those stories offer evidence that classic Christianity has transformed human behavior wherever it has been taken seriously.

The pragmatic test of orthodoxy lies in how it is still actually transforming lives. Classic Christianity depends not upon any particular individual's view but upon how the history of salvation molds a particular person's whole way of living. All who receive that gift are called to bear testimony to how the Spirit has worked to transform their lives.

Autobiography in the classic Christian tradition has a different function than autobiography in modern literary culture because it shows how grace reshapes personal identity. It is not primarily an act of pure self-expression as we see in the great novels of James Joyce and Thomas Wolfe. Rather it is an expression of thanks for God's own coming within time for the whole of time.

It would be presumptuous to assume that my tiny slice of discernment provides any normative pattern for any other. Each one must find his or her own way on the path of recognition.[48] The simple truth is that my life direction was entirely turned around by orthodox Christian faith.

At some point between my boyhood and my young adulthood, personal conversion narratives had become stories of sin and salvation that were cliché-ridden. Compared to Augustine they were warped and devolved. In college days I was wary of the temptation to focus any serious religious argument tied to my own personal experience. Rather I found it more reasonable to appeal to history, morality and empirical evidence. My own early Methodist spiritual formation had rightly emphasized personal testimony to a new birth, but when testimony was perverted or made routine, it became offensive to me. Easy claims of instant conversions often seemed to me to be phony.

In the early 1970s I at times imagined that I was the only one who was on this eccentric path backward from modern accommodation to classic Christianity. That was because I lived cocooned in a university where such things as conversion and new birth were hardly ever mentioned, seldom examined and not talked about without embarrassment. They were purposely avoided for fear of offending someone or appearing out of date or being marginalized. That legitimate hesitation still stands as a constraint on any conversion narrative.

But as I learned to listen to the life stories of others who had similar trajectories to mine, I found their companionship encouraging. Among people I have met and known personally who have traveled along a similar road are four in particular: Avery Dulles and Albert Outler of the generation before me, and Richard Neuhaus and Joseph Ratzinger of my generation. I have been blessed by these four lives and by their telling.

A steady principle of biblical teaching is that only from the end do we understand the beginning. We understand slavery in Egypt from the viewpoint of the exodus, and the wilderness from the viewpoint of crossing the Jordan. We understand the life of Jesus from his death and resurrection. So with me, the meaning of the first half of my life has been made clear by the last half.[49] The prodigal son had to try out every wrong path in a far country before he found the right path home. Only after his testing of futile ways was he ready to come home.

As with Augustine, it was through a journey of the mind that I had a change of heart. I had to learn that my life was more than my mind, and that my journey had to be experienced without my knowing where it was taking me. In the 1970s I learned that it was God the Spirit, prompting, wooing, revealing and guiding the journey.

The 1980s

Charting the Course

◆

WATERSHEDS

The death of my father. Dad's death ended an era for me. I lost my most
reliable guide, my first mentor and the one who inspired me to seek to
live a good life. I have no doubt that his just and good life mirrored for
me the heavenly Father's justice and love. He offered me a pattern for
loving devotion to family, reverence toward the law, food for the poor,
shelter for the homeless and a love for books and knowledge.

Dad's life prompted me to write "My Dad's Death Brought Christmas
'Home'" just after he passed away in 1980. The subtitle was "The Clash of
the Christmas Symbols and the Reality of the Funeral." It was my last act
of homage to Dad.

Our family gathered around Mom as she provided the cohesive center
for our grieving family. I found special strength in my mother and great
joy in her presence. She remained in Altus with a host of dear friends,
most of whom I knew. They were people upon whom her light had
shined and her joy had radiated. She continued to pour her heart into
music and young people until she was eighty-nine: teaching piano,
directing the choir and encouraging young people of all races to enjoy
and make music. When Lily Oden passed away in 1993, the church where
she had so long played the organ was a flood of tears. She had touched
the lives of virtually every family in town.

Long walks in the forest. Returning to New Jersey, I took many long solitary walks in the dense Drew forest. I was always moved by its soaring ancient oak trees, undisturbed for thousands of years, and the deep valleys carved by the glaciers.

We maintained a close connection with our Oklahoma extended family all through our years in Jersey. We saw Tal frequently when he came to New York for national church board meetings. We enjoyed visits from Edrita's retired parents, who traveled all over the continent in their motor home. Her father had a calling card that defined his roving role as "Visiting Methodist." He brought into our family a spirit of encouragement, zest, cooperation and diligence. We named our second son after him. Edrita's much-loved father passed away in 1989.

Our growing family thrived on the theatrical, cultural, historical and sporting events of the New York area. After a precollegiate career as a radio announcer and working with a sonar sound team in search of oil, Clark went back to the University of Oklahoma to finish his degree in electrical engineering. He then went to work for a series of companies in sound engineering and aeronautics: an Austin, Texas, electronics manufacturer, Eaton Corporation, Frontier Engineering in Oklahoma City, and the Seagate Corporation, where he designed high speed hard drives.[1] Edward studied history at Southern Methodist University and proceeded to law school at Washington and Lee, followed by a successful law practice in Charlotte. Laura took leadership roles in church youth mission trips repairing houses of the poor. She went to SMU to study Russian history and literature. In addition, she studied conversational Russian at the Tolstoy Institute in New York. She served as planner and treasurer of the Peace Walk from LA to Washington, DC, in 1987, and then led the first ever Peace March of Russians and Americans from Leningrad to Moscow in 1989.[2]

Edrita accompanied me on many of my lecture journeys, brightening any scene she entered and reducing the frustrations. She was a perennial hostess to the homeless families who resided in our church during their times of dislocation. Then the diagnosis of breast cancer struck once again. My sister, Sarah, and Tal's wife, Jane, did so much to help Edrita through her roughest patches.

Bathed in a glorious light: The ordeal of open heart surgery. In my fifties I had open heart surgery. When cardiologist Stephen Goss did a routine catheterization, he found 99 percent blockages in three arteries leading directly into my heart. The next day I had three-way coronary artery bypass surgery. That required me to shift my priorities and derailed everything else I had been doing. Three decades later I still feel a sense of unmerited surprise that I am still alive.

Open heart surgery at that time was still a highly uncertain surgical procedure. In New Jersey, the nearby Morristown Memorial Hospital had just acquired the services of a brilliant open heart surgeon, Dr. Grant Parr, from Philadelphia's renowned Children's Hospital. I was one of his first patients at Morristown. When I asked him about the likelihood of recovery from three arteries being redirected by grafting, he gave me a tolerable percentage chance of recovery and survival, so I immediately went under the knife with complete confidence in the surgeons.

I was put on a heart-lung bypass machine to provide my body with oxygenated blood. To get access to the heart, they had to open my chest by cutting through the breastbone. That was the part of the operation that required the most healing. They wedged my ribcage apart and re-channeled the blood flow through three different arteries using veins from my leg.

Midway through the surgery the surgeon explained to Edrita that there had been a serious emergency while I was under anesthesia which had required the surgical team to stop and begin all over. They had already grafted my main arteries and sewed me up but then had realized that I was not getting sufficient blood flow to keep my heart muscle from further damage. It was at that point that some slight necrosis (cell death) of heart tissue occurred, thus the surgical team made a decision to redo the entire operation, rerouting the arterial flow and regrafting all the arteries while taking another vein from my leg. This extended the length of the operation to five hours and caused great anxiety as Edrita and Laura waited in the recovery room.

I regained partial consciousness in between those two surgeries and could hear the voices in the operating room and was conscious enough to realize that a serious medical emergency was occurring. During that unforeseen waking moment, I had the clear impression that I had already died. Unexplainably I felt an unexpected sense of relief, joy and entry into a distinctly new world where a bright light was radiating into my soul.

I was bathed in a glorious world of light—stunning, radiant light of a different sort than I had ever seen. The light seemed to be not the light from the operating room ceiling but from somewhere far beyond. I was surprised that I was not at all afraid. After the second surgery, when I woke up I realized that I had not died. Edrita was by my side.

Later Laura entered the recovery room with her bright eyes beaming but wet with tears. Laura held my hand and stroked my hair. I had heard her sob before, but never like that. I realized at that fragile moment how very much my daughter loved me. We had always been close, but never so close as that moment.

The deeper discovery for me was the lasting realization that I was not afraid of dying. This is not a report of a near-death experience but rather an imagined death experience. After that I felt a freedom from the dread of dying that has offered inexpressible comfort to me in the ensuing years. At my lowest point physically I underwent a peak experience spiritually. It was as real as anything I have ever experienced.

Much later an unfolding thought would come to me concerning God's providence. I wondered if there might have been a mysterious purpose in my felt experience when I had been mercifully allowed to live when I might have just as likely have died. The reason to me later seemed evident, although it will doubtless to some seem glib: I felt that I was being given some sort of transcendent permission to complete my vocational agenda that I had only barely begun.

There was far more yet ahead to do. The first volume of my systematic theology was completed in 1986, but volumes two and three remained to be done. In the first volume I had been perplexed and awed over the glorious idea of divine providence pervading every voluntary decision of human life. I was ready to move on to the completing stages of the reasoning of classic Christianity concerning redemption and consummation. If my heart had fallen into irreversible dysfunction, that vocation would have been left unfulfilled. That vision would unfold only gradually after I had completed *Pastoral Theology*, traveled to Cuba and the Soviet Union, and matured through the discipline of prolonged studies in patristic writings. That required time and time was what I now had.

At the time of the open heart surgery in July of 1987, I was told that the recuperation process would take three or four months. Within six weeks after the surgery I was walking five miles a day. I met all my classes that term. By October I was in New York at Richard Neuhaus's apartment conferring with Avery Dulles and David Novak to edit a draft document on natural law. By November I was walking ten miles a day.

MEANWHILE AT THE ZOO

The awkward dance with political correctness. In the 1980s it seemed that almost every decision had a politically correct component. I valued the attempt at fairness in language and correctives to racism and sexism, but if those correctives were made disproportionately at the cost of quality in basic Christian teaching, I was concerned. I supported affirmative action but resisted its abuses. I could not have predicted the high price I would pay.

When complaints poured in from the churches and ordinal boards about the performance of some of our ordinands, I tried my best to defend our seminary and its curriculum. As the seminary became more polarized toward the left, our churches became more nervous about theological education. Yet if anyone talked of accountability of professors to Scripture, tradition or church discipline, howls would arise about academic freedom. The revisionists were gaining ground in the university while losing ground with the grassroots.

Two brilliant women were invited into our faculty while I was either incapacitated or on leave. They both had made widely recognized contributions to knowledge through their writing, but now faculty members were requiring that every new nominee for any faculty position had to pass the feminist litmus test. I who had once thought of myself as sincerely pro-feminist became stereotyped as uninterested in justice. Each new appointment brought the activist majority increased clout until I was a lonely voice amid a chorus of indignant advocates. Though I thought of myself as politically realistic and savvy, my detractors were very clever and outmaneuvered me at almost every level by utilizing the emerging majority now present in faculty meetings. In many faculty meetings and votes I was the only one who raised questions about the directions in which we were going.

During the time I was on leave, the faculty had written a legalistic and speech-limiting fairness code that required all students in all of their sub-mitted papers to replace he or she language with awkward third person substitutes. I followed its rules precisely but was not willing to resort to ridiculous grammatical constructions. I was ordered by our feminist dean to appear for an inquisition. Karen Brown and two of her well-instructed students grilled me on my negligence in language policy rules. I knew the rules and followed them, but I was not shy in setting forth reasons why the language rules tempted the teaching of bad grammar and the exclusion of such crucial words in Christian teaching as "Son of God."

In that atmosphere many evangelical, Catholic and Orthodox students felt marginalized and badgered by those who were promoting a rigid brand of supposed inclusiveness that became brutal in its rejections. Po-litical correctness penetrated the entire curriculum and controlled almost every syllable uttered. Liberty of conscience was not fully respected.

As convenor of the area of theology in the graduate school, one of my duties was to assess the theological competence of candidates for faculty positions. When an opening occurred for a new faculty appointment in the area of theology, all faculty were invited to suggest nominees, but the theology area had special responsibility to review and evaluate fitness.

As a new position actually did become available in theology, the strong contingent of savvy feminist colleagues set forth as their nominee the most controversial epitome of theological feminism at that time, ar-guably the leading feminist voice in North America. In my view she deserved a hearing in which she could set forth her reasoning about issues basic to the teaching of theology on God, providence, salvation, the human condition and the church, since she was being interviewed for a position in systematic theology.

I myself had established a solid record of support of women's rights and causes consistent with Christian teaching and Methodist church polity. I had especially fought to protect women and girls from sexual trafficking, domestic violence, sexual harassment and sexual assault. I had supported affirmative action as defined by the courts, and I had supported equal pay for women. In addition I had supported gender neutrality in English as long as it did not require impossible syntax or attack biblical language about God the Father and God the Son.

As a scholar I had written a book on Phoebe Palmer, arguably the most influential woman of the nineteenth century in American religion. I had long supported the ordination of women, and I had nurtured good and wholesome personal and working relations with the gay and lesbian members of our faculty.

So I set about to give due diligence in carefully reading this nominee's writings, in assessing the balance of her theological temperament and her capacity for collegiality. With the exception of her dissertation, almost all of her writings were focused narrowly on issues of confrontational feminist advocacy. She viewed the Bible as thoroughly sexist. She regarded Christology as inherently anti-Semitic. She sought a radical critique of traditional Christian theology based on gender oppression analysis. She envisioned a wholesale reimaging of all things biblical and Christian from a controversial point of view that focused on male oppression. Her view of social evils such as racism, sexism, heterosexism and classism largely hinged on her allegations of a hierarchy of male domination as the centerpiece of all classic Christian teaching. Though born a Catholic she could not teach at a Catholic institution because of her constant defense of abortion policies and reproductive rights, so she was apparently interested in teaching at a Methodist seminary. Yet she had views contrary to the church polity in the tradition of Wesleyan views of sexuality. This was the candidate proposed to take a central role in teaching Christian theology.

I asked her reasonable questions on the classic Christian teaching on the sacrament of marriage and the covenant bonding of one man with one woman as the basis for nurturing children, on her enigmatic dissertation on Gregory of Nazianzus, on the Trinity and on the biblical language of Son of God, Son of Man. I was relieved when she was not selected, but I paid a high price for asking questions that seemed to me central to the decision we were asked to make. That interview did not dissuade my colleagues from organizing ever more insistently to elect new faculty with similar views as hers. Amazingly it became a virtual heresy to raise basic questions about the theological reasoning of any faculty proposed to teach theology.

That interview was in my view a pivotal moment in the history of Drew Seminary. As the feminist voice gradually became the majority and feminists were tenured, they gained complete control. It caused every subsequent nominee to be examined largely on the basis of feminist issues: gender language, abortion rights, reproductive rights and sexual ethics. I remained at Drew largely for my graduate students, many of whom were hungry for substantive classic Christian historical inquiry.

The well-appointed faculty club, a dining area with round maple tables just large enough to gather six to eight faculty members in close discussion, had been the perennial hangout for faculty dialogue, and I enjoyed being there for debate after debate. Often around our table were Merrill Maguire Skaggs,[3] who was the graduate school dean; Neal Reamer, author of numerous books on the history of democratic theory, genocide, Madison, Marx and Reinhold Niebuhr; and Shirley Sugarman, convenor of the Aquinas faculty seminar.[4] My most enduring partners in dialogue were Harvard educated John Ollom in physics, and the wonderful Dr. George de Stevens, the inventor of hydrochlorothiazide, which is the most widely used diuretic for lowering high blood pressure and is a medication that helped keep me alive for more than two decades. Those were a few of the cast of characters I lunched with regularly. Most of them were not teaching in religious studies but were working in scattered academic fields, often with interdisciplinary models of research. I grew closer to and learned more from these very bright colleagues in fields distant to religious studies.

My closest, most affable and congenial colleague during my thirty-three years at Drew was unquestionably James O'Kane in sociology. An observant Catholic, he unpretentiously embodied traditional Catholic teaching in its most winsome and convivial way.[5] While Will Herberg introduced me to the wisdom of Judaism and applied that wisdom brilliantly to contemporary culture, Jim O'Kane introduced me to the joy of daily Catholic practice, moral life and classic Catholic catechesis.[6]

For three seasons I had my own television show on New Jersey Public Television titled *Authors*. We had our own production facility at Drew University. It was Drew's first attempt to produce a regular television program. I focused especially on authors in the New York–New Jersey area who had recently published books. This program extended my public dialogue with many whom I otherwise would not have met. Among my guests were publisher Malcolm Forbes, sportswriter Roger Kahn, Martin Luther King Jr.'s biographer David Garrow and a notable stream of feminist writers.

Places of serenity. Then there was the haven of the *tertulia*, a Spanish name for a small gathering of like-minded friends with mutual interests. We always met at a quiet restaurant that offered us an informal place for sharing ideas, opinions and repartee. It was a place of respite for good wine, superb food and hassle-free talk.[7] Dubbed the "Triple O Gang," our tertulia was composed of Ollom, O'Kane and Oden.[8] We were the three Os who came from West Virginia, Brooklyn and Oklahoma. Besides luncheons at excellent restaurants, the three of us enjoyed junkets into New York and elsewhere—sometimes a Civil War battle site or a walk across the Brooklyn Bridge or checking out interesting Brooklyn gravesites such as that of Phoebe Palmer. Those were the colleagues who filled my life in New Jersey with fellowship, revelry and an idiosyncratic sort of spiritual formation.

I loved inhabiting the Drew Library. I was usually either in a windowless basement carrel or in a quiet office overlooking Tipple Pond. More than any other place, the library carrel became my retreat, the place to be alone with my thoughts, to read the classics, reflect and write.[9] I tried to keep my research and reading time as separate as possible from my teaching. I enjoyed meeting students informally in the coffee room or in my office, but when I was writing in my hidden carrel I did not particularly want to hear a knock on the door. Everything I needed was in the library, so that is where I usually wrote, disappearing into the stacks by way of an elevator whose sign said: "My name is Otto. Punch me gently."

Though never much of a techie, I became the first Drew faculty member to attempt to use computer technology for teaching and writing. When the university administration shifted to digital information in the 1980s, I was permitted to have a "dumb computer," which was connected to the new CPU for the university administration. That allowed me to edit from my office digital manuscripts that could be printed out on large perforated paper. I had attended an electronics fair in 1982 when the Franklin Ace 100 was on display, and I decided that I must get one and learn how to use it. Self-taught, I used it for two years before I upgraded to an Apple II with its 5¼-inch floppy disks slotted into an external drive. It took hundreds of those disks to write my *Systematic Theology*.

The outdoor place of serenity for me was the large undulating native forest that was a part of the Drew campus. "The Forest" had been used as the identifying location for many books written at Drew in the nineteenth and twentieth centuries. In the forest, the deep quiet valleys helped me gain composure.

The Aquinas Interdisciplinary Seminar brought me into dialogue with British poet and philosopher Owen Barfield, author of *Saving the Appearances: A Study in Idolatry*. Barfield and C. S. Lewis became close friends in 1919 and remained so for forty-four years. Barfield was instrumental in converting Lewis to theism in addition to serving as his legal adviser and trustee. Barfield was a key figure among the Inklings of Oxford. He had an amazing range of wisdom on literature, poetry and especially on the history of language, a subject about which he knew more than anyone else I knew. Another dialogue partner on the history of language was Roger Wescott, a master of etymologies.

At a time when I was struggling to understand historical continuities, those conversations with Barfield and Wescott were formative for me. They helped me understand the transmission of tradition through human speech, deepening my understanding of social continuities, the transmission of ideas and the nature of language. The Aquinas Seminar hosted semester-long resident scholars, including eminent social theorists and cultural observers like David Bakan, Philip Rieff and William I. Thompson. I was most grateful for personal time with Nobel Prize winner and holocaust survivor Elie Wiesel.

Looking out on the spacious picture-book campus of Drew contributed greatly to the joy of my working life. Red brick Georgian style buildings built between 1834 and 1899 were generously spaced. My first Drew office was in historic Seminary Hall, built in 1898. It was a turn-of-the-century collegiate gothic building constructed by Italian masons and artisans, with walnut paneled stairways along with portraits of the early Drew faculty. Its stone portico featured a Guastavino tile ceiling. In the basement of Seminary Hall my friends and I gathered for coffee in Kirby Lounge and for worship under the high ceiling of Craig Chapel. The chapel had a balcony entered through a rickety hidden passageway which I took when late to morning services.

When a large nineteenth-century lecture hall for biblical studies was divided into two Seminary Hall faculty offices, I inherited a spacious, high ceiling first floor office. It was roomy until I filled it up with my books floor to ceiling. I added more and more books as the years went by. By the 1980s the shelves were so high I needed a ladder. Upon Edward Leroy Long's retirement, the largest of all of the faculty offices became available in the three-story red brick Wesley House. During my last years at Drew I occupied that wonderful historic office looking out on the lush landscape from the bay windows of the second floor. From my desk I could see the broad tree-lined space of the gated entryway into the university. That was the gate virtually reduplicated by the Methodist Seminary in Seoul, an aesthetically beautiful echo of Drew. It was one of Drew's most historic buildings, built in the 1890s as the residence for Drew presidents. As it turned out, I needed that space to preserve my extensive working library in a single location.

One day I got a knock on my door. An engineering inspection had occurred and everything had to be moved out, as the entire house was under the strain of the weight of my books. The floors of the historic residence were insufficiently braced for my library.

THE GRATIFYING CAREER OF GRADUATE TEACHING

Mentoring dissertation research. In dissertation counsel I was in my element. I was steadily advising on the conception, organization, chapter-by-chapter drafting and defense of PhD dissertations. I worked with them to move their dissertations to publication whenever feasible, and toward recommending them for teaching appointments. Directing dissertation research was never boring. I wanted my best graduate students to benefit not only from my teaching, critical methods and dialogue, but most of all for the fact that I was a stickler for primary sources.

I deliberately tried to guide dissertations toward scholarly publication, preferably in full-length scholarly books rather than into occasional scholarly articles few would ever read. I took pleasure in seeing Drew PhDs take on leading roles in writing, teaching and as deans and presidents of colleges and seminaries from Korea and Japan to Central America and Ghana.[10] Out of those years many Drew dissertations were published in university presses, trade presses and religious presses.[11] I had the privilege of directing dissertations on Leo the Great, Gregory of Nyssa, Chrysostom and Augustine.[12] Many lifelong friendships emerged out of the bonding I enjoyed with PhD students through the searching discussions required by dissertation research.[13]

Born in Ireland, Finbar O'Kane landed on my doorstep as a PhD student.[14] Finbar was uproariously articulate but had a serious mental block when writing his dissertation, though he was a born writer of poetry. He wrote all of the time, but he was intimidated when it came to organizing his research into a viable PhD thesis. I was his dissertation director, but did not get anything from him that looked like a cohesive dissertation. After years passed, as we discussed this, he told me he kept his writing under his bed. When the seven-year time limit for completing a dissertation drew near, I finally told him to get all the papers under his bed and let me see them. Reluctantly he brought me a Thomas Wolfe-size pile of papers on his thoughts on everything. Some looked like James Joyce sentences. Some were brilliant. Out of that I began to help him shape his remarkable insights into a viable dissertation on Irish history and language. Nobel Prize-winner Seamus Heaney of Harvard, who served with me on Finbar's dissertation committee, was delighted with what he read, and approved.

A century after the founding of Korean Protestantism, the brightest of Korean students were flocking to Drew as their preferred American university for higher education, in part because Drew had played a major role in the founding of the first university in Korea. In May 1884, the whole student body of Drew seminary walked in a parade to the Madison train station to give a sendoff to one of their fellow graduates, Henry Appenzeller, for his unprecedented appointment to faraway service in the hidden land of Korea. There they sang, prayed and wished him bon voyage on the first Protestant mission to Korea. Thereafter the name Appenzeller was venerated in Korea, and for Korean Christians his memory has been forever linked with Drew. Appenzeller's work led to the earliest Western-quality schools and universities in Korea.[15]

This is why my literary efforts found their first Asian translations in Korea. My relationship with Korean doctoral students continued steadily over thirty-plus years. They have become leading theologians in Korea. *Kerygma and Counseling* and *Pastoral Theology* were the first to appear in Korean, followed at last by the twenty-nine-volume patristic commentary.[16] I marveled at how in my early years at Drew my labors in pastoral studies had been so quickly taking root on the other side of the globe.

I have outlived many of the faculty with whom I began at Drew, and most of my colleagues among the Kent Fellows and American Theological Society.[17] In my early years at Drew I was privileged to share an office with the distinguished African American professor George Kelsey, the teacher of Martin Luther King Jr.[18] I could not have wished for better administrators than Paul Hardin (president), James Kirby (seminary dean), Bard Thompson (graduate school dean), Thomas Ogletree (seminary dean) and Merrill Skaggs (dean of the graduate school).[19] My closest colleagues at Drew were in the Graduate School. They included

Oxford educated Dean James Pain and Gabriel Coless, a Benedictine historical theologian. I had two important colleagues at Drew from the Netherlands: Pieter de Jong and Johann Noordsij.[20] Pieter was my closest colleague in theology before and after he became Dean of the Theological School. We had common interests in Teilhard de Chardin, Barth studies, Catholic theology, and existential theology. Ed Long was an especially resilient and insightful partner in dialogue, an unusually wise man with a tough mind and a soft heart.[21]

When I was awarded an American Theological Schools Faculty Fellowship to work on Kierkegaard studies, I spent a semester in the stacks of the University of Texas Library and the Humanities Research Center in Austin, with an office in the Austin Presbyterian Theological Seminary. Although I had been teaching Kierkegaard seminars for years and had lived in constant companionship with his authorship, the perennial Kierkegaardian side of my work did not bear visible literary fruit until I completed a work for the Princeton University Press on Kierkegaard's parables, which was fully two decades in the making.[22]

Resisting the untimely challenge to classic Methodist doctrinal standards. As a born and bred Methodist I could not ignore the follies of the Church that had ordained me. That made it necessary for me to attend the United Methodist General Conference of 1988, where legislative interpretations of the Doctrines and Discipline were debated. That was the crucial year for deciding whether or not to revise established doctrinal standards for the largest Protestant mainline church. The previous General Conference had set aside a large budget for a special committee on the UMC Theological Task. Like sharks, the revisionists were hungering to slacken off on traditional Methodist teaching. My dean at Drew, Thomas W. Ogletree, was on the drafting committee. Since he consulted with me at key stages of the drafting, I became deeply involved in that editing process. I sought to preserve the classical standards that had been in place since Wesley's time, rather than subject the church to an even more hazardous debate over revising them amid the high tide of wild theological experimentalism. Who knows what might have popped out of that Pandora's Box.

Since 1784 the standards of doctrine for American Methodists have been clear. The standard of preaching is Wesley's *Standard Sermons*, the standard model for interpretation of Scripture found in Wesley's *Notes upon the New Testament* and the standard of ecumenical unity within the churches of the Reformation in the *Twenty-Five Articles of Religion*. By constitutional restriction those doctrinal standards are not amendable except by the most unlikely process that requires a vote of "three-fourths of all the members of the several annual conferences," followed by a super majority of two-thirds of the General Conference. A binding legal document called The Plan of Union of 1968 which united Methodists with the Evangelical United Brethren had specified that "Wesley's Sermons and Notes were understood specifically to be included in the present existing and established standards of doctrine." All of that is background for why I became energetically engaged in a three-year debate on Wesleyan doctrinal standards.

The leading initiative for minimizing the standards came from one of Methodism's leading Wesley scholars, Richard Heitzenrater of Duke. He had proposed that the familiar doctrinal standards be abridged to include only the Articles of Religion, excluding Wesley's *Standard Sermons* and *Notes*. I had to make a difficult decision as to whether I would argue a case against one of Methodism's best known scholars or let it go by. Since I could not in good conscience let it go by, I plunged into extensive documentary research and mustered the historical arguments and disciplinary grounds for retaining the traditional standards. That required my taking the challenge all the way to the General Conference, the overall legislative body for 7.7 million United Methodists. To most it was self-evident that the two hundred years of repeated confirmation had made it clear that the standards had been well-defined from the beginning. For the first year of the debate everything seemed to be trending against the traditional standards. To turn the tide I had to set forth the evidence in a full-length book, *Doctrinal Standards in the Wesleyan Tradition*.[23] I had to discontinue everything else I was doing on the *Systematic Theology* in order to get that historical evidence before the church legislators before it was too late. That defense was also pertinent to other

Wesleyan-based churches who shared much of the same doctrinal tradition: the Free Methodists, the Wesleyan Church, the Nazarenes and the African American Methodist church traditions.

Professor Heitzenrater's opinion appeared in the *Quarterly Review* of 1985.[24] To the surprise of many, he argued that Wesley's *Sermons* and *Notes* were not legal doctrinal standards at all and had not been since 1785. The fact that everyone thinks they are, he said, was a mistake of historical judgment. He thought he had "conclusive evidence" that the General Conference of 1808 "did not understand its standards of doctrine to include Wesley's *Sermons* and *Notes*." His supposed "conclusive evidence" was based upon an ambiguous motion made by Francis Ward that the *Sermons* and *Notes* should be retained but also that John Fletcher's *Checks Against Antinomianism* be added to them, thus changing entirely the pattern established by Wesley. That interpretation of the rejected Ward motion would have been a huge innovation and prompted me to write a response.[25] My first efforts did not stem the tide.

No book covering all the relevant sources had been written since the nineteenth century. To establish the traditional argument, I had to do a lot of digging in the United Methodist Archives, which happily were located only a few steps away from my library carrel. With the help of Kenneth Rowe I found the original handwritten manuscript of the General Conference of 1808. The puzzle was figuring out why the 1808 Conference struck the defeated Ward motion from the record, as if to not only defeat it but eliminate it from memory.[26] Heitzenrater argued that that disputed notation was conclusive evidence that the Conference was not willing to go on record as defining its standards of doctrine in terms of any documents other than the Articles, a huge leap in logic.

I took my arguments to the drafting committee. Happily they were not willing to defend the Heitzenrater speculation on the Ward motion. More important was the evidence I found in the Plan of Union affirming the *Sermons* and *Notes* as doctrinal standards for the unification of the Methodist Church with the Evangelical United Brethren Church in 1968. Once it was established that the Plan of Union was a legally binding statement defining the standards, my case was largely won.[27] I felt entirely vindicated when the General Conference once again confirmed that the *Sermons* and *Notes* were explicitly covered by the First Restrictive Rule, which precludes the Conference from amending our "established standards of doctrine." That welcome decision at General Conference resulted in a rewriting of the doctrinal standards section of the Discipline so as to make clear that the *Standards Sermons* and *Notes* remain in place and are protected by the constitution from further legislative tinkering.[28]

Why tell that story? First, it was an intriguing detective story involving disputed manuscript evidence, insider politics, ideological motives, legislative debate and parliamentary maneuvering. Second, because my life story cannot be told without that narrative. Omitting it would miss a significant episode that made a difference. But, third, for me it is the only occasion where I have had a significant effect on a conciliar doctrinal decision that had decisive importance for the future of the Wesleyan theological tradition. Now I feel that I have not performed any service more crucial to the Methodist church than setting forth that evidence in a timely way. My scholarly work has never before or since been focused on church legislative matters, but in that case I was gratified that I was a part of retaining the classical Wesleyan doctrinal standards in my own community of faith.

This caused me to ponder the ironies of providence. I was focused on patristic writings, so why did it fall to me to protect the Wesleyan standards of doctrine? Amid the permissive tendencies of the United Methodist Church, I finally appreciated that the doctrinal standards were the bedrock during a wild period of theological unruliness. Why was I diverted from patristic studies to Methodist doctrine? The answer lies with Mr. Wesley himself, who was a beneficiary of the Oxford revival of patristic studies. He became deeply grounded in the ancient Christian writers and the consensual tradition of ecumenical teaching. He longed for the Societies under his care to not further divide the unity of the church but to maintain her classic ecumenical teachings.

As a followup to this episode, I wrote a full-length study of John Wesley's systematic theology, titled *John Wesley's Scriptural Christianity: A Plain Exposition of His Teaching on Christian Doctrine*, also under the

Zondervan imprint. Later in 2010–2014 I wrote a four-volume work on *John Wesley's Teaching* that discussed the entire corpus of Wesley's homilies, essays, journals and letters organized by themes that are rooted in his own systematic organization of Christian teaching in the first edition preface of his *Works*.[29]

THE CONTROVERSY STIRRED BY *AGENDA FOR THEOLOGY*

The awakening of the young fogeys. In the decade after the *Agenda for Theology* was published in 1979, I was frequently queried as to the intent and practical implications of my call for a postmodern form of classic consensual Christianity. I needed repeatedly to defend and clarify the terms of my proposal on modernity, postmodernity and paleo-orthodoxy. The decade of the 1980s offered an opportunity to begin to carry out the agenda I had proposed in practical ways.

Fogey is a term of derision within the context of modernity. It soon became a term of endearment among young paleo-orthodox believers. A "young fogey" was one who had slogged through the rigors of university education only to become disillusioned by its illusions. They were fogeys in the sense that they loved the most ancient ways, while they themselves were young and being made new. Everywhere I went during the 1980s I met those young people. Whatever their physical age, they were youthful in the hunger for ancient Christian wisdom.

They dived into the study of the patristic writers, the politics of repentance and the celebration of divine providence in history. They were smart, critical, intensely traditional and astute in the examination of evidence. Many told me how they had laughed and groaned their way through *Agenda for Theology* and that until then they had not been able to take seriously any talk of orthodoxy of any kind. Those strong young believers were starved for simple Christian truth telling. Mostly in their twenties or thirties, they showed up in my public presentations and many private conversations, and my correspondence with them increased exponentially throughout the 1980s. The most useful method for them to make their way through the academic maze was social location analysis, where the social location of academics could be shown to affect their research.

Most of what I was learning in reframing *The Agenda for Theology* was coming from young people thirty years younger than I who were searching for reliable interpretations of classic Scripture texts. They had been through a disappointing, expensive university education in which they had excelled, otherwise they would not be in a graduate program, but an education which they were beginning to recognize as largely ignorant of classic Christianity

When I jokingly dubbed them the "young fogeys," the term persisted.[30] I had never heard the term before.[31] Although the term has been erroneously attributed in Britain to Alan Watkins's writing in 1984 in *The Spectator*, it had an earlier history of being debated in American circles since my *Agenda for Theology* in 1979.[32]

Academic elites were seeking upward social mobility within the university, media and culture. While they often viewed themselves as value neutral, they were vulnerable to being trapped in a highly biased value system. I took delight in pursuing a "knowledge elite analysis" of theological trends and commended it to them.[33] Since my Yale days I had been deeply immersed in social location analysis.[34] This is an inquiry whose central question is, "How does your location in society affect your value system?" I urged my students to follow the pecuniary interests on why good Christian teaching had turned into bad historical analysis. Peter Berger's analysis of the "knowledge elites" has been decisive for me ever since I heard him present it in a New York lecture. If the liberal university elites could use sociology of knowledge arguments against classical Christianity, I could use those same arguments to describe the economic interests of the university elites. This was an easy move, but very telling.

Inhabiting the classic Christian mind. When articulated gently, empathically and with good wit, ancient Christian acumen is almost always perceived as a useful contribution to knowledge. It is perceived as "new" only because it has been recently rediscovered. For moderns, ancient truth is only admissible in the court of modernity if it dresses itself in the garb of modern premises. For me that is the garb I have gladly cast aside. I am not convinced that classic wisdom has no caché in the current political realm. Informed believers live within a longer time frame than a book season or an election cycle.

On the invitation of David Neff and Harold Smith, I was welcomed by James I. Packer, George Brushaber and Robert Cooley into the senior circle of editorial leadership of *Christianity Today*. We were assigned the task of keeping watch over the theological quality of America's most widely read religious journal. *Christianity Today's* readership was centrist evangelical, including not only Reformed, Baptist and Lutheran writers, but also Wesleyans, charismatics and Pentecostals. Not so well-known is that many of the *CT* leaders were deeply nurtured by Anglican evangelicals in the British tradition of John Stott and J. I. Packer.

While reaching out from my liberal university base to conservative evangelicals, I was surprised that I was also gaining a growing number of appreciative Catholic partners in dialogue through unexpected networks. Young Catholics were reading *Agenda*. They had not seen many works by Protestant scholars that had dug deeply into the earliest Catholic and Orthodox sources. They could easily see that my key sources were those writings of the primitive church of the ancient Greek East and the ancient Latin West, along with the magisterial Reformation of Luther, Calvin and Wesley. Catholics became interested in the renewal of Protestant theology grounded in pre-Reformation exegesis. They quickly grasped how important its rediscovery was for the unity of the body of Christ worldwide. Three Catholics who first grasped how important the evangelical dialogue was for Catholics were Joseph Ratzinger, Avery Dulles and Richard Neuhaus.

Rediscovering classic pastoral reasoning. By 1980 I had already spent two decades with pastoral issues, but I still felt that I had not completed my task and wondered whether I needed to invest more time in finishing the work I had started. I was invited to serve on the editorial advisory board of the *Journal of Pastoral Care* in 1980. I was still a critic of most of the popular directions prevailing in pastoral care. Fee-based pastoral counseling was increasing, despite my protests, but I cherished those friendships. In 1980 I relaunched my attempt to carry out my intention to provide classic sources for the renewal of pastoral theology.

My continued dialogue on pastoral care required four steps, all involving writing projects: First, in *Care of Souls in the Classical Tradition* (Fortress), I reintroduced Gregory the Great to pastors. Second, in *Pastoral Theology: Essentials of Ministry* (Harper), I wrote a textbook that systematically treated all the perennial issues of soul care from patristic perspectives. Third, in *Guilt Free* (Harper), I took on the questions of guilt and forgiveness. Those were all different approaches to a single subject: recovery of classic pastoral wisdom.

The fourth and most demanding step was to bring that agenda to a fitting conclusion in the publication of the four-volume series on Classical Pastoral Care (Crossroad-Continuum) presenting textual evidence of pastoral wisdom from Irenaeus to Augustine to Thomas Aquinas to Luther.

Those pastoral projects occupied at least half my literary energies for a decade. The other half was largely dedicated to systematic theology.

Agenda for Theology had set forth a blueprint for the classical reconception of biblical exegesis, historical and systematic theology. That general blueprint needed a place to start. The place I first sought to rebuild it was in *Pastoral Theology: Essentials of Ministry*. I began writing it 1979, and it was published by Harper in 1983. The return to pre-Protestant and classic Protestant sources became accepted practice after decades of faddism.

My motive in that book was to distill the best ideas of the two millennia of ecumenical Christian thinking concerning what pastors are and do. *Pastoral Theology* sought to develop an internally consistent grasp of classical Christian thinking about the pastoral task.[35]

No systematic pastoral theology had come out of my liberal church tradition since Washington Gladden's *The Christian Pastor* (1898). Already with Gladden, those classic roots were greatly eroded. Growing neglect of classic sources intensified throughout the twentieth century.[36] My intent was to find roots in the earliest Christian centuries for every major pastoral task.[37] I sought to plant those seeds without harming the valid achievements of contemporary pastoral care.[38] The later pastoral writers based their work on the earliest patristic writers. I knew that if

I held closely to them, it would produce a very different kind of pastoral care than those of the twentieth century.

To my surprise, I found that the classic pastoral tradition held consensual answers to virtually all of the relevant questions of contemporary soul care. Caring for another's soul means to seek the health of the inner life of the person, which involves the mending and nurturing of that personal center of the self, viewing God as the primordial giver of care. Pastoral counsel is soul care in the sense that it seeks to address the inner wellsprings of personal decisions with wisdom, prudence and love. To care for souls means to be accountable for shepherding the inner life of persons through the crises of emotional conflict and growth in responsiveness to God.

Soul is what distinguishes a living being from rocks.[39] That the human soul has the unique capacity among all creatures to behold and reflect the mystery of God is the subject of pastoral care. Tragically, soul is capable of stumbling and falling, of abusing freedom, and of being led into captivity. *Psyche* (soul) is the seat of the emotive and religious life, and of the person's relationship with God.[40]

In the 1980s the pastoral office was fast becoming co-opted into other vocational roles: administrative, political, therapeutic and teaching. The pastor has a special relation with the flock which is different from the usual relationship that prevails between physician-patient, teacher-student, leader-follower, attorney-client and public official-citizen. All of those roles are in some sense analogous to various aspects of pastoral care, yet no single one completely encompasses parish ministry. The difference: the pastor uniquely accepts the call of God to take full responsibility for soul care wherever needed. The minister is "set apart" for a vocation of shepherding souls.[41]

The modern pastoral office hungers to relearn from the classic pastoral office that the Christian community is a covenant community bonded not by politics, race, blood or ideology, but by covenant with God the Father as made known through his Son. Jesus regarded his disciples as sisters and brothers, the Christian community as a nurturing family, and the faithful as children of God. In a local congregation the pastor is called to guide that family in spirit, to care for each member, to wisely nurture that process and to help each member of the family of faith grow to fuller maturity. Such a task requires special personal qualities that can be sought, studied, cultivated and improved, but only by praying for grace freely to acquire them.

In *Pastoral Theology* I sought to reclaim the biblical teaching of admonition. Admonition is a requirement of love because freedom is prone to sin, and because correction needs the wider perspective of caring partners. Solitary self-correction is prone to self-deception. If we are going to live out our lives together in responsible community, we ask accountability among each other commensurable with our age, station and capacities for empathy.[42]

The aim of admonition is the restoration into fellowship of persons estranged from the grace of God. One member of the body of Christ looks to another to help him or her grasp where misdeeds or misjudgments may lie in order to mature more fully toward manifesting our humanity in Christ. Good counsel, called *nouthesia* (admonition) in the New Testament, is required to redress grievances, repair hurts, repay debts and seek reparation.

Gentle admonition is grounded in the empathy that is patterned in the incarnation. It lives out of that love which "covers a multitude of sins." Timely admonition is a gift of the Spirit. God loves us enough to search our hearts when we go awry. Pastoral admonition gives active form to the promptings of the Spirit in our own hearts. The pastor prays for the power to instruct conscience, break through deceptions and heal inner wounds.[43]

Classical pastoral care. Crossroad-Continuum was among the most perceptive and imaginative Catholic publishers in North America, promoting thoughtful theological reflection in the post-Vatican II setting. It was spawned by the huge international publishing group Herder and Herder, based in Germany. The English-speaking expression of that effort was led by the remarkable editor and author Justus George Lawler. Shortly after *Agenda for Theology*, I met with Lawler to discuss ways of introducing classic pastoral sources to both Protestant and Catholic

readers and pastors who had been too long enamored with psychotherapeutic models as a resource for ministry. We all wondered how it could
possibly work for a Protestant author to write for a largely Catholic audience. It was an unheralded leap into a fad-laden pastoral environment
utilizing only established ancient and classical writers.

It took four volumes to complete, published over the years between
1985 and 1988. The series was called Classic Pastoral Care. It first had a
largely Catholic readership and then later had a widely Protestant readership through a Baker Books reprint of all four volumes in 1994. The
four titles provide an indication of the vast arena of this classic literature:
Becoming a Minister (vol. 1), *Ministry Through Word and Sacrament* (vol.
2), *Pastoral Counsel* (vol. 3) and *Crisis Ministries* (vol. 4).[44] The result was
an unprecedented collection of classical sources for a modern pastoral
audience addicted to novelty. It required vision for a large international
publishing group to sponsor the publication of a multivolume series on
classical pastoral care by an author who was largely unknown to its large
Catholic readership.

No one could have predicted the excellent outcome for the four
volumes. They showed that there was an unexpected readiness in
modern Catholic and Protestant readers to dig into classic pastoral
sources after years of trendiness. That series played a major role in
turning the tide from modern fixations to classic wisdom. Each
volume was organized systematically and logically around the prevailing issues that have arisen in every century of pastoral teaching.
Classic gemlike extracts were threaded together by brief introductions
and comments that flowed in a sequential argument. Taken together,
they were a sourcebook of perennial wisdom for pastoral care. It
showed how powerful the classic pastoral tradition had been and how
relevant it has remained.

At last the research efforts I had initiated on patristic sources in the
1970s and proposed as an agenda in 1979 were beginning to bear fruit.
Those volumes became a staple historical resource for both Catholic and
Protestant pastors, counselors and therapists for over three decades.

STAYING THE COURSE

In 1988 Stan Gundry with Zondervan thought that *Agenda for Theology* (Harper, 1979) might have missed its audience with evangelicals. So I substantially revised it for an audience that deliberately included evangelicals under a new title: *After Modernity . . . What?* (1990).

The Zondervan book helped break the barriers in publishing between liberal and evangelical readers, walls that were far higher at that time than they are now. Harper had reached many mainline and some conservative readers, but the Zondervan edition was gladly received by a new evangelical readership that trusted the Zondervan imprint.

It was introduced by the leading evangelical theologian, J. I. Packer. With his encouragement I found a great many evangelicals who were ready to receive the promise of the recovery of patristic exegesis and teaching. For many it was their first introduction to unapologetic paleo-orthodoxy. Remarkably for me it yielded a huge new circle of close personal friends and many readers on three continents: Europe, Australia and North America. The new book helped me connect with many kinds of evangelicals including Reformed, Anglican, Lutheran, Wesleyan and charismatic. They could recognize their own traditions as rooted in the early Christian writers.

This taught me that I had to try to write for three audiences who were not on usual speaking terms with each other: mainline (Harper), evangelical (Zondervan) and Catholic (Crossroad-Continuum) readers. The dialogue that emerged was part of what prompted Richard Neuhaus and Charles Colson to inaugurate Evangelicals and Catholics Together, which unleashed a more fertile form of evangelical-ecumenical dialogue. With the unbridling of that new breadth of dialogue, I was constantly on the travel and lecture circuit interpreting that phenomenal development.

Few mainline authors before 1989 had been willing to risk their reputations in publishing under an evangelical imprint. Thereafter many of the most astute mainline Protestant theologians would find it acceptable to publish with evangelical presses, among them Richard John Neuhaus, Robert Wilken, Carl Braaten, Stan Hauerwas, N. T. Wright and James H. Charlesworth. Although I paid a high price among my liberal colleagues in the 1980s for breaking through those barriers, it was a price worth paying for all of the new friends I made.

An unexpected outgrowth of *Agenda for Theology* and *Pastoral Theology* was an invitation from Westminster John Knox Press to become involved in a new commentary series called *Interpretation: A Bible Commentary for Teaching and Preaching.* Its coeditors Paul Achtemeier and James L. Mays had noticed that I was interested in regrounding biblical studies in the texts of early Christian exegesis. They asked me to write the volume on 1-2 Timothy and Titus. Since then that series has gone into many editions. In it I sought to show how the leading classic Christian writers wrote powerfully on the pastoral epistles with preaching values that are still applicable today.

A map for the journey of the 1980s. There was a pattern of cohesion that steadily unfolded after the *Agenda for Theology.* Since my life has been so closely interwoven with my writing, it is pertinent to recapitulate the chronology of the writings of the 1980s. This path moved in a cohesive sequence through these phases: *Agenda for Theology* (1979), *Pastoral Theology: Essentials for Ministry* (1980s), *Systematic Theology* (1985–1993), The Classical Pastoral Care Series (1985–1988), and toward conceptualizing the recovery of patristic exegesis (1988–1993).

Most of my PhD research seminars in the 1980s were in patristic studies, systematic theology and pastoral theology. The central thread that united all of those was the desire to reground modern ecumenical theology in ancient ecumenical teaching.

In 1989 the Evangelical Theological Society asked me to tell the story of my turn from modern to classic Christian thinking. That plenary address was the first time I had attempted to gather my thoughts on what had happened to me before and after the transformation of the early 1970s.

My address was first presented in New Orleans for the 1989 ETS Conference and later published as "The Long Journey Home" for the *Journal of the Evangelical Theological Society* in 1991. I poured out my heart about the gracious path I was on. I presented the sharp contrast between the overarching unity of the trajectory I had been taking in the 1970s and 1980s that were so different from all my wandering paths of the 1960s.

Next the *Christian Century* wanted an autobiographical piece from me. Every decade since 1939 the *Christian Century* had sponsored a series of articles on the primary preoccupation of the journal: "How My Mind Has Changed." Notice the policy bent of the series: the editorial passion is not on continuity but change. This is a sure clue to *Century's* quintessential modernity.[45] Their direction was exactly opposite to mine. So when asked to write my essay in that series, I focused not on how my mind had changed but how my mind had remained the same. Now in line with the apostolic tradition, my focus has been on continuity, not change, ever since I grew to love the ancient Christian writers. Before that my mind was constantly changing, since I was trying to keep up with accommodating to modernity. After rediscovering the ancient Christian writers, my mind has steadily focused on making no new contribution to theology, but to adhere closely to the unchangeable, irreversible and unalterable apostolic tradition. The *Christian Century* piece was titled "Then and Now: The Recovery of Patristic Wisdom." I enjoyed answering their question exactly as they had stated it by recognizing the unchanging center of Christian teaching.

In 1984 I talked with editor John Shopp about my next Harper project after *Agenda for Theology* and *Pastoral Theology*. He was aware that there had not been a major systematic theology written since Tillich (1951–1963), and it was dominated by a nonhistorical Jesus and a view of God as "Being itself." He urged me to think about writing one. Knowing what I had done in pastoral theology, he hoped I might do something similar in systematic theology. That conversation presented a major vocational challenge to me.[46]

It is fitting here to note that I have had the good fortune of working with brilliant editors over my fifty-plus years as a writer. I could not have done all that I have done without them. As a young writer and a child of mainline liberal Protestantism, my early editors were largely with the mainline presses, Abingdon, Westminster John Knox and Fortress. I had to learn how to move beyond denominationally rooted religious publishers to a much wider audience of both general and scholarly readers.

Harper publisher Steve Hanselman drew me into the board that edited the Renovaré Spiritual Formation Bible. He was followed by Mickey Maudlin, who was my editor for *Classic Christianity*. The Harper organization became my major publisher of the middle period of my authorship. I had started with Harper and Row in 1975, which later morphed into HarperSanFrancisco, then HarperOne. When Princeton University Press published my two books on Kierkegaard, they offered a new look at Kierkegaard, viewed through his parables and comic wit.

The publisher with whom I have most often worked over two and a half decades is InterVarsity Press, who first published my Moscow lectures (*Two Worlds*), but far more importantly were the twenty-nine volumes of the Ancient Christian Commentary on Scripture. IVP has taken huge risks to help their readers enter the arena of patristic studies, but as Andy Le Peau and Linda Doll have written in their book on the history of IVP, those risk-laden editorial decisions have proven to be extraordinarily well-received.[47]

The most exacting and substantively helpful editor I have had over the years has been James Hoover of IVP, who helped me through many volumes to avoid mistakes, anachronisms and repetitions.

I chose to work with a diverse range of religious publishers from Catholic (Herder and Paulist) to Lutheran (Fortress and Concordia), and Reformed (Zondervan, Eerdmans, Baker and Westminster John Knox) traditions. Since consensual Christianity in fact precedes and nourishes all those separated traditions, it was crucial to the agenda to work through and beyond the barriers between church traditions.

Working with many different editors has broadened my vision greatly. My longstanding concern for consensual Christianity brought me into many lecture halls besides those of mainline Protestantism. The more I wrote, the less I wrote for Methodists. *Requiem*, my last book for Abingdon, elicited a sharper break with liberal bureaucratic Methodism, yet I continued my interest in Wesley studies. As my communities of discourse expanded from a narrow range of academics to a centered world of lay orthodox believers, I reveled in many new and extremely valuable friendships.

How the Neuhaus Circle fed my soul. A key figure in that widening circle of friends was Richard John Neuhaus. Ever since the Hartford Declaration and *Agenda for Theology*, Richard has been a genuine defender and advocate for my initiatives as a writer.

Though I was five years older than Richard, he was a key mentor and partner in dialogue for me for over thirty years before his untimely passing in 2008. His repertoire of personal, rational and dialogical skills was amazing. He was ever alert to comic perceptions of moral reasoning, and his wit was quick and engaging.[48]

I first knew Richard Neuhaus as an anti-war leader, then as a brilliant pastor of a renewing Lutheran congregation in one of the toughest neighborhoods in Brooklyn. Later I knew him as writer of the Hartford Declaration along with Peter Berger. From then on he was on track to become a leading writer on public policy and an adviser to presidents. In the early years after the Hartford Declaration, I became increasingly involved in that group of theologians hosted by Neuhaus. Peter Berger was a dominant figure in its early years.[49] Neuhaus had the ear of Pope John Paul II and Pope Benedict XVI as well as many cardinals. He drew me into his circle of friends, who included George Weigel, Michael Novak, David Novak and Robert Jenson.

Richard and I emerged out of similar activist paths during the 1960s, his focusing more on anti-Vietnam protests and mine more on lay theological academies, existential psychotherapy and group processes. He became an articulate spokesperson for classic Christian moral reasoning and fearlessly took on controversial issues. His winsome spirit disarmed critics. With his extraordinary gift of hospitality, he brought minds together and watched them hone their skills by clashing, as they looked for a stable center. His wisdom was sought by Presidents Carter, Reagan and G. W. Bush. He was a frequent voice of reason on television. He founded and edited *First Things*, an ecumenical journal focused on creating a religiously informed public philosophy for the ordering of society.

Our friendship began in 1976 when I was invited by Pastor Neuhaus and Rabbi Leon Klenicki to participate in a Manhattan discussion to explore the potential mutual interests of Jewish and evangelical leaders. That inaugurated a serious dialogue on Jewish-Christian relationships on such subjects as relief for displaced persons, the future of Judaism and messianic theology. I knew of nothing like that dialogue even being conceived until that meeting. There I met Fritz Rothschild, Seymour Siegel and others from the faculty of the Jewish Theological Seminary. Around a massive board room table in a paneled room in New York we came together, about ten distinguished Jewish leaders and the same number of evangelical leaders, all of us wondering what might happen. In that dialogue I witnessed the earliest inklings of reconciliation between conservative Jews and conservative evangelicals, knowing that up until then there had been minimal communication.

My neighbor Ben Armstrong at Drew was the president of the National Religious Broadcasters. Ben, who knew of my close relationship with Will Herberg, asked me to join in the Manhattan discussion.[50]

After that I became a regular participant in the dialogues, seminars, lectures and good times sponsored by Richard Neuhaus, first in connection with the Rockford Institute, and later with the Institute of Religion and Public Life in New York. While Peter Berger was a key figure in the early years, later the leading minds were George Lindbeck, Paul Ramsey and Avery Dulles. Among other Catholic voices that appeared often for various venues in the Neuhaus circle were Edward Oakes, Robert George and Russell Hittinger.

Wolfhart Pannenberg was a star who occasionally passed across the North American horizon and brought his extraordinary mind to bear on the Neuhaus discussions. One of those meetings in New York occurred when the Metropolitan Museum had on display the exhibit "The Glory of Byzantium." I went with Pannenberg, Neuhaus and Robert Jenson to attend a spectacular exhibition of previously inaccessible Byzantine icons, architecture and manuscripts. When the three of us got separated from Pannenberg, we later found him patiently answering complicated questions from visitors, explaining the meaning of the artifacts in fluent English while also giving occasional traffic directions to visitors who must have thought he was a museum employee.

I watched the principled arguments of reason and conscience unfold in Neuhaus's mind for all of those thirty-two years, always in precise and often exquisite language. It seemed he never spoke a sentence that lacked generosity, humor and immense persuasive power. His thought processes ripened into full expression in his 1984 study *The Naked Public Square.*

In Rockford, Massachusetts, David Wells, Timothy George, Robert Jenson, Cornelius Plantinga and I met in 1988 for a seaside dialogue on the future of theology. Over several days, under the sponsorship of the Lilly Foundation, we developed a closeness that has lasted. Out of those conversations David Wells wrote an excellent series of books on the promise and limitations of contemporary theology. A premier teacher at Gordon-Conwell Theological Seminary, David remained for me a thoughtful partner in dialogue. Timothy George had recently become the dean of Beeson Divinity School in Birmingham. He became a leading voice in the Dulles Group, Evangelicals and Catholics Together, and the Manhattan Declaration.

I served with John Leith and Robert Wilken on the Faculty Advisory Committee for the Center of Theological Inquiry (CTI) at Princeton during the early days when it was defining its mission. John Leith was a leading figure among Presbyterians seeking the return of that Church to the basic principles of Reformed theology. Along with Leith the advisers included Robert Wilken, author of *The Christians as the Romans Saw Them*, who set a high standard for theological reflection at the Center.

Carl Braaten and Robert Jenson cooperated in the founding of *Dialog* magazine in 1961 and in 1991 *Pro Ecclesia* at the Center for Catholic and Evangelical Theology at St. Olaf College. Jenson had spent many years at the Lutheran Theological Seminary in Gettysburg, later returning to his alma mater of St. Olaf College. He wrote widely on the themes of Trinity, sacraments, Barth and Edwards. Jenson would later become Senior Scholar for Research at CTI. Those were all dear friends who shared and encouraged me throughout my journey.

How did Neuhaus and I benefit mutually from our three decades of friendship? In Richard's presence I found a community of scholars that provided the collegiality that I could never have gotten from the university. It was meaningful to me beyond words. It combined intellectual stimulus, inspiration and conviviality. My ideas were always being challenged and tested by caring and brilliant friends. Having him nearby was like having a

New York brother with whom I could spar and rely on for honest criticism.

But what did he get from me? I think he got a glimpse into an energetic and high-spirited authorship that he liked. I had written a half dozen books before his first book with Peter Berger.[51] He was one of the first to grasp the agenda for postmodern paleo-orthodoxy. When he wrote *The Catholic Moment* in 1987, he subtitled it: *The Paradox of the Church in the Postmodern World*. He could see that my hopeful and lighthearted *Agenda for Theology* embraced Protestants, Catholics, evangelicals, Orthodox Christians and charismatics. He brought that vision into personal embodiment more clearly than anyone else.

The Dulles Group was a gathering of about a dozen Catholic, Protestant and Jewish theologians who met regularly in New York under the leadership of Avery Dulles, David Novak and George Lindbeck, and was enabled by the hospitality of Richard Neuhaus. The quiet brilliance of Dulles, Novak and Lindbeck brought immense historical depth and good judgment to our deliberations. This group met in the Grant Room of the New York Union League Club three or four times a year over many years for theological discussion on public life issues, theology and ethics.

Out of those discussions came a cycle of Eerdmans-Neuhaus collaborations called the Encounter Series. They featured important essays by Joseph Ratzinger, Paul Johnson, George M. Marsden and Joseph Fitzmyer, They usually began with a defining essay with recorded and edited responses to key questions.[52]

Through dinner sessions in New York I brought Richard Neuhaus into serious dialogue with several evangelical scholars I knew he would want to know, among them Michael Horton and J. I. Packer. Richard became the personal embodiment of the hopes of an increasingly influential network of evangelical Protestants in dialogue with magisterial Catholic and conservative Jewish leaders.

HOW RATZINGER PLANTED THE SEEDS FOR
THE PATRISTIC COMMENTARY

During the 1980s I had been chiefly preoccupied with writing the three volumes of my *Systematic Theology*, which was at every point grounded in patristic wisdom. Until I personally met Cardinal Ratzinger, I did not know how to begin to build the bridge between systematic theology and the history of exegesis. Both were passionate concerns of mine, but I had not yet methodically grasped how patristic consensual doctrinal formulations flowed out of scriptural exegesis. Since my Heidelberg days I had viewed Joseph Ratzinger as a unique model of a grounded systematic theologian who was deeply knowledgeable regarding ancient ecumenical Scripture studies of the first five centuries. He was also keenly aware of the probing spirit of recent biblical criticism. Though I was reading Ratzinger in 1966, I did not personally meet him until 1988. Now we know him better as Pope Emeritus Benedict XVI. He wrote his professorial dissertation on Bonaventure at Munich in 1959, while I was working on mine at Yale on Bultmann.

Both Ratzinger and Pannenberg were well-known theologians before they turned forty. As an American on sabbatical leave in Germany with time to read, it soon became evident to me that the rising luminaries of Catholic and Protestant theology were Ratzinger and Pannenberg. Neither had been translated into English, so in the mid-1960s they remained largely unnoticed in North America.

By the 1960s the discipline of rigorous systematic theology had dwindled to almost nothing except for Pannenberg and Ratzinger. Tillich's earlier work of the 1950s had virtually avoided many key questions of systematic theology, especially divine foreknowledge, atonement and patristic exegesis. Neither Pannenberg nor Ratzinger produced a comprehensive systematic theology in the 1980s, but both were working along similar lines. Both Ratzinger and Pannenberg were searching for deeper historical grounding than that which could be derived from historical criticism alone. So was I. I began reading Ratzinger's essays on conciliar questions at the same time I was reading Pannenberg on revelation as history. Both were brilliantly argued and were for me transforming.

In Rome at Vatican II I had witnessed Ratzinger at work as a leading young *peritus* of the Council, assisting Josef Cardinal Frings of Cologne.[53] I found in Ratzinger a clear, orthodox, critical, passionate theologian who shared my hopes as fully as any systematic theologian I knew. By reading

Ratzinger I grasped the immense usefulness of thinking intentionally out of the history of exegesis, especially in its earliest patristic forms. By reading Pannenberg I was challenged to view the whole of history through the lens of apocalyptic writings, which were focused on the end of history. Most critical historians at that time were focused more narrowly on the here and now, not on the whole of history, including its end.

Ratzinger was a founder of the groundbreaking theological journal *Communio*, along with Hans Urs von Balthasar, Louis Bouyer and Henri de Lubac. I became a regular reader of *Communio* after Vatican II. I entered that circle when I became an author under the Herder imprint of Crossroad-Continuum Press, a North American manifestation of the Communio circle. After the 1978 ten-year retrospect on *Humanae Vitae* at Princeton, I found myself in active dialogue with the American circle of Ratzinger's students.

The vision of the Ancient Christian Commentary on Scripture was a slow-growing and complex conception that would not take firm definition and practical plausibility until I met with Joseph Ratzinger, when he pointed me in the direction of assembling scholarly resources to develop a patristic commentary on the Bible.

The 1988 New York Ratzinger Consultation on biblical interpretation. At last I had a chance to meet personally with Joseph Ratzinger over four days in New York in 1988 in a casual setting that allowed for extended personal conversation. I received an invitation from Richard Neuhaus (then still Lutheran) to meet privately with Joseph Ratzinger along with a small group of Catholic and Protestant theologians.[54]

Those days with Ratzinger would remain important to me for the rest of my life. There I began to consider the deliberate study of the history of patristic exegesis as a paramount personal vocation. I was interested in the potential recovery of the genre of the catena, the ancient method of remembering the church fathers by revealing their verse by verse interpretations of canonical Scripture. I had not yet formulated the method of the Ancient Christian Commentary on Scripture, but I was sure I wanted to prepare myself for much deeper work in patristic perceptions of Scripture texts than my Yale studies had prepared me to do.

The theme of the private seminar in the days following Ratzinger's

Erasmus Lecture was "Biblical Interpretation in Crisis."[55] The setting of the Erasmus lecture was the magnificent new St. Peter's Lutheran Church in Manhattan, encircled outside by a rowdy crowd of LGBT activists with cheeky pickets and strident howls. They made a deliberate attempt to block entry into the sanctuary and tried to break up the lecture as much as possible. Some had even gained entry with ticketed invitations. They were scattered around the large gathering of distinguished invited guests. I was seated on the front row with the dozen scholars who had come to the four-day Ratzinger Seminar after the lecture. The demonstrators outside were exasperated by the Cardinal's upholding of classic Catholic teaching on sexual ethics, which was precisely Ratzinger's assigned responsibility as protector of the doctrine of the faith.

The stereotyped image of Ratzinger was instantly dissipated when he stood up and began to speak—quietly, meekly and thoughtfully. A holy man stood before us, thin, with white hair and a humble spirit. His calm address was punctuated by ardent ovations from the vast majority of the audience as well as loud interruptions by picketers both inside and outside the church. He was unperturbed. Amid the clamor he revealed a lowly heart as an exceptionally learned, witty and reasonable thinker. When interrupted he waited patiently without any sense of being offended. When he started again, loud voices would shout out demeaning phrases. He stood attentively, smiled gently and waited for time to speak.

That was a brilliant lecture and made all the more memorable by its being constantly challenged by harsh distracters. At length a security decision was made to remove the protesters. The police extracted most of them without further struggle. But outside the perimeter of the church, we could see the protesters through glass windows and hear them shouting. In spite of all of this, we settled in for a wonderful lecture and soon were enwrapped in soaring thoughts on how the Bible renews the church.

Ratzinger's theme seemed to be directly addressed to my needs. He explained that the task was not merely to understand the Bible historically, but more so to understand history biblically. Accordingly, the role of modern biblical historical criticism must be acknowledged but in a

way that calls for a deeper critique of one-sided contemporary criticism.
Ratzinger showed how literary and historical criticism was not
equipped fully to grasp the history of God with humanity. Real history
is far more complex than can be dealt with solely by the narrow methods
of present-day historical criticism, however important those methods
may be for understanding the Bible's context, transmission and language.
The Bible's richer understanding of history required what Ratzinger
called a self-critique of historical exegesis. As I heard him unfold his
vision I felt moved and personally confronted.

For years I had been steeped in Bultmann's New Testament demythol-
ogizing criticism, but I had missed something crucial: how the narrative
of God's action in history itself provides a telling critique of modern historical criticism. I had written about the critique of criticism in *Agenda
for Theology* a decade earlier but had not yet seen it spelled out with such
finesse, wisdom and power as a deliberate return to patristic exegesis.

In the paddy wagon with Judge Bork. The uproar around St. Peter's
Lutheran Church at Ratzinger's public lecture was so disruptive that the
New York City Police Department decided that the VIP guests needed a
police escort to a safe haven. All the theologians of the seminar, along
with distinguished visitors, bishops, opinion makers, political figures and
jurists, had been invited to a reception at the archdiocese residence of
John J. Cardinal O'Connor. But it appeared to be too dangerous for us to
walk the several blocks over to the bishop's residence, so all of the distinguished guests had to be steered into a holding room until the police
could arrive with paddy wagons. But it was not the unruly demonstrators
who were placed in the paddy wagons but the distinguished guests headed
for a reception. We were hastily herded into a line of police vans.

I walked back to the last seat in the rear of the paddy wagon, followed
by Judge Robert Bork and his wife Mary Ellen. Judge Bork had recently
been on national television for days defending his record as a US Circuit
Court Judge before a divisive Senate Judiciary Committee hearing for his
nomination to the Supreme Court. Having watched those heated proceedings, I thought Judge Bork had made a brilliant defense of his record
as judge. In the police wagon I leaned over and said to him: "You have

given all of us a seminar in constitutional law in the Senate Committee hearings." He quipped: "I am glad now to be in a safe place—like a New York City Police Department paddy wagon!"

We all got a laugh out of the way we arrived at the archbishop's residence in a police vehicle normally used to transport inebriated revelers. Years later when I was chairman of the board of the Institute of Religion and Democracy in Washington, DC, I had the pleasure of working closely with Mary Ellen Bork, former nun and author, who was one of our most well-informed and wisest board members.

At Cardinal O'Connor's residence I enjoyed thoughtful conversations with leading Catholic figures and New York literary titans. With fine wine and a wonderful meal, it was my introduction to the summit of American Catholic leadership.

Better than that, however, was the quiet scholarly discussion scheduled to proceed over the next few days with selected Catholic and Protestant theologians.

The small theological seminar withdrew from the public sphere to the large walnut-paneled library of a Fifth Avenue private home looking out upon Central Park. There we talked at length with Ratzinger about his lecture and its implications. We heard excellent papers on his proposal presented by eminent Catholic scholars Raymond Brown and Joseph Fitzmyer.

I had much to talk about with Ratzinger during the casual luncheons and coffee breaks in between the seminar sessions. His *Theologische Prinzipienlehre* (1982) was profoundly resonant with my *Agenda for Theology*. I had just completed *The Living God*, the first volume of my *Systematic Theology* in 1987, at the time when Ratzinger's critique of liberation theology (*Politik und Erlösung*) appeared. His work on comprehensive systematic theology would later extend to many more volumes than mine, but we were both interested in the same objective: showing how deeply the ancient consensual Christian writers had permeated the entire history of doctrinal definition.

Through a half dozen extended dinner conversations, I explored with Ratzinger and our colleagues the implications of the recovery of a patristic catena for both Catholic and Protestant theology. At one point I awkwardly revealed to him that I had been writing a systematic theology as a Protestant that I hoped would be sufficiently so catholic (small c catholic) that it could be considered unobjectionable to Catholic teaching. I did so lightheartedly and sincerely. He listened cautiously and quietly said to me, "Yes, send it my way."

Some months later when I sent him volume one and the copyedited manuscript of volume two of my *Systematic Theology*, Ratzinger remembered our conversations and graciously passed it along for an official critical evaluation by his friend Louis Bouyer, cofounder of *Communio*. I still possess the long letter in French from Bouyer that contained several pages of thoughtful analysis. Years later I met Bouyer on the Drew campus where, after delivering his address, I thanked him for so carefully critiquing my first efforts at regrounding Christian doctrine in patristic exegesis.

As we departed New York I mentioned to Cardinal Ratzinger that I was planning a sabbatical leave in Rome in 1991. He invited me to call him upon arrival.

part three

Homeward Bound

7

The 1990s

The Outpouring of Grace

◆

MEETING JOHN PAUL II AND RATZINGER IN ROME

At the Lord's Table with John Paul II. The half-year sabbatical in Rome in the spring of 1991 gave me a chance to change my pace. I was able to stay at Casa Santa Maria through the Jesuit network of Avery Dulles. Cardinal Ratzinger was in the Office of the Congregation of the Faith, and John Paul II was the much beloved pope.

The Casa was the seventeenth-century residence of advanced North American scholars studying for advanced degrees in the graduate division of the North American College of Rome, where Timothy Dolan was rector. Formerly a nunnery, the Casa was where Napoleon had kept his cavalry officers when he invaded Rome.

A quiet residence next to the Pontifical Gregorian University and the Pontifical Biblical Institute on the Piazza della Pilotta, the Casa was right in the heart of Rome.

It was an easy walk to the Coliseum and Forum of ancient Rome. Since I have always loved to walk in cities, it was the perfect location to see central Rome at an easy pace. The Vatican, the Augustinian Institute of Patristic Studies, and Ratzinger's office were a short bumpy bus ride away from the Casa.

I arrived in Rome late evening on January 17, 1991, so late that the Casa guards were already retired and I had to awaken them by repeated knocks. I was weary from the flight, not expecting anything in particular to be happening for me the next day.

It was on that very night that the Persian Gulf War began. While I was sleeping in Rome, a major air strike took place near the Kuwait border by the coalition forces at dawn and the Middle East was aflame.

I was roused out of bed at 5 a.m. by Monsignor Charles Elder, director of the Casa. He had an urgent message that had come overnight from the Papal Secretary. I was told to come immediately to the Vatican. He said, to my surprise, that I had been invited to the private morning Mass with John Paul II, which began in the pope's private chapel at 7 that morning, and I needed to arrive there by 6 a.m.

Having no time to speculate on how this had happened, I leapt out of bed knowing time was short. Father Charles put a bus ticket in my hand with quick instructions on where to catch the bus and where to go when I got to St. Peter's Square. I had to find my way to a certain great bronze door on the north side of the columns of St. Peter's Cathedral. It was still dark when I found my way to the bus stop, but as overwhelmed as I felt, I knew I was on my way to meet the pope personally.

I knocked on the massive door to the Papal Residence, uncertain if I was in the right place. I was promptly and warmly received, and very surprised to be recognized as one of a dozen on the expected guest list. I wondered who had arranged this. The friendly attendant escorted me through a high-ceiling Renaissance hallway of statues to an elevator. I was the last to enter the elevator.

I stood between a towering Irishman and a tiny elderly French nun. "The war has begun, has it?" said the bulky Irishman in a deep brogue. I looked at him blankly and said, "What war?" I had heard no news that morning. The rest of the slow-moving elevator trip was drenched in heavy silence.

The three of us were the last to join the small group that was gathered in a baroque reception room near the pope's private chapel. Leaving our winter coats there, we were greeted and escorted by Father Stanisław Dziwisz, the amiable personal secretary to the Holy Father.

We were ushered into the small, quiet papal chapel where Pope John

Paul II was already at the kneeling rail in humble demeanor, deep in prayer facing the altar. There were no more than fifteen people in attendance. I was grateful to be there but was still feeling astounded that I had been invited. Even though I was aware that I was the only non-Roman Catholic at the pope's private mass, they were not. I took the furthest back row seat on a wooden chair, only a few steps away from the pontiff on his knees.

A stunning bronze figure of Jesus on the cross and white candles on the altar table caught my eye. The prevailing motif was sacrifice: the sacrifice of the crucified Lord and the sacrifice of his followers. Straight ahead was an altar with white stone panels on each side, one on the left portraying the death of Peter, crucified head downward, and one on the right portraying the beheading of Paul. So here I was in the chapel dedicated to Peter and to Paul, who had stood ready to give their lives for the risen Lord, whose living presence we were celebrating.

Glancing up, I saw a colorful stained-glass ceiling depicting the angelic hosts who seemed to be with us in our singing. I imagined that there was a vast choir of angels there praying with us for the peace of a broken world on the first day of a bitter desert war.

Even though I had been told that Pope John Paul II was a man of prayer, I was not quite ready for the intensity and earnestness of his inward struggle in prayer, the labored wrestling of his supplication, the sweat on his brow. What I saw was a man whose head was buried deeply in his hands, whose fingers became entwined in his white hair, grasping both sides of his head intently, both palms pressing on his temples. The intensity of his praying imprinted an unforgettable image on my mind.

The feast I missed. A nun with a guitar accompanied one of the hymns that was sung in Spanish. Next I heard the powerful liturgical voice of the Holy Father, a rugged voice that had come through many Polish afflictions. Here was the man widely credited with actions that prefaced the end of Soviet hegemony. There was something wonderful, resonant and reassuring in that voice, conveying the serenity and comfort of a pastor. He was a caring servant who was wise in the ways of the world without ceasing to be deeply empathic.

The body language of John Paul II was unhurried and confident. As he was being attended by Father Stanislaw with sacramental garb, belted and set for the Eucharist, I felt he was completely at ease with himself. He was fully present.

I had to make a decision quickly: Would I receive the Holy Communion? There was no time for contemplation. I could either accept the generous invitation or let the gift pass me by. To take the host would be to break the canonical rules for Catholic sacraments.

In good conscience, I bypassed receiving the body and blood of Christ from the pontiff's own hands. Why? I had become a very catholic evangelical, but I was not a baptized Roman Catholic. However, was I not baptized into the one, holy, catholic, apostolic church by the hands of a Methodist bishop in historic succession with Anglican ordinations? Yes, but there remains serious doubt among some concerning the authenticity and catholicity of my baptism, despite many warm reassurances of real friendship.

Though I would have been inwardly ready to come, and had been invited, I recognized that I was not properly prepared according to their own canon law and catechetical rules to come forward for bread and wine at the Lord's Table. I did not have the proper wedding garment for this celebration. There was no one there to turn me away except myself—my conscience and my respect for the holy sacrament. I respected the commitment of my Catholic friends to their belief, however much I might see it differently. I felt like a splintered bone in the broken body of Christ.

Each one in the congregation filed forward to receive the broken body and sacrificial blood of the Lord. I alone remained silently behind. I prayed in solitude for the unity of the church.

What a rare opportunity to miss. I would gladly have received it. Honestly, my soul thirsted for it. Any Catholic would savor the great privilege of just being there with one of the great men of the modern Catholic tradition.

I too met the risen Lord that day in spirit, if not in bread and wine. I thought about the ironies of a broken body of Christ, broken on the cross, broken in the liturgy and broken in my heart.

After the benediction, the worshipers who were in the private chapel Mass were ushered into a magnificent Renaissance reception room where Pope John Paul II greeted each one of us personally. By my side was the renowned benefactor of orthodox Catholic teaching, businessman Tom Monaghan of Domino's Pizza, a giant of industry, but here a soft-spoken, unpretentious, meek penitent.

The pontiff warmly enclosed my hands with his large, supple, welcoming hands. At that moment I felt the heat of camera lights flashing all around me. I greeted him on behalf of American Protestant theologians who were grateful for his moral courage, humane spirit and theological discernment. I told him I prayed for his determination to deepen the orthodox faith in American Catholic university and seminary faculties. He smiled knowingly.

When he put in my hand a chain of treasured silver Vatican rosary beads, I realized that I had never held a rosary before. A means of grace so familiar to ordinary Catholics was entirely strange to the hands of a Protestant. Seeing the joyful light in his eyes was a moving experience for me. Later I gave the papal rosary to my closest friend at Drew, Jim O'Kane, who knew what to do with it and felt blessed to have it.

As I walked away from the large reception chatting with Tom Monaghan, we entered the bright sunlight illuminating the vast circle of columns of St. Peter's Square. We talked about how our hearts had been touched by a historic man of prayer on a fate-laden day. Monaghan talked about his plans to build a new kind of Catholic university, later to be called Ave Maria University in Naples, Florida, where some friends of mine, Professors Matthew Lamb and Matthew Levering, would become leaders in the building of its faculty.

As I left St. Peter's Square, I thanked God for the major role this Polish pope had played in the ending of the Cold War.

Back at the Casa Santa Maria, I realized that I was the sole Protestant resident among the Catholic priests of the Casa. I was honored and delighted to be among them. I had my first lunch with seventy of them in the great dining hall. A particular napkin had been set aside for me to be returned to the same napkin slot after each meal. I felt warmly received by that group of quick-witted young Catholic priests whom I would come to know well during the spring semester of 1991. They were all studying for doctorates in various fields, particularly Bible, theology and marriage law.

They wanted to know how it happened that I got an invitation to a private mass with the pope. None of them had ever received such an invitation. Even though I had to say that I didn't know, I quietly pondered if it might have been arranged by Joseph Ratzinger or Avery Dulles, but I left the mystery in God's hands.

That evening I learned that many of the Casa colleagues were gathered in the television lounge hearing the war reported in Italian, so I joined them there. We watched the blow-by-blow onsite report of the tanks moving north through the kill box.

The Rome visit with Cardinal Ratzinger. Weeks later I had my second probing discussion with Cardinal Ratzinger in his office, two years after our New York seminar. As I approached the security entryway of the Congregation of the Doctrine of the Faith, I was keenly aware of the troubled history of that building, and I shuddered to recall that this was the place where Galileo had been interrogated in 1615. It was built in 1452, six years before Michelangelo was appointed architect for the design of the present St. Peter's Basilica. This wing had been built for the purpose of maintaining and defending "the integrity of the faith and to examine and proscribe errors and false doctrines." Just beyond the guarded gate, I saw a bare courtyard surrounded by buildings where prisoners must have been held during the Inquisition. That office was the oldest of the nine congregations of the Roman Curia, housed in the Palace of the Holy Office at the Vatican, adjacent to the great square of St. Peter, and close to the Augustinian Patristic Institute, where I had been studying.

As I climbed the steps to the third floor, I was graciously met by a young man, Father Christoph Schönborn. He was serving as Ratzinger's assistant, later to be appointed Cardinal of Vienna, and even then one of John Paul II's key theological advisers. We visited briefly before he ushered me into the Cardinal's office, where Ratzinger welcomed me, recalling our days of dialogue in New York.

I spoke at length with Ratzinger about the consequences that had unfolded due to our previous conversations in New York. I explained how they had prompted me to begin laying huge plans for a patristic commentary on the whole Bible. Hearing this, his eyes lit up. I explained why I thought it would bring together Protestants, Catholics and Orthodox, who had the same patrimony. While the idea was still in conceptual formation, I wanted his counsel on deciding about its viability, goals, methods and how to proceed. He was quite interested in the prospect of an Ancient Christian Commentary on Scripture and thought Catholic scholars would want to be a part of it. He immediately grasped its relevance for ecumenical dialogue, theology and spiritual formation. I was pleased when he gave me great encouragement to continue with the plan.

I had entered the building with fear and trembling, remembering its dreadful history, but I left with a keen awareness of how far we had come since the conflicts of the Reformation and the Council of Trent. I felt hopeful that the unity of the body of Christ might be healed by a return to Christian Scripture as viewed by its earliest interpreters.

Eyewitness to the Collapse of the Soviet Union

Three weeks after the papal Eucharist I was on my way to Soviet Moscow, on the invitation of the philosophy department of Moscow State University. Five years earlier Soviet president Gorbachev had been calling for an "uncompromising struggle against manifestations of religion." But after the fall of the Berlin Wall in November 1989, fresh winds were blowing in the Soviet universities. A climate for religious studies was emerging. The formerly atheistic society was looking for ways to incorporate vital religious understandings once again into its common life and public discourse. I recalled my own fascination with Marx and socialist revolution, and felt great relief that I was now on a completely different path, just as they were.

Lectures at the Department of Atheism of Moscow State University. The unexpected invitation to lecture in the Soviet Union came from the very professors once charged with intellectually defending official Soviet atheism. Only months before they had been called the faculty of the

Department of Atheism of Moscow State University. The new name under glasnost was the Department of Scientific and Historical Study of Religion and Freethinking. The name change was more than cosmetic. Breaking free from their former status as compliant apologists for atheistic ideology, the professors of the scientific study of religion in the university were beginning to form a curriculum much like what we would call the comparative study of religion. Within that narrow window, the study of Eastern Orthodoxy was guardedly permitted. I had agreed to lecture to undergraduate students on the theme of postmodern Christianity, and to doctoral students on the structure of awareness in time.

I was trudging through the February snows of Moscow trying to get a glimpse of an academic system in identity crisis and radical transition. With some scholars this required a complete ideological reversal. I found my hosts more than casually interested in the spiritual vitalities remaining within the Protestant tradition I represented.

The Moscow faculty laughed when I described the immense popularity of Gorbachev in the West. One joked that the difference between Gorbachev in Moscow versus Gorbachev in Washington was that in Washington he could be elected.

Even from a half mile away, Moscow State University looked like a secularized cathedral with high spires, classic pillars, baroque marble and socialist piety exuding everywhere. Built in massive proportion by political prisoners on Stalin's order, it was one of the largest universities in the world. The main teaching building itself housed thousands of students on an enormous scale. I kept on running into surprises. Due to the paper shortage the department was using old test papers as toilet paper in the bathrooms.

Far from asking purely conceptual questions, I found the faculty and students especially interested in how religious faith could affect the moral underpinnings of a society.

Their questions arose out of their experiences of being cut off from free and lively religious discourse for most of their lives. When I sketched the story of my own former history of romanticizing Marxism, they smiled knowingly. When I told them of my subsequent disillusionment, they understood. I expected resistance but got none.

Marx was a pivotal maker of modernity. I was a theologian who had abandoned modern idolatries and was entering into a nascent post-modern world where classic Christianity was craved. Their newfound interest in Orthodoxy paralleled my interest in the postmodern recovery of classic Christian teaching. Their transition in the 1990s was much more like my transition in the 1970s than I would ever have imagined. They were postmodern in the same way I was disillusioned with modern Marxist ideology. They had me explain postmodern paleo-orthodoxy, and they quickly understood it. I found that they had suffered seventy times over what I had experienced in the failure of modern consciousness.

Ironically, at a time when American university studies in religion were rapidly secularizing, Soviet studies were rapidly desecularizing. They were intensely interested in theology proper—specifically the history of dogma, doctrinal theology and liturgy. I was surprised to find them eager to talk about the meaning of baptism, the homilies of John Chrysostom and the doctrine of sin. At this same time, these theological and dogmatic subjects were almost unmentionable in many American universities. But in Moscow they were driven by passionate concerns for social transformation. Some who spoke with me were considering being baptized.

The university's most widely published expert on atheism was experiencing a midlife crisis, since she could not find a publisher. Atheism had lost its status as an officially supported state ideology. They knew very little about Protestantism because they had had no firsthand experience of it. They had only seen it as a stereotype. They had a blurred awareness of the Russian Orthodox tradition, but had little understanding of what Luther, Calvin and Wesley had been doing. That was a memory void that I had to try to work around.

They were mourning not for a centralized economy but for an organic, stable social order with a moral center. They were pondering the recovery of the thousand-year-old Russian cultural tradition that had been saturated with classic Christian teaching and liturgy. They wondered if being baptized would reconnect them with seventy years of lost memory. I had arrived at a Rip Van Winkle moment in Soviet history.

The reflections of Russian women on Western feminism. Especially remarkable to me were the strong and sensible voices of Russian women. Five of the faculty members in religious studies were women. All were accomplished scholars with PhDs and numerous publications, but none of them were feminists in the American sense.

The women students of Moscow State University were eager to talk about the status and role of women in the Soviet system and America. Russian women had great difficulty connecting with the mentality and aspirations of the pampered American women's movement. I heard them argue insistently that Soviet women through all the social dislocation of Russia had remained basically happy, spiritually healthy, tough and inwardly centered. These Russian women thought of themselves as resilient, sensible, secure and confident in overcoming obstacles. They did not feel that they were being victimized as they saw Western women claiming to be. They felt that they were more at home with their gender identity than many American women whom they had seen portrayed in American movies. I found them to be strongly resistant to any premature imposition of Western feminist values on Soviet society. "Let us find our own way," they said. Women in the Soviet system have a long tradition of working hard and long. Many have had child care provided since wartime days. Women had excelled in medicine, math and engineering. All had struggled with cramped multifamily housing and small budgets.

They were astonished when I reported to them that approximately one-third of our Protestant candidates for ordination were women. I pointed out that in 1980 most of my women students were active feminists, but by 1990 many were becoming either moderate or critical feminists who overtly disagreed with many of the excesses of popular feminism. I explained that many of our women theological students had strong pro-life convictions on abortion and deep concerns about the loss of legitimacy of the nuclear family and felt that sexual experimentation did not protect the interests of children.

The Moscow State University women expressed deep concern that impressionable Russian young people might be vulnerable to taking on Western habits and values from punk rock, porn, sexual permissiveness and drug-oriented music. I too wondered if Russian university students might soon be determined to try all of the mistakes that American university students had been making. They wanted to discuss the rising incidence of sexually transmitted diseases and the religious blessing of homosexual unions, eager to hear how I dealt with these issues as a theologian.[1] I had just stepped away from an American academic ethos of permissive sexuality and rigid political correctness. Quickly I learned that American feminist issues were not on their wavelength.[2]

I explained that if feminism is defined as defending equal political, economic, and social rights for women, especially in education and employment, then I have been a sincere feminist since 1964, when I first read Betty Friedan. My hesitations about feminism came gradually from women writers, especially the Jewish thinker Midge Decter and evangelical teacher Elisabeth Elliot. In those days of the early 1990s, I was pondering the consequences of some of the wild speculations of Germaine Greer and Mary Daly. Much of my critique of exuberant feminism was lavishly furnished by former feminist writers who were wisely seeking deeper insights into the dynamics of victimization, the mutual benefits of sexual complementarity and the narrowness of arithmetic egalitarianism.

Young Moscow University women wondered why American women were so unhappy. They thought American women were well-off financially but deeply discontented. They plainly described Russian women as mostly positive about their lives, but they were especially intrigued when I mentioned the hypothesis of "the feminization of poverty," an idea then under discussion in the United States, arguing that the feminist insistence upon the independent identity of women had unexpected negative consequences for women's economic status. The feminist idealization of women having children without men, and public policies that encourage fatherless children, increased the vulnerability of children and family continuity. The Soviet women were puzzled and could not easily feel sorry or even empathize with American feminists.

My last lecture ended on a personal note. I explained that by my presence there in Moscow I was following in the footsteps of my daughter,

who had engaged in so many peace initiatives. While Laura had studied
Russian language and literature in college, she had felt a strong sense of
responsibility to organize the first joint peace walk of Americans and
Russians in the Soviet Union. Over two hundred young Americans were
joined by young Russians to walk, and walk they all did, from Leningrad
to Moscow during the height of the Cold War in 1987.

I passed around her picture with much "oohing" and "ahhing" from
them as they realized instinctively that some Americans really care about
them and were willing to go out of their way to reach out to ordinary
Russian citizens.

The session ended not with any further comment on my lecture but
with the department chair expressing how grateful they were to Laura.
Her act of self-giving seemed far more important than anything I had said.

I left Moscow State University clutching a bundle of letters that Russians had given me to mail in the United States. When I indicated that I
would not return to the United States for some weeks, they laughed:
"What is a week in relation to our postal system? All we want is to be as-
sured *that* they will be mailed, not *when*."

When I returned to Rome, it was late and the Casa door was locked. I
was loaded down with heavy baggage, which included some liturgical
books I had bought in Moscow and a pewter Russian cross with a bullet
hole through it. My most prized possession was a tattered Russian Bible
given to me by the Moscow Bible Society, which had survived the seventy
years of official atheism.

Not able to arouse anyone by knocking, I went to the back at Piazza
della Pilotta and shouted for someone to come to the door and got no
response. Seeing that all of the windows were dark, I went to the Jesuit
Center near the Gregorian and found Father Gerald Collins, who made
a call to the Casa. Finally I was welcomed back from Russia.

The second Russian trip after Yeltsin's coup. I returned to Moscow a
half year later, representing a "citizen's diplomacy initiative" focused on
person-to-person interaction between American and Russian citizens.
In September 1991 I joined Democrat Kathleen Kennedy and Republican
Frank Keating in the people-to-people visit to Russia. The eldest daughter

of Robert Kennedy and the future governor of Oklahoma were reaching out in order to build trust through personal conversation, in the spirit of post–Cold War glasnost. Ironically we met in the center that had been used to teach Soviet propaganda to non-Russians, in a building that featured a huge white statue of Lenin inside the entryway. It had been long associated with international espionage efforts, but now was serving as a venue for welcoming conferences with foreigners.

A genuine revolution had occurred in the short time between my Moscow lectures and my personal diplomacy efforts. By September of 1991 it was no longer the Soviet Union. The Soviet Union had collapsed. Seventy years of repression had suddenly come to an end. I was there just after the Russians made Boris Yeltsin the first freely elected president in the history of their country when he ran against the Communist Party and won a hearty endorsement from the Russian people. In August 1991 the Communist Party attempted a coup d'état to oust Gorbachev and reestablish an authoritarian central regime. Russian President Boris Yeltsin famously stood on a tank to defy the Communist Coup in 1991. I arrived three weeks later

I saw the streets around the Moscow White House when they still had debris left over from the barricades. After my second visit to Russia, I felt that my 1979 "end of modernity thesis" had been vindicated in 1991. The evidence was best seen in a space that had been set aside for the broken and tumbled statues of Stalin, Lenin and KGB chief Felix Dzerzhinsky. As I strolled around the Statue Graveyard in Fallen Monument Park, I knew that a turn in history had been made.

I went to Russia because I wanted to test out the viability of my paleo-orthodox hypothesis in a post-Communist non-Protestant environment. I wondered if the death of modernity and birth of postmodernity in America might be analogous to what was happening in the failing Soviet Union. To me, the wind in the fallen statues whispered yes.

The dramatic collapse of Soviet modernity provided a revealing mirror for me in viewing the death of modernity in America. That was when I decided to write *Two Worlds*, published in 1992, which reported my university lectures and related cultural observations. The Cold War officially ended during the period when I was in Moscow. I saw the Russian people in an ecstatic period of genuine people's liberation, unlike the kind of liberation falsely promised by waring Marxist-based forms of liberation theology.

Witnessing the Evangelical Revival in Cuba

New birth in Cuba. Not long after visiting Russia, I wanted to visit Cuba firsthand, but could not get in. It was virtually impossible to enter Cuba without both US State Department approval and a personal invitation from the Cuban government, both very difficult to get. Since US evangelicals were hearing about a significant revival of Christian witness in Cuba, I wanted to investigate it firsthand.

Through the intervention of Cuban Methodist bishop Joel Ajo of Havana, a way opened up for me to get into Cuba in 1993. As a young Methodist pastor, Joel Ajo had been arrested and sent to a Camagüey concentration camp, but now he was bishop of the Cuban Methodists. I accepted a special invitation to give five lectures on "The New Birth" at Seminario Evangelico de Teologia in Matanzas, Cuba.

My motive was to hear exactly what the Cuban Christians were saying and to bring their witness back to North America. I was accompanied by my translator and colleague, Douglas W. Ruffle, who had spent ten years (1978–1987) in Argentina during the revolutionary times when the Mothers of the Plaza de Mayo were protesting the disappearance of their sons. Doug was writing his PhD dissertation on Eusebius under my direction. Fortunately for me, he was well-prepared to help me navigate the Cuban church situation.

For years there had been a motley parade of American ecumenical bureaucratic clergy who had made their way to Cuba to pay homage to Fidel and blame America for Cuba's problems. This had caused a distortion in perception. The irony was that the only link between conservative Cuban evangelical congregations and the North American Christian laity was an ultraliberal church bureaucracy in America. Thus religious news sources from Cuba echoed Communist Party language. The ecumenical bureaucrats had bought their way into Cuban hospitality by supporting the regime.

On the highways I saw old Chevys, Dodges and Studebakers that I had not seen for years. The American-made automobiles on Cuban streets had been built in the 1950s. They were kept running by clever Cuban mechanics long after they had disappeared from the streets of the United States. Under frugal economic circumstances, the suffering Cuban people had become very creative.

Cuba felt to me like a return to Dust Bowl conditions where we seldom threw anything away and repeatedly recycled what we had. Most people were lean and gaunt. Cuban parents were patient and proud as they engaged in a daily battle to provide enough food for their families.

We were told that there were more professionals in Cuba than in any other Latin American country, especially medical professionals. Anyone could acquire a free education, but just having an education did not mean you had a job, income or even food, much less civil liberty or free speech.

The sight of the lean faces of Cuban children looking into the window of a government sponsored tourist "dollar store" was unforgettable. Only there were dollars permitted, but just for foreign tourists, not Cubans for whom possession of dollars was illegal. On the outside of the windows, Cuban children gazed upon the dazzling consumer world of soap, shoes and radios from which they were barred. Cuba was trying to teach them that a free economy was dangerous.

Still, this paucity of worldly goods did not seem to be diminishing the hope in their eyes. They were living within austere limits without whining, as a result of years of grinding poverty that had taught Cubans to be extremely creative economically. They bargained and bartered among themselves. If someone's brother worked in a factory making coffee, his wife might find ways of marketing coffee privately. If another cousin worked in a plumbing parts factory, he became a part-time plumber, largely by bartering his skills.

Collectivist educational policies had disrupted ordinary family life. Young people were routinely separated entirely from their parents for long periods to go off to study socialism and work in rural cooperatives. With rampant prostitution, AIDS hit Cuba with a vengeance. An HIV-positive diagnosis was like a prison sentence. The sufferer would be treated inhumanely, thrown into a permanent quarantine and isolated from everyone. Despite this agony, Cuban Christians were experiencing a wave of genuine spiritual revival, with many narratives of personal faith in Jesus as Lord.

The American church bureaucrats were not well-prepared to understand this turn of events. The news conferences following their visits painted the Cuban church as strong advocates of liberation theology. If so, I wondered, what were they doing speaking in tongues? Charismatic Catholics and Protestants were increasing in holy boldness.

Nearby the seminary I passed by the Vietnam Bookstore with titles displayed such as *The History of Precapitalist Economy, How to Build a House*, a medical textbook and *The More Transparent Region* by Carlos Fuentes. I walked past a run-down movie theater in Matanzas whose paint was peeling on the outside, but the lobby inside had elegant marble floors and mahogany panels from past days of splendor. A handmade sign announced the next movie: *Falling in Love in the USA*—in color.

I did not meet a single Cuban Christian who was speaking of counterrevolutionary violence, as that would have been utterly futile and harshly treated. If I were taping a conversation I would be signaled quietly to turn off my recorder. They were less anxious about reprisal to themselves than to their children.

The evangelicals in Cuba when I was there were growing more confident despite the totalitarian society. They could see the socialist dream crumbling. Many pastors had been imprisoned, and many more were subject to intimidation. They were willing to suffer if necessary to continue their witness. Every baptism was charged with a sense of great potential consequence, since it risked reprisals and vulnerable jobs.

Among ordinary laity, there was a sustained commitment to unobtrusive person-to-person evangelism. They did not want money, nor did they ever solicit outside support, because that would only complicate their lives. Their desperate poverty created by a controlled economy which suppressed free economic exchange did not undermine their faith. They remained proud and were persevering with patience and wit.

Contrary to the glowing reports of Cuban socialism from ecumenical leaders, I found that socialism was a joke among many with whom I talked. It had long ago lost the moral high ground. Liberation theology was discredited among Cuban evangelicals and Catholics long before it had withered on the vine in American seminaries. On Cuban streets I recalled the revulsion I had felt on the streets of Geneva when I first woke up to the prospect of a world ecumenical movement tied to socialist dreams. In Cuba I was seeing the bizarre fruits of those dreams.[3]

The church in Cuba was determined to stay close to the people. A choice that touched every Cuban family was to stay and make do or leave if they could. Some left not only their property but their family in Cuba, but not their heart for Cuba. Those who left still loved Cuba and longed to share in its future. However, Cubans remaining in Cuba knew that most who departed would never return. Many who left in the 1950s had been gone for four decades. That left the residue of a divided conscience which continued to vex the Cuban people. Most families had relatives abroad with whom they could communicate only with great difficulty. The view was strong that all Cubans belonged to one family, both at home and abroad.[4]

The growth of the house-church movement was not planned but was an outgrowth of government policies that made it illegal to either renovate churches or start new ones. The faithful quietly invited people to their homes for prayer, testimony, singing and Bible study. The resourcefulness and vitality of the Cuban lay revival has grown silently out of these conditions. The evangelical revival that emerged was led by the laity and the youth more than by clergy, who were either no longer there or had been silenced. There were reportedly 1,600 baptisms of Catholic young people the month I was there. They came to baptism with a hunger to transcend their atheist education.

I interviewed Jaime Ortega, Catholic archbishop of Havana, who also had endured forced labor camps along with Methodist bishop Ajo. When I asked whether there were any serious bilateral ecumenical interactions between Protestants and Catholics, I got the same answer from the archbishop that I got from the Protestant leaders. There were intermittent fraternal relations, but overall there remained deep fractures between

Catholics and Protestants. Catholics felt that the Protestant liberation theologians had been too cozy with Fidel and his principles. Evangelicals thought that Catholics were unnecessarily defensive about Protestants disrupting their majority status.

The voices of the Cuban evangelical revival. I got a glimpse of the revival at the seminary at Matanzas, but got a closer look when I went into out-of-the-way parishes. I visited an Afro-Caribbean Methodist Church on the sprawling fringe of Havana. The simple frame church building was jam-packed. Many congregants were young families with children. In the chancel sat an electronic keyboard, a tangle of percussion devices and an accumulation of steel guitars and maroon tambourines. Cuban Christian renewal was clearly coming alive to an Afro-Caribbean beat. The charismatic black pastor invited anyone in the congregation to come forward who had never before been to church. A couple brought up an infant—not for baptism but for earnest prayer looking toward a possible future baptism. Baptism was a deliberate countercultural decision in Cuba. As the "Glory Singers" led the congregation in rafter-raising voices, whole families swayed together, hands uplifted. I was very moved. It was a vivid, unforgettable occurrence of new birth within the wilderness of Fidelismo.

I had come to Cuba to teach seminarians about the new birth. Now in the revival movements in the churches I was seeing it for myself. This was the gentle but certain work of God the Spirit. The evidences of revival were the fervency of prayers, the intensely felt presence of the Holy Spirit, lives being morally transformed, behavior patterns reconstructed and courageous decisions being made. I knew instantly I was among the living members of the one body of Christ, just as I had known when I was in the papal chapel. As the cadence mounted, the lights went off unexpectedly—a frequent feature of Cuban life at the time. A bright kerosene lantern was quickly lit, brought in and hung, swaying from the ceiling, illuminating the singing, rocking congregation.

The preaching was as impassioned as the praise. Its power was palpable as I heard the words telling all of us that it was about a war with Satan in the hearts of each one of us. We were told that although the final outcome at the end of history is already known to the faithful, the struggle continues this side of the end. We face an adversary who presents himself as a friend, and we cannot afford to be naive about this combat. As you are mocked by others who do not understand and will scold you, do not complain. Be ready to view sacrifice as a privilege of participation in the way of the cross. Rejection is to be expected, even within your own family. You are called now to make a decision that could be the most important decision of your life: receive Jesus in your heart and trust him for forgiveness of your sins.

The Spirit was ricocheting through the packed hall. That night fourteen answered that invitation, willing to put their lives and careers on the line. Several were young people, one a mother with a baby in her arms, another a lean, tall, strong man still in his work clothes. Many other congregants of all ages came forward to pray for the sick. From that moment on I knew that this was the most consequential event I had seen going on in Cuba: the work of the Spirit in prayer with a distinctively Cuban rhythm.

Back at Matanzas seminary, I learned that the most loved person in the school was an aging Presbyterian professor emeritus René Castellano. He was the one person who could tell me the most about recent Cuban Christian history. He had witnessed three generations of Cuban crises and had watched the birth and struggle of the seminary from its beginnings in 1946, a decade before Castro took over Cuba.

In his spare apartment, he carefully measured a spoonful of black Cuban coffee, steeped it in boiling water and served it in a demitasse with sweet cinnamon torticas. In his seventies, he was very thin but healthy. He had a closely trimmed white beard and a radiant face. He lived alone under conditions that would be regarded as the lower end of the poverty scale in America. I heard that professors were being paid in pesos the equivalent of $15 US per month, yet there was not a hint of any acrimony. He had no desire for the seminary to become dependent on foreign support.

The aging professor had been imprisoned early in the Cuban revolution and was now considered a saint among the seminary students. He told in clear, moving English: "God only illumines the next step, not long distances ahead. We would prefer God to illumine the way for a long distance ahead, but the flickering light of the Word shows only the next step. God called Abram, 'Leave Ur. I will then tell you where you are going.' To Paul the Spirit said, 'Go to Macedonia. I will tell you there what next.' The risen Lord said to his disciples, 'Go to Galilee. You will find me there.' It is humbling for the pilgrim to not know what is over the hill, to have no more foreknowledge than the next person. But this is a part of our spiritual growth: to take small steps without knowing what is ahead but trusting God to bring good out of evil."[5]

We talked of music and dancing in the Cuban church. Spritely he showed me some features of the Cuban form of dancing with free movement of the hips and hands.

Shortly after returning to the United States I got a call from the office of John J. Cardinal O'Conner in New York. He had been reading my *Agenda for Theology*. Knowing I had just been to Cuba, he invited me to come in to his office for a visit. We had met once before at his reception for Cardinal Ratzinger in his archdiocese house. He was preparing to go to Cuba and sought discernment about what to expect.

Edrita hugged me tightly when I returned from my travels to Russia and Cuba. She was able to understand that my vision had been enlarged and that the hazards had been worth risking. Her support meant everything to me.

THE BIRTH OF THE PATRISTIC COMMENTARY

The dream of an Ancient Christian Commentary on Scripture. The path ahead would lead from the Ratzinger conversations to pivotal conversations with Howard and Roberta Ahmanson in picturesque Corona del Mar, California. The dream of a patristic commentary that had been conceived in the Ratzinger seminar of 1988 began to become a reality in 1992. During that interim four-year period I had been searching for a practical way to make the commentary into a viable project.

It was like looking for a needle in a haystack to find a match between a biblical text and its patristic commentator. It sounded easy when we first sought to do it, but it proved arduous. The primary sources in documents and manuscripts were scattered all over the globe in neglected manuscripts, codices and printed books in archives and research libraries. Our challenge was to correlate each biblical verse with pertinent comments by the church fathers. I was warned that that would take hundreds of scholars at least as much time as it took Jacques-Paul Migne to produce his momentous Patrologia series (1836–1875), but I persisted anyway despite that sober forecast.

I became convinced that the newest digital search technologies would be necessary to look into the oldest Christian texts. The Ancient Christian Commentary on Scripture could not have been accomplished without state of the art computer technologies able to do global searches into vast data bases in the original ancient languages. Those search engines were not yet developed at that time, so the commentary had to start with undeveloped technology.[6] I had to convince others that a patristic commentary on the whole of Scripture was doable, that it had been delayed too long and that digital searches would open the door to making it possible for the first time in Christian history.

At that time most of these technologies were still in testing phases, and none had yet been applied smoothly to patristic sources. This enigma could not be conquered by hand searches of paper books alone. It required searching digitalized data bases of patristic texts in Latin, Greek and Syriac sources, but many of them at that time were not yet digitized.[7] Even with digital help, that would still leave a tremendous amount of work for editors, translators and publishers. My first task was to draw together some trusted colleagues who could help me find a more efficient way to identify specific Old or New Testament comments on specific texts in Greek, Latin or Syriac. We began by selecting a particular text, like Romans 3:24, and asking, How did Augustine and Cyril of Alexandria comment on it? How, for instance, do you find what Origen said about the plagues of Exodus or Rahab of Jericho?

Few historians were delving into complex Boolean searches of ancient texts. The patristic guild was largely disdainful of technology, preferring 3x5 library cards and hand searches. Most patristic scholars were wedded to paper and physical evidence, unaware of the digital hurricane that was on its way to transform their paper havens. The paper, the fabric, the smell of leather in library stacks had always been a part of the library's mystique and the historian's passion. History, therefore, was one of the last departments in the university to make the switch to digital.

I wondered why had there been no catena (chain of patristic comments on biblical texts) published in English for generations.[8] No one I knew was talking about a comprehensive correlation of every biblical passage with the best thoughts of patristic writers from the first to the eighth century.[9] Those ancient writers had stood for so many centuries as authoritative interpreters of the text, but I could see now how inaccessible they were to nonspecialists.

I had a visual image in mind for how the page design might look for ACCS. It would be modeled after the Steinsaltz edition of the Talmud, which itself was modeled after medieval scribes before the era of printing.[10] I had found no similar Christian commentary for classic exegetes. Most of the Talmud was written during the same centuries as the patristic writers. Why hadn't its methods of comparison been done with the early Christian biblical interpreters? The worshiping community needed a classic commentary for its spiritual formation and homiletic wisdom. Historians needed better access to the history of exegesis. I needed a usable patristic commentary for my own spiritual formation. But the need was most strongly felt and expressed by my own PhD students. I searched but could not find any model in recent times to compare with the classic Greek or Latin catenae that featured chains of patristic comment on a particular verse.

There was an immense gap of neglect in biblical studies. The previous generation of biblical scholarship had been so intently focused on recent historical and literary methods that it had left the worshiping community with a longing for simple, straightforward explanations of what the texts said and what they meant. Many were unaware that the earliest biblical commentators had been doing just that. Most of those ancient writers had also been responsible for pastoral care and had written simple homilies on how a text was interpreted in a way faithful to the apostolic tradition. They had shown what that text meant in relationship to the whole course of scriptural revelation. The difference was that they had been responsible to worshiping congregations, not to university history departments.

As I reviewed the biblical literature around 1990, it was evident to me that modern biblical scholars had been largely uninterested in what Basil or Ambrose might have said about understanding the meaning of a particular text for church teaching, since they were almost never quoted. They thought the church fathers could be dismissed because they lacked modern empirical methods of investigation—or so it appeared.[11]

My doctoral students knew how my life had been changed by reading the ancient Christian writers. Many of my students were engaged in historical, literary and redaction criticism of particular passages of Scripture, but they lacked the sources to compare ancient with modern. All they found were endless stacks of historical-critical studies. They knew those studies could not easily be turned into teachable moral reflection or personal transformation. They had limited power for spiritual edification. My students wanted to connect the critical exegetical work they were doing now with the insights of the earliest Christian memory. I recommended that they go to the volumes of Biblia Patristica, *Index des citations et allusions bibliques dans la littérature patristique.* Almost cost prohibitive, what they found there was only the reference citations and not the texts themselves, which would have been filled with passion and depth. They needed a source that provided the actual texts, but even that would require hundreds of volumes. They wanted a selection of the most important and representative texts in a single printed series. Seeing that the need was clear, I began to feel a claim upon me to help provide what was needed.

Not wanting to take this task on myself, I tested the idea out with other patristic scholars, who thought it was conceptually splendid but practically impossible. I knew that no one was working systematically on the whole Bible as seen by the early Christian writers. I also reasoned that it would require significant funding and finding a publisher willing to take substantial risks.

As it turned out, Robert Wilken, renowned author of *The Land Called Holy* and a leading figure in the North American Patristics Society, called me on his way from Virginia to New Hampshire. He wanted to drop by my house for a casual visit. Over the years I had learned a great deal from

him, and had sparred amiably with him many times before as a participant in the Lindbeck and Dulles Groups in New York and at professional society meetings.

Usually he overnighted in New York with his old friend Richard
Neuhaus, but this time he wanted to come by Drew to talk with Edrita
and me. We arranged a room for him on the Drew campus and spent
an evening together. I introduced the idea of a patristic commentary.
He had been reading my *Systematic Theology* and valued my attempt
to reground theological reasoning in the ancient Christian writers.
Cautiously I told him that I had been contemplating a comprehensive
patristic commentary. He looked stunned. I asked for his candid
opinion about its viability. At first skeptical, he conceded that it might
be done, but only with great difficulty. Even then his vision of it was
constrained by his strong conviction that only a few books of the Bible
had sufficient line-by-line commentaries, but he was intrigued by the
boldness of the idea.

From the outset we had two different visions. He thought the commentary would be primarily for scholars; I thought it should be for
everyone who reads the Bible regularly, including scholars. We spent the
evening talking about the possibilities and limitations of the idea. Edrita
was concerned that I would not have time for this project.

The Ahmanson initiative. Howard Ahmanson had been reading my
book *After Modernity . . . What?* Roberta had also read it, and they
wanted to meet me. This turned out to be the beginning of a lasting
friendship with the Ahmansons and an immensely fruitful collaboration
that has grown deep over two decades.

Our meetings in California always occurred at the Ahmanson's house,
high above the Pacific coast. The cove of the Crown of the Sea (Corona
del Mar) with its fine sand beach and huge black wave-worn volcanic
rocks was a truly spectacular vista, which I enjoyed tremendously.

I received an invitation from the Ahmansons to explain *Agenda for
Theology* to some of their friends in California. They had invited a group
of young film producers, artists and musicians to discuss their varied
work in the media environment, which was known to be skeptical about

religion. Howard had sent them a copy of my book on lively paleo-orthodoxy within the collapse of modern idols.

The young artists were bright and disarming. All were engaged in creative projects in film, sculpture, fiction, rock music or the visual arts. About forty of them filled the living room area to overflowing. They had high spirits, camaraderie, imagination and interweaving interests.

That was my first glimpse into what the remarkable Ahmanson family was all about. For years they had been inviting educators, pastors, students, architects and theologians for stimulating evenings of buoyant discussion. Roberta's vocation is Christian hospitality: bringing people together for synergies of mind and heart.

The Ahmansons are voracious readers of art, history, science, travel and cultural criticism. Roberta had been reading Calvin and Thomas Aquinas at the time, and Howard had been reading on local governance and comparative linguistics. And even though their son David was very small, he showed me their Noah's ark collection of animal statues in a long row leading to the ark.

A return to California was arranged for me by Steven Ferguson, who was extremely important to the story of the patristic commentary, more than anyone would guess. He was serving as the assistant to the president of Biola University, Clyde Cole. Together they planned for me to meet with some of their faculty to talk about the vulnerabilities of modern ideologies. These fallen gods had given new life to classic Christianity as it applied to university teaching. Those attending the faculty seminars were attempting to integrate classical Christian teaching into their university teaching. The Ahmansons viewed nearby Biola as a test case for what they were seeking in the deep reform of Christian colleges, universities and seminaries.

That initial exploration led to more extended venues arranged through Ferguson. I agreed to meet periodically over a semester with a select group of Biola's key faculty members to guide them in their thinking about their vocation as teachers.[12]

I invited Edrita to come along with me on one of those trips to California. Edrita's adroit conversation style was flawless, hilarious and winsome, and Roberta and Howard enjoyed her immensely. As we had dessert on the veranda overlooking the Pacific, I was thinking that the evening was almost over when suddenly Roberta asked me a totally unexpected question: What do you want to do with the rest of your life?

While I had not anticipated this question, I had an immediate answer, "Develop a patristic commentary on the whole Bible." Howard wanted to know more about why it was needed and how it could be accomplished, so I explained that an ancient Christian commentary on Scripture would bring back together evangelicals, Orthodox Christians and Catholics. Later Ferguson urged me to write a project design for reflection by the Fieldstead staff. (Fieldstead is the philanthropic arm of the Ahmansons.) The remainder of my life has been wrapped up in its consequences. It seemed to me to have happened in the twinkling of an eye. The shape of my future was clearer than it had ever been before.

Seldom having spoken about special providence, although I had written about it as a universally received Christian teaching in the first volume of my *Systematic Theology*, I had always delighted in the biblical promise that God prepares the way long before we take a step on a journey. I knew the abuses of that doctrine: exaggerated claims of private revelation and the sad history of how often it has been used for egocentric purposes. But the course of the events leading to that conversation on the veranda and its subsequent invitation made me reflect on providence in a new way. That moment was the beginning of a new phase of my life and literary work.

We returned to Drew University, where the digital research began. There in two basements of the university, which we called the "skunk works," the work on the first complete patristic commentary on Scripture in modern times was launched. The first three pieces of my vocational puzzle had been found: Herberg's admonition, Ratzinger's vision and now the Ahmansons' interest in making it possible.

The conception, the publisher and the design. I invited a gathering of patristic scholars in New Orleans on the balcony of Broussard's Restaurant, where I set forth the basic proposal for an ancient Christian commentary on Scripture. It turned out to be an auspicious moment for beginning to gather a team of notable patristic and exegetical scholars who would provide counsel on how to proceed. The next step was a feasibility study that considered practical options and set forth a workable plan. Robert Wilken was a senior scholarly adviser at the conceptual stage.

I made a formal appeal to the Drew University president and administration to designate Drew as the academic home of the project. Through an orderly process, the Drew University Patristic Commentary Project was thoroughly discussed, duly processed and approved by the university.[13] The Drew administration then authorized me to invite leading patristic scholars to Washington, DC, in 1993 to judge the viability of the project based on the feasibility study. I selected a dozen scholars, many of them from the New Orleans conversation, to evaluate that assessment. There was general agreement that the project was profoundly needed but could be done only with volume editors of high international repute. It was agreed that the project should begin as soon as possible, and that I was to draw together an editorial advisory board, develop sufficient funding and find a publisher.

Shortly thereafter I was invited to submit the formal proposal for the patristic commentary to Fieldstead to go through their regular review processes. Receiving the news of a very generous grant effectively launched the project. I began making arrangements with Drew University for logistic support for a project that promised to resurrect Drew's long reputation as a research-oriented academic center.

With high respect to alternative conceptions, there were compelling reasons why we decided to write for a general audience of informed lay readers, as distinguished from a small audience of advanced patristic scholars. If we could succeed in serving those general readers sensibly and persuasively, we knew that the texts, translated by world-class patristic scholars, would also be utilized in university libraries, seminary courses and advanced studies and research.

We had zero competition since no one else was considering producing a patristic commentary on the whole Bible. The advisory team decided not to limit our searches to a few preferred commentaries but wanted to include allusions and references from the whole range of patristic literature, including homilies, letters, poetry, hymns, essays and treatises. That decision followed the pattern of the early catena traditions. We paid special attention to major, detailed, line-by-line commentaries such as those by Origen, Cyril of Alexandria, Theodoret, John Chrysostom, Jerome, Augustine and Bede, but went far beyond them into occasional writings. Out of this excess of raw materials, we encouraged the volume editors to select the best, wisest and most representative reflections of ancient Christian writers on any given biblical passage.

We intentionally sought international editors who would be more likely to be trusted by the readers of Scripture globally rather than allow a North American stamp to be put on it. The next crucial step was to secure a good match in a publisher. Competitive economic conditions had put the major trade publishers like Harper and Oxford in a defensive, risk-aversive mood for such a huge project. Some editors of a Catholic press doubted that Protestants would be able to produce such a commentary. A token number of mainline Protestant publishers did not quite understand the need for it.

The resolution of all of those issues occurred in the annual meeting of the American Academy of Religion in Chicago in 1994, where a decisive conversation with Robert Wilken, Brian Daley, Christopher Hall, Publisher Bill Eerdmans and me occurred. Robert had previously worked with Eerdmans and I had not. I had previously worked with the Inter-Varsity Press (IVP) and Robert had not. Two visions clashed. Chris and I preferred the vision of a large multivolume series with world-class editors covering the whole Bible that would address an international nonprofessional audience. Wilken's alternative vision had a North American focus on producing only a few volumes for largely a professional readership. Bill Eerdmans tried to mediate, but could see there was no easy way to reconcile the two visions. At that crucial point Chris, who became the ACCS associate general editor, took me aside and confided to me that further attempts to work in that direction would be unavailing. Chris had a strong hunch that our publisher should be Inter-Varsity Press. I still hoped that we could reconcile with Wilken, but I finally saw the wisdom of trusting my long-term colleague.

The conceptual battle was over. We contacted the IVP editors and set forth the basic idea for the Ancient Christian Commentary on Scripture, projected at that time to be about a twenty-seven volume series.[14] After I submitted a detailed proposal, IVP invited Chris Hall, Joel Scandrett and me to engage in a two-day planning session. We came out with an agreement to proceed with a major subscription effort.

I was determined to stick to my original vision that the Ancient Christian Commentary on Scripture should have three clear goals: the renewal of Christian preaching based on classical Christian exegesis, the intensified study of Scripture by lay persons who wanted to think with the early church about the canonical text, and the stimulation of Christian historical, biblical, theological and pastoral scholarship toward further inquiry into the scriptural interpretations of the ancient Christian writers. Those goals have guided every step along the way.

Boolean digital computer searches were especially useful in combing through the Greek and Latin texts. They have the capacity to specify the selection of specific words or word combinations.[15] The digital search team identified a profusion of exegetical materials on virtually every narrative in Scripture. Many of those ACCS editorial assistants went on to teach in seminaries and universities.[16] We agreed to the common practice in defining the patristic period as early Christian writings from Clement of Rome to John of Damascus, covering seven centuries of biblical interpretation, from the end of the New Testament to mid-eighth century, including the Venerable Bede (A.D. c. 673–735).

"Our core team" has been the four colleagues who have been together for almost twenty years: Christopher Hall (former seminary dean and chancellor of Eastern University), Michael Glerup (chief executive officer of the Center for Early African Christianity), Joel Elowsky (research director of ACCS and CEAC as well as professor at Concordia Universities Wisconsin and St. Louis) and me.

We have worked closely together over many years of intense productivity. Together we have written, edited or produced the twenty-nine volumes of ACCS, the five volumes of the Ancient Christian Doctrine series, the more than a dozen volumes of the Ancient Christian Texts series, three volumes on early African Christianity, and founded the press of the Institute for Classical Christian Studies. Those colleagues have provided me with enduring friendships, a picture book full of memories and companionship in travel to dozens of countries from China, India and Russia to Johannesburg, Nairobi, and Cairo to Rome and Oxford. They have been cooperators in every enterprise in which I have been involved since 1993.

In the early 1990s I entered into conversation with the Electronic Bible Society hoping to interest them in the digitization of the thirty-eight volume Ante-Nicene and Post-Nicene Church Fathers, which at that time had not been digitized. With a generous supplementary grant from our benefactors through ACCS, that crucial data base was made available in digital form.

Enlisting preeminent international patristic scholars. In Rome I renewed my friendship with Cardinal Ratzinger in followup conversations in 1991 when he was prefect of the Congregation for the Doctrine of the Faith. He remembered our pivotal New York conversations four years earlier.

Then in 1996 I met once again with Ratzinger at his office, where we talked about working together on a film exploring the common theological concerns of evangelicals and Catholics. He was well aware of the Neuhaus and Colson initiative on Catholics and Evangelicals Together and the groundbreaking work we were doing together. He was interested in its ongoing discussions and their current issues. It was clear that new bridges were being built between Catholics and evangelicals, particularly from joint efforts in the defense of the unborn and in joint statements on justification, Scripture and tradition, and the church as a communion.

From Ratzinger's office in the Vatican Palace, he and I walked over to a nearby restaurant on the Via della Conciliazione, where I reported to him on the current developments on the patristic commentary which his New York symposium had stimulated. We discussed potential Catholic patristic scholars as nominees for editing particular volumes of the Ancient Christian Commentary on Scripture. His brilliance was bathed in humility. By that time I knew that he had become Pope John Paul II's closest theological adviser.

I was especially grateful to Edward Cardinal Idris Cassidy of the Pontifical Council for Promoting Christian Unity of the Vatican for his blessing and wise counsel in our visit to Rome concerning the ACCS and the evangelical-Catholic dialogues between the World Evangelical Alliance and representatives of his office.

I actively sought out world-class scholars who understood our high academic requirements and our nonprofessional audience. I had little difficulty enlisting an international team of proven and eminent scholars who were able to reach a global audience that bridged all of the major communions of Christianity. As had been planned, a large proportion of the editors were not from North America.

I did a great deal of intercontinental traveling from 1993 to 1998 to consult with key figures in Oxford, Cambridge, Edinburgh, Tübingen, Athens, Cairo, Rome and the Pacific Rim, drawing together a global team of volume editors. A wide series of ecumenical consultations sought the best nominees. I consulted personally with Greek, Russian, Coptic, Armenian and Syrian Orthodox patriarchs and primates. I solicited their counsel on the most competent scholars in their traditions in the history of exegesis, capitalizing on their hopes for a viable classic Christian commentary.[17]

In Rome my key partners in dialogue were Professors Angelo Di Berardino, Basil Studer and Robert Dodaro of the faculty of the Augustinianum. At Princeton both Professors Bruce M. Metzger and Karlfried Froehlich were crucial advisers from the very earliest stages. In New York I consulted with Professors Robert Wright and Thomas Hopko, and in Washington with Augustine Di Noia of the Dominican House, and with Sidney Griffith of Catholic University of America. No one who knew international patristic scholarship could doubt the high reputation of those advisers and volume editors. I had frequent opportunities to visit with America's leading Catholic theologian Avery Dulles before and after his elevation to the cardinalate. When we needed expertise in the interpretation of sacred texts in the early Jewish tradition, I turned to David Novak, Rabbi David Dalin and my colleague Peter Ochs. Major Protestant traditions did not lack representation.[18]

I was grateful that the first primate to give his official and heartfelt blessing to the commentary was the Ecumenical Patriarch Constantine Bartholomew, leader of the Greek Orthodox Churches all over the world. Through the intervention of Orthodox theologian George Dragas, the patriarch warmly received us in Istanbul (Constantinople). I returned to visit with him in 2002 to report on what we had done, with his support and approval.

At that time I was also pleased to accompany the Ahmansons for a visit with the Armenian Catholicos Aram I, the Armenian Patriarch of the Holy See of Cilicia. He was already well-informed about the patristic commentary and was eager to do all he could to further our work. I then went to Jerusalem to seek the blessing of Patriarch Irenaios of the Orthodox Church of Jerusalem. His blessing was later confirmed by his successor Patriarch Theophilos III. When the Russian edition was published, ACCS received the blessing of the primate of the Russian Orthodox Church, His Holiness Patriarch Kirill of Moscow.

I was especially privileged to meet His Holiness Pope Shenouda of the Coptic Church, and to consult with Coptic bishops Seraphim and Moses. I was elated that there was immediate receptivity among both Copts and evangelicals to the project of an Arabic edition of the patristic commentary.

Orthodox Bishop Kallistos Ware was one of our earliest ACCS senior scholar advisers and advocates. He was present at the first editorial selection planning meeting in Oxford in 1995, when we were seeking to correlate the best volume editors with the most fitting books of Scripture. On the advice of Sister Benedicta Ward of Oxford, we established standard protocols to ensure that texts from often ignored traditions were fittingly represented and that both patristic and matristic writers were considered.[19] In the company of Baroness Caroline Cox, her son and Roberta and David Ahmanson, it was a special joy to make the long pilgrimage to Armenia to the Mother See of Holy Etchmiadzin.[20] We traveled in a small van across the disputed no man's land of Nogorno-Karabakh, which was brimming with people holding automatic weapons. Baroness Cox was my guide to the fabulous culture of Armenia. I came to deeply appreciate her dauntless courage in her tireless care for the needy. Her work had taken her to the most hazardous places on earth where children suffer, notably Sudan, Darfur, Armenia, Rwanda and Myanmar. In Armenia we were privileged to visit a home for abandoned children she had founded.

Upon returning to London, we unwound with a memorable visit to the House of Lords in the British Parliament. As a prominent member of the House of Lords, Baroness Cox invited us to have a formal lunch in the elegant Peer's Dining Room only steps away from the parliamentary proceedings. Steven Meyer (of the Discovery Institute of Seattle) and I were on the planning committee for the formation of her charitable foundation. We selected the name Humanitarian Aid Relief Trust, with the symbol of a hart (HART), for the North American branch of her charity. Strolling down the corridors of the Peers felt like a walk through British history as we were then allowed to sit in the reserved space above and to the back of the Lord Speaker in the Peer's Court to observe a session of the House of Lords at close quarters.

Having secured the affirmation of Catholic and Orthodox prelates, we visited a wide range of Anglican and Protestant leaders from Reformed to Pentecostal, and from Lutheran to Baptist traditions.[21]

The Ancient Christian Commentary on Scripture was at every turn viewed as a new and distinct ecumenical event. It was a fresh expression of the unity of the body of Christ coming not only from ecclesial but also academic voices. In less than twenty years we brought together patristic scholars of diverse Christian traditions who were drawn much closer together by the consensus of the earliest commentators on Scripture.

The Oxford Patristic Conference became the gathering place for triennial consulting with many in our international team of editors. I felt that all of the traveling I was doing was necessary to garner that broad consent before the first volume was published in 1998.

Two of the leading women scholars in patristic studies assisted our first steps: Sister Benedicta Ward of Oxford and Professor Frances Young of Birmingham. From the outset I thought it especially important to include the voices of women such as Macrina, Eudoxia, Egeria and the sayings of the desert mothers for contemporary readers of the Bible. We wished we could have found more, but wars and fire were not kind to the women writers of the early church.

While in Oxford I consulted independently with the inimitable Henry Chadwick, the dean of patristic scholars at Oxford, as well as with Elizabeth Wright of Oxford, the longtime editor of Studia Patristica.[22] Then I went back to Rome, where I met with Angelo Di Berardino, Robert Dodaro and the most famous scholar of patristic exegesis on the globe, Manlio Simonetti of the University of Rome.[23] Shortly thereafter we commissioned Orthodox theologian Andrew Louth of Durham for Genesis 1–11 and Sever Voicu of the Vatican Library for the Apocrypha. From then on we knew there would be no question about our world-class scholarship.[24] The ecumenical range of our editors was stunning in both quality and variety. Lutherans contributed greatly to the editorial tasks.[25] Over four hundred people from five continents were involved in our international team working as translators, editors and cooperators. Under the guidance of Avery Dulles and Angelo Di Berardino, we enlisted leading Catholic scholars, among them Mark Sheridan of San Anselmo University in Rome, Jesuit Joseph Lienhard of Fordham and Father Francis Martin of Washington, DC.

Conditions for optimal outcomes. Five ingredients were essential to the realization of this undertaking: right conception, a publisher who understood the hunger of the readership, a willingness to take heavy financial risks in hopes of long-range results, an incentivized editorial process, and a graduate school at a major university with a long history of multivolume scholarly research. The story of how those five ingredients came together is worth telling.

The conception was timely and rightly defined. It was clear to us from the outset that there was virtually no portion of Scripture about which the ancient Christian writers had nothing useful or meaningful to say. The church fathers studied the Bible thoroughly with deep contemplative discernment, comparing text with text, often memorizing large portions of it.

Our mission was not to circumvent the work of textual critics but to better acquaint the readers with the range of the most ancient sources. Many of those selections had not been translated into modern languages.

Others had remained deeply hidden in library archives as unnoticed manuscripts or codices in Latin, Greek or Syriac.[26]

Unprecedented advantages accrued from using digital research techniques that were untested at that time. Those included an efficient and cost-effective employment of human resources, an abundance of potential material for future studies in the history of exegesis and an enormous residual data base to be used for varied purposes.[27] Without those new digital search-and-storage techniques, this series could hardly have been accomplished short of a vast army of researchers working by laborious paper searches in scattered libraries around the world.[28] The ACCS provided a model for patristic biblical references that can be globally searched. It led the way for studies using those methods of research, and for achieving useful results.[29]

IVP understood our project conception better than any other publisher did. The IVP leadership quickly caught our vision and strongly agreed with its viability. In addition they were willing to invest considerable funds in design, marketing and in building an astonishing list of continuing subscribers.[30] At first we thought we could break even with one thousand first year subscribers. Within twelve months we had ten thousand subscribers and felt vindicated. Subscribers cascaded in from libraries, professors, students and pastors, along with many nonprofessional readers.

A decade later, when ACCS had sold a half million copies in the English language, I had a mirthful conversation with my friend Bill Eerdmans. He was as usual very good-humored and upbeat. We could not resist musing about the outcomes of IVP's ACCS compared with the progress of the Eerdmans-Wilken project on The Church's Bible commentary series. I told him I was glad that both conceptions of a patristic commentary were making their way into print and glad they would reach diverse audiences.[31] My hope had been to build into the editorial apparatus an expectation that the project would not drag out into decades, as so typically happened with multivolume series. We constantly monitored the pace of publication.[32] Our earlier aim to produce three or four volumes per year proved viable in the later stages, but not in the earliest years. Though we were unable to meet those targets in the first four years, we were able to make up for them in the middle years.[33]

In fact our research did indeed find its way to a worldwide audience of Catholic, Protestant, Orthodox and charismatic lay readers who had been hungry for deeper grounding in the study of sacred texts beyond the scope of the historical-critical methods that had dominated biblical studies. Libraries found it a "must have" series. Many unexpected types of religious communities were being drawn toward those classic sources for spiritual formation.

Drew University benefited significantly from sponsorship of the ACCS. In its first hundred years Drew University established an impressive reputation as a publishing faculty equal to its early competitors, Syracuse and Cornell. The university assisted in the nurture of major long-term multivolume scholarly projects extending as far back as the very beginning of Drew. The *New York Times'* Arno Press has kept in print the major twelve-volume work of Drew president John McClintock and Drew professor James Strong in their *Cyclopaedia of Biblical, Theological and Ecclesiastical Literature*, begun in 1867 and completed in 1887. As the *Cyclopaedia* took almost twenty years to complete, so did the Ancient Christian Commentary on Scripture.[34] The last major academic series to come out of Drew was the thirty-four volume edition of Chinese Christian Classics, which had been translated in the Drew Library in the 1940s. Now Drew University had renewed that tradition, generously contributing sufficient working space for the project along with its logistical, library and computer services, as well as overhead costs estimated at about a quarter million dollars.

The outcome of the ACCS vision was akin to the outcome of the work of an earlier Drew professor, James Strong, who wrote *Strong's Exhaustive Concordance of the Bible*, an English cross-reference of every Hebrew and Greek word in the Bible (KJV), a fifteen hundred page reference that has remained in use for over a hundred years. Still in active use, it has inspired a reference system used by later concordances that still can be found on the shelves of most libraries in the English-speaking world. Fortunately for us, the office from which Strong had produced the *Exhaustive Concordance* became the office for ACCS.

The Search for Consensual Exegesis

Producing documentary evidences of consensual remembering. By means of a chain (catena) of memorable classic wisdom emerging out of Scripture text, the reader is linked with the earliest apostolic tradition and offered consensually received ancient Christian writers a venue without extensive comment from the compiler.

Text by text the consensus appeared, shining through differences of time, culture and language. The sociological evidence: only those links persisted that were reused again and again. They survived dozens to hundreds of generations by consent. Their consent was proved by their intrinsic value to ongoing generations of believers. I took this as durable evidence of a democratic grassroots way of selection, much more reliable than turning selection over to the knowledge elites. Hence there was a deep and hidden democracy at work in consensual teaching. If a text appeared in a catena, it had already survived a highly selective process extending over countless generations and cultures.[35] That was evidence for the broad consent for which I was searching. It verified the Vincentian method. Those texts would not have persisted without consent. The test of orthodoxy was accurate remembering over many generations of human change. The catena celebrated the basic early Christian memory.

When I searched for others in modern literature who had stated that principle, I could find no better expression of it than Vincent. The early catena was the historic prototype of all subsequent biblical commentaries. Yet contemporary biblical scholars have demeaned it since it lacked the one criterion necessary for them: modernity. Its context was simply the worshiping community. Because of that, I had to show why that evidentiary method was central to the earliest forms of Christian memory. Since *Agenda for Theology* I had felt called to establish that understanding and make it understandable.

The impact of those patristic chains of comment on doctrinal teaching were embedded in the early ecumenical conciliar decisions, as in the councils of Ephesus (431), Chalcedon (451) and Nicea II (787), where doctrinal decisions were frequently supported by venerated quotations from the earliest and most widely respected biblical exegetes.[36] That conciliar procedure of trusting major consensual writers developed into a wide-spread tradition that produced the first biblical commentaries.[37] I took great comfort in the recognition that the pattern of research I used in the 1990s was no different from the pattern of research leading up to the conciliar process of early Christianity. It is also important to note that as historical criticism emerged, the catena receded. An unwritten book at some point will be written on that theme.[38] The catena approach to Scripture study has been more systematically ignored in the last century of Christian scholarship than in any previous century. Jews had the Talmud and Midrashim. Christians had the catenas. Why had contemporary Christians remembered less profoundly than contemporary Jews?

Liberating the sacred texts from hypermodern interpreters. As a former disciple of Rudolf Bultmann, I had personally lived through dozens of iterations of various cycles of literary and historical criticism that sought to expound and interpret the text in an ever-narrowing way. About every third year we came to expect a supposedly new form of biblical criticism—redaction criticism, Formkritik, source criticism, feminist criticism, canonical criticism and the like. Those were often expressions of the desperate hunger for upward mobility occurring within the history guild.

Every one of the ACCS volume editors had thoroughly studied those forms of criticism, but most were seeking to reach beyond them. Those critical methods had left pastors to sail through troubled waters of contemporary culture armed only with the ever-changing layers of modern historical speculations. As a result, weakened preaching invaded the pulpits. The worshiping community found those outcomes largely unsatisfying and wanted a more instructive alternative. That was the starved context in which our regeneration of the patristic catena entered and immediately produced fruitful consequences. Many of the catenae had never been translated into modern languages. The catenae were written by fifth- and sixth-century biblical scholars who were quoting the second, third and fourth century apostolic interpreters. They were focused on relating each discrete verse to the whole testimony of sacred Scripture by the analogy of faith, comparing text with text, on the premise of *scrip-*

turam ex scriptura explicandam esse, by which each passage was illuminated by the stream of other passages and by the whole gist of the history of revelation, as was done in the rabbinic tradition. The catena was not intended as a format for extensive technical opinions but for concise content interpretation.

The texts we most actively sought out were those sufficiently self-evident that they did not require extensive contextualization in order to be understood by ordinary laity. We scoured the vast literature for classic patristic comments that had rhetorical strength and metaphorical power to convey the depth of Scripture's intent.[39] As general editor charged with making the whole series cohere, I was constantly looking for those texts that represented the central flow of the ecumenical consensual exegesis. In each verse I tried to find classic texts that best represented the mind of the believing church.

A debate emerged as to whether ACCS was a biblical commentary by modern standards, but I can assure you that ACCS is a biblical commentary by the standards of those who came long before and decisively shaped the entire subsequent history of biblical commentary, defining the very idea of a commentary.[40] A modern biblical commentary on patristic comments could be an entirely different project at some future date, but even then the classics texts would speak for themselves.

The patristic commentary as stimulus to Christian unity. Contemporary readers are now finding common ground in the earliest biblical interpreters regardless of their sectarian memory. Persons from all of the traditions have an equal right to appeal to the early history of Christian exegesis.[41] The patristic commentary morphed into an ecumenical symphony.

That was an unanticipated joy. Without a sacrifice of intellect or conscience, the readers were finding their own history in the wisdom of texts common to them all. They were finding common faith in listening together to their common roots. Those who had been longest deprived of those patristic texts have had the greatest desire for them.

That eagerness has been especially strong among evangelical communities. The evidence for that fact was found in the growing numbers of leading evangelical seminaries who only after ACCS have set up new chairs in patristic studies. Twenty years ago it was hard to find references to John Chrysostom and Cyril of Alexandria in the evangelical vocabulary, but now references abound. That was demonstrable in the flood of serious books and articles on patristic subjects among evangelical publishers that ensued. Evangelicals have often been caricatured by avant-garde historians as critically backward and hermeneutically challenged. Now it is arguably the historians who appear critically deficient.[42]

Nonprofessional readers of the Bible have responded to a deep need that ACCS helped make clear. They are recognizing their need for biblical resources that go far beyond those that have been made available to them in both the mainline, pietistic and historical-critical subcultures. The recognition of affinities between modern evangelicals and the ancient Christian writers has influenced every field of seminary studies: biblical, historical, doctrinal and pastoral.

Given the obvious weaknesses of much preaching in our time, the ancient Christian homilists have become a dynamic source for the renewal of modern preaching. Lay persons have reveled in their inspiration.[43] Those who have read deeply in the ACCS have often indicated to me that they regarded patristic Bible study as a key element in their own spiritual formation.

The ACCS has now been translated into the languages of half of the world's population. Lay readers in vastly different cultural settings in Asia and Africa are asking how they might grasp the meaning of sacred texts under the instruction of the great minds of the ancient church. ACCS unapologetically claims its rightful place as an essential source book in the history of religious literature.

REQUIEM FOR THEOLOGICAL EDUCATION

The dilemma of meeting the goddess at the Lord's Table. I came back home to the New York area after my sabbatical in Rome in the spring of 1991 and settled back into teaching. Soon after returning I realized that we were increasingly having strange things happen in our seminary chapel services. The chapel services had become viewed by some as an opportunity for liturgical experimentation or political tirades with visual props and an entertainment mentality.

None was more surprising than the Sophia Communion experiment. The majority of women students at Drew Seminary had come as moderate to conservative believers from small towns. Many were devoted moms with growing families. Meanwhile a small cadre of feminists conceived of themselves as chosen to speak for all of the women in the seminary, regardless of age and experience.

The Thursday service that particular week was announced as a special event sponsored by the women's caucus. It was led by a highly visible guest feminist leader with an uncommon fixation on the advocacy of the goddess Sophia as an object of adoration.

I have followed Wesley in viewing Holy Communion as a uniting and converting sacrament, uniting the body of Christ and converting the heart for service. In all of my years of coming to the Lord's Table, I had never once seriously considered withdrawing from a Holy Communion service. I had read *Wisdom's Feast*, coauthored by our guest homilist, so I knew that she had frequently spoken of Sophia as a goddess to be worshiped, referring to Sophia as "a strong, proud, creative goddess within the biblical tradition."[44] Our liturgist had invented and written about the strategy of introducing Sophia worship into permissive old-line churches in order to move through calculated stages in which the goddess character of Sophia would be introduced only gradually and then legitimized.

In a five-tier process the homilist planned to first attempt to conceal the goddess character of Sophia by a "basic and unobtrusive reintroduction" but then would later reveal her overtly in a faux Eucharist which addressed feminist issues by celebrating the "Jesus-Sophia connections" and her "presence in all things."[45]

As an orthodox theologian, I approached the service with some uneasiness. I wondered if it might be best to not attend at all. Then I recalled that that seminary chapel welcomed all, including me, to the Table of pardon. I tried to practice the "duty of constant communion" as set forth by Mr. Wesley. My intent was to listen carefully and fairly, then join the community at the Table of divine forgiveness. I had come with the expectation of hearing the word preached and receiving Holy Communion. The first hymn was on Sophia as lover, comforter and counselor, sung to the tune of Salve Regina, a touching hymn I had so often sung in Rome with the priestly residents of Casa Santa Maria, sung in honor of the blessed Virgin, mother of the incarnate Lord.

As I listened to the revised liturgy I began to feel more queasy and manipulated as I wondered whether I was in a place where some other lord was being worshiped. For the first time in my life I felt like the second-century Christian witnesses must have felt when required to bow to the gods of Roman civic religion and surrender their Scriptures to the authorities. Some, like the five women of the African church in Scilli (A.D. 180) had given their lives rather than deny their faith in the sole lordship of Christ.

Then came the feminist homily mostly addressed to feminist activists. It was far beyond the range of easy tolerance for many traditional women in the seminary. In the name of inclusiveness, all other hearers were marginalized and to some extent demeaned. When that docetic-gnostic view of wisdom was mated with feminist political objectives and bootlegged into the liturgy, the faithful women students found it hard to sit by compliantly.

The quandary. It was becoming clear to me that the god worshiped in this service was not the triune God made flesh in Jesus Christ but the mythic voice of the goddess Sophia, entirely distinguishable from the One celebrated in the Christian liturgy. Was my conscience requiring me to leave? Just at that moment the homilist urged the congregation not to delay in asserting their convictions. She argued that the longer feminists delayed asserting their authority in worship, the more intractable it would be. She then offered the invitation to come to the Lord's Table not in the Lord's name but in the name of the goddess who was swapping roles with Jesus. The invitation came not on behalf of the Lord of glory crucified on a cross but the idea of wisdom seen through the lens of feminist political activism.

That did it. I decided that she was inadvertently correct that I could not delay making some attestation of the lordship of Jesus Christ in the

Holy Communion. Therefore, as the peace of Christ was exchanged, I greeted two or three women sitting nearby and quietly, inconspicuously, left the service.

The predominant theme of the 1993 Re-Imagining Conference was the audacity of reimagining God, using Sophia worship as its key liturgical expression. It was sponsored by the National Council of Churches in Minneapolis, touted as a major ecumenical event and funded by United Methodist, United Church of Christ and Presbyterian boards and agencies.

It sought to transform the way Protestants ought to think about God by using the Sophia model as a central feature. It presented itself as an "ecumenical convergence," but it became the most ecumenically divisive event in recent memory. Triune language and the atonement were belittled. The liturgists ridiculed the blood of the cross as a primitive way of thinking. Those were all intentional, inflammatory, counterecumenical ploys that the conference organizers deliberately designed. As I later listened to the audiotapes, I wondered how a modern "ecumenical" conference that was intentionally divisive and contrary to ancient ecumenical teaching could possibly label itself as ecumenical with a straight face.

The perplexity of the laity about theological education. My book *Requiem* (1995) sadly pointed to the death of the old liberal seminaries. I grieved because it could have been different. The seminaries were not forced to become slaves to modern ideologies but chose and celebrated their choices.

Requiem was not a book primarily for religious professionals but rather it was about professionals charged with preparing people for ministry. I wrote that book to address a primarily nonprofessional audience to help them understand what was happening in the seminaries that were sending young pastors to their local pulpits.

Worshipers in mainline churches were often baffled by the ideological rhetoric coming out of the mouths of their own ordained ministers. They were much more distressed by what clergy were forgetting to say than by what they were saying. Many in the pews wondered where in the world their ministers had gotten their bizarre ideas.

Eventually it became a matter of conscience for me to open that Pandora's box. I knew that patient congregations were seething with frustration over what they were hearing from their sacred pulpits. They had been socialized to be compliant, to not raise embarrassing questions, to not enter into disputes, especially regarding their own local pastors.

Eccentric, wild pockets of free-floating church bureaucrats and idealists seemed to dominate church policy, yet were accountable to no one, least of all to those who funded them. The congregations found their church agencies impenetrable. Laypeople were drifting toward despair about whether any real changes could ever be made. At that time they began to vote with their feet in increasing numbers. With each local attempt, they met the brick wall of the bureaucracy. I hoped someone else would explain that descriptively, but no one did.

Requiem was not about my faculty directly but was far more concerned with the larger dilemma of theological education in North America generally. The Sophia liturgy was the straw that broke the camel's back for me.

While writing *Requiem* I constantly pretested my arguments through lectures in widely diverse ecumenical audiences. I spoke frequently to seminary audiences, scholarly societies and pastoral retreats. I wanted to put my assessments up for critique before they were published in 1995.[46] Traveling a lot, I listened to the pain of those who had suffered from their theological education as well as to the outrage of professional colleagues who were infuriated by any challenges to it.

For me that situation was a timely opportunity for teaching classical Christianity as the healthy survivor of failed ideologies. I urged young orthodox believers not to leave the liberated seminaries but stay and transform them. I was criticized for not walking away, more by my conservative colleagues than anyone else. It seemed to me unthinkable to abandon a once-distinguished theological teaching tradition, its intellectual achievements, its libraries, its alumni and its laity. So many of the patient faithful had for so long been committed to sustaining those institutions of higher learning. To me the seminaries could not be abdicated.

By the late 1990s many seminarians realized that the old game was unsustainable. They could see that the passing permissive generation was desperately on the defensive and its claim of legitimacy was vulnerable, as I had been warning since *Agenda for Theology*. Faithful seminarians were faced with dealing simultaneously with the severe debt crisis in theological education and the reconciliation of an alienated laity. I, who so loved the academic life and wanted to renew it, was caught in the irony of challenging its misdeeds in order to spare its collapse.

The decisive question was whether the secularization process could be reversed and transcended by a rediscovery of classic Christian faith. That had occurred many times before in Christian history, and I knew the Spirit had plenty of time. But did the seminaries?

I decided to stay in the church that had baptized me as long as its doctrinal confession and constitutional guarantees remained intact. If those doctrinal standards did not remain intact, I would have to ask my conscience whether there was any reason to remain. But I did not believe that was going to happen. I knew the strength of those historic constitutional guarantees.[47]

The study of biblical and Christian history had devolved into a deconstruction of sacred texts. The study of ethics had become both an oppressively legalistic rulebook of political correctness and a license for permissiveness. The study of liturgy had declined into an experiment in balloons, guitars and bad poetry. I did not feel anger or pity about those absurdities, but I did feel the lightness of the laughter of God toward our human follies, including my own.[48] A basic rewriting of the counterproductive rules that allowed tenure abuses was required.

My leaving the Sophia service became a firestorm of controversy, first with feminist groups, then with some of my faculty colleagues and finally with the Abingdon publishing imprint for the United Methodist Publishing House, who had been publishing my books since 1968. I got two kinds of feedback: the first from the women students who shared with me the annoyance they had felt during the service and thanked me for my action; the second from the feminist activist minority who wanted to make a public cause célèbre out of that quiet incident which for me was a private act of conscience.

Meanwhile as the goddess liturgy grew in public awareness, I, as consulting editor of *Christianity Today*, provided a brief one-page report of what had happened in my seminary.

The inquisition: Stop the presses! In drafting and redrafting *Requiem*, I worked very closely with my Abingdon editors, who were eager to publish the book. The final manuscript went through two full rounds of serious redrafting to make it more palatable. Just before publication it received another full review by the publishing committee of the United Methodist Publishing House. In due course it was accepted and scheduled for publication in late 1994.

The final galleys of *Requiem* were complete and the copyedited book was in production when a strange thing happened. Unknown to me, a letter-writing initiative had emerged from unidentified persons who were trying to get the United Methodist Publishing House to rescind the decision to publish *Requiem*. I heard in whispers that a few activists wanted to stop the presses. I was out of the loop but I got occasional reports from persons who knew what was going on. I was told it was a close call.

Since I knew I could get another publisher, I made no effort to find out exactly what was going on. Also I knew that the publishing committee worked confidentially, but eventually I was told the gist of it. The publishing committee is an agent of the United Methodist Church under the supervision of the General Conference in connection with its imprint Abingdon. I later learned that the board of publications of the United Methodist Church had met to debate whether *Requiem* production should be cancelled, but the Abingdon editors were eager to see it in print and defended their editorial decision.

The editors' judgment was approval, and *Requiem* was published and soon became a favorite on the Abingdon list. When one of my friends tried to buy it at an Abingdon Bookstore, the store managers could not find it. After searching they found it hidden under the cash register and not available on the shelf. The clerk gingerly put it in a brown paper bag when my friend purchased it.

I was gratified when the published book was positively reviewed and widely read. It became obligatory reading for mainline seminary deans.

My purpose was to convey to the laity and to traditional seminary students a glimpse of what was happening in many mainline seminaries, particularly throughout all of the mainline Protestant churches.

Back home the controversy was not over. After *Requiem* was finally in print, I got word from my seminary dean at Drew that my book would be the sole subject matter of the next regularly scheduled faculty retreat on May 5, 1995. I welcomed the encounter. As a tenured member of the faculty since 1970, I was at ease and ready to answer all questions.

Most of the dialogue was civil, but it was like walking on eggs. After that retreat it was clear to me that my effectiveness as a member of the faculty was now limited. I had already helped build up the faculty academically as much as I could, so I voluntarily withdrew from all faculty committees and focused, to my delight, on my research and writing, along with teaching my usual annual class load.

RETREAT TO CHICKASAW NATION

Back in the saddle again. It was a perfect time for an exit and withdrawal, not from teaching or research but from seeking to be responsible for the follies of theological education.

Days after that turmoil, I quietly sought out a remote retreat on a hidden lake in the Arbuckle Mountains of Oklahoma to write my book on Kierkegaard's theory and practice of comic perception. It was a large manuscript long overdue from a contract signed with the Princeton University Press.

I can think of no writing project I have ever enjoyed more than *The Humor of Kierkegaard*. Princeton University Press gave me wide freedom to do that book as I saw fit. I set forth Kierkegaard's little-recognized idea that humor is intrinsic to Christianity since it speaks first of incarnation, which is intrinsically a contradiction, and contradiction is the essence of humor. The gospel is a story about a king who appears as a plumber's assistant.

I reviewed the whole of Kierkegaard's corpus for yarns and stories that exemplified his remarkable wit.[49] At Five Lakes I gained a renewed will and wit. It was time for some laughs. It was my time to get some distance from Drew with a sweeping change of pace under a big sky.

What a great respite I had in the Oklahoma hills, where the largest town nearby was less than five thousand in population. The lake was in Chickasaw Indian Nation country with lots of cattle and catfish. It was the perfect place for me to be.

I felt like a prisoner who had gotten a reprieve. I was literally

Back in the saddle again,
Out where a friend is a friend,
Where the longhorn cattle feed
On the lowly gypsum weed,
Back in the saddle again.[50]

I took my guitar with me back to the same county in Oklahoma where the inspiration for that song had occurred. At Five Lakes I lived near the tiny village in Chickasaw country now named Gene Autry, Oklahoma, which had a population of ninety-nine, where the singing cowboy, son of a country Methodist preacher, and then owner of the Los Angeles Angels, had been born.

In the Chickasaw Nation, where many Chickasaw Indians still live, I found a welcomed quietness, with lots of hiking, bird watching and fresh air to breathe. I realized how much I had missed the unpretentious people of rural southern Oklahoma. Edrita was working as a communications consultant and did not want to leave her clients, friends and neighbors in New Jersey, so I went on my one-semester sabbatical alone. By that time the children were all out of college and into jobs in Washington, DC, Austin and Dallas. At Five Lakes I lived a quiet, solitary life. I was drawn to the monastic pattern of ordered prayer, study and work. I had read a lot about it, and now I wanted to practice it.

I stayed on in Five Lakes until classes called me back to New Jersey in January, when I taught my last Kierkegaard seminar. After that I returned to my Oklahoma retreat as often as I could. In 1996 I deeded the lake house to Tal and Jane, and purchased a lovely brick lakefront home on Lansbrook Lake in Oklahoma City.

Returning to Drew, my teaching was largely limited to combinations of January terms, summer terms and full semesters sufficient to make an annual full load of teaching.

I taught my last rounds of systematic theology lectures and Wesley seminars through the change of the millennium. I did not give my colleagues at Drew any more trouble and sustained pleasant relations with all of them.

All that time I remained project director for the Ancient Christian Commentary on Scripture, traveling the globe to keep up with my volume editors and translators. By that time the commentary had grown into a huge international organization involving large numbers of researchers, linguists, editors and cooperators scattered throughout Europe, North America and the Pacific Rim.

The growing circle of young orthodox teachers. Between my *Agenda for Theology* of 1979 and *Requiem* of 1995, I was watching a growing stream of young conservative theologians in search of classic Christianity. *Requiem* was evidence of a reversal already occurring among young educators open to the hope of a promising era.

Jest was their trademark. Their calling cards were light satire and ironic wit. With a wink and a smile, that style of reasoning was beginning to flow into the stodgy streams of contemporary academia. Since serious theology was largely without courage and historic boldness, it was time for comic perception. This light form of heavyweight argument was best exemplified by Kierkegaard, Berger, Neuhaus, Hauerwas and Willimon.

At the end of *Requiem* I listed those theologians whom I regarded as forerunners of the recovery of orthodox teaching after the end of modern ideologies. Among them were many names not present in *Agenda for Theology.* By 1995 many of them had produced a body of work that advanced or exemplified the agenda.[51] That list was much more robust than the few theologians I named in 1979 as portents of postmodern classic Christianity.

A sea change was occurring. If the list were done today, it would be five times as long as it was in *Requiem* in 1995. I look back with gratitude for them all. Not all agreed with me, but we knew we had a common beginning point in the joys of classic exegesis.

Harare and the Collapse of Modern Ecumenism

The next stage shifted my attention from Euro-American circles to Africa.

Wisdom from Africa. In December 1998 I went to Harare, Zimbabwe, on press credentials to report for *Christianity Today* on the World Council of Churches World Assembly. With its debt crisis and loss of constituencies, rumors abounded that Harare might be the last WCC General Assembly.

In Africa I experienced the stark contrast between the bold and vibrant life of African Christianity and the WCC bureaucracy. The utopian temperament that I had first seen on the streets of Geneva was dying, while the work of the Spirit was flourishing all over Africa among Copts, Catholics and Pentecostals.

Africa helped me regain a borderless vision of the recovery of multicultural classic Christianity. On the African continent I could see how the ancient Christian faith was coming alive with astonishing power. I glimpsed how Africa might be the unique place in the world to find a new foundation for Christianity beyond the prevailing ideologies of Western modernity because it had not yet been fully Westernized. I found it to be a place where the world could relearn the long-lived wisdom of ancient African apostolic Christianity.

Each of the three World Assemblies of the WCC I have attended in my lifetime symbolized a phase of the history of the modern ecumenical movement: Evanston 1954, creation; Geneva 1966, the fall; and Harare 1998, demise.[52] Politicization choked its spirit. I went to Harare hoping that Genevan ecumenism had turned a new leaf, but that was not so.

The first major event in Harare was a love fest between the perennial African political bully Robert Mugabe and the bureaucracy of the World Council of Churches.[53] The shared political objective for both was the idealistic idea of immediate world debt cancellation. With both the country and the World Council in a spiraling debt crisis, it was not surprising that the featured public issue of the entire world conference at Harare was debt forgiveness.

For years the Council had been unable to pay its bills. It was getting almost no support from its member churches because of its political extremism. Increasingly it was forced to turn to far left-leaning international corporate funders to keep its bizarre political agenda alive. Harare had been selected as the favored location to try to make that political point, but the cronyism and coverups of the Mugabe regime made this the least likely place to make that point convincingly. The untamed spending by Mugabe with his political co-conspirators had made Harare a nest of corruption. Deeply in debt themselves, the WCC decided to make international debt forgiveness, regardless of any financial correctives, their major theme.

Harare's economy was already in a tailspin, and soon it would take wheelbarrows of Zimbabwean currency to buy a sack of corn meal. As I went downtown for a television interview for PBS to report on the Harare gathering, I had ten dollar units of Zimbabwean currency in my pocket that was worth about 17 cents and declining with every breath. Who would have known that soon it would take 7,000 of those bills to buy a single biscuit.

The Jubilee debt forgiveness theme gave the Council the opportunity to twist an important biblical metaphor to serve one more desperate political initiative. In the Bible, debts are to be avoided, or when incurred, paid back. Several academic studies have shown that the recurrent cycle of over forty years of debt forgiveness had reinforced cronyism and dependency, with Zimbabwe being one of the most conspicuous examples. The Conference was not about the grace that leads to repentance and faith, but the reinforcement of a dysfunctional cycle of dependency which turns into an addiction. If you were a Marxist, you would certainly want the Conference to be focused on the redistribution of wealth, and the Conference did not disappoint. Meeting in one of the most devious socialist regimes in Africa, the collusion between crony military governments and leftist religious bureaucracies was never more evident.

Discovering the ancient faith in the Ethiopic Orthodox liturgy. After many days of struggle at Harare, several Orthodox and evangelical participants heard about an Ethiopic Coptic Eucharistic service. Together we decided to attend. It was deeply moving. It confirmed our profound affinity with the most ancient sub-Saharan African Christian tradition.

The service was in a makeshift tent. The faces of the priests were living icons. The robust voices of chanting women and elderly black men with white beards penetrated the night air. Visually, we seemed to be attending a great royal event, as if a king were coming for a banquet.

There was one white-bearded elderly celebrant who had piercing eyes and a kindly bearing who gave us the impression of a carved ebony face. Central casting could not have produced a face more saintly.

I was hearing the liturgy in one of Africa's oldest living languages. I realized that I had entered into an arena not far removed from the earliest centuries of African Christianity.

The liturgy that night rehearsed the Scripture story. The empty tomb was before us. The priests disappeared into the sacred space of the inner sanctuary of the tabernacle where the Ark of the Covenant was kept. They were preparing to offer the body and blood of the incarnate and crucified Lord. The fire of the Holy Spirit was being rekindled in a way I had never experienced before. It dawned on me that for almost two millennia the risen Lord has been meeting with sub-Saharan Africans at his Table.

All of this reminded me that Jesus is no newcomer to Africa. He was here as a baby whose family was in flight. In the Nile Valley he began to grow in wisdom, stature and favor with God and humanity. According to early African Christian memory, even as an infant the incarnate God was holding the world together.

Our feet were planted in Africa. Our hearts were beneath our feet. Africans were offering up prayer to the risen Lord on behalf of the cares of the world. We were a small cluster of believers, but the center of changing space seemed to be right there with us in that Holy Communion.

A green and gold curtain enclosed the consecrated elements. The candle's fire proclaimed the presence of the Spirit. Beneath the curtain we could see the sandals on the black feet of the presbyters, moving and shifting in a rhythm of praise.

The curtain was suddenly opened. In gestures that have survived in Africa for centuries, the incense was dispensed to the tiny community at prayer. The sweetness of the Spirit invaded my nostrils. The beauty of the holiness of the Lord was beheld, breathed and sung in rising tones. As the host drew close, the voices rose. The women with shawls approached the host and tasted the bread laid out on a linen cloth. The cup of suffering was offered to all. When Communion was over, the mystery once revealed was returned to its holy place and concealed.

I was deeply moved, and after that my heart began to turn toward Africa. The next day we realized that the Orthodox had been reaching out for evangelicals in a surprising gesture of reconciliation.

I had come to Harare to report for *Christianity Today* specifically on whether the WCC's earlier promises to evangelicals were being fulfilled. The previous WCC World Assembly at Canberra in 1991 had formally mandated the World Council of Churches to strengthen relationships with evangelicals, Pentecostals and charismatic movements. But that had never been implemented except at the most routine and ceremonial bureaucratic levels. Permissive evangelicals had been carefully chosen to represent the evangelical conservatives. The only evangelicals in the conversation had been selected from the Geneva spin room.

Although the WCC pretended it had already fulfilled the mandate of Canberra, as was officially reported to the Harare Assembly, there was little evidence to show that any signs of reconciliation had made a plausible beginning. Evangelicals were clearly outsiders. Even with the most generous interpretation, the effort to include evangelicals had been only sporadic and half-hearted.

Orthodox and evangelical Christianity had been betrayed by temptations to accommodate to the common ideologies of modernity at the cost of the classic Christian center. But amid that situation, a new ecumenism was taking shape among the Orthodox and evangelicals.

It was only after Harare that I could clearly discern how damaging the old WCC ecumenism had been to the very cause of unity it purported to advance. The WCC had fostered the disunity of the church. Ironically, nothing had been more deeply divisive in contemporary Christianity than the very movement intended to unify it. The disunity had been caused by those WCC ecumenists who had largely forgotten the ancient ecumenical consensus.[54]

The old Geneva ecumenism had assumed that it owned unending proprietary rights to the term *ecumenical*. By Harare it was clear that the World Council of Churches was not the sole legitimate heir of the office of bringing unity to the body of Christ. It would not be corrected by circumventing North American evangelicals, Roman Catholics and most Orthodox believers.

At Harare I gave up on the old Geneva-based ecumenism. Happily a new post-WCC ecumenism was emerging among Catholics, Orthodox and evangelicals. While the institutions purporting to be ecumenical were falling apart, the Holy Spirit had been all along at work to create forms of unity in world Christianity far beyond chic ideological politics.

Classic Ecumenism

The narrative of my participation in international ecumenism has been a massive part of my spiritual formation and intellectual history. It was first as an aficionado, then as a skeptic and finally as an advocate for a new ecumenism.

I have personally participated in WCC World Assemblies at their earlier, middle and later stages. What began with promise in 1948 (Amsterdam) reached it apogee in 1966 (Geneva) and began falling to its death bed in 1998 (Harare).

My original ecumenical history had begun a year before the Amsterdam Conference when in 1947 I had joined in the peace movement by organizing and advocating for the World Federalist Campaign for World Government. From then on I moved steadily into greater involvement with that ecumenical leadership.

After Harare. Not until after Harare did I get it straight that the nineteenth-century evangelicals were the chief architects and precursors of the WCC. The World Evangelical Alliance and its associated mission organizations were crucially responsible for calling together the mission conferences that led to the Edinburgh Conference of 1910, which led to the founding of the World Council of Churches in 1948. No one had mentioned that, and I finally understood that that story had become buried history. Moreover the eighteenth-century revivals and mission societies had anticipated the impulses to Christian unity that later gave birth to modern ecumenism of the WCC. That became a house that needed sweeping.

Harare put on display a tiring movement captive to viewing all things through the eyes of permissiveness and run-amok egalitarianism. Meanwhile, the very modernity to which the Genevan ecumenism was seeking to adapt was now in the process of dying intellectually.

Fortunately for me, during my seminary days I had been theologically tutored by two mentors, both key figures on the World Council Commission on Faith and Order: Albert Outler, who had drafted the document "Tradition and Traditions" in Montreal of 1963, and John Deschner, who had drafted the document "Baptism, Eucharist, and Ministry" at Lima in 1982. They were the exceptions to the modernity that was promoted after 1966. Thankfully, Outler and Deschner had taught me the best of ecumenical thinking during its wisest days. By the end of the twentieth century the soundest element of the old WCC ecumenism, the Faith and Order Commission, had been virtually booted out of the elite WCC leadership circles.[55]

The irony was that early Geneva-based ecumenism was in sound continuity with international missionary societies that had created the World Evangelical Alliance in 1846, and it was not until 1966 that this WCC ecumenism took its radical turn toward an imaginary revolution. From 1946 to 1966 I had been mesmerized by all things ecumenical and had read everything I could get my hands on to understand the movement in order to further its goals. Meanwhile, at Harare I was witnessing behind the scenes an unprecedented reconciliation between the Eastern Orthodox traditions and the global evangelicals who were recognizing that Orthodox ways of reading Scripture were truer to the text than they had previously been perceived. A rapid and basic reversal of mood was occurring as evangelicals realized that Orthodox liturgies of the East were not the ogre that stereotypes had portrayed.

It happened more quickly than I would have imagined. After centuries of caricature, those two forms of Christian memory were coming closer together. For too long evangelicals had remained distanced from the liturgical practices of Orthodoxy. The evangelicals had often ruled themselves out of Orthodoxy dialogue because of a distrust of what seemed to be its cultural narrowness, ethnocentric temptations, superstitions and antidemocratic hierarchies. The failure of bureaucratic ecumenism had led me toward a very different historically rooted evangelical and catholic view of the unity of the body of Christ.

The unifying effects of patristic exegesis on a renewing ecumenism. It was a stunning fact of the 1990s that worldwide evangelicals were increasingly drawing closer to patristic exegesis. The Ancient Christian Commentary on Scripture came along at just the right time to encourage that dialogue, and it became obvious to us that the evangelical traditions (Reformed, Baptist, Lutheran and Wesleyan) were starting to realize that they had been too long deprived of vital contact with the classic exegetes.

The ancient exegetes most respected by evangelicals were Tertullian, Augustine and Chrysostom.[56] With more acquaintance with the church fathers, it became possible to see more clearly the similarities between the patristic writers and the eighteenth-century leaders of the evangelical Great Awakenings (Wesley, Edwards and Whitefield), who held a high view of the inspiration and authority of Scripture, and an incarnational Christology.

Our patristic commentary played a modest but at the same time a significant role in strengthening communication between evangelicals, Orthodox and Catholics.[57] Today the world of Orthodoxy has become intriguing to evangelicals worldwide. As young Orthodox meet young evangelicals, they recognize their kinship almost instantly. Each side has missed something the other side could have given to them. Evangelicals have continued to flourish, living out of a history of revivalism that has often been thought to be philosophically immature or historically naive. But now evangelical, charismatic, Baptist and Pentecostal traditions are rediscovering the actual twenty centuries of the history of the Holy Spirit. Among the children of the Great Evangelical Awakening, a reawakening in orthodoxy teaching is emerging, in part grounded on consensual exegesis.

The first time I publicly attempted to set forth my view of this new ecumenical situation was in Washington in the Senate Office Building in

1999, only a few months after Harare. Anglican bishop Deng of Sudan was being honored by the Institute on Religion and Democracy (IRD), with the occasion being the tenth anniversary of the IRD. I was invited to give the anniversary lecture and chose to focus on what I was perceiving as "the new ecumenism."

All of us who were committed to the new ecumenism had survived a thousand failures of the old Genevan ecumenism and were yearning to reground in apostolic teaching. The uniting work of the Holy Spirit was taking form on a breathtaking world scale. Meanwhile it was being manifested not in institutional expressions but primarily in quiet and inconspicuous ways through casual conversations in local churches, parachurch ministries, food relief, Bible studies and grassroots service projects.

That reaction had come out of an entrenched WCC habit of falsely presuming that the embodiment of the body of Christ depended largely upon institutional negotiations, human ingenuity, rhetoric and cleverness. What I now understood to be the new ecumenism was not fixated on management, strategy, political action or formulas for wealth distribution, ecological salvation or social planning.

I came to believe that the emergent ecumenical dialogue would likely happen more through parachurch mission initiatives, associations and social service ministries than through long-established denominational bureaucracies, and realized that this was already happening through such unanticipated vehicles as World Vision, evangelical publishing houses and relief agencies.[58]

The new ecumenism was living out of the undeniable awareness that God was doing something far more unexpected, diffuse and magnificent than any bureaucracies or movements could achieve. The old ecumenism began in 1948 at Amsterdam, while the new ecumenism was becoming aware that it had a history dating back to the Council of Jerusalem, A.D. 48.

After the Berlin Wall fell on November 9, 1989, most could see that world Christianity no longer needed to remain captive to a Marxist vision of social change at a time when Soviet Marxism was disintegrating. Liberal denominations had spent enormous amounts of energy, moral capital and money on ecumenical politics directed toward regulatory politics. Little to none of it had been spent either on telling the gospel story or in regrounding in the apostles' view of the unity of the body of Christ.

The old Genevan ecumenism wholeheartedly accepted the canons of modern consciousness as a permanent feature of every conceivable future, while the new ecumenism was not intimidated by recent forms of modernity because it had been through many modernities.

Breaking stereotypes: Evangelicals and Catholics Together. The fruitful dialogue that emerged prompted Richard Neuhaus and Charles Colson to inaugurate Evangelicals and Catholics Together (ECT). The early participants included Avery Dulles, J. I. Packer, George Weigel, Bill Bright, Michael Novak, Elizabeth Achtemeier, Richard Land, Mary Ann Glendon and Timothy George. Incisive critiques by D. James Kennedy, John F. MacArthur Jr. and R. C. Sproul prompted further clarification and ensuing documents on justification by grace through faith, authority of Scripture, veneration of saints and the Blessed Virgin. Bill Bright wrote a clarification of "Why I Decided to Become a Signatory" to the first document. ECT allowed a more fertile form of ecumenical dialogue than was possible through the old official ecumenical channels centered in Geneva. I participated in virtually every session until 2009 when struck by advanced lymphoma cancer.

ECT resulted in the first major attempt in North America to bring together two circles of voices by leading theologians to speak out on the neuralgic issues between Catholic and evangelicals: grace, salvation, justification, communion, baptism and culture of life. Some Reformed evangelicals took heat from those early efforts, but the outcomes were remarkable. Although it was composed of North American scholars, it was closely watched from abroad, especially by the Vatican, with high approval because it had international consequences.[59] Unlike the ecumenical dialogues of the Faith and Order Commission of the World Council of Churches, which represented church bodies, we were not formally representing organizations but speaking out of our own commitments to our diverse histories hoping for reconciliation wherever possible.[60]

Richard Neuhaus was a radiant light for me in debates about religion and public life, and had been since our first meeting in 1976. I watched the evolution of his transition from Lutheran to Catholic. He stunned the Lutheran world by receiving ordination with the Roman Catholic Church, under the sponsorship of Avery Dulles. I was with him on the day he was received into full communion in the Catholic Church by Cardinal O'Connor. As anticipated in *The Catholic Moment*, he came to view the Catholic Church as the most promising heir of culture formation in American society, poised to become a major force in constructing a religiously informed public philosophy.[61] In his note to his friends on his conversion, he argued that the separated existence of Lutheranism, if once necessary, is not necessary any longer, and if so, such separated existence was no longer defensible. With all my anguish with the United Methodist Church, I considered becoming Catholic or Eastern Orthodox, but concluded that my vocation was in the church that had baptized and ordained me.

I experienced Evangelicals and Catholics Together much like being in an intense postgraduate seminar with probing questions, rigorous argument and delight in achieving consensus. The Reformed tradition and Baptist evangelicals took the greatest risk by merely being there, especially Harold O. J. Brown, Bill Bright and Charles Colson. I had been in conversation for years with many of the Catholic participants, including George Weigel, Michael Novak, Edward Oakes and Thomas Guarino. Not one was in that conversation without risks of criticism from either reluctant Catholics or defensive Protestants.

I served as a drafter for the second document, "The Gift of Salvation." Since I had been writing on evangelical catholicity since the 1970s, the role I played in the ECT was as mediator between very traditional Catholics and very traditional Reformed voices, both filled with good intentions.

Many observers of ECT were unaware that the initiating crisis that had brought us together was the conflicted situation of Christian mission efforts in South America, with Pentecostal missions growing exponentially while Catholics theologians had been struggling with liberation theology. At the height of those discussions, a joint meeting of South and

North American Catholic prelates was held in New York to seek discernment on evangelical growth and liberation theology.[62]

Avery Dulles and I were the only participants in Evangelicals and Catholics Together who also had seven years of experience with the dialogue going on between the World Evangelical Alliance and the Roman Catholic Pontifical Commission on Christian Unity (WEA–RCC). So we were able to keep each dialogue informed about the other. ECT was North American and produced five consensus documents. WEA-RCC was worldwide in scope and produced only one document while I was involved. I have been privileged to share in those pivotal conversations for more than two decades. As one of the oldest surviving original signers of all of the documents of Evangelicals and Catholics Together, and as drafter of the WEA-RCC document on Communio, I have been deeply blessed by those friendships where all present have experienced joy in the unity of the body of Christ.

The risk-laden questions were on justification, scriptural authority, the Blessed Virgin and the culture of life. The risks of dialogue proved fruitful beyond imagination. A year after the second ECT document was published, most of the opposition had died down.

The 2000s

A Time of Harvest

THE CUSP OF THE MILLENNIUM

The end of the 1990s and the beginning of the 2000s was a fitting time to reflect on the long range of human history and what the new millennium might hold.

The beginnings of Orthodox-evangelical Dialogue. During this time several brilliant Orthodox theologians befriended me and welcomed my consuming interest in patristic exegesis. Some were among the most astute Orthodox teachers of our time, including John Breck, Thomas Hopko, Stanley Harakas and Leonid Kishkovsky. I also relied heavily upon my own former Drew PhD protégées Vigen Guroian (Armenian Orthodox) and David Ford (Orthodox Church of America).

The Society for the Study of Eastern Orthodoxy and Evangelicalism, which met annually at Wheaton College, invited me to lecture on Orthodoxy as a healthy survivor of modernity. That drew me closer into a growing question regarding what to do about the controversial evangelical presence in the world of Orthodoxy. These obstacles between evangelicals and Orthodox were chronic and tender.

The misery that evangelicals were causing the Orthodox was viewed by the Orthodox as unwelcome proselytizing in lands that had a Christian history stretching over millennia. The misery which the Orthodox were causing for evangelicals was in restricting freedom of assembly, rights to purchase property and free speech. Evangelicals were appearing everywhere in the Orthodox world, hoping to proclaim the gospel to a culture perceived to be deficient in the teaching of justification by grace through personal faith in Jesus Christ. Additional crucial differences in church doctrine and sacramental teaching made the divide even greater. The Orthodox at that time could hardly regard evangelicals as legitimate partners in dialogue.

The 1991 WCC Assembly at Canberra had frustrated the Orthodox delegates, due especially to the proposed revisions in language concerning the classic doctrine of God the Father and God the Son. Feminists were refusing to speak of Father and Son. Experimental liturgies at Canberra were gender focused.

The evangelicals had been promised a seat at the table in Canberra, but then were ignored and represented only by the evangelical house pets of Genevan ecumenism. Evangelicals agreed with the Orthodox on classic trinitarian language, but continued to pursue questions on religious liberty in Orthodox lands.

At that point I became involved in the attempts to reconcile the conflicts that had emerged, both on gender and civil rights. I was invited to two meetings where these issues were frankly and rationally examined. The first was in a Württemberg Evangelical Lutheran retreat center near Stuttgart in 1993, sponsored jointly by the World Evangelical Alliance and representatives of the Ecumenical Patriarch of Constantinople. Some progress was made in listening to each other through the personal good will of the participants. I was on the drafting committee that proposed a formula for evangelicals to discuss the definition and dangers of proselytism if the Orthodox would consent to discussing guarantees of religious liberty.

This became the key working premise of the second Orthodoxevangelical dialogue in Egypt in a retreat center hosted by the Coptic Orthodox Church in Alexandria from July 10 to July 15, 1995. Considerable progress occurred by respecting these two conditions in future dialogue.[1]

The cave of St. Anthony. It was immediately after that reconciling week on the Alexandria coast that I took off on my own and traveled to

Cairo to seek out the church historians of the Institute of Higher Coptic Studies. There I met Father Ibrahim for conversations about patristic exegesis. In that conversation I expressed my deep desire to visit the cave of St. Anthony even though I did not know how to get there. Generously he agreed to set aside all of his responsibilities and take me in his car all the way across the eastern desert to the Monastery of St. Anthony. Anthony was the founder of Christian monasticism (A.D. 251–356).

On the road through the desert it felt as though I was on pilgrimage to nowhere. No matter how deep into the desert we went, it seemed as if it would go on forever. But I was intent on visiting the isolated place where St. Anthony spent many years in the desert seeking to live the holy life.

After long, barren stretches of emptiness, Father Ibrahim and I arrived on the coast of the Red Sea. We turned south for another long stretch with Mount Clysma on our right and the Red Sea on our left. At length we came to an isolated turn on a dusty road toward the mountains. Never have I felt I was in a more remote place. In the distance I saw an oasis of trees surrounded by a high wall. There we sought admission into the monastery from a gatekeeper who was perched in a high tower above the ancient gate. During previous times of Bedouin attacks, the only access had been by a basket lifted to the upper level of the gate. Since we were expected, we gained admittance through a small door in the gate. The inside was a like a garden with a tiny stream flowing, and where fresh fruits and vegetables were being cultivated. I was able to visit the small chapel, but was not able to gain access to the library. We were happy to be offered sparse but comfortable quarters there.

The next morning, Father Ibrahim and I climbed a steep walk of a thousand feet up to the Cave of St. Anthony of the Desert. The well-worn path led to the place where Anthony had spent so many years of his life alone in prayer. With candle in hand, I squeezed into a slender rocky cell, barely tall enough to stand up straight. The rock walls in the cell were black basalt.

That cell, a natural cleft in the rocks, reached a hundred feet deep into the heart of the mountain. At the far end of the cave was a small room, hand carved from the rock. As I rested my head on the rounded stone that according to tradition served as Anthony's head rest, I knew that a fundamental recognition was occurring in this long-awaited moment.

In that cave with the tiny candle light flickering off dark walls, I realized that true silence and solitude had been missing in my life. Remembering how much I had at times dreaded solitude, now I wondered if I might be consoled by it. After the cave, solitude became a central feature of my spiritual formation.

The passing of the beloved companion. Back at home, with the children out of college, Edrita's career path had shifted to new horizons as a communications consultant. She developed her own business in corporate communications for biopharmaceutical clients in New Jersey and Pennsylvania. After that she served for five years as executive officer of the Drew Alumni Organization, where she planned and hosted many events for the alumni family.

Despite limitations, Edrita had chosen to continue an active life, insofar as possible, performing in documentary films, college productions and local theater productions. Her last role was as Meg in Harold Pinter's *The Birthday Party* in the Drew Theater. The ingénue roles that she once played so wittily were a thing of the past, and now she was focused on character roles during the heyday of the theater of the absurd. Even though her illness had been difficult for her, she still had all of her charisma and magnetism as an actress.

Our children were thriving in other parts of the country, but Edrita was struggling with her own slow battles of strength and pain. Clark was working in aeronautical engineering, Edward was practicing law, and Laura had developed her own eco-friendly business in Washington, D.C. Still associated with many of her friends in the peace movement, Laura was actively organizing crosscontinental peace marches.

Edrita was always the glue that had held the family together. It was devastating, therefore, when she faced several years of dealing with a series of life-threatening illnesses that began with several breast cancer surgeries, and then in early 1997 she was diagnosed with an insidious stomach cancer. After that she faced a decisive battle that turned out to be an incurable cancer of the appendix, which is usually diagnosed only after it is too late. When we had run out of options in New Jersey, I took her to Washington, D.C., hoping that major surgery under the renowned Dr. Stanley M. Sugarman might remove the cancer.

By August 1997 she was back home recovering, but with many complicated followup medical routines. She did not want hospice status until there were no other options. When palliative care was the only option, I became the caregiver with some wonderful help from Sarah my sister and Jane my sister-in-law, and some visiting hospice help. I learned how to perform many of the home care nursing procedures, maintaining a saline drip, administering intravenous medicines and keeping surroundings sterile.

Because everything was not working out well for Edrita, I looked for a way of bringing her nearer to our extended families in Oklahoma. She hesitated as long as possible to leave her friends and neighbors in New Jersey. Jane and I managed to bring her back to Oklahoma, where she was able to spend precious times with her family and enjoy the support of our extended family in Oklahoma City. Edrita's parents were living only eighty-five miles away in Ada. I tried to offer her palliative comfort, but increasingly to no avail.

She faced the difficult summons of slow, lingering illness, repeated hospitalizations and the spiritual challenge of remaining resolute amid severe physical limitations, which she invariably did. Her struggle ended mercifully on January 28, 1998. She had been a courageous survivor of cancer for many years. In her final illness she was undaunted by death and literally full of life and charm in her last days.

On a cold night in January she slipped away close by my side. Now she is gone. To the courageous and gracious woman who accompanied me through forty-six years of faithful companionship, I was and still am deeply bonded by our love, our children, our memories and our close mutual understanding.

She brought unutterable splendor to my life. If the woman is the glory of the man, as Paul wrote, she was the particular glory of my life. Nothing else comes even close. I celebrate her radiance and the mystique of the one human I most loved. Every phase I went through, she went through with me. She accompanied me along my unpredictable, hazardous odyssey, and in a way still does. Sometimes she was puzzled about where we were going or grieved over where we were, but it was always the two of us who were facing it together. She knew me inside out and understood every foible, every hidden vice and every short-coming I ever had. She bore with my infirmities, forgave my sins and filled my life with mercy. I have missed her every day. Her death left me devastated. I had to pick up my life again without her. Now life felt like a puzzle with so many missing pieces. We had been one; now I felt half of one.

William Butler Yeats had written:

All through the years of our youth
Neither could have known
Their own thought for the other's,
We were so much at one.[2]

So it was with us.

Out of our love she had woven together a family of beautiful children and grandchildren spreading out all the way from Alaska to North Carolina. Each one of them grew more and more to be an incalculable gift to me in her absence.

Our daughter, Laura, in Alaska was pregnant during Edrita's last weeks. With dire warnings of Edrita's deteriorating condition, Laura had flown in from Anchorage to be with us. Laura was a great comfort to me, as were Clark, Jeanne and Ed with all of the care they extended.

Within two weeks after saying goodbye to her mother, Laura gave birth to Chloe in Alaska. At this writing my granddaughter Chloe is sixteen, full of life, very bright, with a future full of promise. She is an incessant reader and a born writer, already producing stories and films.

Meanwhile the families of our three children have grown to six grandchildren and two great-grandchildren. It has helped me to re-focus from grief over Edrita to the special joy of watching our children, grandchildren and great-grandchildren flourish.

How the Confessing Movements Began to Turn Around the Mainline

Founding the Confessing Movement. Some years earlier I had met in Shaker Village, Kentucky, with the twenty Wesley Fellows for their Christmas Conference in 1993. After that I participated in a small preliminary planning session that would eventually lead to the founding of the Confessing Movement. A few days later this initial planning group asked Bishop William Cannon and the president of Asbury Theological Seminary, Maxie Dunnam, and me to call together key Methodist Church leaders to attend a conference seeking to unify faithful moderate and traditional voices in the church.

The week after Easter 1994, ninety-two national leaders came together in Atlanta to respond to our call. They represented the leadership of more than a dozen different national renewing and confessing Christian organizations from all of the Methodist jurisdictions. There they unified their efforts and chose the name The Confessing Movement Within the United Methodist Church.

The key word was *within* because we wanted to stay within the UMC and reform it rather than separate from it. A rising initiative was born that would soon have 600,000 adherents and correspondents. I chaired the committee of theologians who were asked to draft their founding document for the Confessing Movement. Leicester Longden, Scott Jones and Gregory Galloway were also among the drafters. Senator Pat Miller of Indiana, who was an experienced legislator with gifts for mobilizing action, agreed to serve as director.

This unifying initiative among Methodists was followed with apt variations by similar confessing movements among Presbyterians, Anglicans and others in North America, the United Kingdom, Europe, Australia, New Zealand and elsewhere. The major tenet under attack for all of those organizations was the authority of Scripture. Urgent issues included those on classic Christian teachings on matrimony, financial accountability, ordination and the fairness of representational systems with regard to concentrated bureaucratic interests. We knew that those issues might cause irreparable setbacks if all of the confessing movements did not become unified and effective. Some were worried that such an imminent attack might be successful legislatively in the largest North America's mainline denominations—Methodist, Episcopal, Presbyterian and Lutheran.

As chairman of the board of the Institute on Religion and Democracy in Washington, I also served as the consulting theologian for the Association for Church Renewal (ACR), composed of the executive officers of confessing and renewing movements within member churches of the WCC. It was the first cross-denominational alliance of church renewal organizations in the mainline churches, a coalition of executives of more than two dozen active renewing and confessing movements.[3] ACR was the only venue where the voices of all those national renewing movements came together regularly. Those national renewal groups included Presbyterians for Renewal, Disciples Renewal Fellowship, Good News, Confessing Movement Within the United Methodist Church, Presbyterian Laymen and many others.

By 2002 we realized that this burgeoning movement needed a guiding confession for biblically grounded policy advice. Philip Turner, the former dean of Berkeley Divinity School at Yale, and I decided to call together the best-informed theological minds of all of the confessing and renewing movements in the mainline denominations. Each of the eighteen theologians selected were astute on key issues within their own denominations and had shown courage and moral fiber in speaking out boldly for church reform despite resistance from their church bureaucracies. Most were young. They were from churches whose lay people had grown restless after they had come to understand their church's lack of political balance.

We met in 2002 in Fort Worth through the hospitality of Episcopal bishop James Stanton. Collectively they composed "A Letter to Confessing Christians," a powerful appeal to the churches of the mainline. They addressed not only the sexuality issues but also issues on financial accountability, scriptural authority, the culture of life versus the culture of death, and the world mission of the church. They spoke as one in the form of a pastoral letter addressed to the faithful of the renewing and confessing movements, not primarily to the press or to the cultural elites.[4] No one around that table was serving in the renewing movements without cost, professional risk and in some cases potential reprisals.[5] All were willing to give clear voice for an untold number of unheeded traditional and evangelical voices in the mainline.

The end result was that those renewing movements experienced significant growth and vitality, and were no longer braced in a defensive stance. Their cause was theological integrity within their churches in which the lay believers totaled over twenty million persons.[6] Thereafter worldwide evangelicals no longer thought of renewal as occurring only within the boundaries of discreet denominations, but more so in union with the intergenerational worldwide body of confessing Christians of all times and places.

Turning around the mainline. In the period between 1990 and 2010 with so much of my attention focused internationally on patristic studies, China and Africa, I found I could not turn my back on the struggle for the soul of the mainline churches in America. The deeper I became involved in these three initiatives (ACR, IRD and the Confessing Movement), the more I felt that an introduction was needed to the issues, themes and documents of the mainline churches and renewal movements. So I wrote *Turning Around the Mainline* as a report of the progress being made by confessing Christians in those churches. I included a practical case study of the most pressing issue of the day: the property rights of churches.

Mainline here refers to the largest liberal bureaucracies of the Protestant churches in North America, all closely associated with the National and World Council of Churches, who often assumed that they represented the voices of all Protestantism in the halls of legislatures. Even though those old-line bureaucracies felt empowered to proceed with their own agenda, they found they had diminishing influence within their local congregations.

Liberal preaching had considered it a virtue to be doctrinally laissez faire, liturgically experimental, disciplinarily nonjudgmental, politically correct, morally broad-minded and above all, sexually lenient and permissive.[7] Now those churches were in precipitous decline. Even while old-line liberalism declined, we were witnessing an extraordinary rebirth of orthodoxy that was emerging within these denominations. The decline itself provided a grace-filled opportunity to call for scriptural accountability and lay consensus.

When some in these groups wanted to leave these denominations, I tried to provide plausible reasons for why they would do better to stay and fight for their reform. To flee a church is not to discipline it. Discipline is fostered by patient trust, corrective love and the willingness to live with incremental change insofar as conscience allows. An exit strategy is tempting but self-defeating, since it forgets about the faithful generations who have given sacrificially to build those churches. It would be a dishonor to them to abandon the church to those with aberrant faith.

Turning Around the Mainline set forth a reasoned argument for the faithful to stay in their pews, boards and legislative processes to fight and win this battle. We learned that the Spirit intends to reclaim the worshiping communities created by the apostolic witnesses to the Lord's death and resurrection. The authentic advocates of the unity of the church are those who care about its discipline and holiness, and do so with humility and gentleness. The faithful church is promised imperishable continuance even if particular churches, local bodies or denominations stumble.

WRITING IN THE NEW MILLENNIUM

The Classic Christian Readers series on justification and good works. During the years when I was editing the patristic commentary, I was also working on several other writing projects: *The Justification Reader* (2002), *One Faith* (with Packer in 2004), and *The Good Works Reader* (2007). I would be remiss if I did not account here for the purpose of those books and the puzzles they tried to solve.

With Bill Eerdmans I began writing a series of books in 2000 to set forth major patristic readers on the key themes of the Reformation. In the Classic Christian Readers series I showed that Reformation teachings on justification, good works and sanctification were profoundly rooted in the most consensual patristic writers in a way consistent with Reformation reasoning. A thousand years before Luther the church fathers were closely examining the justification texts of Paul, James and John. I limited my source texts to only those parts of that teaching on which there was substantial agreement between traditions of East and West, Catholic, Protestant and Orthodox, including charismatic and Pentecostal teaching on salvation by grace through faith. My task was to show textually that all of those doctrines had been anticipated in large measure by the most consensual patristic writers.

The Justification Reader focused on classic Christianity's struggle against *works without faith.*[8] *The Good Works Reader* focused on the opposite error of cheap grace, or *faith without works* of love.[9] In these two patristic Readers I used only ancient consensual sources to present an orthodox model for faith and ethics that was consonant with Luther, Calvin, Lutheran orthodoxy and classic Reformed teachings. Anyone who might prematurely conclude that salvation depends on our good works will find strong resistance in the consensual Christian writers and the Reformers.

I set out to show how there was indeed an early Christian consensus on justification from which Protestant, Roman Catholic and Eastern Orthodox believers all could learn. I knew that goal could only be accomplished textually by presenting direct quotations that demonstrated that consensus. The church fathers' teaching on justification was restated almost verbatim by the sixteenth-century Reformers. Hence the consensual patristic teaching on justification can still be confessed in good conscience by Reformed and evangelical Christians. Protestants who need to continue the argument against Catholic teachings of justification do well to recognize the difference between medieval scholasticism and the classic Christianity held by both the patristic and Reformation writers in harmony.

God's justifying action on the cross did not depend on human merit of any kind. Major patristic voices here were Irenaeus, Athanasius, Gregory of Nazianzus and Augustine. That wisdom was firmly established in the earliest generations of biblical interpretation long before Luther or Calvin or the debates of Augsburg and Trent. I simply followed the modest, inductive approach of the Vincentian rule to textually set forth a patristic consensus.

I argued that both Luther and Calvin were deeply grounded in classical pre-Reformation Christology and atonement teaching. I have long admired the strongest and most courageous advocates of classical Reformed tradition teaching such as David Wells, Michael Horton, Albert Mohler, R. C. Sproul, John Piper and Harold O. J. Brown, and have rejoiced when they recognized their own substantial grounding in Athanasius and Augustine.[10]

The Good Works Reader showed the affinities of the Fathers and the Reformers on the life that flowed from justification by grace through faith. Catholics accused Protestants of ignoring good works, while Protestants accused Catholics of making good works the basis of salvation. The consensual patristic writers corrected both of those tendencies.

Each of those good works cited in Matthew 25 had an inspiring history of interpretation by the patristic writers, notably: Cyprian, Basil, John Cassian, Leo the Great, Ambrose, Augustine and Gregory the Great. My purpose was not to diminish the writings of the Reformers on grace-enabled good works following faith but to show their roots in ancient consensual exegesis.

In simplicity I asked the patristic writers to teach me clearly whether the poor in spirit are blessed; whether God has a preference for the poor; whether the poor have a responsibility to make something of their God-given freedom; whether penury is commended; whether the poor are more likely to be rich in faith; whether the incarnate Lord, though rich, became poor for us; whether we reinforce slothfulness by rewarding it; whether we are to lay up riches for ourselves; whether we are actively to seek out the poor; whether faith takes special care for the plight of the fatherless and widows; whether our own choices determine our eternal destiny; whether all good works are summarized by feeding, quenching, welcoming, clothing, relieving and visiting; whether the faithful are without excuse if they ignore the hungering, thirsting, shivering and homelessness; whether the gospel was first proclaimed through food offered and hurt healed; whether the conditions of finitude in creation justly permits famine and drought; whether we live by bread alone; whether Christ is known in the breaking of bread; whether Jesus offered himself as food and drink; whether the incarnate Lord experienced hunger and thirst; whether we meet the Lord when we meet the stranger; whether the incarnate Lord willingly depended on the hospitality of others; whether hospitality depends upon the worthiness of the receiver; whether we entertain angels unawares; whether the glory of our original nakedness has fallen; whether God provides clothing that does not wear out; whether it is possible to care for the body in proper balance without anxiety; whether the holy family themselves were displaced persons and refugees; whether the prayer of the righteous is effective; whether faith is tested in my meeting with the next one I encounter. In all these questions, the consensual answers were clear. The heart of the gospel is God's good work for us. What we do in response is a story every believer lives out. It is the story of *faith becoming active in love*.

My last plenary address to the Evangelical Theological Society in 1997 was on the patristic exegesis of Romans 1:27, titled "Without Excuse: Classic Christian Exegesis of General Revelation," published in the *Journal of the Evangelical Theological Society* in 1998. ETS president Norman Geisler, one of Reformed theology's most conservative advocates, brought me to that plenary to show how the ancient Christian writers dealt with that highly contested passage of Scripture.

Amsterdam 2000: Working with J. I. Packer on One Faith. Ten thousand world evangelical leaders, on the invitation of Billy Graham, gathered in Amsterdam to celebrate world evangelical initiatives and to pray for the next millennium. This immense conference brought together the largest gathering of Christian international ministries ever held. One of the major objectives of Amsterdam 2000 was to seek a consensual view of world evangelical theology. I was asked to be a theological consultant for that part of the assembly's agenda, which was headed by J. I. Packer, Timothy George and David Neff.

Meeting with Jim Packer and his wife, Kit, in the airport boarding room after the assembly, I mentioned to him that no one had ever attempted to compare the hundred or more confessional texts of international evangelical missions to see what they had confessed in common. When I asked if he would be interested in coediting such a collection, he readily agreed.

So Packer and I set out in 2000 to gather major modern evangelical confessions written since 1950 in a book of systematically ordered selections, which was published in 2004 and titled *One Faith: The Evangelical Consensus*.[11] It showed the consensus of worldwide evangelical movements on point after point of confessional Christian teaching. The reason this data was significant is that evangelicals had long been caricatured as belligerent independents, infighters and separatists lacking in love of the unity of the body of Christ.

We gathered over a hundred statements of faith from major evangelical gatherings in Amsterdam, Iguassu, Manila, Berlin, Chicago, Willowbank and Seoul, showing points on which evangelicals worldwide concurred. We included statements of faith by international and regional seminaries and mission agencies. From all over the world we combed the sources for documents written as confessions by evangelical organizations such as World Vision and World Relief.

Packer and I stayed away from documents that were primarily the work of a single author, since we were looking for consensus. We focused instead on statements that had emerged from deliberate dialogue that had led to serious confessions by international evangelicals. It is this grounding in the ancient consensus of faith that made those confessions truly ecumenical. We were simply asking how those statements of faith agreed with one another.

One Faith showed that the world evangelical consensus could be demonstrated textually on a documentary basis as an evangelical expression of the same conciliar process that had been used to define biblical essentials dating back to the earliest Christian centuries. In a time when liberal denominations were blurring Christian distinctiveness, evangelicals were becoming clearer about their firm unity on essentials. No such documented consensus had been attempted prior to the Amsterdam Assembly. Those evangelical confessional texts dispelled the myth that evangelicals have represented a one-sided fringe of Christianity.

For many years before this book, Dr. Packer and I were serving together as senior editors of *Christianity Today*. We also collaborated in the search for evangelical consensus, first in Evangelicals and Catholics Together beginning in 1993, and then in "The Gospel of Jesus Christ—An Evangelical Celebration" in 1999.

Evangelicals now have vast new audiences through their energetic publishing of books, magazines and using online media. Any reader can easily recognize the pattern of evangelical unity that corresponds with the core of the patristic consensus.

As one who has lived through most of a century of rootless mainline Protestantism, I can attest that when these core teachings have been diluted, the result is not a gain but a loss to the unity of the body of Christ. The cohesion of those statements of millions of believers worldwide is heartening. Its durability through time is sociologically unique. The Holy Spirit is ceaselessly seeking to engender unity in the body of Christ.

THE OUTCOMES OF THE COMMENTARY

Expanding international translations. I had made good friends at the University of Peking through five years of visiting there for symposia. Back at Drew I got a letter from the chairman of the Department of Religious Studies at the University of Peking (Beida), where the ACCS translations project had begun. The premier Chinese university had commissioned six of their faculty to come to Drew and other American campuses to investigate the structure of college curricula in religious studies. Drew University was their first stop. We showed them how we were using digital searches to identify key ideas and terms in the ancient religious texts.

I mentioned to them that I had documented some facts about how Methodist missionaries in the nineteenth century had a part in founding the Boys School that later became Huiwen University, which later morphed into the modern Peking University. Explaining that some of those missionaries had come from Drew, I took them to see the evidence in the Drew Archives. They were incredulous as I showed them early photographs of the John Leighton Stuart President's House, which had been built before the founding of Peking University. They instantly recognized the pagoda in which we had been holding our meetings. We marveled at the small world we lived in and the unheralded historical intertwining of our two universities, Drew and Peking.

One of the most difficult challenges of our ACCS work was the oversight of our expanding international translation teams. Benefiting from the work done by Joel Scandrett and Michael Glerup, Joel Elowsky, who became the operations manager for the entire project in 2000, graciously agreed to take hold of this far-reaching and difficult task after we had all agreed that the Chinese, Arabic and Russian translations would have great potential for impact upon hundreds of millions of readers who otherwise might not find access to Christian wisdom. We began with China.

Almost every year after those beginnings in Beijing, we added another international translation team: first Spanish, followed by Italian, Polish, and Korean.[12] Motivated by a strong desire to publish editions in Hindi and Arabic, I circled the globe seeking out the best translators. This took me on a long trajectory from Singapore to Beijing to Shanghai to Hong Kong to Taiwan to Delhi to Bangalore to Cairo.

While in India, I was invited by Principal Bruce Nicholls and his wife, Kathryn, to give a lecture at the Union Biblical Seminary in Pune, India. At first we aspired to produce an affordable edition in Hindustani or Urdu, which might make the ACCS more accessible to many of the one billion people in India, but that turned out to be a bridge too far, and not a better option than the English edition, since English had become a second language for a large percentage of educated Indians. After this respite in Pune, I took a memorable train trip over the mountains to Mumbai and continued on to Cairo by air to explore the viability of translating ACCS into Egyptian Arabic.

In Cairo we had to make a decision on whether we should have an Egyptian Arabic translation or one done in Lebanon or Cyprus in standard Mideastern Arabic. After much deliberation we decided to partner with University of Balamand in Lebanon to produce selected volumes of ACCS in Arabic. This left Egypt, the largest nation of

Christian Arabic speakers, without a good translation into basic Egyptian Arabic.

Back in Europe we talked with both French and German scholarly publishers, but in both cases a twenty-nine volume series was not viewed by them as financially viable or needed in their respective languages initially. With the Oxford Center for Mission Studies (OCMS) drawing together excellent doctoral students from all over the world, they asked me to come there to explain to them how the classic consensual agenda for theology was being manifested in the recovery of patristic exegesis. From then on OCMS and Wycliffe Hall Oxford were on the regular circuit of stops for us in finding the best ways and people to proceed with our seven modern language translations.

The ACCS core team of leaders gradually morphed into an international consultancy for integrating patristic sources into Christian colleges and seminaries all over the world. In Thailand, Kuala Lumpur and Singapore I was finding great interest in how the intellectual leadership of the early Christian writers might become a potential model for reconceiving postcolonial Christianity in modern Asia. They were recognizing a new relationship with early Christian biblical interpreters who had lived on the Asian and African continents.

In connection with my growing involvement in the World Evangelical Alliance, I went to Tokyo in 1999 to lecture on those themes at Japan Biblical Seminary. There I reconnected with my former doctoral student Sam Fujimoto, who was now serving as dean of the Methodist Seminary of Tokyo. While I was in Korea, Bishop Oh of Seoul invited me to preach in Korea's largest Methodist church, followed by my attending a mountain retreat with pastors from Wesleyan-based churches, where I met again many of my former Drew PhD students who were now providing crucial leadership for over thirty different universities and seminaries in Korea. I found that a non-Western focus for patristic studies was emerging everywhere I went.

I had come a long way since the Herberg faceoff. Some who had known me before 1970 hardly recognized me now. They simply were unable to connect the dots of my unique history.[13] When I tried to clarify the continuity of work from *Agenda for Theology* in 1979 to the ACCS two decades later, it seemed to them to be obscure and disconnected.

Two popes bless the patristic commentary. Two years after having met Cardinal Ratzinger in New York in 1988, I met Pope John Paul II in January 1991. Twelve years later, in 2003, the Italian editors of Città Nuova generously arranged an occasion for our whole editorial team to meet the great pope to receive his blessing upon the Ancient Christian Commentary on Scripture and to present him with copies of the patristic commentary in both Italian and English.

After this memorable event, we gathered together all of our Italian translators and volume editors to celebrate the progress of the translation in Italian. Remembering the role of Cardinal Ratzinger in the conceptualization of the project, we felt deeply blessed to be received by John Paul II. While in Rome, our core team was allowed access to the closely restricted quarters of the Vatican library and to the Vatican papal secretariat offices, guided by Dr. Sever Voicu, our ACCS volume editor for the Apocrypha. I regarded that volume as one of the great achievements of our commentary. No one in the world could have understood and translated so many different language sources as well as Dr. Voicu did.

I wept when John Paul II died four months after we received his blessing, and then I was brought to tears of joy when I heard the name Joseph Ratzinger pronounced from the Vatican balcony as he was named Pope Benedict XVI. I marveled that the dream of a patristic commentary on Scripture had been first envisioned in conversation with the person who was now the new pope. Ratzinger the theologian had been the one best prepared to understand what I as an evangelical Protestant had been doing in patristic exegesis. Only special providence could explain how all of this had come to fruition.

The patristic commentary as spur to successor projects. After about two million words in 8,700 pages and fifteen years of active editing, our team was gratified to complete the English edition of ACCS in 2009. That still left the task of finishing the international translations into mainland Chinese simplified script and Polish.

As we neared completion of the ACCS, our core team set about complementing it with four derivative projects:

The Ancient Christian Doctrine (ACD) five-volume series (2009–2010). The Ancient Christian Texts (ACT) twelve-volume series (2009–2013). The Ancient Christian Devotional (ACDev) multivolume series (2007ff.), and The Early African Christianity (EAC) multivolume series (2010–2011).

Directing the editing and publication of those multivolume series derived from patristic comment has filled my agenda in the early years of this new millennium. I was quietly working as general editor of all these projects in Oklahoma while these international translators and editors were working all over the world.

Gerald Bray and I drew together five distinguished scholars from different traditions of Christianity to write and edit the series in Ancient Christian Doctrine.[14] Then from major worldwide traditions we selected a distinguished board of reference to help set the editorial criteria.[15] The volume editors set forth the textual evidence organized around key themes of the Nicene Creed: God, Christ, salvation, the Holy Spirit, the church, and the future. They covered every crucial teaching necessary and sufficient for faith.

The five volumes of the Ancient Christian Doctrine series presented a phrase-by-phrase commentary on the ancient consensual creed of A.D. 325, bringing together the classic scriptural arguments about what each of these phrases meant and how they were consistently grounded textually in the Hebrew Bible and the Christian canon of Holy Writ. It was designed to serve as a practical teaching guide to the earliest layers of ecumenically received orthodox scriptural teaching.[16]

The unifying text was the Nicene Creed, the most widely received of all ancient confessions. Phrase by phrase our volume editors showed how each article had been worked through exegetically in detail by the major venerated interpreters of the Ante-Nicene period: the Didache, Ignatius, Irenaeus, the Apostolic Constitutions, Clement of Alexandria, Tertullian and Athanasius.

The scriptural basis of the creed shows textually how the early church fathers sustained apostolic continuity under the guidance of the Spirit through the written word. Christians all over the world still appeal to these confessional statements as the most reliable rule of the faith received in baptism.

The second major project that sprang out of the ACCS was as the Ancient Christian Texts Series, now with twelve volumes of full-length patristic commentaries on a particular book of Scripture, and more to come.[17] All of these volumes were previously unpublished, inaccessible or not recently translated. ACCS readers who desired to go deeper into a single patristic teacher on a single important commentary could now do so.

The third series responded to many daily readers of Scripture who were hungering for a deeper spiritual formation shaped by the fathers. For those who wanted to learn to pray with the fathers, we offered daily meditations through the Christian year based on ancient Christian prayers and homilies. Those multivolume works grew out of the ACCS and gave further expression to its intent and purpose. At the same time Christopher Hall began a series on reading Scripture, learning theology and worshiping with the fathers.

Producing the fourth series on early African Christianity has been my predominant preoccupation for the period following 2007. The rest of this book will tell that story.

The rebirth of Orthodoxy and classic Christianity. Around 2000 I began to read sociological reports of the burgeoning renewal of Jewish Orthodox communities. A sharp reversal was occurring in our culture which proved that as modern secular and political ideologies were continuing to wane, Jewish and Christian communities of traditional faith were thriving more than ever. The more traditional, the more flourishing.

This resurgence showed itself in widespread efforts to reclaim the classic spiritual practices: the close study of Scripture, daily prayer, regular observance in a worshiping community, doctrinal integrity and moral accountability. This rebirth was characterized by a return to orthodoxy that was gathering momentum across denominational lines.[18]

Two millennia have passed since Christianity flowered forth from Judaism. During those two thousand years the Christian faith has had adherents in innumerable cultures and sustained its vitality through huge historical crises in widely different historical challenges without substantive changes in its central affirmations.

The core of that consensus is found in the conclusions of the seven ecumenical councils ranging from A.D. 325 to A.D. 787, a consensus about the central narrative of Scripture. The means of grasping this consensus was simply stated by Vincent of Lérins, "In the worldwide community of believers every care should be taken to hold fast to what has been believed everywhere, always, and by all." This is called orthodoxy (derived from *orthos*, "right, true" and *doxa*, "common teaching, opinion"), which means that which is commonly confessed as the truth of apostolic teaching, which itself is an interpretation of the Hebrew history of salvation. This commitment to orthodoxy has not only survived into modern times but beyond the collapse of leading modern ideologies. All I needed to do was show evidence of this fact.

The growing number of orthodox renewal movements is only a part of the evidence. Scratch the surface of any mainline church congregation and you will find believers who hunger for a return to classic Christianity, by which one may trust in the work of the Holy Spirit to bring fallen humanity to a redeemed consummation fitting to the mercy and justice of God. The contemporary doctrinal shallowness of modernity can only be corrected by a return to deep theology that has stood the test of time and links us to the prophets, apostles, saints and martyrs of the earliest times.

I have discovered that I belong to a vast family of orthodox Christian believers of all times and places, which includes historic Eastern Orthodoxy, Roman Catholicism and Protestantism. The Christian family is far wider, broader and deeper than most of us have commonly thought of it as being. Those who can recite the Apostles' Creed with full integrity of conviction and live out Christian moral norms, as well as worship in spirit and truth, are all part of a classic consensual family of faith. This great cloud of witnesses helps me feel at home in all of these settings. Since God's Word is addressed to all humanity, orthodoxy embraces a scriptural inclusivism that is much broader than a politically correct inclusivism.[19]

In 2005 I heard from the HarperOne publisher Mickey Maudlin that they would like me to revise the three-volume *Systematic Theology* into a revised, compact, single volume by condensing 1,200 pages to 900 pages. Since writing the original in 1987–1992 was followed by all of the work I did on the patristic commentary (1992–2006), it was imperative that the original version be entirely replenished yet without substantive changes.

I took the time to engage in a thorough rethinking of the three volumes, which had been titled *The Living God, The Word of Life* and *Life in the Spirit*. The 2006 version of *Classic Christianity* deepened the patristic roots, tightened the systematic structure and reached out for general lay readers. Many seminaries, however, still use the original three volumes, and Henderson Publishers has continued to reprint that original version.

TURNING THE HEART TOWARD AFRICA

Recognizing the "south to north" flow of third century intellectual history. When I left the cave of St. Anthony in the far eastern desert of Egypt, I knew that part of my heart was left in Africa. From then on, wherever I was I yearned for a much more intense focus on early African Christianity. I began probing into the earliest monastic writers: Poemen, Palladius, Pachomius, Shenoute and Paphnutius. When I read John Cassian, I realized that he had transported the wisdom of the African monks to Europe, out of which followed the Augustinians and Benedictines, who took monastic teaching from Africa to the northern Mediterranean. The original home of all Christian monastic thought and practice was in Africa.

By Africa, I mean the continent of Africa, not simply the North African dioceses of the Western Latin tradition. If Cairo is in Africa, then it is possible to view all the locations along the whole length of the Nile as indigenously African. Some Egyptian Christians do not prefer to be called African, but they still live in Africa. Since Egypt and Tunisia are in Africa, the continent of Africa includes both the Maghreb and the Nile Valley, and all to the south.[20]

As I studied how doctrine was formed, I realized that African biblical interpreters had played the decisive role in daily spiritual formation in world Christianity. They established that every Old Testament text anticipated fulfillment in the New Testament, and every New Testament text fulfilled the promises of the Old. That has been a defining principle since the beginning of Christian preaching (Acts 2:14-40), but the particulars and methods of showing how promise and fulfillment were related were formulated first in Africa. Athanasius and Augustine both demonstrated great maturity in conveying this method of reading Scripture to a worldwide received tradition. The earliest layers of Latin Christology and ethics passed through the hands of Tertullian and Cyprian before Augustine passed them on to the West. The Bible was first translated into Latin not in Europe but in North Africa.

Finally it dawned on me that the biblical interpreters from the north were depending on the biblical interpreters from the south—primarily from Africa. Close inspection showed that the scriptural interpretations of Christians from the Mediterranean north and east typically pointed back south to Christian writers on the continent of Africa. Gradually it became clear to me that a basic fact in the history of the transmission of texts had been neglected.

The flow was from Africa to Europe. It was not that Europeans brought Christianity to Africa as I had been taught. This "south-to-north hypothesis" became evident to me the more I studied the flow of patristic exegesis.

When Africans read our Western textbooks, it often seems as if the great ideas of Christianity first came from Europe and few if any from Africa. This bias has elicited major faulty characterizations and omissions, especially the founding role of Mark in African Christianity and the absence of huge territories such as Ethiopia, Sudan and Libya from textbook discussions.

My brother Tal and I had just returned from Algeria. We had traveled with a research group who had fortunately received an academic permission from the Algerian government to visit. In a time when American access to Algeria was strictly limited to government-approved travel, our group had been allowed to travel under priority police security protection. We visited Christian archaeological sites in the Maghreb from Hippo to Cherchell to Tagaste. We had also been able to trace the steps of Augustine from Numidia to Carthage.

The need for a more inclusive study of early African Christianity. On April 21, 2006, I was enjoying the company of Howard, Roberta and David Ahmanson at Egret Point, my home in Oklahoma City. Roberta and I had benefited from many reflections on questions of vocation, both hers and mine. We had often discussed how providence had worked to bring time and events and people to a decisive point where something that had seemed entirely out of reach appeared doable. I was in the completing stages of editing the patristic commentary, and Roberta wanted to know what my trajectory might be after the commentary was complete.

I described to her my growing conviction that Africa had shaped the Christian mind far more than anyone had recognized. This especially seemed to me to have been unnoticed by many Euro-American historians.

My hypothesis, although not proved, was that the flow of intellectual leadership in early Christianity had been south to north, from Africa to the Near East and Europe. I was eager to learn why such an important fact had remained largely uncommented upon in the historical literature. I knew that early Christian readings of Scripture were far more sophisticated in third-century Africa than in Palestine, Cappadocia or Europe. Aware that indigenous African roots of early Christianity had more often been viewed as Greco-Roman or Palestinian imports into Africa, I thought someone needed to find reliable, fact-based answers to those questions.

Having compared tens of thousands of patristic texts over fifteen years, I tried to explain to Roberta exactly how it happened that our team of ACCS scholars had gradually become aware of the chronological priority of major African exegetical insights among early Christian interpretations of Scripture. I told her how difficult this had been for me to grasp because the stream of Eurocentric assumptions that had been part of my education had flowed the opposite way. Roberta wanted to know what this would mean to Africans. There are nearly a half billion Christians today in Africa, including Copts, Catholics, Protestants and many sorts of charismatic believers, all having in common an unrecognized patrimony of significant early sources from the continent of Africa. I had a growing hunch that the awareness of early African sources might become prized as a treasure for every believer in Africa, where there were few who seemed aware of their early pre-Islamic roots.

Roberta wondered about the social implications of this insight. I stated my reasons why I thought it could play a supportive role in transforming the identity of postcolonial African Christians. They had suffered so long from colonial domination that their own patrimony obviously had been overlooked. The intellectual self-esteem of African believers could be profoundly affected by learning of their early African Christian intellectual tradition. That recognition could also cast in a new light the Christian-Muslim conflict on the African continent.

Roberta wondered whether this recognition might build bridges between Christians in North Africa with Christians in the south of Africa. I knew that all of the conditions were present for Copts to discover Pentecostals as common bearers of the work of the Spirit. With few exceptions, such as the work of Bishop Antonios Markos, this potential link had remained hidden. Similarly I thought that the rapidly growing charismatic movements in the South might be poised to recognize their affinity with Copts. Although their historical memories and languages differed, both view the work of the Spirit as central to their common life.

Next Roberta inquired as to the time and effort required to confirm this south to north stream of Christian intellectual history. My thought then was that we could probably bring together some key people to help us assess whether it is worth researching this untested hypothesis. If it were confirmed that the Christian intellect blossomed first on the African continent a century before it found full formation in Asia and Europe, that could mean a great deal to Africans.

Together Roberta and I decided that the first step to take was to call together a dozen or so of the best African theological minds to think about whether and how it might be done. In a short time we had put together a list of those who might be invited within a few months to consider the viability of an entirely unanticipated offspring of ACCS, a center for study of early African Christianity.

Founding the Center for Early African Christianity. After the Ahmansons left Egret Point, I thought back to my childhood, pondering my persistent thirst for knowledge about Africa.[21] As an adult I had taken every opportunity to travel to Egypt. Twice I had been to Tunisia to see early Christian artifacts and architecture. At different times I had traveled to many sites in North Africa from Carthage to Alexandria to the Nitrian Desert early monastic sites, the Delta, Thebes and the Upper Nile. I had lodged for a time in Hierapolis and explored the shores of the Mediterranean west of the Alexandria. I had also experienced Africa's deserts and great waterways.

Each time I had visited I had become more intrigued with Africa. I discussed with the core team the idea of a multiyear investment of our time in Africa as the ACCS editorial demands were concluding. As all of our core ACCS team pondered the south-to-north hypothesis, we wondered if it could be confirmed. With that conversation the seeds of the Center for Early African Christianity were planted, and they would grow exponentially through our ensuing explorations.

Three months later I met with sixteen selected invitees at Egret Point on September 7, 2006, to make a plausibility assessment. Since I was a white guy from middle America I was wondering whether I would be taken seriously in African studies. The answer came from Tite Tiénou, formerly from Mali and who later served as president and dean of Faculté de Théologie Evangélique de l'Alliance Chrétienne in Abidjan, Côte d'Ivoire, West Africa, before becoming the dean of Trinity Evangelical Divinity School. He told me emphatically not to worry about the color of my skin since I would be calling Africans to their own roots. I am glad that I took his advice with absolute seriousness because the question of my ethnicity never arose in Africa.

Classic consensual Christians do not admit skin color as a criterion for judging Christian truth. They never have and never will. African Christianity is not primarily a racial story but a confessional story of martyrs and lives lived by faith active in love. To judge truth by race is itself heretical since it denies the Great Commission. At Pentecost the church was sent to all nations, so any temptation to treat Africa as the sole source of all enduring Christian truth must be avoided. That would encourage an ideological bias contrary to the catholicity of the faith. But Africa was the first continent in which the concept of catholicity was first tested.

As we formed ourselves into a board for the Center for Early African Christianity (CEAC), they asked me to begin writing an exploratory book on my thoughts on early African Christian history, especially the south-to-north hypothesis. I began drafting it around the basic argument that I had presented to the planning group. Bob Fryling, publisher of InterVarsity Press, strongly encouraged this book as a first step.

Eighteen months later with the help of my IVP editor, Jim Hoover, that manuscript became *How Africa Shaped the Christian Mind: Rediscovering the African Seedbed of Western Christianity*. It served to break open the hypothesis for public discussion and also served as a proposal for a long-term research plan. As director of CEAC, I began a long process of consultation in Africa to assess needs, define research methods and search for consensus.

In those consultations the core of the problem was defined, centering on the common misperception that Christianity in Africa is a relatively recent arrival coming from Europe and the West. The future task is to show through the texts that the most brilliant Christian intellectual formation had occurred earliest in Africa, especially around philosophical and scriptural interpretation.

Out of the profound spiritual exercise of listening to Old and New Testament Scripture as seen by African eyes, I came to a deepening respect for the African textual and intellectual tradition. Those in CEAC came to realize that virtually all later Christian theologians after Tertullian, Clement, Origen, Cyprian and Athanasius were impacted by one or more of these five guides to the study of Scripture. They shaped the classic Christian consensus following A.D. 180 before Nicaea.

Ever since Mark's Gospel was first read and preached on the African continent, the African mind has been shaping the Christian mind. From

Tertullian in Carthage to the Catechetical School in Alexandria, those great intellects on the African continent were emulated wherever Christians later went.

African Christians gave the whole historic church its earliest and deepest clarification of the history of salvation in Jewish and Christian Scripture. They adhered faithfully to the preaching of the apostles, planting the Word and watching it grow in almost every known part of Africa. The most widely received list of the scriptural canon was formed in the bosom of Alexandrian Christian inquiry into the earliest of the apostolic witnesses. It stimulated a consensual form of exegesis that provided reliable Scriptures for reading in the worshiping community. That exegesis was transferred from Origen to Eusebius to Jerome and on to Rome. Those African writings have since become the common patrimony of all Christians everywhere. Many crucial doctrines prior to Nicea (325) were settled first in Africa through consensus by African church councils (incarnation, the true humanity and true deity of Jesus as fulfiller of the promises of Israel, the authority of the prophets and apostles). Later they became accepted by churches all over the Mediterranean and beyond.

I could see this most clearly in the history of Scripture interpretation, especially in the clear succession from Origen to Gregory Thaumaturgus, from Egypt to Cappadocia, and from the Old Latin Bible of Africa to Cyprian and Augustine. Africa was in the forefront of the surging current of intellectual imagination that matured into doctrinal agreement. Africa was the continent that excelled in systematically describing the relationship between the Old and New Testament. Christians in second-century Alexandria were living in the midst of a huge Jewish population. It was in the setting of advanced Jewish scholarship that the principle of analogy of faith was first clearly articulated for Christianity.[22]

At first this south-to-north hypothesis was for me merely a hunch, then it gradually became a matter of factual inquiry, observation and assembling evidence by a widening team of experienced scholars. Only then did it turn into a phenomena that could not be ignored, and then became a conviction underlying the work of the Center for Early African Christianity.

Africa's vast effects on Europe have not been adequately understood to this day. Many African-born scholars who have been trained in the West have not yet fully grasped that the flow of intellectual creativity in early Christianity moved from Africa to Europe, not vice versa.[23]

This elicited an alteration in the course of my life work. I refocused my efforts on the vast potential social consequences of the African roots of Christianity. As our ACCS team refocused its patristic research upon Africa, we increasingly confirmed the hypothesis in the texts of Clement, Origen, Didymus the Blind, Cyprian and Athanasius.[24]

A major logjam was broken when I began to trace the long, circular trajectory of monasticism from Africa to Lerin to Ireland and then to Europe and Portugal, only to return again to Africa as a Europeanized experiment. This is one of the most astonishing of all the stories of the preservation of civilization. We learned to trace the path of Scripture interpretation back from Africa to Antioch, Jerusalem, Rome, Constantinople, Nisibis, Lerin and Ireland. We learned this only from pursuing the ancient African sources directly.

This inattention to this south-to-north flow of intellectual history has left Africa without a sense of having a distinguished literary and intellectual history. Overcoming this esteem deficit was a major aim of CEAC.

I was puzzled by the demeaning prejudice that had crept into historical lore that these great figures were not Africans at all but merely Europeans in disguise. According to that careless reasoning, the greater those competencies, the less African they appeared to be.[25]

How World Evangelical Alliance networks dovetailed with the Center for Early African Christianity. Before the Africa initiative began in 2006, I had already been engaged in the World Evangelical Alliance for years. I was asked to give a plenary address for their International Theological Conference in London on consensual Christianity. This became the beginning of many international friendships for me. Soon I was appointed to their international Theological Commission, which provided an unusual opportunity for me to meet leading evangelical theologians from around the world. It was my first immersion in evangelical leadership on a world scale.[26]

Those friendships helped me to put my concerns into a global perspective. From then on I was thinking less in Western terms and more in international terms about the emerging opportunities of classic Christian teaching. After that I was invited to join the working group on a heated consultation between the World Evangelical Fellowship (later World Evangelical Alliance) and the Roman Catholic Pontifical Council for Promoting Christian Unity, usually referred to as the WEA-RCC Conversations.[27]

From 1999 to 2009 I participated actively in those global evangelical-Catholic dialogues in the same way as I had in the ongoing Evangelical and Catholics Together dialogue in North America. Those conversations required dealing with complicated and prickly issues between Protestants and Catholics, especially in South America, Russia and the Middle East, where there were longstanding, polarized points of discord. Many evangelicals considered that entire dialogue dangerous and felt that it was contaminating to have any significant doctrinal conversations at all with Catholics. The subject was so enflamed that the whole dialogue was almost cut off entirely by evangelical suspicions and stereotypes of Catholics. Only through the determined efforts of Professor Rolf Hille of Tübingen did they continue.[28]

Traveling with Avery through the Galilee. Near Jerusalem at the Ecumenical Institute of Tantur, representatives of the WEA Theological Commission met with the Pontifical Council representatives to finally get a preliminary agreement on a document titled "Communio" that I helped draft, which sought to break through the polarization. Those days at Tantur proved to be the most productive session of the evangelical-Catholic dialogue.[29] Previously polarized positions yielded to empathic listening.

While at Tantur, within a stone's throw of Rachel's Tomb on the border between Israel and the Palestinian Territories, and only a mile from Bethlehem, I took the opportunity to seek out the remote Monastery of Mar Saba in the Judean desert. With some unease, I drove from Bethlehem south and west into the Palestinian Territories, through the rough Judean desert hills to try to find the renowned monastery where so many great Eastern theologians had resided, among them John of Damascus.

The monastic form of celebrating the liturgy of Mar Sabas had become a standard form of public worship throughout much of the Eastern Orthodox Church. It was a holy place in Judean monasticism, and is still considered to be one of the oldest continuously inhabited monasteries in the world.

As I drove through a tiny Palestinian village west of Jerusalem, the boys of the village threw rocks at my car, probably because I had an Israel tag. Cautiously I continued driving slowly south to the end of a long, rutted road where the monastery stood in a valley with steep cliffs nearby. I rang the outer bell hoping for some response, and after some time a shy monk came cautiously to the door. I told him I was a theologian interested in the history of ancient Judean Christian monasticism. Hesitantly he opened the huge door. I was in a fortress-like situation, dark, quiet and with few signs of hospitality until they brought me to a talkative young monk from Brooklyn, who ushered me around the ancient monastery, its chapel and halls, warning me of the danger of studying monasticism without living it.[30]

On the last day of the Tantur consultation, when I mentioned to Avery Dulles that I was going to spend a few days traveling in the Galilee, he told me he had never been there. I was surprised since he was a much-traveled Jesuit who had studied in Germany and spoke French and Italian, and had lectured all over the world. He was the son of the renowned John Foster Dulles, who had played key roles in the founding of the United Nations and the World Council of Churches before he became US Secretary of State. In jest I once introduced Avery as the only theologian who had an airport named after him.

If Avery had not seen the Galilee which I had visited several times, I asked if he might join me in a road tour of the north of Israel. I showed him my small Fiat rental car, wondering if he could fit into it. Avery was very tall, about six feet five, with such long legs that I could not see how they would fold up into my minivehicle. Always amiable and gentle, he tried out the front seat with the seat pulled far back. Since we were talking about sharing the driving, he tested out whether he could get into the driver's seat. Although he could barely fit in the Fiat, he rearranged his plane reservations to Louvain, where he had a lectureship coming up.

With that change Avery and I headed north from Tantur to the Mount of Olives. We headed toward Shiloh to Mt. Gerizim, Bethsaida, Mount Tabor and Nazareth. We feasted on delicious St. Peter's Fish in Tiberius. We spent some time at the synagogue in Capernaum and visited the ancient "House of St. Peter." We stood on the ruined ramparts of Megiddo (Armageddon) looking out over the Plain of Esdraelon, the scene of many battles throughout early history and prophesied as the final battle of human history. We traveled far north in Israel to Caesarea Philippi to the place where Jesus said to Peter: "You are the rock," charging Peter to shepherd the church. We mused by the huge wellspring that marked the headwaters of the Jordan, which to the faithful symbolized the eternal grace that flows from baptism. That moment was the high point of all of my times in Israel.

As we toured around every corner of Galilee, I was constantly learning from Avery about his own personal story as son of America's chief diplomat, as a Manhattan-born Presbyterian who became Catholic, a Harvard student who became a Jesuit and as a polio patient who learned to walk tall. Every few hours Avery would retire to pray the Divine Liturgy. That was when I learned the spiritual power of the Book of Hours that ordered time in relation to the light and dark cycle of daily prayer.

That week of traveling with Avery was one of the most memorable in my life. His intellect and piety had a decisive effect upon my life with God. As we returned from Acra through Caesarea to Tel Aviv, I felt blessed to have been able to spend almost a week of uninterrupted days with America's greatest living Catholic theologian.

AFRICA'S GIFT

The first stage of the Center for Early African Christianity in Nairobi 2006. I served for seven years on the WEA Theological Commission. Our annual meetings rotated between the continents. Significantly, 2006 was our year to meet in Africa. This offered an exceptional opportunity to introduce our work in Africa to the African Evangelical Alliance.

Two weeks after the founders meeting of the Center for Early African Christianity in September 2006, I took off for Nairobi, Kenya, with Mike Glerup to attend a meeting of the Theological Commission of the World Evangelical Alliance. Our task was to evaluate projects for study on behalf of global Christianity, but since we were in Africa we paid special attention to research and action proposals on African Christianity.

As I strolled through banana trees and lush vegetable gardens of Nairobi, I felt like I was in a horticultural Eden. The ripe corn and avocado trees lined the flagstone walkways of the seminary. The WEA Theological Commission gathered in the Nairobi Evangelical Graduate School of Theology (NEGST, later changed to African International University). Students from all over Central and East Africa had come to study there in the quiet suburb of Karen, with an excellent faculty and a splendid library. Tea on the grounds was served every mid-afternoon in this flourishing and fragrant setting.

It turned out to be perfect timing for melding the interests of the WEA in Africa with our newly founded Center for Early African Christianity. I presented a short summary to the commission that outlined our research proposal on the contributions of early African Christianity to world Christianity, with special attention to their social consequences for today. I proposed that the commission sponsor an official international study group of the WEA Theological Commission on early African Christianity. It was approved unanimously, and I agreed to direct it.

The Center for Early African Christianity had been created precisely to do this task. CEAC instantly became a project of WEA.

The mutuality of interests between WEA and CEAC was providential. It promptly opened many doors with Africa's foremost figures in academic and ecclesial leadership. Without the previous work of the patristic commentary, those two alliances would not have met. The serendipity of interests was instantly recognizable by all of us.[31] Our CEAC team explored with the seminary faculty and administration the idea of developing a course of studies in early African Christianity. To our knowledge that focus had never been proposed before.

It required developing a website (earlyafricanchristianity.com) and an international digital and printed book press (ICCS Press), and translating our early African research into the regional languages of Africa. We organized the International Consultation of African Theologians (ICAT) with twenty-five leading African theologians to advise us.

In Nairobi we opened up conversations with Catholic, Protestant, Coptic and Pentecostal scholars and their academic faculties in East Africa, and were warmly greeted by the Catholic University of Eastern Africa. For years that faculty had been active in historical and theological publications on African Christianity. We met several of their faculty and the university president, and at their publications office we obtained numerous volumes of published works by leading Catholic theologians serving in East Africa.[32]

We had good reason to develop partnerships with the African Instituted Churches (AIC) movement whose offices were in Nairobi. Their purpose was to bring together independent African Churches who had no history of connection with Western missions. They did not depend on any Western-based religious support or tradition. They showed keen interest in the thesis of *How Africa Shaped the Christian Mind* since they had never considered themselves a product of any Western mission movement or organization. They wished to have no indebtedness to colonial Christianity in any form. Since our work focused on the period fifteen hundred years before colonialism in Africa, we were right in tune with their work. They had always thrived on indigenous forms of African Christian worship, theology and social organization, and had flourished exponentially in thousands of small villages and cities all over Africa. One estimate put their probable numbers at sixty million members. AIC found a scholarly vision in our work that complemented their own.

This movement of African instituted churches has been sweeping Africa over many years. It is easy to see why the leaders of those churches have shown such an active interest in learning how African patterns of Scripture study spread from Africa to Europe. They are now in the process of rediscovering their ancient roots from the ancient indigenous African expressions of Christian faith rooted in the Nile Valley and the Maghreb.

A member of our CEAC board, Coptic bishop Markos Antonios of Johannesburg, had previously played a founding role in the inauguration of the Organization of African Instituted Churches. In 1978 Bishop Markos invited the originating leaders of African Instituted Churches to come to Cairo to meet the Coptic patriarch Shenouda III, and discover their deep similarities with Christians of the North of Africa. Bishop Markos is to this day one of the most energetic exponents of our scholarly efforts in Africa.

The purpose of the African Instituted Churches movement was "to locate their faith within the wider Christian faith tradition." They celebrate the local African cultures as the unique venue for the reception and interpretation of the gospel. They see part of their future as learning more about their ancient African ancestors of the earliest decades of Christianity. No wonder they were vitally interested in learning more about the unexplored African memory of Mark.

I met Bishop Arthur Kitonga, who was the founder of hundreds of congregations of Redeemed Gospel Church Kenya, one of the fastest growing missionary church initiatives in Africa, with many branches in Kenya, Tanzania and South Africa. Those congregations were impressive expressions of the African Instituted Churches movement. Bishop Kitonga generously invited me to preach in his church, Victory Temple, the next Sunday. It was a huge congregation located right in the impoverished center of the Mathare area of Nairobi. In that neighborhood I realized how difficult the conditions are for urban ministry in East Africa. Surrounding the church were thousands of small and crowded makeshift huts of corrugated tin or wood with improvised roofs.

The bishop brought me before the largest audience to which I had ever preached—about four thousand congregants. Extemporaneously I preached on Jesus' invitation to "knock and the door will be opened." After I had spoken at length and was exhausted, Bishop Kitonga continued with an accelerating tempo of ardor, ending with an invitation for hearers to come to the altar. Streams of people came down. Tears were shed. I laid my hands on their heads. They expressed feelings of extraordinary blessedness.

In Nairobi we also visited the faculty of Nairobi International School of Theology (now International Leadership University). Upon hearing our concerns, they generously invited us to consider making their campus our East African home.[33]

Returning to New York I had dinner that evening with Chuck Colson, Timothy George and J. I. Packer, key leaders in Evangelicals and Catholics Together, to explain what we were doing in Africa. I talked in detail with Neuhaus about how the CEAC was seeking to develop a significant relationship between evangelical and Catholic theologians in Africa. He and the others grasped instantly the ramifications for unifying Christian witness in Africa.

In November I went to Washington, DC, to the annual meeting of the Society for Biblical Literature and the Evangelical Theology Society, where I had called together a group of leading African-born theologians living in the United States.[34] Our purpose was to reflect on the recovery of African Christian unity by means of the recovery of ancient Christian teaching.

All this happened so quickly, with a converging cascade of collaborators from many important and diverse quarters. In our first months in Africa we were well on our way to solving one of our earliest tasks—discovering our natural partners in Africa and preparing for the next major consultation in Uganda.

As if in a chain reaction, we were invited to attend another much larger all-Africa conference in Entebbe in November of 2006. There I addressed the Ninth General Assembly of the African Evangelical Alliance (AEA), celebrating the fortieth year since its founding in 1966. We met in a stunning venue overlooking the magnificent Lake Victoria, with wild baboons in the surrounding trees, shorebirds galore and superb hospitality. At Entebbe we met another layer of the core of African evangelical leaders: bishops, leading pastors, deans and parachurch mission officials, in addition to theologians. Those occasions offered a well-timed opportunity to meet our future partners and have leisurely conversations with them exploring how our research might serve curriculum and teaching needs in African educational institutions.

It was there in Entebbe that Steve Ferguson first began asking me to consider writing my spiritual and intellectual autobiography as a narrative reflection on the struggles of our times. I was too busy to think about it then, and in addition I did not think of myself as an effective writer of personal narration.

The conjunction of those meetings in Nairobi and Entebbe was a huge blessing. If we had attempted to meet that variety and quality of influential leaders by making appointments one by one, traveling from place to place, it would have taken many months. Since the General Assembly of the AEA meets only once every four years, and the WEA Theological Commission meets in Africa only once about every six years, the conjunction of those great assemblies provided a rare and unforgettable congress of mutual interests and the meeting of minds.

We met the Reverend Moses Masai on his way to Darfur, Sudan. When I asked him about his mission in Darfur, he said his sole purpose was to serve the hungry and preach to the refugees. He had no external support. He told us that he would find it as he went. He would live with the refugees, eat whatever food they had and do what he could to heal and teach. Moses arranged a meeting for us with Bishop John Obechef, former Anglican who broke away as a Charismatic Episcopal bishop in order to create hundreds of churches in several East African nations—Uganda, South Sudan, Kenya and Tanzania, and now in faraway Darfur.

We met also with French-speaking West African leaders from the Faculté de Théologie Évangélique de Bangui in the Central African Republic. Their leading theologian, Isaac Zokoué, was the first to go back to the Central African Republic to develop a Master of Arts curriculum specifically in early African Christianity. Geoff Tunnicliffe, executive director of the WEA, came to Entebbe and helped us solidify the new link between the patristic commentary, the WEA and the African evangelical leadership. As we said goodbye to the 150 leaders present in Entebbe, we praised God that we had been offered the hand of fellowship with most of the major evangelical leaders of the continent of Africa in such a short time, only four months after the founding of the Center.

Strategic meetings with Anglican bishop Anis Mouneer and Coptic theologian Tadros Malaty helped us formulate a practical plan for developing early African Christian studies in seminaries in Egypt.

I accompanied Howard and David Ahmanson to Cairo in February 2007 to meet Coptic and Anglican prelates and students, guided by Arne Fjeldstad. We met in Alexandria with the eminent Father Malaty, arguably the world's leading Coptic theologian. He had served in many Coptic churches and seminary faculties around the world, from Sydney to Jersey City. This winsome and saintly priest greeted us in his own renowned parish, St. George in Alexandria, and provided us with a grass-roots parish perspective on Coptic Egypt.

Father Malaty's parish featured a well-fitted Coptic bookstore, the best I had seen. I had been looking for Coptic theology resources for years. Although most were in Arabic, here I found many in English, published for diaspora Copts. Most were locally produced for specific congregations and hence have received little circulation outside Egypt. Here was a wealth of literature with many volumes pertinent to my research. I came away from that bookstore with an armful of books, many by Father Malaty, which helped to orient me toward the Coptic view of history, liturgy and prayer. His books on Origen and Mark became wellsprings of resources for my books on early African theology and on the African memory of Mark.

When we visited the St. Mark's Church in Klot Bek, which is the Coptic Cathedral in Alexandria where the tomb of St. Mark is located, we fortuitously met Bishop Bishoy, who served as secretary of the Coptic Church's Holy Synod. Bishoy was a major Coptic theologian and confidant of Coptic pope Shenouda. We visited the traditional marturium of St. Mark.

When Anglican bishop Mouneer heard about our presence in Cairo, he graciously invited me to speak to the students of the Alexandrian School of Theology. The school had classes largely in Arabic, but some were in English, meeting both in Alexandria and Cairo. The whole student body was having a semi-annual retreat at which I spoke in English and the bishop translated into Arabic. That school meets near the location where the first catechetical school in Christian history had been developed under the esteemed leadership of Pantaenus, Clement and Origen.

I spoke to those young Arabic-speaking ordinands about how the recovery of the School of Alexandria today has consequences for the whole of Africa and of global Christianity. The students were coming from Anglican Churches in Egypt and Sudan, as well as from other places in North Africa. I was elated to find such a robust Anglican effort in theological education in Egypt, whose effects were being widely felt in Sudan, Ethiopia and Libya. We began laying plans for a graduate-level course of studies on early African Christianity, which Michael Glerup would lead, along with David Eastman, Joel Elowsky and Andrew Walls.

Our most inspiring moment in Cairo was the visit to Manshiyat Naser, also known as Garbage City, a slum settlement on the outskirts of Cairo. There amid the debris was the spectacular Cave Cathedral, St. Sama'ans Church, reputed to be the largest church in the Middle East, with seating for fifteen thousand people. Living under marginalized dhimi status for centuries in the Muslim society, Christians have been blocked from many occupations in Egypt, but one exception is garbage collection. Muslims in Cairo have left trash collection up to Christians for reasons having to do with Muslim law. Sorting, selling and recycling garbage has been a life-sustaining occupation for Cairo's Coptic poor. Garbage for the huge city was dumped at Manshiyat Naser. We drove through street after street of mounds of refuse being sorted under temperatures above 100 degrees, where about fifty thousand Christians live out an undaunted faith. We marveled at their perseverance.

In Addis Ababa, Ethiopia, in 2008 we brought together the twenty-five most eminent African theologians for an assessment of our first year of work in Africa.[35] We knew that many of them had not had the opportunity to meet each other, separated as they were by long African distances as well as the worldview and emotive distances between the Christians of the north and south of Africa, as well as those of the east and west. Those men and women were selected in a way that represented all regional sectors and most major traditions of African Christianity: Coptic, Catholic, Protestant, Pentecostal and African Instituted Churches.

Some were Africans teaching in European universities. Most were teaching in some of Africa's most distinguished seminaries and universities. All were published scholars, highly respected in their separate communities. To them I presented my "Core Hypotheses for Discussion"[36] This was the beginning of a heartening conversation in which those theses were well-received, and the group requested subsequent meetings to continue pursing them.

The goal was to produce previously untranslated texts for scholars, and in due time to help the parents of Africa to tell the stories of the saints to the children of Africa. All this was emerging through our on-the-ground workshops, seminary classes, publications and website. We found a strong desire among sub-Saharan Christians to connect with their brothers and sisters in north Africa. From that point on there was a substantial consensus that the early African Christianity project should be carried out, that they were eager to participate and carry on in the work. We not only enjoyed good fellowship in Addis but looked forward to coming together later in French-speaking Dakar, Senegal.

Ongoing tensions between the Coptic Orthodox Church and the Ethiopian Orthodox Church had continued for over twenty years. The Coptic Orthodox bishop said to be closest to Coptic pope Shenouda was Bishop Bishoy, secretary of the Holy Synod, who was one of our twenty-five key African theologians. He had been sitting with us every day in our consultation in Ethiopia. Since he had written extensively on sensitive theological issues, he was the one we asked to represent Coptic Christianity in Addis.

Prior to our consultation, there had been ambivalent overtures to reconciliation between Egyptian and Ethiopian churches, but those had apparently lacked public confirmation by the two patriarchs. Bishop Bishoy was among the last to accept our invitation to the consultation but became an active participant in all of it once it began. An articulate Coptic theologian, Bishop Bishoy engaged actively with sub-Saharan voices around the large table. All agreed that a deeper plunge into Coptic dialoque was timely.

Midway through our conference, Bishop Bishoy brought unexpected good news to our deliberations: Pope Shenouda was on his way to Addis to be received by Abune Paulos, pope of the Ethiopian Orthodox Church, to officially celebrate their long-awaited reconciliation. He brought the personal greetings of Pope Shenouda to our gathering of African theologians. Ethiopian patriarch Paulos sent an official delegation to our consultation to welcome us to Ethiopia. On the last day of our consultation, the reconciliation of longstanding conflicts between the two Orthodox patriarchates was formally celebrated by a foot-washing ritual.

Bishoy indicated that the timing of this reconciliation was made more auspicious by our presence in Addis at that time, and to some extent our consultation may have prompted Pope Shenouda to conclude the reconciliation during our week in Addis. Spontaneously we all arose and cheered in gratitude for both patriarchs sending us their blessing on the occasion of their reconciliation. It felt like an iconic event.

Our mission to Mozambique in far southeast Africa was directed especially to young Africans. In 2008 our core CEAC team attended the All Africa Conference of Churches (AACC) in Maputo, Mozambique. I spoke to African youth who had gathered from all over the continent. I presented the central evidence for how Africa shaped the Christian mind and focused on the theme "Rediscovering the African Seedbed of Western Christianity." I watched their young faces light up as we set forth evidence of the intellectual strengths of early Christian teaching in Africa. In subtle ways they grasped instantly that they had not yet been given sufficient access to those crucial resources, and that they must lead the way in the rediscovery of the brilliance of ancient African Christianity.

I asked them to savor a simple point unhurriedly: the Christians living on the African continent south of the Mediterranean had originally taught the Christians of Europe and the Middle East. Africans had informed and educated the very best of Syriac, Cappadocian, Greek and Latin teachers. Since they could not easily find those African sources in modern Western textbooks, I urged them to discover this information for themselves and rewrite all of this new information into a fair-minded history. They celebrated that Christianity on the African continent had a much longer history than was portrayed by many of its modern colonial expressions.[37]

The first seven years in Africa. By 2008 we completed six decisive consultations at Nairobi, Entebbe, Mukono, Alexandria, Cairo and Maputo. Our African partners knew that the Center for Early African Christianity had no hidden purposes other than to make contemporary African Christianity strong in intellectual leadership. We were met by welcoming and encouraging believers everywhere we went in Africa to present the vision of the unnoticed treasure of early African Christianity. They were grateful that we were providing them with evidence of the intellectual strength of their own Christian ancestors. Our sole purpose in being there was to highlight the brilliant Christian minds of ancient Africa and to share with those we met how deeply we appreciated their spiritual birthright. We were there to communicate to Africans how deeply we ourselves had been moved by their heritage.

During our first seven years in Africa, CEAC has gathered key leaders from all four quadrants of Africa: North Africa, Francophone West Africa, South Africa and East Africa. Through conferences, workshops, curriculum planning and scholarly dialogues they are voluntarily setting local agendas for the recovery of early African Christian teaching. Though we were determined to reach out to African Americans who understood our mission, we had decided from the outset that our crucial partners were on the continent of Africa. Desta Heliso, dean of the Ethiopian Evangelical Seminary said, "We need you to help us rediscover ourselves historically."

By these efforts, ministries of prayer, scholarship, preaching and social service discovered fresh vitalities that had been slowed down by modern colonial-period divisions. Ancient African writers were introduced by Copts to sub-Saharan Pentecostals. Together they reaffirmed the power of the Holy Spirit in history to bridge cultural and language barriers.

We held our first consultation in Ethiopia because it was a bridge between the north and the south of Africa. Early Christians are not to blame for not having the technology to penetrate further south than Ethiopia in the first fifteen hundred years. The goal since Pentecost had always been to bring good news to the ends of the earth, even if the ends were not then known. The stubborn limits of African geography prevented the earliest Christians from penetrating further south beyond the highlands of Ethiopia. Sub-Saharan explorations had to await technologies of shipping and commerce in order to move further.

The Coptic tradition from Egypt and Ethiopia has had the most sustained experience with persisting for centuries under conditions of repression, and has shown tremendous staying power. We took pleasure in showing that the biblical core of Coptic Christian triune teaching and Christology was not substantively different from that which is being taught today by sub-Saharan Catholics, evangelicals and charismatics.

We voiced our heartache that sub-Saharan Africa has remained linguistically distant from the north of Africa. The ancient Christian traditions of the north of Africa have maintained this intrepid witness on behalf of all contemporary African Christians for two thousand years. The south of Africa has benefited far less than it could have from the wisdom of Christians in the north of Africa, but this can be corrected by expanding our historical memory. Meanwhile sub-Saharan Christians still have rich spiritual gifts to offer Christians of the north. Only together will these voices become better prepared for the hazards of Africa's future.

Even if African Christians might be called to face another thousand years of Islam, they will face it better with an accurate memory of their own six centuries of pre-Islamic vitality as well as their history of courage, sacrifice and determination since Islam.

The earliest African councils of the third and fourth centuries provided a world model for achieving consensus and proximate unity in the body of Christ. The Councils of Carthage and Alexandria showed Europe how to resolve issues by conciliar consensus. The African exegetes held that it is the Holy Spirit who creates the unity of the body of Christ worldwide. These African councils made far-reaching decisions out of the apostolic teaching that echoed throughout early Christianity.

The African martyrs from Mark to Black Moses provided a model for believers all around the world to discover that through persecution a world community of faith was emerging that transcended national borders. The road to doctrinal consensus in world Christianity was decisively hammered out in Africa during the horrific period of martyrdom and state-required idolatry. A century later the search for consensus would appear in France, Italy, Spain and Syria. All who have excavated the rich history of the earliest councils have found themselves immediately digging into African texts.

The Institute for Classical Christian Studies (ICCS), parent body to the Center for Early African Christianity, created a publishing house, ICCS Press, to insure that the works of early African Christian writers will be made available at low cost to African Christians. Looking toward a high tech future for Africa, this press focuses on providing searchable digital texts and giving scholars and pastors the ability to access the wisdom of early African Christianity. It helps pastors by providing easy searches of key biblical words, subjects and key classic African authors. Internet and digital technologies will in time provide vast databases for thorough revisiting of the history of the earliest African writings. ICCS Press will stay on the growing edge of these technologies. High costs in book distribution currently constitute an obstacle in Africa, but that obstacle is being gradually overcome through digital technology and print-on-demand publishing of digitally stored texts. The scholarly publications of the Center for Early African Christianity are focusing on African sources and texts written before A.D. 1000 in Coptic, Geʻez, Arabic, Greek, Latin and Syriac. Young Africans scholars will play the decisive role in the rediscovery of their birthright. They will be able to publish their findings through ICCS Press.

Even young children can grasp the basic elements of the stories of Moses the Black, who was a very bad man before he met Christ, and Mary the mother of Mark, in whose house in Jerusalem the Lord's Supper was instituted. Children can learn to follow Athanasius in his exile, Anthony in the desert, and the brave women and men of Scilli who refused to yield the Scriptures to the authorities. Ultimately these stories will find a global audience, but first they must find a way to be heard by the African child.

The story of early African Christianity is not a myth but a real history.

It is the story of African believers facing life-and-death choices, centuries of demeaning slavery and dehumanization. As this reality unfolds, an African grandmother will tell the stories of the saints of Africa to her grandson and granddaughter. These are stories of heroic proportions, replete with courageous characters and surprise endings that will likely result in the children of Africa embracing their Christian ancestors. These stories can be told simply in a way that echoes the courage of their faith. For this reason the CEAC is planning a Children's Book Series that will help these stories come to life in the imagination of the African child.

The twenty-five preeminent African theologians who met in Addis Ababa met again in 2009 at Dakar, on the far west coast.[38] While English is the most widely spoken international language throughout the whole of Africa, huge populations in West Africa and North Africa speak French or Portuguese in addition to their regional language. In Senegal we reached out to the French speaking West Africans by translating *How Africa Shaped the Christian Mind* in French and circulating ten thousand copies. Bishop Mouneer of Egypt has sponsored a teaching program in Alexandria to provide a graduate-level academic program in early African Christianity. That led to the development of a graduate-level program in Cairo that included faculty from the St. Leo's Patriarchal Seminary in Maadi, the Institute of Patristic Studies, Regis Jesuit University, Jamia University at Al-Azhar, Cairo, and the Alexandria School of Theology.

After the Dakar Consultation in West Africa, Joel Elowsky and I headed directly to São Paulo for a meeting of the Theological Commission of the World Evangelical Alliance. I fell very ill due to incipient lymphoma cancer and had to return home immediately for treatment. For six months I completely lost my voice when my vocal chords refused to resonate properly after I had a lymph gland biopsied.[39] I was encumbered by these illnesses for two and a half years, but this did not stop me from continuing a regular pace of research and writing.

The 2010s

After Eight Decades

◆

EGRET POINT

My place. After having faced so many exciting and adventurous years with Edrita, I am now facing my future alone. This has been my time to draw closer to life with God. My constant prayer is simply for grace to live a full life of accountability to God.

Still, I was reminded of her at every turn.

My months of greatest spiritual growth were the months that followed her loss and the birth of Chloe. It was as if Edrita had left me my grand-daughter as a reminder of her ongoing love.

Eight years before, Clark had married Jeanne, who brought with her three wonderful children, all of whom were blended into our family seamlessly. Edward's two girls in Charlotte brightened my life as well. I increasingly felt that I had a new future in order to do something worthy of the privilege of nurturing this awesome family that Edrita had given me.

It took me a long time to move from withdrawal to engagement, but after a continuing period of grief and healing I found new spiritual energy. One day as I was sitting not far from the weeping willow I had planted in Lansbrook Park in Edrita's memory, an elegant Great White Egret landed near me. Somehow I felt that beautiful bird was a signal that it was time to pick my life up again.

There was no map for this inward journey. I watched doors open and close as they led me into this phase of my life. I studied and practiced the daily order of the hours of prayer of early monasticism, ordering my days according to the cycle of darkness and light through every day.

I was longing for some place to recover the peace that had flown away with her. At Egret Point I found a serene place for me to thrive. It is a quiet point on the lakeshore where the Great White Egret families gather in large numbers from April to October.

A string of seemingly disconnected events brought me to this new place on the lakeside I love. The most striking house in the neighborhood was the first house built directly on Lansbrook Lake by the architect who first developed the area. It was constructed with a beautiful brindled gray local stone from the nearby Arbuckle Mountains. The site had taken advantage of the unusual location right where the lake turns sharply from a westerly to a northerly flow under a bridge, down a waterfall and on past the park. With this most stunning vista on the lake, no other house in Lansbrook was so favorably located, so isolated, so quarantined from traffic and so aesthetically appealing. It was the only house on the lake that immediately faced the water on the south where the egrets gather and the water on the west where the prairie sunsets are widest.[1] I called it Egret Point.

The Great White Egret is a large, majestic shorebird with exceptional grace in flight or quiet shore fishing. Some of the largest egrets remain in Oklahoma year round, but most with young go south to the warmth of Aransas Pass in Texas during the cold weather. The growing families arrive back in Oklahoma in April and remain until October.

In the late evening people who visit Egret Point love to watch these huge birds with 56-inch wingspans come in from their favorite fishing spots and circle above the trees while slowly losing altitude until they arrive at their preferred nesting point, which is only fifty yards from my back door in the towering trees by the lake. On one occasion I counted 128 egrets at sunset in four trees nearby. When I am on my back porch at any hour of the day, my entertainment is simple: open my eyes to the lazy turtles basking on logs, the striking fish, the squirrels leaping from tree to tree, the geese and ducks in formation, the cardinals, the cooing doves, the herons and the incomparable dignity of the egrets. I became a keen observer of ever-changing tints of light on water, where the heavens meet the breeze in ever new forms of natural beauty.

In March 2004 I brought Judy Cincotta on to our team as my executive assistant. An experienced businessperson and wife of a former FBI agent, she has helped me do everything I have attempted to do in the last decade. She has been my rigorous editor, my sounding board, my financial agent and my organizational assistant in every way possible. My life would have been much diminished without her. She has read every line of this story a half dozen times, each time refining my intention.

In search of solitude: The liturgy of the hours of darkness and light. Throughout the changing hours of light and shadow and breeze I went back to the Anglican Diurnal Order of daily prayer, the Benedictine daily liturgy and the four-volume Divine Liturgy of the Catholic tradition that Avery Dulles taught me to pray daily. Over many days in the Galilee I had noticed how consistently he withdrew regularly and observed the hours, inconspicuously in a quiet practice of daily prayer. This daily liturgy now sustains me through all seasons.

The traditional sevenfold order of daily prayer hinges on the believer's relationship with light and darkness. When the world is sleeping, it is the Hour of Vigils. When the world is awakening, it is the Hour of Lauds. Then when the believer is entering into the world of work, it is the Hour of Terce. When the morning work world is winding down, when the world is hungry and being fed, it is the Hour of Sext—the sixth hour after dawn. When the mid-afternoon sun is descending, it is the Hour of None. When the world is bathing in the glory of sunset, it is the Hour of Vespers. And when the world is yielding and retiring, it is the Hour of Compline. During these alternations of ascending light and descending darkness my life with God deepened. This pattern follows the psalmist's sevenfold ordering of the times of prayer (Ps 119:164).

The heaviness of my struggle after Edrita's death is hard to convey. My mending heart found halting expression in a series of seven weeks of meditations later published under the title *In Search of Solitude: Living the Classic Christian Hours of Prayer*. There were three voices in those personal prayers and reflections, which included You (Lord), me and her. These meditations were ordered around the ancient prayers and chants of the Book of Hours.

In the years since Edrita's passing my deepest wish has been for solitude, to be left to my books and thoughts, and a quiet life with family and friends. Many friends, colleagues and deeply caring family have stayed in touch with me and remained in my life since my contemplative years began. I have appreciated their love more than they will ever know. In recent years I have continued to write, but not travel, teach or lecture. I have enjoyed living a low-profile life.

But this story does not end on a downer note of boring retirement and withdrawal. Exactly the opposite. Following my retirement from Drew after Edrita's passing, I moved permanently to the place where my extended family resides in Oklahoma, finished the ACCS editing in 2006 and launched the vast project in Early African Christianity that required a great deal of mobility until 2009, when I faced lymphatic cancer. I had many productive years of teaching in the university—fifty-three years from 1960 to 2003—but the most prolific years of my life have been since I took up a full-time life as an author on Egret Point. From here I have poured my heart into the Africa project with great pleasure and fruitfulness. Although I loved teaching, lecturing and coordinating a world-scale mission, I have loved the centered life of writing more. This is why I sought out a tranquil semi-monastic life of praise, study, writing and enabling the mission to Africa.[2] I cannot leave the narrative without a word about that mission.

THE AFRICAN TRILOGY

The African memory of Mark. After writing *How Africa Shaped the Christian Mind*, I focused on the single person who epitomized the whole narrative of early African faith: Mark the Evangelist. Mark was the first person to set pen to paper to record the events of the ministry of Jesus and the first person to bring the gospel to Africa.

My purpose was to show specifically how Africans have remembered their first-century beginnings as shown in the ministry of Mark in the Cyrenaic Pentapolis and in Alexandria. All African believers have become the sons and daughters of St. Mark. According to African memory, Mark the Evangelist was chosen by the apostles to be the first apostle to the continent of Africa.[3] Though much revered in African iconography and history, Mark's original African identity has never been understood or explored in the modern West. According to Coptic memory, Mark was born in the Pentapolis of North Africa, now northeastern Libya. Cyrene was the most likely place of Mark's birth. Alexandria was, in my view, undoubtedly the place of his death.

As St. Patrick is widely honored as the first apostle to all of Ireland, and Thomas to India, so is Mark honored as the first apostle to all of Africa. In these cases the material and literary evidences are stronger than typically believed by Western historians. Those evidences come from archaeological, numismatic, epigraphic and stone artifacts, as well as written texts. I drew together physical and literary evidence that the Markan martyrdom sites in Alexandria corresponded exactly with the events reported in the primordial African narrative. The location of the earliest churches in Alexandria pinpoint the events of Mark's arrival, his first convert, his first congregation, his first Christian school, his challenge to idolatry, his arrest, his dragging by horses to death, the attempt to burn his body, his burial and the veneration of the site of his martyrdom. These archaeological pointers became for me the most persuasive material evidence that Mark taught and was martyred in Africa, being the first of many African martyrs.

African patriarchs and church leaders of early times appealed to the authority of Mark and prized their direct lineage from that African expression of apostolic succession. African Christianity has typically viewed its core apostolic authenticity as closely related to its factual and historical founding by the apostle Mark. For Africans to neglect Mark is analogous to Armenian Christians overlooking Gregory the Wonderworker or Jews forgetting Jacob.

I examined the evidence that the house of Mary the mother of Mark was the location of the institution of the Lord's Supper and of the coming of the Spirit in Pentecost. I laid out the arguable evidence for Peter's visit with Mark to Babylon of Old Cairo, and for the close interconnection between the families of Peter and Mark. Mark was the first writer of the history of Jesus. Despite hundreds of books on Mark, the story of Mark had not yet been sufficiently told from the point of view of early African texts and sources.

Early Libyan Christianity. The third volume of the African trilogy, and clearly the most difficult, focused on the most neglected arena of early Christian studies, Libya. Of the thousands of books on early Christianity, no one to my knowledge had given book-length treatment to Libya, the vast land where Christianity flourished unnoticed for five hundred years.

I was invited in 2008 to speak to Islamic university students in Libya on the centuries of pre-Arab Christian history in their country. The joint invitation came from Da'wa Islamic University and Anglican primate Anis Mouneer, and was accompanied by the generous cooperation of officials from the civil government.

My special motivation for telling the Libyan story was much deeper than issues of modern politics, revolution or economy. I wanted to demonstrate that Libya had played a significant role in the specific aspects of the formation of Western culture at the apex of its civilization during the first five Christian centuries. My book *Early Libyan Christianity* sets forth the evidence. It is a prototype narrative of early African Christianity: once important for doctrinal formation, then after five centuries forgotten.

My university lectures focused on the physical and literary evidences of a significant Christian presence in Libya in the years before Islam. I was also reporting on the archaeological finds that had been buried in the antiquity of that region.[4] From the first to the seventh century Christians were firmly planted in Libya. They had bishops, churches and councils for which there remains both civil and ecclesial documentation. The archaeological evidence of early Christian life in Libya is abundant and on display in the museums of Tripoli, Qasr Libya, Cyrene and Sabratha. Those centuries of Christian presence created a robust Libyan Christian culture, hence an early African form of Christianity dating back to the mother of the Evangelist John Mark.

In *Early Libyan Christianity* I laid out the interweaving evidences that Tertullian may have been Libyan, born in the same city as the Roman emperor Septimius Severus. I described the struggle of Synesius of Cyrene as the leading bishop of the Pentapolis. Early Libyan Christians had a feisty record of entering into lively disputes over scriptural interpretation, particularly on the eternal divinity of Christ.

At a formal dinner at the British Embassy in Tripoli I was sitting at the same table with the Anglican primate of North Africa, the British ambassador, and several Orthodox and Catholic bishops in addition to distinguished Muslim scholars. I received questions from all quarters, but the one most engaging was why Egyptian Christianity survived and Libyan did not. I argued that Libyan Christians had already suffered much more from the tribal uprisings than those in the Nile Valley. The crucial military answer was the absence of a Byzantine navy.[5]

For most Libyan Christians of the seventh century the Arab sweep meant either conversion to Islam or frenetic flight to safety if they had the means. The result was the gross depopulation of Christian Libya, which did not happen in Egypt. That was followed by the mass movement of the marginalized Libyan Christians to safer havens such as Sardinia and Sicily.

Later in 2011 Coptic bishop Markos Antonios of South Africa asked me to trim and simplify *How Africa Shaped the Christian Mind* for translation into many of the regional languages of Africa. I did this by reducing two hundred pages to fifty and eliminated all technical terms. It was titled *Africa's Gift*. Already it has been translated into Kiswahili and Zulu, with translation projects now underway in Hausa, Shona and Ndonga, and projected in Igbo, Yoruba, Lingala and other regional languages. Ultimately "Africa's gift" refers to African Christianity's gift to world Christianity both then and now.

Each time I went to the hospital for chemotherapy, I took my computer with me, of course. The nurses got some laughs. Visitors thought I should give myself permission to leave the books and laptop at home, but I considered the hospital more like a quiet respite than an ordeal. The congestive heart failure limited my treatment options for lymphoma, but I tolerated chemo very well. The battle with cancer proceeded during

2009 to 2012, when I was researching and drafting for *The African Memory of Mark* and reading and researching in order to write *Early Libyan Christianity*.

I was pronounced free of cancer in 2013, but my susceptibility to infection has prevented further travel. That meant that my contribution to the Center for Early African Christianity would have to be largely in the form of research and writing rather than the life on the road to which I had become accustomed. My last flight was in July 2009 from Dakar, Senegal, to São Paulo, Brazil, to a joint session of the WEA Theological Commission and the Evangelical-Catholic Conversation, which I had to leave due to illness. From then on it was testing, biopsies, diagnosis and numerous hospital rounds of chemotherapy.

The further I pursued the Africa thesis, the more I confirmed that out of early Africa came Christianity's most brilliant early intellects (Tertullian, Cyprian, Clement and Origen) and texts (philosophical, religious and moral) that would put a permanent stamp on Western European culture, and would come to dominate much of Western thought. This African priority was recognized and acknowledged in the fourth century by Cappadocians (Basil, Gregory of Nazianzus), Syrians (Ephrem), Greek writers (Evagrius Ponticus), and Romans (Rufinus), but the African roots of these consensual teachings were later disregarded, not remembered by Europeans.[6]

The evidence became ever more compelling that the birth of the European *university* was anticipated within African Christianity. I set forth the evidence for how Jewish and Christian interpretation of sacred texts—*exegesis*—first matured in Africa. I showed how African thinkers shaped the core formation of Christian *doctrine*. I described how the early African councils set the pattern for worldwide ecumenical decisions that bought greater *unity* to world Christianity. I explained how Africa shaped Western forms of *spiritual formation* through communities of prayer. I set forth clear evidence to show how Neo-Platonic *philosophy* moved from Africa to Europe.

If Islam is viewed as a traditional African religion, as it should be, how can the five centuries of indigenous Christianity that preceded it not have been even more traditionally African? It is hard to name any other living religious tradition that possesses a continuous written record of survival over two thousand years that is more stable and durable than Judaism and Christianity. Islam began in A.D. 622, five centuries after Christianity was firmly implanted in Africa.

When we study African Christian sources of the first millennium, the challenge of Islam is seen in a different light. Islam is not a meaningless challenge but a strange providential gift to Christianity calling the faithful to courage and faith. For this challenge modern Africans need the consolation of knowing their own history so they can celebrate the intellectual gifts of the most brilliant minds of early Christianity as indigenous Africans.

To imagine that African Christianity is destined to come to nothing is the least plausible of all conjectures. The earliest African Christians faced challenges far more hideous than do believers of this century. They were enabled to pass that wisdom along to Europe and the world in the first five centuries. Classic Christian teaching today is poised to thrive in Africa beyond all expectations despite the many obstacles of poverty, malaria, immune deficiency diseases, stalled economies and government corruptions as well as the challenge of Islam.

LOOKING BACK

A tiny slice of history glimpsed. Steve Ferguson for years begged me to write my life story, but I was resistant until Africa gave me a reason. Through many unforeseen journeys I finally realized that the continent of Africa had become my spiritual destination and most worthy scholarly investment.

Although reading autobiographies has always been for me a favorite pastime, I did not want to do my own. Taking it on as a duty, now it has become a joy. At last I can see why some of my closest colleagues (Steve Ferguson, Roberta Ahmanson, Judy Cincotta and Michael Glerup) thought it must be done. It has been restorative for me and an illuminating review of recent theology.

But classic Christianity resists focusing exclusively upon personal narrative for a good reason. Its subject is God far more than individual experience. Our human stories are indeed worth telling, but they remain small when measured in relation to the incomparable One whose story is told in actual universal history from creation to consummation.

No matter what my story has been for others, for me it has been a story of providential leading along a long road. By discovering the joy and meaning of consensual Christianity, my life has been enriched over two decades. It was by the grace of God that I had a change of heart and found what I had always been seeking.

This has been a very personal story, but at the same time a chronicle of a society lost in the wilderness, a culture in crisis and a faith being reborn. The major social crises of our times have been its backdrop: depression, war, recovery, boom, the 1960s' experiments, the gender revolutions and finally the rebirth of classic consensual Christianity.

As this story has unfolded once again in my memory, I have come to realize how unusual my specific path has been. I have faced problems common to all, yet it still amazes me that after living such a fragmented life for the first forty years, I have come out of it with a clear identity, a sustainable sense of self and unity of purpose grounded in salvation history. Many times I have disagreed with myself when I have compared one stage with another, but those changes have seemed to me to be the core events in my spiritual formation. Those unexpected turns *are* the story.

Funny I was put on the path to a genuine Christian new birth by a Jew. I who had once been a social radical became a "mere Christian" and finally became a theologian after having only pretended to be one.

In Judges 7, Gideon's army was first composed of more than twenty-two thousand soldiers. God said, "Too many." Then it was gradually reduced to three hundred. Only then did the Lord commission them to make way for the people of Israel to go to the Promised Land. I regard my serious readers as a great blessing because they have proven to be more important than thousands of standby observers. I still follow the hope of Kierkegaard in his authorship that he might reach out for "that one single individual." I feel as he did, that if I have only one, a single truly listening reader, I will be grateful. And I know the angels will be singing.

Acknowledgments

I am sincerely grateful for those who have reviewed all or part of this manuscript while it was in formation, especially Steve Ferguson, Michael Glerup, Joel Elowsky, Christopher Hall, Jim Hoover, James O'Kane, David Ford, Max Bunyard and Michael Ryan. To my executive assistant, Judy Cincotta, who has been many times over every sentence, I owe incalculable thanks. To the women in my life since my wife's passing— Sarah Oden Hampson, Jeanne Oden, Janet Oden, Adrienne Oden and the late Jane Oden, I offer my deepest gratitude for their caring love. I am forever grateful to our benefactors, the Ahmansons, whose unassuming maxim is *non nobis* ("Not unto us, not unto us, O Lord, not unto us, to your name we give glory" [Psalm 115:1]). This story tells about a dream that could not have become reality without all of these dear people and many more whose names appear in these pages. I am grateful to HarperCollins, Zondervan, Abingdon and InterVarsity Press for allowing the adaptation of some portions of previously presented episodes without which this narrative would be incomplete.

Writings by Thomas C. Oden

1960s

The Crisis of the World and the Word of God. Nashville: Methodist Student
  Movement, 1962.
*Radical Obedience: The Ethics of Rudolf Bultmann, with a Response by Rudolf
  Bultmann.* Philadelphia: Westminster, 1964.
The Community of Celebration. Nashville: Methodist Student Movement, 1964.
Experience therapeutique et revelation: un Symposium. With A. Godin and A.
  Chapelle. Louvain: Nouvelle Revue Theologique, 1965.
Kerygma and Counseling: Toward a Covenant Ontology for Secular Psychotherapy.
  Philadelphia: Westminster, 1966.
Contemporary Theology and Psychotherapy. Philadelphia: Westminster, 1967.
The Structure of Awareness. Nashville: Abingdon, 1969.
The Promise of Barth: The Ethics of Freedom. Philadelphia: J. B. Lippincott, 1969.

1970s

Beyond Revolution: A Response to the Underground Church. Philadelphia: West-
  minster, 1970.
"Optimal Conditions for Learning: Toward a Clarification of the Contractual
  Learning Process." *Drew Gateway* 42 (Fall 1971): 3-23.
The Intensive Group Experience: The New Pietism. Philadelphia: Westminster,
  1972.
After Therapy What? Lay Therapeutic Resources in Religious Perspective. Spring-
  field, IL: Charles C Thomas, 1974.
Game Free: The Meaning of Intimacy. New York: Harper & Row, 1975.
*Should Treatment Be Terminated? Moral Guidelines for Christian Families and
  Pastors.* New York: Harper & Row, 1976.
TAG: The Transactional Awareness Game. New York: Harper & Row, 1976.

Parables of Kierkegaard. Princeton, NJ: Princeton University Press, 1978.

Agenda for Theology: Recovering Christian Roots. San Francisco: Harper & Row, 1979.

1980s

Guilt-Free. Nashville: Abingdon Press, 1980.

Pastoral Theology: Essentials of Ministry. San Francisco: Harper & Row, 1983.

Care of Souls in the Classic Tradition. Philadelphia: Fortress, 1984.

Conscience and Dividends: The Churches and the Multinationals. Washington, D.C.: Ethics and Public Policy Center, 1985.

Crisis Ministries. Vol. 1, The Classical Pastoral Care series. New York: Crossroad, 1986.

Becoming a Minister. Vol. 2, The Classical Pastoral Care series. New York: Crossroad, 1987.

The Living God. Vol. 1, *Systematic Theology*. New York: Harper & Row, 1987.

Phoebe Palmer: Selected Writings. Sources of American Spirituality. New York: Paulist, 1988.

Doctrinal Standards in the Wesleyan Tradition. Grand Rapids: Zondervan, 1988. Revised edition, Nashville: Abingdon, 2008.

The Word of Life. Vol. 2, *Systematic Theology*. New York: Harper & Row, 1989.

Pastoral Counsel. Vol. 3, The Classical Pastoral Care series. New York: Crossroad, 1989.

Ministry Through Word and Sacrament. Vol. 4, The Classical Pastoral Care series. New York: Crossroad, 1989.

First and Second Timothy and Titus. Interpretation Commentary. Louisville: John Knox, 1989.

1990s

After Modernity . . . What?: Agenda for Theology. Grand Rapids: Zondervan, 1990. Reprinted 1992.

Life in the Spirit. Vol. 3, *Systematic Theology*. San Francisco: HarperSanFrancisco, 1992. Reprinted 1994, 1998.

Two Worlds: Notes on the Death of Modernity in America and Russia. Downers Grove, IL: InterVarsity Press, 1992.

The Transforming Power of Grace. Nashville: Abingdon, 1993.

John Wesley's Scriptural Christianity: A Plain Exposition of His Teaching on

Christian Doctrine. Grand Rapids: Zondervan, 1994.

Requiem: A Lament in Three Movements. Nashville: Abingdon, 1995.

Corrective Love: The Power of Communion. St. Louis: Concordia Publishing House, 1995.

Christology. Vol. 3, The Albert Outler Library. Lexington: Bristol Press, 1997.

General ed. Ancient Christian Commentary on Scripture. 29 volumes. Downers Grove, IL: InterVarsity Press, 1998–2010.

2000s

The Justification Reader. Classic Christian Readers. Grand Rapids: Eerdmans, 2002.

The Rebirth of Orthodoxy: Signs of New Life in Christianity. San Francisco: HarperSanFrancisco, 2003.

with J. I. Packer. *One Faith: The Evangelical Consensus.* Downers Grove, IL: InterVarsity Press, 2004.

The Humor of Kierkegaard: An Anthology. Princeton, NJ: Princeton University Press, 2004.

General ed. Ancient Christian Commentary on Scripture CD-ROM. Windows and Macintosh editions. Downers Grove, IL: InterVarsity Press, 2005.

Turning Around the Mainline: How Renewal Movements Are Changing the Church. Grand Rapids: Baker, 2006.

How Africa Shaped the Christian Mind: The African Seedbed of Western Christianity. Downers Grove, IL: InterVarsity Press, 2007.

General ed. Ancient Christian Devotional. 3 volumes. Downers Grove, IL: InterVarsity Press, 2007–2011.

Good Works Reader. Classic Christian Reader Series. Grand Rapids: Eerdmans, 2007.

Classic Christianity: A Systematic Theology. San Francisco: HarperOne, 2009.

General ed. Ancient Christian Doctrine. 5 volumes. Downers Grove, IL: InterVarsity Press, 2009–2010.

General ed. Ancient Christian Texts. 15 volumes scheduled. Downers Grove, IL: InterVarsity Press, 2009–.

2010s

In Search of Solitude: Living the Classic Christian Hours of Prayer. Grand Rapids: Zondervan, 2010.

The African Memory of Mark: Reassessing Early Church Tradition. Downers Grove, IL: InterVarsity Press, 2011.

General ed. with Joel C. Elowsky. *On the Way to the Cross: 40 Days with the Church Fathers.* Downers Grove, IL: InterVarsity Press, 2011.

Early Libyan Christianity: Uncovering a North African Tradition. Downers Grove, IL: InterVarsity Press, 2011.

God and Providence. Vol. 1, *John Wesley's Teachings.* Grand Rapids: Zondervan, 2012.

Christ and Salvation. Vol. 2, *John Wesley's Teachings.* Grand Rapids: Zondervan, 2012.

Pastoral Theology. Vol. 3, *John Wesley's Teachings.* Grand Rapids: Zondervan, 2013.

Ethics and Society. Vol. 4, *John Wesley's Teachings.* Grand Rapids: Zondervan, 2014.

Consulting ed., with Angelo Di Berardino, general ed., and Joel C. Elowsky and James Hoover, consulting eds. *Encyclopedia of Ancient Christianity.* Downers Grove, IL: InterVarsity Press, 2014.

A Change of Heart: A Personal and Theological Memoir. Downers Grove, IL: InterVarsity Press, 2014.

Notes

PREFACE

[1]In the Depression all hands, including third graders, were needed to bring in the cotton crop. Cotton harvest is work intensive. The time was ripe to get the cotton from the fields to the gin, where it was pressed into large bales. A favorite entertainment for boys was visiting the cotton gin to watch the big machinery and the moving trains. In our arid county we prayed for rain to help the cotton grow and then prayed that the fields would soon be dry enough to plow.

CHAPTER 1: THE 1930s

[1]The eldest son of I. G. Clark was Dave Clark, who excelled in mechanical engineering at Purdue University and remained to teach on the Purdue faculty, researching and testing huge diesel railway locomotives. The younger son, my uncle Ira, took a history PhD at Berkeley, then became professor of history at New Mexico State University, and wrote on railway history and water rights in early New Mexico, Texas and Arizona.

[2]In subsequent years, when these values have often been mocked or derided, I have wanted to ask faultfinders what was so wrong with them. Scouting was splendid training for the future that was awaiting me. In Troop 33 I learned I could make things on my own, solve problems, and care for the unfortunate. Though many honors were bestowed on Dad, none was more treasured than the Silver Beaver Award for lifelong outstanding service to the Scouts.

[3]Tal had the rare privilege of being baptized with water from the River Jordan, brought by Brother Ball from his trip to the Holy Land. I was baptized by water from the city reservoir—but I supposed with the same effect. As an infant I received my Christian name (Thomas for my grandfather Oden and Clark for my mother's family name). Later I understood that my baptism needed my free confirmation and called for my willing response.

CHAPTER 2: THE 1940s

[1]Worldwide casualty estimates range from 40 million to 71 million.

[2]Few farmhands in those days worked by the hour or day. Most worked by risk-laden sharing of the profits of actual produce, which was a great motivator for efficiency. There were both good and lean years, with fervent prayer for rain and interminable uncertainties on a semi-arid prairie.

Chapter 3: The 1950s

[1]In those days pacifist and socialist forms of idealism were intimately joined. The American Civil Liberties Union (ACLU) grew out of the civil liberties and conscientious objectors program of the International Fellowship of Reconciliation (IFOR). These two parallel organizations intermeshed. Among prominent ACLU leaders were Eugene V. Debs, Felix Frankfurter, John Dewey and William Z. Foster. The Garland Fund was a major source for the financing of Communist Party enterprises, including Brookwood Labor College, which was founded by the IFOR. Branching off from IFOR was the Workers Defense League (WDL), which focused on the legal protection of labor organizers, sharecropper organizers, migratory workers and persons subject to deportation proceedings.

[2]From Professor Stanley Kaufman I got a rich introduction to English poetry from *Canterbury Tales* to T. S. Elliot. On my first day in modern philosophy class under the German philosopher Gustaf Mueller, he literally filled the blackboard with all the major figures with whom we would be dealing. At the center was in large caps "HEGEL," with all satellites and subthemes branching out from the center: Kierkegaard, Fichte, Schelling, Heidegger, Husserl and many others, as if they were planets revolving around the sun. After a deep immersion in Hegelian philosophy, I was even more deeply challenged by Carlton Berenda, who introduced his students to an entirely different galaxy: notably the Vienna Circle, Rudolf Carnap, A. J. Ayer and R. B. Braithwaite.

[3]I was drawn early into the orbit of Harry F. Ward, chief author of *The Social Creed of the Churches*, the most widely circulated statement of the Social Gospel. In the 1950s I belonged to the Methodist Federation for Social Action, which Harry Ward founded and which is still persisting in activist Methodist leadership. Few Methodists realize that the author of this diluted creed, which became a standard statement of faith among Methodists, was written by one of the most influential self-described socialists among American clergy. Despite occasional criticisms of Soviet excesses, Harry Ward left a record of conformity to changing socialist positions throughout most of the 1930s. This did not prevent him from teaching in highly influential seminaries, first at Boston University and then in Union Theological Seminary. He never formally joined the Communist Party, but he became one of the party's most active and influential fellow travelers and also taught me how to be one.

⁴My most public guide into the socialist world was Norman Thomas, the former Presbyterian minister turned Socialist candidate for president. Six times he ran. After serving as the pastor of New York's East Harlem Church, he left his parish to join the Socialist Party and then became a leading figure in the Fellowship of Reconciliation. He helped found the American Civil Liberties Union and served as codirector of the far left League for Industrial Democracy. He ran as the Socialist Party's candidate for governor of New York, and twice ran for mayor of New York City. He was my model for lofty ideals and persistence. After World War II he campaigned for nuclear disarmament as chairman of the Postwar World Council and worked tirelessly for civil rights, labor and peace groups, including the ACLU, NAACP, CORE and SANE. He was my most durable template for social thought and public policy.

⁵My mentor in pacifist teaching in the 1950s was the gentle John Swomley, a Methodist minister who in his later years served as professor of social ethics at the St. Paul School of Theology in Kansas City. I admired him deeply for his courage and for the moral power of his arguments. He had been the director of the National Council Against Conscription during World War II and throughout my college years, when scores of Methodist ministers became conscientious objectors. He became the president of the Methodist Peace Fellowship, where his idealism penetrated deeply into the thinking of many young Methodist pastors, including me.

⁶I was a member of the International Fellowship of Reconciliation and an avid reader of the *Pendle Hill Papers*.

⁷In 1955 Richard Niebuhr was commissioned to direct a major review of North American theological education. Its results became widely known in three ensuing books: *The Ministry in Historical Perspectives* (1956) edited by Niebuhr and Daniel Day Williams, *The Purpose of the Church and Its Ministry* (1956) and *The Advancement of Theological Education* (1957), which Niebuhr wrote in collaboration with Dan Williams and James M. Gustafson. Their task was to visit seminaries all over the continent and write a definitive book on the future direction of theological studies. For this Niebuhr spent a year making extensive visits to major seminaries. This brought him to SMU-Perkins, where I had a rare opportunity to interview him.

⁸No one else had ever mentioned Hartmann to me, but I was captivated by his brilliance and holistic moral and philosophical thinking. Few today will recognize his name, but he was the first writer to give me a sense of the unique world of value. Hartmann advanced penetrating ideas about the laws of multiple levels of moral complexity, including inorganic, organic, emotional and intellectual values. The world of moral awareness that he described had inexhaustible splendor and meaning, and when rightly grasped was full of wonders and glory. In his three volumes of *Ethics*, he astutely analyzed and described the dynamics of moral phenomena, moral values and moral freedom. Though Hartmann's work is almost

impossible to find, I recommend it as basic education to any reader of philosophy or theology. My first published attempt at a field theory of ethics arose out of that period of intense reading of Hartmann. It hinged on what I called "multiple simultaneous value actualization." It was derived from Hartmann's description of the moral universe, celebrating the capacity of the will to actualize many values within the great chain of being in a single moment; that is, I can breathe, eat, converse and learn all at the same time in those distinguishable spheres of moral choice. I attempted to build upon that ethic in my study *The Structure of Awareness* in 1968, but the seeds were in Hartmann, and I have Liston Pope to thank for that.

[9]The prolific literary productivity of these Kent colleagues of the class of 1957 is revealed in the work ethic prevailing at that time. Among them was the irrepressible rabbinic scholar Jacob Neusner. No authorship in our time has exceeded Neusner's work in quality, quantity and critical acumen. Neusner was working largely alone for many years at Brown University, publishing volume after volume on the great classic texts of Judaism, while I was working with an international network of patristic scholars on the Ancient Christian Commentary on Scripture and its international translations. We were doing two analogous projects in the early history of exegesis of sacred texts, one Jewish, one Christian. We first met in 1957 in this same small class of Kent Fellows, and worked on parallel projects for over five decades. In this community of discourse I learned how important it was to test out my ideas with trusted friends.

Chapter 4: The 1960s

[1]George MacLeod had taken a small group of Scottish students to the island to rebuild the ruins of the thousand-year-old abbey church. Their work was the beginning of an experimental, ecumenical community that preceded the semi-monastic ecumenical community of Taizé, France, under Roger Louis Schütz-Marsauche. Faith and Life would later strongly affect the wider ecumenical scene in North America when it moved to Chicago a few years later and expanded into lay theological seminars taught all over the world.

[2]Joseph Wesley Mathews left seminary teaching at Perkins to go to the University of Texas to build an intensely committed lay theological academy. Mathews was dedicated to bringing his existentialist theology into the practice of community life among college students in America's largest university. He was developing an off-campus ministry that might be described as a Protestant monastic order of work, worship and service.

[3]Enid is on the path of the Great Chisholm Trail. The town was founded on the day of the Great Land Run of the Cherokee Outlet in 1893. At 50,000 inhabitants, it is Oklahoma's ninth largest city.

[4]I had the unusual good fortune to come to Phillips Graduate Seminary as a tenured associate professor, soon to be promoted to full professor with a manageable teaching load and the expectation that I would continue my research and writing.

[5]I was thrust into the role of editor early in my first year of teaching. Editing was a task I began early and continued for fifty-plus years. The unheralded writers in that modest student movement series would later prove to be key figures in church renewal, although at that time most were not well known. I was twenty-nine years old. That series included a description by Joseph Mathews of *Common Worship in the Christian Faith and Life Community*, which described the daily order of the remarkable community of work and worship at the University of Texas. I edited the narrative by George W. Webber titled *The East Harlem Protestant Parish*, which became a prototype for inner-city ministries in the early sixties, often inviting the brightest young theological students to plunge into the deepest pockets of poverty. In the same series I edited Arthur Brandenburg's *A Community of Lay Scholars in North Carolina*, Robert A. Raines's *The Recovery of Mission in the Local Church*, and T. Ralph Morton, the leader of the Iona Community, on *Work and Worship in the Iona Community*.

[6]Tal's daughter Dr. Amy Oden has carried on this tradition as dean of Wesley Seminary in Washington, DC. My cousin, Bishop William Bryant Oden, became historian of record for the history of the Council of Bishops.

[7]Some of its rudiments were found in Reuel L. Howe, *Man's Need and God's Action* (New York: Seabury Press, 1962).

[8]Thomas C. Oden, *The Crisis of the World and the Word of God* (Nashville: Methodist Student Movement, 1962). Only a thousand copies were published of the earlier soft cover book, most of which have disappeared. But it remains the most concise entry into my earliest work in systematic theology. As early as my unpublished senior sermon at Perkins Chapel in 1956, that threefold understanding of human awareness in time formed the core structure of that sermon and the rudimentary argument of *The Structure of Awareness* (Nashville: Abingdon, 1968).

[9]All good things in time and space can be valued anew in the light of that One from whom all things come and into whom all things return. Creaturely values become more deeply significant, not less, in the light of their finiteness. They are not gods, so they can now be valued in relation to the Giver of the finite world. We can value them realistically and work for their realization. All values in creation are valued anew in the light of the Giver of value. Lowly things have new worth. Elevated things lose their terror. Whatever is now known to be good is good in the context of the One who is incomparably good. All of our enemies become friends in relationship to the friendship of this first and last reality.

[10]Among my essays that further explored this premise were "Analogia Fidei und Psychotherapie" in *Evangelische Theologie*, "Theology and Therapy: A New Look at Bonhoeffer," in *Dialog*, and "Ecumenics and Psychiatry" in the *Christian Century*.

[11]I had not yet embraced the classic Christian teaching of the incarnation as an event in history.

[12]These analogies were further explored in *Kerygma and Counseling* (Westminster, 1966), which was later selected for reprint for the Harper and Row Minister's Paperback Library Series.

[13]Carrying our luggage from the train station to Ziegelhausen proved to be our first endurance test. It looked easy on the map. With great effort on the part of all of us we crossed the Old Bridge over the Neckar and walked a half mile more to the pastor's residence, where we were staying until we could locate an apartment.

[14]My research in Heidelberg took place a decade before the contributions of Irvin David Yalom, who is often considered the founder of the existential psychotherapy movement in America.

[15]He wrote his Freiburg doctoral thesis on "The Doctrine of Judgment in Psychologism" and had been an assistant to Edmund Husserl. Husserl provided a critique of what he called "psychologism" in the method he called "phenomenology"—the study of structures of consciousness as experienced from within the subject self. It was literally the logic of "that which appears" (*phainómenon*).

[16]Van den Berg's ground-breaking work paralleled contributions by Viktor Frankl, Karen Horney and Otto Fenichel.

[17]Among those published in 1965 were *Gaudium et Spes, Pastoral Constitution on the Church in the Modern World, Dignitatis Humanae, Declaration on Religious Freedom, Ad Gentes, Decree on the Mission Activity of the Church, Dei Verbum, Dogmatic Constitution on Divine Revelation*, and *Apostolicam Actuositatem* (*Decree on the Apostolate of the Laity*).

[18]See "Geneva 1966—Ethical Challenges Still Relevant Today," World Council of Churches, September 5, 2006, www.oikoumene.org/en/press-centre/news/geneva -1966-ethical-challenges-still-relevant-today.

[19]Its networking connections with the Saul Alinsky circle were evident to anyone familiar with the Urban Training Center and the Industrial Areas Foundation. A chief activist in the Detroit Conference was Stephen C. Rose of the Youth Division of the WCC, editor of *Renewal* magazine and *RISK*.

[20]The crux of the existential theology I taught in the late sixties can be summarized in a tight formula: Amid our experience of an anxious future, a guilty past and a boring present, we have sought to achieve self-fulfillment through "the gods," meaning the elevation of limited causes and creaturely goods to give ultimate meaning and value to our lives. In our glorification of these causes and valued

objects, which have become our gods and deliverers, we have increasingly distanced ourselves from that singular One from whom all things come.

[21]*Guilt Free* (Nashville: Abingdon, 1980) was an invitation to take guilt seriously, according to the analogy of God taking guilt so seriously that he died on the cross to redeem it.

[22]See details of how the connections were made in *The Structure of Awareness* (Nashville: Abingdon, 1969).

[23]Later one of my Drew graduate students, psychologist Stephen M. Maret, wrote his PhD dissertation under my direction on Frank Lake's *Maternal-Fetal Distress Syndrome*, later published as *The Prenatal Person*. Maret's book stands out in my mind as one of the most useful and significant academic projects I directed at Drew. Its prenatal research deepened my pro-life convictions.

[24]I was pleased to rediscover the extraordinary joy of parish ministry. A year later I was asked to serve a small Methodist church in Waukomis, Oklahoma, as an interim appointment from 1968 to 1969. Those rural churches brought me back from my speculative life to the reality of those dear communities of believers.

[25]As varied as Fritz Perls, Kurt Lewin, Abraham Maslow, Alan Watts, Alfred Adler and Karen Horney.

[26]In the mid-sixties, Fritz Perls was the principal trainer in Gestalt therapy at the Esalen Institute. Jewish philosopher Martin Buber provided the intellectual foundation, which he called "personal encounter," so much so that it became known as "the encounter culture." In role reversal, one person takes the role of another. It develops empathy and reveals relational dynamics.

[27]The stellar cast of theological titans in those colloquia included Hans Jonas, Rudolf Bultmann, Robert Funk, Fritz Buri, Paul van Buren, Schubert Ogden and Will Herberg. Though those names are largely forgotten now, they were on the lips of everyone who was immersed in the growing edge theology of the 1960s.

CHAPTER 5: THE 1970S

[1]Johnny Mercer, "I Want to Be a Dancin' Man," *The Belle of New York*, 1952.

[2]I was eager to discover more about my new friend. I found that he was born in the shtetl of the small czarist-Russian village of Liachowitz near the river Neris between Minsk, Belarus and Vilnia, Lithuania, on June 30, 1901. His immigrant Russian Jewish parents managed to flee to New York City, where he grew up in one of Brooklyn's most impoverished neighborhoods—Williamsburg. His father died when he was ten years old, leaving him to be guided by a mother who believed strongly in self-taught learning. He and his brother, Ted, assisted his impoverished mother in knitting and making belts, her only means of income. Like Reinhold Niebuhr, his academic degrees were less noteworthy than his critical mind, which

was deeply shaped by secular Jewish values strongly oriented toward New York Jewish intellectual circles.

He was an ethnic New Yorker through and through, as much as I was a dustbowl Oklahoman. He spoke German from childhood, learned Russian in order to read Lenin, sang Yiddish, studied Hebrew and French to physical exhaustion, and read in basic Italian and Spanish. He entered the College of the City of New York in 1918 and remained until 1920 when dismissed for absences and trouble-making in military science. From there he chose to commit himself completely to the Communist Young Workers League, where he rose quickly in the ranks of leadership.
[3]In their early twenties, Herberg and his wife, Anna, had become activist organizers and editors for the Young Workers League. They deliberately decided not to have children in order to be completely free for Communist Party service. He served as director of agitation and propaganda (agitprop) for the journal *Young Worker*.
[4]He understood precisely what it meant to say Jesus is Messiah, but never said it for himself.
[5]After he abandoned this bad dream, he wrote a pivotal essay in *Commentary* in 1947 titled "From Marxism to Judaism: Jewish Belief as a Dynamic of Social Action." There he recounted his long journey from communism to Judaism. He interpreted socialism as a secular distortion of the Jewish and Christian messianic vision. Herberg's disillusionment with Marxism paralleled other narratives of post-Marxist disillusion by Alexandr Solzhenitsyn, Malcolm Muggeridge, Irving Kristol and Boris Pasternak.
[6]Later I found the huge bibliography of pre-1941 articles from the communist New Workers School and *Workers Age* publications in the Herberg Collection at Drew Library. Herberg was writing both theoretical and practical essays on Marx, Lenin, labor, revolution, race, historical materialism and art criticism. They show how publicly articulate he had been in socialist advocacy. He contributed numerous articles to the *Daily Worker*, *Revolutionary Age*, the *New Republic* and *Workers Age*. His literary activity was prodigious from 1929 to 1940, when it abruptly fell silent.
[7]Herberg plunged into the study of classic Judaica, rabbinic exegesis and modern Jewish philosophy with all of his heart. He dove into deep reading of the formative classic Jewish texts (Torah, Midrash and Talmud). He probed contemporary Jewish theology, especially the writings of Franz Rosenzweig and Martin Buber, along with his friend Fritz Rothschild. From 1935 to 1948 he worked as research analyst and education director of the huge International Ladies' Garment Workers Association.
[8]Out of sheer brilliance and relentless reading, Herberg became a leading conservative Jewish writer, social philosopher, intellectual and a unique kind of Jewish theologian. He founded the learned quarterly journal *Judaism* with Robert Gordis and Milton R. Konvitz, and became a commentator on culture, religion and pol-

itics. He became religion editor of the *National Review* and long-term friend and adviser of William F. Buckley. Through traveling on the college lecture circuit over many years, he mentored many young conservatives who were being shaped by Edmund Burke, Reinhold Niebuhr and Russell Kirk.

[9]See the autobiographical portion of his *Judaism and Modern Man*; cf. David G. Dalin, ed., *From Marxism to Judaism* (1989), pp. 22-37.

[10]Will Herberg's study *Judaism and Modern Man* helped me to understand the contemporary debate in Jewish theology and philosophy. In his lectures he constantly challenged the false idols of political or social utopias on every hand. I most admired his great work of American sociology, *Protestant-Catholic-Jew*, in which he brought together theological and sociological wisdom in the description of the ways Americans were religious.

[11]There is no better way to glimpse the tenor of our dialogue in 1970 than to cite a few of Herberg's crisply written marginal responses while he was reading my book *Beyond Revolution* in the first months of our relationship. Here are several examples:

When I defended "group processes, sensitivity training, and the encounter lifestyle" as "akin to the pietistic tradition," Herberg joked in the margin, "That's exactly what's wrong with it." When I applauded "emerging forms" of culture, he quipped, "What's so special about 'emerging forms'? They may well be seriously deviant." When I argued for the legitimacy of public demonstration and a protest style of politics as well as an increase of inclusiveness in representational systems, Herberg retorted, "Wildly exaggerated." When I wrote that the role of the revolutionary is to awaken the need for change, he jotted, "Actually he does the very opposite: He engenders counteraction which is always the stronger."

When I wrote that "revolution means destruction and renewal," he countered "destruction, yes, but revolution itself is incapable of renewal." When I wrote that religion has become "deeply indebted to obsolete social assumptions in disrepute among the majority of the emerging world," Herberg's marginal notes recorded, "Just what are these obsolete social assumptions" and "who says they are bankrupt?" When I observed that the liberal Christian tradition is magnificent, he crossed out "is" and inserted "was." When I rashly observed that the younger generation has permanently left religion, Herberg noted public opinion research to the contrary.

When I spoke of YHWH as a "cryptic symbol," he could not resist cautioning me that "this was originally a personal name," not a symbol. When I marveled at the underground church's "achievement of plausibility," he commented, "Among whom? Always fraudulent." When I described the "death of God" as having caused the religious consensus to "splinter into a million parts," he wrote, "This utterly exaggerates the influence of the 'death of God' absurdity." When I applauded the welfare state, he pointed out that many of its effects have been deplorable for the poor.

Finally, I confidently stated my conclusion which read, "The emerging church should accept not merely the idea but the reality of the welfare state, and not try to perform a host of governmental functions which it has been trying to do rather ineffectively through private charity." Herberg protested, "this replacement of religion and the church by politics and the state as a source from which all blessings come seriously undermines the relevance and effectiveness of the church." In the end page of *Beyond Revolution*, Herberg remarked, "This is entirely a Protestant book." It is "completely oblivious to Roman Catholicism." As I pondered those criticisms I concluded that he was right on every count. His critique was always quick, clear, tough and constructive. They could be acid, but always with a deeper, gentler instructive purpose.

[12]Irenaeus, *Against Heresies*, 1.28.

[13]God reminded the people of Israel, "I the LORD do not change. So you, O descendants of Jacob, are not destroyed" (Mal 3:6 NIV). The apostles knew that "every good and perfect gift is from above, coming down from the Father of the heavenly lights, who does not change like shifting shadows" (Jas 1:17 NIV).

[14]Thomas C. Oden, "Ist die Forderung Gottes zweideutig?," *Zeitschrift für Evangelische Ethik* 5 (November 1961): 321-39; cf. "Is the Demand of God Ambiguous: An American-European Dialogue." *Ecumenical Review* 13 (January 1961): 153-71.

[15]The prevailing therapeutic theories and methods ranged from mainstream Freudian and Rogerian psychology all the way through the colorful spectrum of behaviorists B. F. Skinner, Joseph Wolpe and O. Hobart Mowrer. Each of those psychologists was welcomed and accommodated into the practice, language and values of Christian ministry.

[16]Needing to test out my hypothesis that the classical pastoral tradition had been abruptly forgotten in the twentieth century, I gathered metrics on the "most frequently referenced" authors in the teaching of pastoral theology from the nineteenth century compared with the twentieth century. The ten most important classical pastoral writers in the first eighteen centuries of Christianity were easy to identify by the numbers of editions and copies sold, and by the times they were quoted in the nineteenth century. Cyprian, Tertullian, Chrysostom, Augustine, Gregory the Great, Luther, Calvin, George Herbert, Richard Baxter and Jeremy Taylor were found to be most widely representative of classic pastoral teaching. I showed their frequency of reference in seven standard works of pastoral theology in the nineteenth century, those by William G. T. Shedd of Union (Presbyterian), Patrick Fairbairn of Glasgow (Scottish Presbyterian), James M. Hoppin of Yale (Congregationalist), Charles Bridges (Church of England), Heinrich Koestlin of Giessen (Lutheran), Washington Gladden of Columbus (Congregationalist) and Daniel Kidder of Drew (Methodist). I found that every nineteenth-century author

unfailingly quoted Chrysostom, Augustine, Luther, Calvin, Herbert and Baxter. I then gathered data on "most referenced" pastoral authors of the twentieth century. The number of references to the same classic figures had dropped to zero. That provided evidence that the attentiveness of contemporary pastoral writers to ancient pastoral writers was virtually nil. The results were set forth in *Care of Souls in the Classical Tradition.*

[17]I spent much of 1970 preparing a publishable manuscript for the Fuller lectures. I did not know that these lectures would open a door for me to other key scholarly evangelical circles with which I had no previous contact: Zondervan Publishing House, *Christianity Today*, the Evangelical Theological Society (ETS) and the World Evangelical Alliance (WEA). They showed me how wrong I had been to previously hold them at arm's length or consider evangelical scholarship lackluster.

[18]Among respondents to my lectures were H. Newton Maloney, who founded the International Society of Psychology and Religion, and Dean Neil Clark Warren, who created the first national network of ministry to singles based on rigorous empirical psychological research. Warren became the founder of eharmony.com.

[19]For a fuller bibliography of this literature see *After Therapy What? Lay Therapeutic Resources in Religious Perspective, the Finch Lectures by T. C. Oden, with Responses by N. C. Warren, K. B. Mulholland, C. R. Schoonhoven, C. H. Kraft, and W. Walker* (Springfield, IL: Charles C Thomas, 1974). Essays that developed from these lectures appeared in the *Christian Century, Journal of Pastoral Care, Journal of Humanistic Psychology* and *Drew Gateway.*

[20]This critique was led by Thomas Szasz, O. H. Mowrer and Paul Vitz, all of whom I would be privileged to meet in Drew's Aquinas Seminars in the 1970s.

[21]My first article that signaled an emerging affinity with evangelical scholarship came shortly after the Fuller lectures in 1972. It was on "The Human Potential and Evangelical Hope," published in *Dialog*, but also in revised forms in the *Journal of Humanistic Psychology* and the *Drew Gateway.*

[22]The syllabus included Plato's *Phaedrus*, Aristotle's *Perì Psūchês*, Gregory of Nazianzus on vocation, Augustine on psychological autobiography and Gregory the Great's *Pastoral Care.*

[23]See Thomas C. Oden, *Care of Souls in the Classic Tradition* (Philadelphia: Fortress Press, 1984).

[24]Others key figures in the classic pastoral literature were Bonaventure on the journey of the mind; Thomas Aquinas's *Summa Theologica* on happiness, fear, anger, the emotions, the dispositions, love and desire; and Hugh of St. Victor on preparation for confession, anointing of the sick, and care for the dying. Then followed the magisterial Reformation tradition of pastoral care as seen in Martin Luther's *Table Talk* and letters, Zwingli on the pastoral office, Calvin's letters,

Martin Bucer on visitation of the sick and poor, Gilbert Burnet's influential discourses on pastoral care and the astute English tradition of pastoral direction represented by Anglican bishops Wilson, Spratt, Gibson and Hort. Among early evangelical writers on pastoral theology were Philip Doddridge, Count Nicolas von Zinzendorf, Jonathan Edwards and John Wesley. All of those great writings had been ignored for about a century while American pastoral counseling was trying to accommodate itself to Freud, Jung, Perls and Rogers.

[25]The leaders of the Institute on Religion and Democracy at that time were Kent Hill, Diane Knippers, Alan Wisdom, Helen Rhea Stumbo and Mary Ellen Bork.

[26]Thomas C. Oden, *Conscience and Dividends: Churches and the Multinationals* (Washington, DC: Ethics and Public Policy Center, 1985).

[27]Notably Richard McCormack.

[28]Out of this study came the conclusion that there are rigorous constraints against prematurely withholding the medical means of life survival; namely, if there is permanent loss of all cognitive function corroborated by medical consultation so as to offer no reasonable hope of recovery, and if there is irrefutable evidence that biological death is imminent or where the dying process is assessed by medical practitioners as being in its last stages, and if the family members unanimously concur with the attending physician that active treatment of emergent complications should not be pursued, and if the patient's preference in such a circumstance is known by written document or reasonably implied. Only then may the family justifiably consent to withholding active treatment on new complications or emergencies, while continuing life support already instituted, so as to allow the terminal illness to take its course. The results of that study were published by Harper and Row in my 1976 book *Should Treatment Be Terminated?* In those exchanges I became convinced that the arena of ambiguous and contested public policy was not where I was most suited to fulfill my vocation.

[29]I also wrote an "Opinion on the Quinlan Case" in the *Union Seminary Quarterly Review*. I made an appeal for "Judicial Restraint in the Quinlan Decision" and commended "A Cautious View of Treatment Termination" in the *Christian Century*.

[30]Among them Joseph Fessio, Francis George, John J. O'Connor and Donald Wuerl.

[31]None of the neo-orthodox theologians had adequately rediscovered the consensual center of classic patristic teaching. Bultmann had demythologized the resurrection. Barth had trounced many aspects of classic Christian natural-law reasoning. Tillich had turned the gospel into an uneventful philosophy of "being itself." Reinhold Niebuhr abandoned classic ecclesiology in favor of political actions and arguments. All four had influenced me decisively. I had written books on two of them (Bultmann and Barth). Yet none had followed the classic consensual (Vincentian) method. None broke through the illusion of the permanence

of modern ideologies. What neo-orthodoxy lacked was the pre-Reformation core of classic Christian exegesis—before Luther, before Calvin, before Harnack.

[32]My own descriptions of postmodern culture dating back to 1968, 1970 and 1979 were set forth before North America had heard of Jean-François Lyotard or Michel Foucault. Accounts of American postmodernism that make the assumption that these hypermodern writers of the 1980s were its first exponents have missed the point entirely. The chief writers on so-called postmodern theory and criticism came belatedly into wide public notice in North America several years after my discussion of postmodern culture appeared in *Agenda for Theology* (1979). Michel Foucault, who earned his doctorate a year after I did, preempted the term *postmodern* some years after I set forth the *postmodern* paleo-orthodox thesis. Classic Christian postmodern theory was well-developed before being harassed by hypermodern writers like Jürgen Habermas (1981), Jean-François Lyotard (1984) and Francis Fukuyama (1989). These writers were then followed by a tribe of hypermodernist theological imitators who tardily called themselves postmodern and for a few short years became a fad of pop theologians. That fad has now thankfully almost disappeared. I speak of the writings of Gabriel Vahanian (*Anonymous God* [Aurora, CO: Davies Group, 2002]), Mark C. Taylor (*After God* [Chicago: University of Chicago Press, 2008]), and Marcus Borg (*Putting Away Childish Things* [New York: HarperOne, 2010]). Since not one of these writers took with full seriousness the death of modernity, they could not be rightly called postmodern, and are better viewed as hypermodern lovers of waning modernity.

[33]Those who refuse to comply with modern assumptions are functionally heretics within the intellectual culture. Although the word least mentioned today is *heresy*, the modern period defends itself against its homegrown forms of heresy. The definition of a heretic is one who dissents from apostolic teaching. But amusingly my work did not make me a heretic because *heresy* is the least modern of all words. There was no doctrinal heresy in the liberal worldview.

[34]Another relatively unexplored hypothesis. The more important question is why no one mentions it.

[35]After *Agenda for Theology* in 1979, the outcomes would be a systematic theology (the 1980s), a recovery of patristic exegesis (the 1990s and 2000s) and a mission to Africa (since 2006). The variants and ramifications of that modest original proposal have been more fruitful and diverse than I could ever have imagined.

[36]I had been struggling with external and internal battles that left me with many aftereffects—dyslexia, vertigo, tinitis, insomnia and travel anxieties, but none incapacitating. In 1976 I had a retinal tear while on sabbatical leave in Austin, Texas, that threatened my vision in one eye. I had to go immediately into surgery for a scleral buckling operation where a silicone plastic band was installed around my eye.

[37]After Dean Ault came Pieter de Jong (1972–1975), James E. Kirby (1975–1981), Thomas W. Ogletree (1981–1990), Robin Lovin (1991–1994), Janet Fishburn (1994–1995), Leonard Sweet (1995–2000) and Maxine Clarke Beach (2000–2010). I was also fortunate to have welcome access to the university presidents during all my years at Drew: Robert Oxnam (1961–1974), Paul Hardin (1974–1990), and former New Jersey governor Tom Kean (1990–2005).

[38]As Herberg had been brought to Drew in 1956 to help rebuild the graduate school into a world-class program of study, so was I brought to Drew fourteen years later to help rebuild a theological faculty injured by faculty losses.

[39]After Lawrence McIntosh left Drew to become chief librarian for the University of Aberdeen in Australia, the need arose to select his successor in teaching the Wesley Seminar. Since I had taught the Wesley Seminar at Phillips during the 1960s, I was asked to take on that crucial graduate school assignment, noteworthy because Drew held the premier collection in the world of Wesleyan historical documents, and because there were so many PhD students desiring to write dissertations out of that unique storehouse of primary documents. So in the late 1970s I began teaching the regularly offered PhD seminar on John Wesley. The seminar participants read the full range of Wesley's 150 major homilies and many treatises. That curriculum continued over the next quarter century, with many excellent PhD students going through its rigors. Wesley Studies was a strong graduate program at Drew, with leadership from excellent colleagues Kenneth Rowe, Charles Yrigorian and James Pain. I was an informal adviser to many Wesleyan-based students (African Methodist Episcopal, AME Zion, Free Methodist, Wesleyan, Nazarene, Pentecostal and United Methodists) for all the years I was at Drew.

[40]In each year following 1974, 30 to 40 percent of men and women in ordained ministry had dropped out of ministry within ten years. From 1974 to 1994 the number of men ordained to Methodist ministry had dropped from about 700 to 400. Within the five years between 1974 and 1981, 46 percent of our male theological students and a whopping 54 percent of women students were dropping out from parish ministries. One conference had an 83 percent attrition rate for women. Many seminarians ended their theological education with a huge debt and nowhere to take their edgy ideological idealism. The costs to young pastors and congregations were immense.

[41]At Drew I was reluctantly cast in a role of seeking to encourage the Methodist bureaucracy to retain its funding for theological education no matter what reservations I had on what was being taught or how it was faltering in the parish. The euphemism for this role was "bringing balance to theological faculty," a balance that required keeping our traditionally oriented students reasonably happy going to classes with largely antitraditional faculty sentiments. I was supposed to calm

fears of a growing number of evangelical students who by their first year discovered they were living in a hostile environment. In required Scripture studies many were subjected to ridicule if they held to a high view of scriptural authority. In required classes on social process and egalitarian idealism they were shunned if they raised questions from a conservative point of view. Each Methodist seminary was receiving around $1 million per year from church coffers through the General Conference Ministerial Education Fund, which was supported by apportionments administered by the General Board of Higher Education and Ministry. My brother, Tal, served on that General Board for many years, keeping me apprised of the dilemmas being faced within the educational bureaucracy.

[42]After many quiet efforts to seek reconciliation of a divided church, I would finally have an opportunity to make my criticisms heard in 1995 in *Requiem*, after which my usefulness to the seminary became diminished. The church's later official Retention Study of 1997, looking back on the previous years, provided a painfully detailed picture of a denomination "bitterly at odds with itself."

[43]My most fruitful years of dialogue with process theology took place in my early years at Phillips Seminary with my close colleague Eugene Peters, a strong and deliberate advocate of Charles Hartshorne's vision of process theology, and with my closest colleague Don Browning.

[44]Ogden's differences with Bultmann prompted me to defend Bultmann. I paid a price for tangling with him. He left a loyal brigade of followers in the Southwest.

[45]Selected by invitation.

[46]Many Wesleyan scholars remained very resistant to the ETS focus on inerrancy, a controversy that was settled for me by studying carefully the Chicago Statement on Biblical Inerrancy and the Chicago Statement on Biblical Application, consisting of two position papers made in 1978 and 1986. Subsequently when asked how I possibly could have joined ETS as a Wesleyan, I always encouraged those who questioned me to read the two Chicago Statements and then I would talk about substantive disagreements with them. Under the coaching and sponsorship of both Stan Gundry and Timothy Smith, I cautiously joined the Reformed-led ETS.

[47]At the time I joined ETS, few evangelicals had any thought of patristic exegesis. Only a few, like Norman Geisler and Wayne House, were in significant dialogue with Catholics.

[48]Spiritual autobiography is familiar to historic orthodoxy, as epitomized by St. Gregory of Nazianzus, St. Augustine, St. Bonaventure, St. John of the Cross, John Wesley and Phoebe Palmer.

[49]The number forty in the Bible is often associated with a period of probation, a time of testing, ending with the possibility of new life. Israel was in the wilderness for forty years before entering the land promised to Abraham. Jesus was tempted in

the wilderness for forty days, reliving the forty years of Israel's journey. My life has unexpectedly fallen into a forty-year period of trial and error, followed by a forty year period of a new life that I could never have imagined.

Chapter 6: The 1980s

[1]In 1992 Clark married Jeanne McAteer Thigpen in Tulsa, whose three children brought marvelous gifts into our family. They settled in Oklahoma City, where she continued her work with the largest advertising agency in the state. Their presence in Oklahoma City was one of the main reasons I returned to Oklahoma in the late 1990s. Having Jeanne's children in my life has been an incomparable blessing. After serving as a naval officer in the Persian Gulf, Cory pursued advanced studies at Rice. Amy completed advanced studies in the Yale Graduate School in architecture, and Mary, who studied psychology, works in New York City with an investment firm.

[2]After developing her own environment-oriented business in Washington, DC, Laura moved to Anchorage, where she works with a hospital serving Inuits and native-American Alaskans, and enjoys a lively avocation as a singer-songwriter.

[3]Merill was sister to John Maguire, one of my close friends from Yale days.

[4]One of the regulars was Merrill Skaggs, dean of the graduate school, an expert on Willa Cather, William Faulkner and Walker Percy. Historian Jonathan Rose, an expert on the history of the book, was always ready to talk wittily about Edwardian literature, Orwell, Churchill, the intellectual life of the British working class or almost any subject at hand.

[5]A specialist in population studies and urban criminology, O'Kane was a quintessential New Yorker, and his brisk Brooklyn speech contrasted with my leisurely Oklahoma accent. For me O'Kane was a great friend who was by my side in all of the difficulties I had while in Madison, with Edrita's long illness, unavailing efforts at university reform, the gradual marginalization of moderates in the faculty and our struggle against ideological excesses in the university. A product of parochial schools in Brooklyn, O'Kane had a deep commitment to living out Catholic teaching in his family and personal life. His Irish wit got me through many down days. A superb raconteur, there was seldom a serious comment made in our dialogue that escaped a split second comic perception from O'Kane.

[6]O'Kane also brought me into dialogue with the Catholic Theological Society, the pro-life community and Catholic lay spiritual formation.

[7]When I was in northern Turkey, south of Pontus near the Black Sea, visiting the remains of Hattusa, which was an ancient Hittite palace dating to the Bronze Age, I actually saw an ancient inscription of a prince named Tertulia. He was talking and bearing a large amphora of wine.

⁸Ollom was a part of the scientific team gathered together in 1944 in Los Alamos, New Mexico, by General Leslie Groves and J. Robert Oppenheimer to coordinate scientific research on the Manhattan Project, which created and tested the first nuclear fission weapons. In World War II, Los Alamos was host to thousands of employees living in remote, primitive conditions, including many Nobel Prize-winning scientists, in a totally secret location.

⁹The basement carrel was small, with steel metal shelving and a small desk upon which my IBM electric typewriter barely fit. Tal had mercifully given me the older IBM he was discarding. The more I wrote, the more I realized I needed to exercise astute time management and benefit from technological efficiencies.

¹⁰The first doctoral student whose dissertation I advised wrote on the protection of innocent life. He was a Dominican Father, Philip A. Smith, who later became president of Providence College in Rhode Island. My first Orthodox student was Vigen Guroian, who raised my consciousness on the Armenian genocide, and whose dissertation on Reinhold Niebuhr prepared him for a teaching and writing career in Loyola Baltimore and the University of Virginia.

¹¹One of the most original dissertations was Neil Anderson's *A Definitive Study of Evidence Concerning John Wesley's Appropriation of the Thought of Clement of Alexandria*, for Texts and Studies in Religion. When Kenneth Brewer proposed a dissertation topic on Hans Küng, I directed him toward Tübingen to write his dissertation with Professor Küng.

¹²Joel Elowsky's dissertation on Theodore of Mopsuestia and Cyril the Great was one of the best. I directed three dissertations on John Chrysostom. The first was that of David C. Ford in his important work on Chrysostom's teaching on male and female, correcting the stereotype of misogyny, and readying him for his lifelong teaching at St. Tikhon's Orthodox Seminary. I directed Steve McCormack's dissertation, *John Wesley's Use of Chrysostom* (1983), and the dissertation on Chrysostom's teaching on providence by Christopher A. Hall. I set the bar high as a tough Socratic questioner in their doctoral defenses. Leicester Longden, having completed his dissertation on Albert Outler, coedited with me a book of Outler's essays and went on to teach in Dubuque Theological Seminary.

¹³Several of my longest-lasting relationships came from among my Drew Graduate students. Christopher Hall became my associate editor for the twenty-nine volume Ancient Christian Commentary on Scripture and was the key figure in bringing the Center for Early African Christianity to Eastern University in Philadelphia, where he served as Eastern's chancellor. Michael Glerup and Joel Scandrett came into the PhD program the same year. Both were in my Kierkegaard seminar, wrote splendid dissertations and played major roles in the conceptualizing and execution of the patristic commentary, especially with the development of digital searches in

Latin and Greek data bases, and with correlating that mass of data with particular texts of Scripture using digital searches. Both became key administrators of the complex process of research, data management, editing and traveling on behalf of the ACCS international translations.

[14]From Ireland, one of Jim O'Kane's clan from "the glen" near Derry.

[15]For over a century Drew University and Korean cultural formation were closely interwoven. That included strides in democratic development, education for women and freedom of religion. I was privileged to shepherd to publication the defining dissertation on the beginning of Christian missions in Korea, written by Daniel Davies in 1985. The Methodist Theological School of Seoul was patterned after Drew literally, even to the design of its gateway, its architecture and its curriculum.

[16]My first of many trips to East Asia occurred in 1979 in Korea for an international consultation on science and culture. In Korea I visited the school that Appenzeller founded, Pai Chai Hak Dang, the first modern Western-styled school in Korea and the predecessor of several Korean universities. In the 1980s I returned several times to Korea for seminary lectures and to visit my former PhD students who were occupying chairs in theology and pastoral studies and giving leadership to Korean Christianity.

[17]I miss especially those now gone: Henry Lambdin, George Kelsey, Bard Thompson, Robert Bull, Neal Reamer, Roger Wescott, Nelson Thayer, Robert Chapman and Niell Hamilton. Among those still living are Russell Richey, Kenneth Rowe and Jim Pain.

[18]As a young teacher at Morehouse College, Dr. Kelsey became a soul guide, mentor and lifelong confidant of Martin Luther King Jr., cited by Dr. King as one who had a decisive influence on his life. Their long-running correspondence now resides as a jewel of the Drew archives. Officing with George Kelsey offered me a sense of reconnection with my earliest days in the civil rights movement in Oklahoma. Kelsey held the chair of Henry Anson Buttz Professor of Christian Ethics for twenty-six years at Drew. After his retirement I was honored to succeed him in that named chair.

[19]With Ed Long I was working in the presence of an unusually wise man with a tough mind and a soft heart, a main voice in North America on the study of Christian ethics.

[20]In 1985 I began meeting regularly for lunch with psychiatrist Johan Noordsij of nearby Summit, NJ. We had many mutual interests in linguistics, existential philosophy, psychology and theology. He asked me to become a consultant for his dissertation in the University of Amsterdam. I benefited greatly by his friendship. His expertise was in language and meaning, along with many other competencies in Freud, Jung, Jacques Lacan and existential psychology. After Edrita's surgery for

breast cancer, Johan was generous in providing counsel for her, and later for both of us together. Johan served as teacher and dissertation adviser for graduate students in the Psychology and Religion Program in the Graduate School.

[21]I benefited especially from his methodical and programmatic idea of "comprehensive complementarity" in *A Survey of Christian Ethics* (New York: Oxford University Press, 1982).

[22]No nineteenth-century thinker has influenced my whole body of work as deeply as Søren Kierkegaard. I still doubt that the analytical powers and psychological insights of Freud and the post-Freudians have equaled those of Kierkegaard. The first edition of that collection of the *Parables of Kierkegaard* appeared from Princeton University Press in 1978 and became a perennial source for college classes.

[23]Thomas C. Oden, *Doctrinal Standards in the Wesleyan Tradition* (Grand Rapids: Francis Asbury Press, 1988).

[24]Richard P. Heitzenrater, "Full Liberty: Doctrinal Standards in Early American Methodism," *Quarterly Review* 5, no. 3 (1985): 18.

[25]See Thomas C. Oden, "What Are 'Established Standards of Doctrine'?: A Response to Richard Heitzenrater," *Quarterly Review* 7, no. 1 (1987): 41-62.

[26]The motion was lost, with an unexplained handwritten note in the margin that said, "It was voted that this motion be struck out of the Journal," accompanied by a single large "X" through it.

[27]The draft presented to the General Conference, however, still failed to make the authority of the *Sermons* and *Notes* unambiguously clear constitutionally. In the General Conference I was invited to the bar of the Committee on Faith and Order, where I supported a compromise that kept the traditional standards in place.

[28]Many legislators told me that without the evidences presented in my book *Doctrinal Standards in the Wesleyan Tradition*, the decision likely might have been different. Another irony is that that book was published by a Reformed-tradition press. Only years later did Abingdon decide to reprint it.

[29]*John Wesley's Teachings* (Grand Rapids: Zondervan, 2012–2014). The four volumes are on God and Providence, Christ and Salvation, Pastoral Counsel, and Ethics and Society.

[30]Writer A. N. Wilson belatedly described himself as "the Original Young Fogey" in the *Daily Mail* of December 16, 2010. Wilson is known for his biographies of C. S. Lewis, Tolstoy and Jesus, and for numerous works of fiction, and for editing *The Faber Book of Church and Clergy* (1992). By the mid-1980s it was being applied to architecture and dress. Irish broadcaster Ryan Tubridy identified himself as a "young fogey." British Member of Parliament Jacob Rees-Mogg was portrayed as a "young fogey" after his 2010 election to Westminster. In its current usage "young fogey" is more broadly said to be a term humorously applied, first in an

American context, then in an Australian and British context, to younger-generation believers who had gone through the illusions of modern ideologies and found them vulnerable.

[31]"Young fogey" to me expressed the comic irony of the situation of my graduate students. More telling is that *The Young Fogey Handbook: A Guide to Backward Mobility* by Suzanne Lowry (1985) became an alternative literary classic. The term as I had used it pointed to a small but growing group of believers who found its comic twist useful to point to the incongruity of their intellectual situation.

[32]Andrew Greeley in *Priests: A Calling in Crisis* (Chicago: University of Chicago Press, 2004) wrote most perceptively of the "young fogeys" as a new cultural recognition that "The Church fathers broadened the canons of scriptural interpretation, invited other churches and denominations to engage in friendly dialogue, and attempted to understand the strengths of the modern world." As a sociologist Greeley describes the Catholic young fogeys as "a generation of conservative young priests on the rise in the U.S. Church. These are newly ordained men who seem in many ways intent on restoring the pre-Vatican II Church, and who, reversing the classic generational roles, define themselves in direct opposition to the liberal priests who came of age in the 1960s and 1970s."

[33]I had grown up with the works of Peter Berger: *The Noise of Solemn Assemblies* (1961), *Invitation to Sociology* (1963), *The Social Construction of Reality: A Treatise in the Sociology of Knowledge* (1966), *The Sacred Canopy* (1967), *A Rumor of Angels* (1969), *The Homeless Mind* (1973), and *Facing Up to Modernity* (1979).

[34]In reference to the sociology of knowledge thinkers like Émile Durkheim, Max Scheler and Karl Mannheim, and for me personally from conversations with Peter Berger, J. H. van den Berg and Thomas Szasz.

[35] Jesus himself called and commissioned the apostolic tradition that engendered a continuation of the work of the apostles into succeeding generations. That means that each new generation is called to renew the ministry of Christ and the apostles. Jesus himself intended to provide a means by which not only his teaching but also his living presence should continue to be vibrantly alive in subsequent generations.

[36]I recognized some solid strengths in the serious attempts at pastoral theology among evangelical scholars such as Frank Segler (Southern Baptist), Armin W. Schuetze and Irwin J. Habeck (Wisconsin Lutherans), and Jay E. Adams (Orthodox Presbyterian). But they were all prone to miss large segments of the broader pre-Protestant classical tradition.

[37]The principal classic works on pastoral theology on which I came to rely were from the earliest Christian centuries. The names of the best of them need to be recalled: Ignatius of Antioch (d. 107), Cyprian (d. 258), Gregory of Nazianzus (d. 389), Nemesius (c. 390), Gregory of Nyssa (d. 395), John Chrysostom (d. 407), Augustine (d.

430), Leo the Great (d. 461) and Gregory the Great (d. 604). After the patristic period came others like Rabanus Maurus (d. 856), Thomas Aquinas (d. 1274), John Wycliffe (d. 1384), Martin Luther (d. 1546), Martin Bucer (d. 1551), George Herbert (d. 1633), Jeremy Taylor (d. 1667) and Richard Baxter (1691).

[38]I had previously offered detailed treatments of Carl Rogers and client-centered therapy (in *Kerygma and, Counseling*), of Seward Hiltner, Paul Tillich, Rudolf Bultmann and others (in *Contemporary Theology and Psychotherapy* and *Radical Obedience*). I had already taken into account the existential psychologists, from Kierkegaard and Binswanger to May, Boss, Caruso and Frankl (in *The Structure of Awareness*). More so I had dealt extensively with experimental encounter groups, T-groups and growth groups (in *The Intensive Group Experience*). I had already entered the arena of Transactional Analysis (in *Game Free*) and behavior therapy (in *TAG: The Transactional Awareness Game*). A new beginning was needed. I called it *Pastoral Theology: Essentials for Ministry*.

[39]Rocks do not have soul. Humans do. We are alive. Animals do not have the more fully responsive soul that characterizes human freedom.

[40]When the apostle John wrote to Gaius, "I know it goes well with your soul" (3 Jn 2), he was referring to the inner citadel of spirituality in the life of the person. When Paul used the term *psyche* (soul) he referred to the *life* that is enlivening the body, that which enables freedom and responsiveness to the giver of life. Psyche is the center of desire, affection and emotion. The soul is subject to temptation and can become to some extent separated from God the Spirit by willful sin.

[41]Soul care places the person in the moral and spiritual context of salvation history. Every person's history is lived out in the setting of universal history and seen in relationship to eternity. However competent, other professions do not share that operative assumption. That has made ministry far more like a familial bond of kinship than any of the other professions. So the pastor, by tradition and unwritten invitation, is often intimately present with individuals and families amid critical situations of birth, marriage, sickness and death, a presence that is not expected of salespersons, bureaucrats, mechanics and brain surgeons, however dedicated they might be.

[42]This interest in deliberate behavior change in the individual is correlated with a concern for forthcoming purification of the believing community insofar as fallen wills can conceive it. Christ "loved the church and gave himself up for it" to consecrate it, cleansing it by water and word, so that he might present the church to the Father glorious, without stain or wrinkle. Christ filled the church with gifts of the Spirit. Meanwhile every member of the church body remains exposed to temptation, anxiety and the risk of freedom's falling into sin. Though Christ is guileless, undefiled and holy, the church, which embraces sinners, is both holy and always

in need of purification, and thus constantly seeking repentance, announcing forgiveness and seeking reconciliation of sinners with God.

[43]The truly recalcitrant may not be prepared to exercise self-responsibility. The argument for withholding Communion on occasions of repeated impenitence
hinges on this point: In order to prepare for Communion the believer must be
penitent. One who thinks he or she deserves the grace offered in Holy Communion is not ready to receive it as sheer grace.

[44]The volume on *Becoming a Minister* provided a stream of mainly patristic but also
some later medieval and classical sources of wisdom on the pastoral calling, preparation for soul care, the biblical pattern of shepherding, ordination and pastoral
authority. That was followed by a volume on *Ministry Through Word and Sacrament*, which dealt with incisive classical selections on preaching, prayer, baptism,
confession and communion counsel. The volume on *Pastoral Counsel* sought to
establish textually that virtually all of the common issues of modern counseling
had already been extensively treated in the patristic period: empathy, congruence,
body language, the timing of seasonable wisdom and the dynamics of willed
choices. The last volume, *Crisis Counseling,* dealt with interpersonal conflict,
physical illness, despair over suffering, marriage and family, poverty, and death.
Textually my point had been vindicated that there was little in modern pastoral
care not treated in classic pastoral care.

[45]When Albert Outler was asked to write one of those articles in 1984, he laughingly
titled it "Ordeal of a Happy Dilettante." He was a happy, very funny man, even in
the midst of his ordeals. But he was never a dilettante. Of all the theologians I have
known personally, he was centered and balanced in every step along the way,
deeply grounded in classic Christianity.

[46]1989 was a landmark year for me because I had four volumes I had been working
on for five years ripen for publication during that year: *The Word of Life,* volume
two of *Systematic Theology*; *Pastoral Counsel,* volume three of Classical Pastoral
Care Series, *1-2 Timothy and Titus,* a volume of the *Interpreters Biblical Commentary,* and *After Modernity . . . What?* Although I had been working simultaneously on various phases of all four of them for the previous five years, I had to ward
off jests that I had written four books in one year. But they all were published the
same year.

[47]Andrew T. Le Peau and Linda Doll, *Heart. Soul. Mind. Strength: An Anecdotal
History of InterVarsity Press, 1947-2007* (Downers Grove, IL: IVP Books, 2006).

[48]The story of Neuhaus's entrance into Concordia Lutheran College in Austin, Texas,
was among the most hilarious of his many rollicking stories. From Pembroke, Ontario, he showed up for college at Concordia Austin without having processed any
application. Having no diploma with him, he persuaded the registrar that he was

serious about education. He was admitted and became the college's top alumnus.
[49]At first, Alan Carlson of the Rockford Institute was providing support for those conversations in New York, until he and Neuhaus split up. I met Berger's protégé, James Davison Hunter, who became an ongoing partner in dialogue. I participated in some of the meetings of the Ramsey Group on ethics, which Neuhaus organized in honor of Paul Ramsey. Some of America's leading ethicists were principals in those conversations, including Stanley Hauerwas, Robert Benne, Max Stackhouse and Gilbert Meilaender.
[50]Through Neuhaus I became close friends with Fritz Rothschild. I audited his course on Franz Rosenzweig. Without Will I would never have had the opportunity to enter into the circle of leading New York Jewish intellectuals that included Midge Dechter, David Dalin and Fritz Rothschild.
[51]The 1960s books I had written are *Radical Obedience, The Community of Celebration, Kerygma and Counseling, Contemporary Theology and Psychotherapy, The Structure of Awareness, The Promise of Barth* and *Beyond Revolution*.
[52]Personally each of these dialogues was formative for me. They provided the core of my intellectual development during the late 1980s. All were published by Eerdmans as edited by Richard Neuhaus and Paul Stallsworth under the titles *Unsecular America* (May 1986), *Virtue—Public and Private* (April 1986), *The Bible, Politics and Democracy*, with Ed Dobson (November 1987), *Jews in Unsecular America* (December 1987), *The Believable Futures of American Protestantism* (May 1988), *The Preferential Option for the Poor* (September 1988), *American Apostasy: The Triumph of "Other" Gospels*, with Peter L. Berger and Robert W. Jenson (April 1989), *Biblical Interpretation in Crisis: The Ratzinger Conference on Bible and Church* by Joseph Ratzinger, Paul T. Stallsworth and Raymond E. Brown (May 1989), *Reinhold Niebuhr Today* (July 1989), *Guaranteeing the Good Life: Medicine and the Return of Eugenics* (August 1990), *Theological Education and Moral Formation* (January 1992), *Augustine Today*, with Ernest L. Fortin, William S. Babcock and Robert J. O'Connell (September 1993). Any contemporary reader who studied that series carefully would get an unsurpassed perspective on public ethics.
[53]*Peritus* is the term for a Roman Catholic theologian appointed to give advice and input to an ecumenical council.
[54]The Catholic scholars present were Avery Dulles, Joseph Fitzmyer, Raymond Brown, Augustine DiNoia and Michael Waldstein. I was humbled to be among the five Protestants, led by George Lindbeck and William Lazareth.
[55]The literary outcome of those conversations may be found in *Biblical Interpretation in Crisis: The Ratzinger Conference on Bible and Church*, ed. Paul T. Stallsworth (Grand Rapids: Eerdmans, 1989). The new edition is titled *Opening Up the Scriptures:*

Joseph Ratzinger and the Foundations of Biblical Interpretation, ed. Jose Granados, Carlos Granados and Luis Sanchez-Navarro (Grand Rapids: Eerdmans, 2008).

CHAPTER 7: THE 1990S

[1]I explained my view of holy matrimony as a sacramental event that seeks to maximize enduring love and the protection of children. Intercourse between persons of the same sex cannot lead to generative life or natural birth. When I argued that the civil rights of those with "alternative sexual lifestyles" must be vigilantly protected without conceding the moral viability of their claims to social legitimation, they applauded. When I argued that marriage was by definition an enduring covenant between one male and one female grounded in the potential gift of sexual generativity in a sacred and durable covenant relation enhanced by sexual bonding, I heard cheers from the Soviet women. I reported that after decades of chemical and sexual experimentation, thoughtful Americans were gradually starting to reaffirm the enduring sexual covenant between a man and a woman and the protection of the children they are given. I found the politically correct mentality which was so prevalent in the American media almost totally absent in Moscow. [2]They were surprised to hear that feminist activism had declined from its apex year in 1984, when the Equal Rights Amendment had been rejected, but they were even more surprised to hear that the Amendment went down due to the active opposition by women who saw it as a diminution of their rights and traditional privileges under law. After the demise of the E.R.A., the movement was more sober about gender-blending fantasies that ignored the obvious differences between women and men. [3]Cuban evangelicals were insisting on independent nonidentification with any political ideology. There was much quiet frustration directed at the old system of socialist education that split families, took over the church properties and imposed a command economy. What mattered to Cuban Christians was not how long the regime would last but whether the church would continue to accompany the people faithful to the narrow way that leads to life. [4]Cuban Christians could not forget how schools founded by the churches had been destroyed or used as storage facilities. They were also mindful of how church properties had been vandalized after the revolution. Decades after the fact they remembered that the old Christian school in Santa Clara was converted to a Communist Party headquarters. But there still remained a will to forgive and move on. [5]He explained his view of providence, that before Constantine, when the road was extremely difficult, the church was empowered by the Spirit through crisis after crisis. Then came the period of Constantine. It offered the church a comfortable place in the world. That is when its deepest spiritual temptations appeared. Our faith calls us

to live in the world but not of the world. In a Marxist society it is no social advantage to be a Christian. Christian existence becomes an exciting, risk-taking, counter-cultural summons rather than a boring obsession with establishment safety.

[6]The back story of this huge project had its antecedents in the digital library exhibit at the Seattle World's Fair in 1962, when I got a timely glimpse into the information technology library of the future. I was instantly captivated by the World's Fair digital exhibit, designed to envision the role of technology in future libraries. It featured a Univac computer programmed to print out a portion of electronically stored text entered from a printed book. As one who loved the printed book unabashedly, I was able to reluctantly concede that information technology specialists at Seattle had accurately predicted the critical role that technology would play in the library of the future. By 1990 this conviction had grown deeper, with a clear momentum toward the deliberate, orderly recovery of neglected patristic texts.

[7]These databases had either not yet been invented or not yet been made fully operational. Project Gutenberg was emerging but as yet not practically operable. At the time we began, Perseus was still being refined but not yet widely implemented. *Thesaurus Linguae Graecae* (TLG) was in a developing stage, as was the Cetedoc library of Christian Latin texts.

[8]The prevailing way the Bible had been studied over so many centuries—by catena and glossa ordinaria—had been neglected for many generations. The idea of a patristic commentary seemed outdated, methodologically flawed, unnecessary or overwhelming to most guild professionals.

[9]The patristic guild was at that time far more interested in the social location analysis of ancient Christian writers in their cultures or texts that had political significance for some cultural or gender or social stratification agenda. Patristic historians were instead more likely to be talking about book-length examinations of one particular writer or text, but there was no literary vehicle that would send the reader of a biblical text to its patristic commentators. I wanted not merely a map to the reference locations, as found in Biblia Patristica, but to present the patristic extracts themselves correlated with the sacred text.

[10]A leading model of early printed editions of the catena was Nicholas of Lyra. There each page of biblical text was printed in the center of the page and surrounded by classic commentators from the early rabbinic and patristic centuries. This arrangement followed the traditional pattern of the pre-Gutenberg medieval manuscript copying of biblical commentaries, such as the Bodmer Library's twelfth-century handwritten codex 25 miniscule of Matthew, which showed the biblical text surrounded by patristic commentators. It was from this medieval manuscript hand-copying tradition that the first published texts of the Talmud were derived, after the invention of printing.

[11]To many modern critics, relevant knowledge began only with Harnack, Schweitzer and Dibelius. In their view, ancient Christian exegetes had little to contribute to historical understanding.

[12]I commuted to Biola from New Jersey. We had five sessions over fourteen weeks. I wrote a rigorous syllabus after they chose intriguing topics partly shaped by their reading of my books and partly by their own active research interests. Our purpose was to reassess the relationship of classic Christianity to their research projects, their teaching practices and the university's mission. About fifteen faculty members participated in the seminar, including professors from psychology, physics, art, philosophy, literature and other departments.

[13]The project idea received steady cooperation and encouragement from the Acting President Scott McDonald, followed by support from the former governor of New Jersey, who became the new Drew president, the honorable Tom Kean, as well as the Graduate Dean James Pain. It was later sustained through a series of theological school deans—Thomas W. Ogletree, Robin Lovin, Leonard Sweet and Maxine Clarke Beach.

[14]Later we added the Apocrypha to make twenty-nine volumes.

[15]By this means we could, for example, find references in Augustine's Latin or Cyril of Alexandria's Greek as they pertained to a particular biblical text. In the case of the Synoptic Gospels, we could usually identify which Gospel writer the patristic exegete was referencing, even when the same phrase appeared in another Synoptic Gospel. We coaxed those hits out of computer databases. The early Boolean digital searches were accomplished by the intensive labor of a dedicated team led by Joel Scandrett, Michael Glerup and Joel Elowsky, with major contributions from Russian Orthodox scholars: Konstantin Gravilkin, Sergey Kozin, Alexei Khamine, Vladimir Karlamov and Elena Vishnevskaya.

[16]Among those now holding professorial positions are Vincent Bacote of Wheaton College, Warren Calhoun Robertson of Gardner-Webb University, Thomas Buchan of Nashota House Episcopal Seminary, Robert Paul Seesengood of Albright College and Scott Kisker of Wesley Theological Seminary. From Canada came Bernie Van De Walle, who is now teaching at Ambrose University of Calgary; from Korea came Meesaeng L. Choi at Asbury Theological Seminary. From Germany came Michael Nausner, now teaching at Theologischen Hochschule Reutlingen in Germany. Those were among the brilliant colleagues that made the ACCS an unprecedented artifact of modern religious publishing.

[17]Among leading international authorities I visited early in the consultation and project design were Sir Henry Chadwick of Oxford, Bishop Kallistos of Oxford and Bishop Rowan Williams then of Monmouth, all former patristics professors at Oxford, and Bishop Stephen Sykes of Ely, formerly Regius Professor of Divinity at Cambridge.

[18]Among ACCS editors deeply involved in the Reformed tradition were John R. Franke of the Biblical Seminary and Mark W. Elliott of the University of St Andrews in Scotland. Baptists were well represented by Chancellor Craig Blaising of Southwestern Baptist Theological Seminary and Steven A. McKinion of the seminary at Wake Forest.

[19]The volume editors were asked to seek an appropriate balance of Eastern, Western and African traditions. We intentionally attempted to include Alexandrian, Antiochene, Roman, Syriac, Coptic and Armenian traditions of interpretation. We could not manufacture texts that had been lost or destroyed over the course of time, but we did mourn their absence.

[20]We were warmly greeted at the pontifical residence by His Holiness Karekin II, Supreme Patriarch and Catholicos of All Armenians. As the 132nd successor to Saint Gregory the Illuminator, he graciously blessed our efforts and suggested scholars who were thoroughly familiar with the early Armenian literature.

[21]I consulted with key Anglican bishops for their suggestions and nominations on ACCS volume editors, among them Bishop Michael Nazir-Ali of Rochester, Bishop Kenneth Stevenson of Portsmouth, and in the United States Bishop FitzSimons Allison. Bishop Rowan Williams of Monmouth was especially encouraging to the Ancient Christian Commentary on Scripture efforts in its early conceptual stage. After many years of patristic teaching at Cambridge and Oxford, he became Archbishop of Canterbury. Especially important to us were the consultations of James I. Packer of Regent College in Vancouver, and senior editor of *Christianity Today* Kenneth Kantzer of Trinity Seminary, and Timothy Smith of Johns Hopkins University.

[22]My earliest visits to Oxford and Cambridge brought Mark Edwards of Oxford, Andrew Louth of Durham, Gerald Bray of Tyndale House Cambridge and Mark Elliott of St. Andrews into our circle as our first four selected volume editors. In Cambridge I received valuable counsel from Bruce Winter, Christopher Sykes, Markus Bockmuehl, William Horbury and others.

[23]Simonetti played the key role of preparing two volumes on Matthew that brilliantly introduced the New Testament half of the series.

[24]Soon we had Anglican bishop Kenneth Stevenson of Portsmouth and Episcopalians J. Robert Wright and Peter Gorday commissioned to write volumes.

[25]Lutherans were led by a trio of wonderful scholars from Concordia Ft. Wayne: Arthur Just, William Weinrich and Dean O. Wenthe. Other Lutheran editors included Philip D. W. Krey and Erik M. Heen of Lutheran Theological Seminary at Philadelphia, Joel Elowsky, and Quentin Wesselschmidt of Concordia Seminary in St. Louis.

[26]Where a viable English translation of a passage was already available, we compared it to the original language text appearing in consensually received critical editions,

such as Patrologia Orientalis, Patrologia Syriaca, Sources Chrétiennes and Texte und Untersuchungen.

[27]Talented Drew Graduate School students in various PhD programs over many years had a hand in digitally researching, developing and producing the ACCS. The heroes of the ACCS were those mostly unknown, unassuming bright advanced scholars with superb linguistic skills who were dedicated to seeing it through. They worked long hours in a dank basement without any fanfare, but their names were recorded in the volumes on which they worked. Many were international students who came to Drew with superb linguistic skill sets from Russia, Germany, China, Korea, Ireland and the United Kingdom, in addition to those from North America.

Housed first in the basement of the former dean's residence, the ACCS was later moved to the former vice-president's house, then to the graduate school basement and then also to the upper floor when the humidity grew too intense. In those quarters every day for over a decade, ACCS staff members were huddled over computers engaged in complex Boolean searches in the original patristic documents, proofreading, checking references and providing each volume editor with large quantities of potential Greek and Latin references from which the volume editors would make their quality selections.

[28]The digital research team at Drew University supported each volume editor individually by performing global searches of the Greek and Latin patristic writers from Genesis to Revelation, seeking to match Scripture text with ancient commentator. The Drew ACCS office supplied each volume editor with a very large read-out of Greek and Latin comments on each verse or pericope of Scripture text. Only a small percentage of those raw, original language materials made the grade of our selection criteria for inclusion and translation. The intent of that process was to achieve brevity and economy of expression by exclusion of extraneous material and not to go into critical-explanatory detail.

[29]Some have noted that the methods used to obtain those outcomes made ACCS a unique event of modern publishing but my view was that it was the people gathered that made the difference.

[30]I was grateful for the patient editors at InterVarsity Press, especially James Hoover, Andy LePeau and Robert Fryling, who contributed vast hours and a substantial investment of resources into the editorial production and accomplishment of those goals. They significantly shaped the editing and producing of that publication miracle.

[31]Intermittently I have had friendly exchanges with Bob Wilken at scholarly society meetings. He marveled at how we had been able to get so many subscribers in advance and efficiently procure manuscripts out of eminent scholars in a reasonable time frame.

[32]Our original goal was to complete the series within a decade. Most of that work was done by 2006, but the last volumes stretched to 2010. Thankfully our benefactors were patient and devoted to the cause.

[33]In those cases where we really wanted to get the manuscript in without untimely delays, we offered incentives if the manuscript arrived on time. For those who lagged behind agreed-upon target dates for first draft and finished drafts, we offered modest gratuities for prompt completion, and in only three cases did we have to give up on a particular volume editor due to failure to meet those target dates. After being reassigned, some volumes took years longer to complete than we expected, but they were worth the wait, as in the case of the excellent volume by Sever Voicu of the Vatican Library on the Apocrypha.

[34]Our work had restored a tradition of major multivolume scholarly publishing efforts that Drew had sustained for eighty years but which had been largely inactive since the mid-twentieth century.

[35]Less than 1 percent of the writings of the church fathers survived in any form. They were confiscated by the authorities, burned, systematically destroyed or rotted away. Michael von Faulhaber, the cardinal who ordained Joseph Ratzinger as priest, presented evidence that as many as half of the early comments on Scripture are today extant only in catena form. They earned the stamp of consensuality the hard way, by being repeatedly selected as worth knowing.

[36]There were Protestant compilations such as those of Johann Gerhard and John Pearson. Among English writers the last major expression of the catena goes back to 1644 when J. A. Cramer of Oxford began publishing his eight volume *Catenae Graecorum Patrum* (Chain of Greek Fathers on the New Testament, now online at archive.org.). For its last expression in German one has to go back over a century to 1899 to Karl Holl's *Fragmente vornicänischer Kirchenväter aus den Sacra Parallela*. No modern editions existed in English until the Ancient Christian Commentary on Scripture. Historians of exegesis and doctrine appeared unaware of how long the catena tradition had been neglected.

[37]The first known Greek catenist was Procopius of Gaza, followed by the first Latin catenist, Primasius of Hadrumetum in North Africa, then followed by Andrew of Caesarea, and a large lost work of *Sacred Parallels* attributed to John of Damascus but likely related to the *Capita Theologica* of Maximus the Confessor. That was the patristic pattern inherited by the early medieval period and seen in the catenae of Rhabanus Maurus (d. 856) and Paschasius Radbertus, upon which Thomas Aquinas built his *Catena Aurea* (the Golden Chain) of patristic commentators on Scripture.

[38]I am referring to the editing of catenae by Franciscan father Jean de la Haye on Genesis (4 vols.), Exodus (3 vols.) and the Apocalypse of John (3 vols.). His major

works were *Biblia Magna* (5 volumes, 1643) and the *Biblia Maxima* (19 volumes, Paris, 1660), which brought together previous sixteenth-century catenae by University of Paris chancellor Jean de Gagny (d. 1549), Dutch commentator Willem Hessels van Est on Paul's letters and the Catholic Epistles (d. 1613), Portuguese Jesuit Manuel de Sá (d. 1596), who wrote *Scholia in Quatuor Evangelia*, Giovanni Stephano Menochio (d. 1655), whose magnum opus was *Brevis Explicatio Sensus Literalis Sacræ Scripturæ optimus quibusque Auctoribus per Epitomen Collecta* (Cologne, 1659), and Belgian Jesuit Jacobus Tirinus (d. 1636), whose major work was the *Commentarius in Sacram Scripturam* (1645).

[39]The discerning labor of selection was done by each volume editor independently, after which Christopher Hall and I reviewed them. As general editor I served as volume coeditor for only one volume, *Mark*. Hall and I chose Mark because some scholars had cast doubt on the possibility of even finding enough quality material from patristic sources on Mark. So we deliberately made Mark our first volume.

[40]In the wake of ACCS, the word *commentary* can no longer be restricted to those using only modern historical critical methods. Under that restricted definition, the classic Christian exegetes are by definition always going to appear to such critics as dated, quaint, premodern and for some as inadequate. Through ACCS, the ancient Christian writers constantly challenge those modern assumptions.

[41]The series brought together Christians who had long ago distanced themselves from each other by separate and competing church memories. I found to my surprise that the study of the church fathers on Scripture energized significant interactions between Protestants, Catholics, Orthodox and charismatics on issues that have divided them for centuries on such subjects as justification, authority, Christology, sanctification and eschatology.

[42]The presence of evangelical scholars at the Oxford Patristic Institute has increased tenfold since ACCS began in 1993. Baptist and Pentecostal seminaries are appointing patristic scholars to their faculties for the first time. Before our publication the deep study of patristic exegesis was not a priority for many evangelicals, but now leading evangelical faculties such as Fuller, Wheaton, Gordon-Conwell, Dallas, Regent College, Vancouver, Beeson, Trinity and all of the major Southern Baptist seminaries have specialists in patristic studies. Evangelicals and charismatics can now relish pre-Reformation texts and find a common faith to which all believers can appeal, as did Luther, Calvin, and Cranmer.

[43]Pastor Rick Warren wrote, "For years I have been meaning to write you and thank you from the bottom of my heart for your work on the Ancient Christian Commentary set. They are, without a doubt, my favorite commentaries, even though I have a personal ministry library of over 20,000 volumes. As a 4th generation pastor, I inherited many out of print classic English commentaries, but I keep returning to

what the early Fathers said. *Glossa ordinaria* is so much more meaningful than all the hyper historical-critical ramblings of academics who seem to write just to impress each other. Also to understand the truly catholic (whole) meaning of a text as understood by the historical community is far more valuable than the thoughts of a single contemporary commentator. Reading ACCS is a conversation about the text instead of a single lecture. You and IVP have done all of us pastors a great service in making the richness of these pastors and theologians accessible. You gave me tools of patristic exegesis that we would have never had otherwise so you have had a direct part in the health and growth of Saddleback Church. Rick Warren."

[44]Susan Cole, Marian Ronan and Hal Taussig, *Wisdom's Feast: Sophia in Study and Celebration* (San Francisco: Harper, 1989), p. 190.

[45]Ibid., p. 148.

[46]I spoke candidly of virtually all of the opinions I would write in *Requiem* to audiences in General Theological Seminary (Episcopal) in New York, Ontario Seminary in Toronto, Chester College in England, Concordia Seminary in St. Louis, Beeson Divinity School, Elmhurst College, West Virginia University and Asbury Theological Seminary.

[47]By now those strategies had gone through a cycle of losing the confidence of the local church laity, creating a hemorrhage of membership and a general disillusionment over democratic fairness. *Requiem* was an attempt to describe those processes as I was actually experiencing them. Evangelicals had long served on that plantation as pariahs in the liberal quest for prestige. They were often stereotyped as grumbling misfits. In *Requiem* I discussed all of those issues. One of its features was a whimsical "Open Letter to Evangelical Students in Tradition-Impaired Seminaries." It was a survival map and an appeal to transform the seminary.

[48]The democratic spirit in church polity was constantly being undermined by clever manipulators who insisted on artificial imbalances in representation. That resulted in grassroots democratic bodies not being able to work their own will according to conscience. Those who now did the planning took on the role of a new bureaucratic nobility. Finding that they could not win free elections or popular referenda, they turned to Alinsky-type strategies for manipulating policies. By the 1990s the ideologists had captured and overrun many universities, diminishing both freedom of speech and critical dialogue, strategies familiar to totalitarian rule.

[49]At the insistence of the Princeton University Press, I wrote a very unfunny scholarly introduction to Kierkegaard's theory of comedy, in relation to his aesthetic, ethical, ironic and religious stages (Socratic Religion A and Christian Religion B) along life's way.

[50]Gene Autry and Ray Whitley, "Back in the Saddle Again," 1939.

[51]On my *Requiem* list of leading young fogeys (paleo-orthodox authors) I had eight

Eastern Orthodox, eight Roman Catholics, six Anglicans, ten Lutherans, thirteen in the Reformed tradition, seven Baptists and eight from Wesleyan-related traditions—all younger than I. Together they represented to me a new momentum in postmodern paleo-orthodoxy. Among them were George Weigel, Alister McGrath, James Davison Hunter, Peter Stuhlmacher, Mark Noll, Robert Jenson, Timothy George, Richard Hays, Nicholas Wolterstorff, Stanley Grenz, David Dockery, Kevin Vanhoozer, Eleanor Stump, Paul Vitz, Robert Webber, Vigen Guroian, John Breck and William Abraham. Above all there was the inimitable Richard John Neuhaus, who while still a Lutheran wrote *The Catholic Moment: The Paradox of the Church in the Post-Modern World* (1986), and who carried out the agenda of postmodern paleo-orthodoxy more brilliantly than anyone I knew. Those were my companions in theology.

[52]In my lifetime I witnessed a sad deterioration away from the vast energy of the young ecumenical movement at Evanston. Then came the turn of the WCC toward pop social engineering in Geneva, and sadly the final gasps of a viable WCC in Harare, Zimbabwe. I personally watched and participated in the modern ecumenical movement from its birth in 1948 to its youth at Evanston in 1954 to Geneva in 1966 and finally to its demise in Africa in 1998. It came and went in fifty years. Present at key stages of its history, I was first enthralled, then engaged, and finally deceived and abandoned by it.

[53]The ultimate symbol of Africa's political corruption and financial denouement was the president of Zimbabwe, Robert Mugabe, who was lionized and venerated by the World Council of Churches leaders, who had continued to maintain a cozy relation with the autocratic Zimbabwe regime. The council refused to criticize his oppressive land policies that had for years served his cronies, fueled by American aid. Mugabe made the opening address to the WCC delegates with cheers and fanfare.

[54]What began with Amsterdam's ideal vision ended with Zimbabwe's pathetic *Padare*, a Shona word for get-together that was corrupted to mean a broad platform for absolute toleration of all conceptions of God as equal, relativizing the Jewish and Christian memory of the history of salvation.

[55]The preliminary attempts at evangelical-WCC reconciliation promised at Canberra lacked integrity. There was a halfhearted effort to develop a WCC-Pentecostal working group, but that was limited primarily to only a few individuals. It did not reach out to the vast and rapidly growing Pentecostal populations over the world, especially in Africa. Little recognition was given to the fact that evangelical constituencies within those WCC denominations were growing rapidly while the mainline was declining. Evangelicals in the long-established churches were now reluctant supporters of the WCC but remained unwitting financial supporters through their WCC member churches even though they were being

disenfranchised. Later the WCC officials admitted that they had not grasped fully the depth of the resistance of the Orthodox and evangelicals on questions of economics and sexuality.

[56]Origen, whom biblical critics read selectively but not with sufficient care, was caricatured as a symbolist uninterested in the plain sense of Scripture. That was an error being corrected by letting him speak for himself on the literal sense of Scripture, as distinguished from his successors, the Origenists, who were rejected by the fourth ecumenical council in A.D. 431.

[57]Profound ongoing differences remained between evangelicals and Catholics on papal authority, transubstantiation, Mariology and prayers to the saints, but the dialogue became beneficial in the arena of early Christian Scripture studies. That was assisted by both sides being able to appeal to Athanasius and Augustine. For me personally that was a period of unfolding wonder at the lofty theological minds of von Balthasar, de Lubac, and Ratzinger. I relished my very significant conversations with the leader of Ratzinger's international circle of students, Father Joseph Fessio, S.J., who founded the Ignatius Press, and who was, more than anyone I knew in America, attuned to the import of Ratzinger's conciliatory thinking and its relevance to Protestants.

[58]Living examples of this new ecumenism were found in Anglican John Stott, Presbyterian Richard Lovelace, Baptist Timothy George, Christian Reformed Richard Mouw, Quaker Richard Foster and Pentecostal Vinson Synan.

[59]Among original or early participants were powerful minds such as those of Edward Oakes, Augustine Di Noia, Nathan Hatch and James Hitchcock. Later key participants included Neal Plantinga, R. R. Reno, Sarah Sumner, Cheryl Johns, Joel Elowsky and Kevin Vanhoozer.

[60]I joined with James Packer and Timothy George in "An Open Letter About 'The Gift of Salvation'" in *Christianity Today* in 1998.

[61]Neuhaus was debating internally with himself and with his closest Lutheran friends, Robert Wilken, George Lindbeck, Robert Jenson and Paul Hinlicky, on becoming a Catholic.

[62]Most of these conversations were held in the Grant Room of the Union Club on Park Avenue. Neuhaus served as moderator and demonstrated keen sensibilities to all viewpoints. Senior voices like those of J. I. Packer, Avery Dulles and Charles Colson were listened to with much respect and benefit. I was stuck by the sincerity and deep faith of the participants and their hunger for embodying the body of Christ. My role in those conversations was a mediating role I shared with Anglican John Rodgers, Dominican Augustine Di Noia and Baptist Timothy George.

Chapter 8: The 2000s

[1]These conversations were reported in Huibert van Beek and Georges Lemopoulos, ed., *Proclaiming Christ Today: Orthodox-Evangelical Consultation, Alexandria, 10-15, July, 1995* (Geneva: World Council of Churches, 1995).

[2]William Butler Yeats, "O Do Not Love Too Long," 1904.

[3]I followed Donald Bloesch as their theological adviser. In 1984 many of these same core leaders wrote the Dubuque Declaration.

[4]These stellar young theologians included Ephraim Radnor (Anglican), Bruce McCormack, Mark Achtemeier, Andrew Purves (Presbyterian), Bruce Marshall and Russell Saltzman (Lutheran), Donna Hailson (Baptist), William Abraham and Leicester Longden (United Methodist), and R. R. Reno (at that time Anglican, now Catholic).

[5]The full text of the joint statement is found in chapter five of my book on *Turning Around the Mainline* (Grand Rapids: Baker, 2006).

[6]A biblical text emerged as their key theme to comfort and encourage the embattled soldiers of the Confessing Movements: "God's solid foundation stands firm, sealed with this inscription: 'The Lord knows those who are his'" (2 Tim 2:19).

[7]As a former full-time card-carrying liberator, I know from experience how mesmerizing this enchantment can be.

[8]Thomas C. Oden, *The Justification Reader,* Classic Christian Readers (Grand Rapids: Eerdmans, 2002).

[9]Thomas C. Oden, *The Good Works Reader*, Classic Christian Readers (Grand Rapids: Eerdmans, 2007). I hope in due time to pursue the last volume on sanctification and the holy life.

[10]This I have argued in book length detail in *The Justification Reader.*

[11]Thomas C. Oden and J. I. Packer, *One Faith: The Evangelical Consensus* (Downers Grove, IL: InterVarsity Press, 2004).

[12]I went to Navarre University to consult with Professor Marcelo Merino Rodriguez, who became our Spanish translation general editor. He supervised translating our selections from the original languages into Spanish under the imprint of Ciudad Nueva of Madrid. Out of the successful publication of the early volumes of the Spanish edition came the initiative to translate ACCS into Italian with our Spanish publisher's counterpart in Italy, Città Nuova.

[13]Connecting these dots is my motivation for writing this memoir. This continuity was briefly stated in two short essays, "Postmodern Paleo-orthodoxy" in *An Introduction to Christian Theology*, edited by Roger Badham in 1998, and "Back to the Future," in *Postmodernizing the Faith: Evangelical Responses to the Challenge of Postmodernism*, edited by Millard Erickson in 1998. In a cassette series for Touchstone, I reported on the young scholars who were "Turning Hearts to the Fathers."

[14]They were President Angelo Di Berardino of the Augustinianum Patristic Institute in Rome (Catholic), Professor Mark Edwards of Oxford (Anglican), Professor John McGuckin of Union Theology Seminary, New York (Orthodox), Professor Gerald L. Bray of Birmingham (Anglican), and the Reverend Joel Elowsky (Lutheran).

[15]Bishop Kallistos Ware (Orthodox), Archbishop Augustine Di Noia of the Congregation of the Doctrine of the Faith (Catholic), Professor Steven Sykes of Durham (former Anglican bishop of Ely), and Dr. James I. Packer of Vancouver (Anglican evangelical). The Ecumenical Patriarch of Constantinople Bartholomew and Cardinal Avery Dulles of New York gave their wise counsel in the formation of the doctrine series.

[16]For example, the first word of the creed is *credo* ("I believe"). The persecuted early Christians who first said "credo" did so at the risk of their lives. Those prepared to sacrifice their lives for their belief have a special authority that safe observers lack. Saying "I believe" implied the willingness to suffer and if necessary die for the faith.

[17]Among those previously inaccessible or inadequately translated commentaries were those of Jerome on Jeremiah (Michael Graves), Eusebius of Caesarea on Isaiah (Jonathan Armstrong), Origen on Numbers (Thomas P. Scheck), Theodore of Mopsuestia on John (Marco Conti), two Greek Commentaries and two Latin commentaries on Revelation (William Weinrich), two volumes by Cyril of Alexandria on John (David Maxwell), two volumes by Ambrosiaster on the Pauline Epistles (Gerald L. Bray), two volumes on the previously untranslated *Incomplete Commentary on Matthew* (James Kellerman), and others on Severian, John of Damascus and Bede.

[18]They are the studies by which I would hope that my body of work might be carefully assessed.

[19]Thomas C. Oden, *The Rebirth of Orthodoxy: Signs of New Life in Christianity* (San Francisco: HarperSanFrancisco, 2003).

[20]If the writings of Philo, Synesius, Victor of Vita and Shenute of Atripe had all been written in France, they would be called European. Though they were written in Africa and emerged out of African soil, it has been difficult for some to call them African. And as they used poetic imagery and metaphors rooted in African cultures, they cannot reasonably be viewed as residues of European imports.

[21]When I was nine years old I saw the 1939 movie *Stanley and Livingstone*. The adventurous Stanley was assigned to find Livingstone in Africa. This required a hazardous trek into the unexplored wilds of East Africa in 1871, ending with the famous line "Dr. Livingstone, I presume." As a youth, this film really stirred my imagination. Here was a servant of the Lord in the heart of Africa quietly and happily healing the illnesses of small African villagers near the Zambezi River, while the world was worried that he might be dead. That was a powerful model for a young boy like me.

[22]The analogy of faith was the method by which each passage of Scripture was illuminated by other passages and by the whole story of Scripture. This unity was first understood in Africa by intense investigations of the relationships of people of Israel and the New Israel. Every New Testament passage had to be interpreted in relation to Old Testament narratives, and every Old Testament narrative had to be seen in relation to the history of its fulfillment in the history of Jesus, as perceived by the apostles. The thoroughness of this practice was Africa's gift to world Christianity.

[23]Kwame Bediako is a brilliant exception. From the beginnings of CEAC he has been our best African model in theology. His voice is deeply missed.

[24]Many leading themes of the writings of Gregory Thaumaturgus, Eusebius and Gregory the Great followed Origen, Didymus and Athanasius in spirit as well as in many specific details. While Origen's critics were rejecting his disciples' excesses, they continued to depend on Origin's language studies and historical method.

[25]This prejudice has meant that the African continent could not embrace as its own even Didymus the Blind or Mother Sarah or the Tall Brothers. Even more unconvincing was the treatment of Numidian-born Optatus or Thebian-born Paphnutius. Their contributions had been packaged neatly into prevailing European motifs, as if with almost no indigenous roots in the Maghreb or Upper Nile.

[26]Key figures in the Theological Commission at that time were Rolf Hille of Tübingen, Henri Blocher of the Faculté Libre de Théologie Evangélique de Vaux-sur-Seine, west of Paris, Vinay Samuel of India and Oxford, and Ward Gasque of Vancouver.

[27]Among those eminent Catholic and evangelical theologians were Avery Dulles, Samuel Escobar of Peru and Peter Kuzmič of Croatia. In 1997 I presented a paper for this group titled "The Holy Spirit Challenges Evangelical Theology," published in the *Evangelical Review of Theology*. I joined those dialogues just at the decisive point when many Latino evangelicals were in disagreement as to whether those conversations should proceed at all.

[28]In a related venue, I was asked to address the Fellowship of European Evangelical Theologians on the future of European evangelical theology. That was my first opportunity to present the classical ecumenical arguments of *Agenda for Theology* to an audience of European evangelical scholars, and my first public attempt to challenge Eurocentric assumptions about African Christian history. The world Catholic-evangelical conversations proceeded with intensity over many years. We met at an evangelical retreat center in Derbyshire, UK, then at Geneva Lake, Wisconsin, followed by Kuala Lumpur, Malaysia, and one near Cologne, Germany, and then others at Philadelphia and São Paulo, Brazil. Those representatives were carefully chosen from five continents to meet in different regions each year. Avery Dulles led the Catholic delegation and George Vandervelde and Rolfe Hille led the evangelicals.

²⁹At Tantur I renewed my friendship with Tom Stransky, the Paulist Father who had guided me around during my visit to Vatican II in the fall of 1965. Border guards stood nearby and manned a checkpoint between Israel and the Palestinian Territory. Tantur was on the site of a sixth-century monastery. I spent early morning hours meditating on that sloping hill of ruins. Each morning I would see workers coming across the ancient monastery site from Palestinian villages to work in Israel, walking through fruit trees to avoid the nearby security guards.

³⁰The Mar Saba library is where Morton Smith found the manuscript of the "Letter to Theodore," alleged to be from Clement of Alexandria.

³¹There were fourteen regional theological commissions linked with the African Evangelical Alliance (AEA), which was the African expression of the World Evangelical Alliance. Their organizational links with African theologians saved us years of effort in contacting key cooperators in our early African Christianity research project. WEA immediately gave us our natural partner network for all of Africa as well as for global Christian theologians interested in Africa.

³²Michael Glerup and I made contact in Nairobi with the late Dr. Tokunboh Adeyemo, general editor of the *African Bible Commentary*, which had been written by seventy African scholars under his direction from all parts of Africa. As a Nigerian working in Kenya and connected with scholars all over Africa, Dr. Adeyemo was astute in advising us concerning the particular scholars on the continent of Africa who might be able to make unique contributions to our research. Another crucial conversation was with Edinburgh-educated Dr. Zac Niringiye, Anglican bishop of Kampala, Uganda, who offered thoughtful counsel for our planning along with advice on potential problems.

³³We also visited the campus of Uganda Christian University at Mukono, near Kampala, in 2006. There I renewed my friendship with its Chancellor Stephen Noll, formerly dean of Trinity School of Ministry in Ambridge, PA, who guided us around that booming campus, where we visited with faculty and students, hoping to envision how studies in early African Christianity could be incorporated into their curriculum.

³⁴Chief among those were Tite Tiénou, president of Trinity Evangelical Divinity School, Chicago, and former dean of the Evangelical Seminary in Côte d'Ivoire, the late Ogbu Kalu of McCormick Seminary, who had written on African Pentecostalism, and James Nbama of Kenya now at the Southwestern Baptist Theological Seminary. We also consulted with Professor Jehu Hanciles of Sierra Leone, teaching at Fuller, and Yale professor Lamin Sanneh of the Gambia, who later joined our board. His contribution to our presence in Africa has been enormous.

³⁵Kwame Bediako was the patriarch of evangelical theologians in Africa. He advised me on invitees, but became very sick and was unable to attend. John

Mbiti was planning to come but other matters intervened. See n38 below for a larger list.

[36]See for the complete version of this founding document "Core Hypothesis of CEAC" at http://earlyafricanchristianity.com/education/core-hypothesis-of-first -consultation-on-early-african-christianity.html.

[37]Throughout the first millennium (in Nilotic, Berber, Pharaonic, proto-Coptic, Ethiopian and Meroe cultures) African Christian teaching had taken root in indigenous, traditional and primitive African cultures. Inland African cultures of the Nile and Medjerda basins had been the main testing grounds for showing the ability of classic Christianity to live in different cultures without changing its memory of the history of salvation. African Christianity was not merely a coastal phenomena but penetrated deep into Africa in the first millennium.

[38]Among the distinguished African-born theologians, representing major universities of Africa, who met at Dakar were Lamin Sanneh, Mercy Oduyoye, Tite Tiénou, Bishop Mouneer, Thomas Oduro, John Azumah, Benezet Bujo, Doug Carew, Walter Obare, Bulus Galadima, Celestin Kouassi, Michel Limbambu, Isaac Zokoue, Desta Heliso and Tolbert Thomas Jallah Jr. Each of these theologians has wide visibility in his or her region of Africa, and many are recognized internationally.

[39]I regained my voice through state-of-the-art surgery provided by Dr. Keith Clark in Oklahoma City. Oncologist Craig Reitz shepherded me through my battle with lymphatic cancer. Dr. Philip Adamson, an internationally known specialist in congestive heart failure, has kept my heart pumping at 35 percent efficiency through a defibrillator and brilliant medical care.

CHAPTER 9: THE 2010s

[1]As I was getting ready for a professional meeting in Denver, I had taken a different path in my usual solitary lakeside walk that day. I noticed a newly posted for sale sign on this lakefront house I had always admired, and when I knocked on the door, I was invited in. I immediately felt right about the house. I knew it would disappear if I went to Denver without making an offer. From Denver I learned the house was mine. My life in this house has been an exceptional blessing for me.

[2]A very special event happened in Jerusalem in 2007, when I met with Petra Heldt, Lela Gilbert and the Ahmansons to confer with the Jerusalem Orthodox patriarchs (Greek, Syriac, Coptic and Ethiopian) on patristic studies opportunities in Jerusalem and in Africa. It was there that the Thomas Oden Patristic Studies Institute (TOPS) in Jerusalem was formed with the purpose of providing Jerusalem with a patristic studies center accessible to students from all over the world. As moving as it was to me to receive three honorary postdoctoral degrees,

or receiving the Vestigia Award from Wheaton or the Herberg Award from Drew, this honor blew me away.

[3]Thomas C. Oden, *The African Memory of Mark: Reassessing Early Church Tradition* (Downers Grove, IL: InterVarsity Press, 2011).

[4]Many of these Islamic students were not Libyan. They had come to Libya from all parts of Africa. All were Muslims chiefly interested in law, political science and family counsel.

[5]See the other arguments in *Early Libyan Christianity*.

[6]None of the most eminent historical theologians of our time (Harnack, Schaff, Dollinger, Troeltsch, Hillerbrand, Pelikan, Lossky, Calhoun) sufficiently grasped or explained this anomaly.

Index of Names and Institutions